One Step from the White House

One Step from the White House

The Rise and Fall of Senator William F. Knowland

Gayle B. Montgomery
and James W. Johnson

in collaboration with Paul G. Manolis

UNIVERSITY OF CALIFORNIA PRESS

Berkeley / Los Angeles / London

*The publisher gratefully acknowledges
the contribution provided by the General
Endowment Fund of the Associates of
the University of California Press.*

University of California Press
Berkeley and Los Angeles, California

University of California Press, Ltd.
London, England

Library of Congress Cataloging-in-Publication Data
Montgomery, Gayle B., 1934–
    One step from the White House: the rise and fall of Senator
William F. Knowland / Gayle B. Montgomery and James W.
Johnson in collaboration with Paul G. Manolis.
        p. cm.
    Includes bibliographic references and index.
    ISBN 0–520–21194–4
        1. Knowland, William F. (William Fife), 1908–1974.
    2. Legislators—United States—Biography.   3. United States.
    Congress. Senate—Biography.   4. United States—Politics and
    government—1945–1989.   5. Republican Party (U.S.: 1854–   )—
    Biography.   6. California—Politics and government—1951–
    I. Johnson, James W., 1938–   .   II. Manolis, Paul.   III. Title.
    E748.K67M66   1998
    973.92'092—dc21   100230724 8   97–50545
    [B]   CIP

Printed in the United States of America
9 8 7 6 5 4 3 2 1

The paper used in this publication meets the minimum requirements
of American National Standards for Information Sciences—Perma-
nence of Paper for Printed Library Materials, ANSI Z39.48–1984.

Contents

Preface

Senator William F. Knowland, the former majority leader and editor of the *Oakland Tribune*, died in 1974. Since that cold February day, we envisioned writing a biography of a man who was so influential in our professional lives and in the lives of so many Americans. We waited, however, until time had softened the pain for those close to the senator. The last years of his life were unpleasant for many members of his family, but now, more than twenty years after his death, it is time to tell his story.

The senator was one of the finest statesmen of the 1950s, a man of principle who spoke his mind, stood behind his ideals, and damned the consequences. As the Republican leader of the U.S. Senate, Knowland was one of the most influential figures in America in those early cold war years. He initiated an Asian policy that is still part of our international direction. He was a public figure recognized and respected by millions of Americans: Dwight D. Eisenhower, with whom he often disagreed, called him "impeccably honest, courageous, studious and serious" and praised him in particular for his leadership in the battle for civil rights legislation in 1957. Yet few really knew him, for he was a shy man, with a stony countenance often mistaken for arrogance.

The senator also had a dark and self-destructive side, and no biography would be complete without an examination of his tragic downfall. In a show of stubbornness, ambition, and self-assurance bordering on feelings of divine right, Knowland took his state Republican Party down to defeat in 1958. He ended his own family's political dynasty in California and gave the Democratic Brown family power that would last into the 1990s. Not coincidentally, he ended the careers of several other major California Republicans.

Time has dimmed the memories of Californians and others. Few people under the age of fifty know Knowland's story. No biography has been written before, and his name has been relegated to mentions in indexes of books about his contemporaries, most of whom could not measure up to his stature. Many have forgotten the contributions he made to his hometown of Oakland, after he returned to run the *Oakland Tribune* when his political career was over. In the final fifteen years of his life, he was a powerful force helping to shape Oakland into the major city that it is today.

We worked closely with the senator during the years after his return from Washington, Johnson as an editorial writer and Montgomery as political editor at the *Oakland Tribune*. We grew to admire him and to appreciate his contributions. We didn't always agree with him, but we always respected him. It would be fair to say that he may not always have been right, but he always was the boss.

Senator Knowland's family and friends have given us the opportunity to explore the life of a great American. We hope we have lived up to their trust and faith.

Acknowledgments

No biography can be written without the contributions of dozens of people. Because of Senator Knowland's national stature, those who contributed to *One Step from the White House* are spread throughout the United States. Through our personal contacts with the senator and interviews with dozens of close associates, the personality of this complex American leader emerged; a full list of interviews is given in the bibliography. Many people no longer living left oral histories, letters, books, and magazine and newspaper articles that expressed their views, and we are indebted to their insights.

First and foremost, our thanks go to Bill Knowland's son, Joe, and daughter Estelle. As painful as it may have been to discuss some aspects of their father's life, they never backed away from answering tough questions. Their aid in bringing this story to publication went beyond what we could have hoped for. They arranged interviews with reluctant relatives and offered us intimate, revealing letters, insights, and hours of their time. Most important, they trusted us to treat their father fairly and with sensitivity. They were interested in preserving his rightful place in history and we hope we have helped them fulfill that goal.

We also are deeply indebted to Paul Manolis, the senator's close friend and longtime aide. He shared with us his experiences of many years and helped with questions on Knowland's life that even his family could not have answered. Manolis spent hours in interviews with us, providing documents and photographs that were invaluable in painting this portrait. The numerous letters to and from the senator quoted in the book were provided by the Knowland family and Manolis.

Kay Sessinghaus Paolinetti and Steven Sessinghaus, the children of Ann Knowland, the senator's second wife, talked to us openly and honestly about the couple's tumultuous marriage. They recognized Ann's human failings but wanted us to see the good side of their mother as well.

The book also draws on the recollections of dozens of our former colleagues at the *Oakland Tribune*, who shared their personal insights, anecdotes, and feelings about the man who signed their paychecks.

To our wives, who were understanding and supportive during our four years of work, we owe a debt of gratitude. Marilyn Johnson labored tirelessly on research and transcriptions of interviews, as well as providing feedback. Roseanne Montgomery surrendered her house to computers and boxes of documents and never hesitated to provide a personal assessment of our work.

Librarians scattered across the country were always cooperative, no matter how demanding we must have been. Our special thanks go to Michael Parrish at the Lyndon Baines Johnson Library in Austin, Texas; Dwight Miller at the Herbert Hoover Library in West Branch, Iowa; Susan Naulty at the Richard Nixon Library in Yorba Linda, California; Paul Wormser at the National Archives in Laguna Niguel, California; and Bonnie Hardwick at the Bancroft Library at the University of California at Berkeley. Special thanks also go to the staff of the small branch library in Providence, Rhode Island, and to librarians at the Dwight D. Eisenhower Library in Abilene, Kansas; the Harry S. Truman Library in Independence, Missouri; and the California State Archives in Sacramento.

Sam M. Stanton, one of James Johnson's former students, gave us invaluable help in providing information from the library at the *Sacramento Bee*. Another former student, Theoden Janes, often rescued Johnson from computer problems.

Ruth Austin, Don Paff, and Lance Williams provided us with vital links to elusive Las Vegas sources. Dr. Franz Wassermann of Walnut Creek, California, gave us a psychiatrist's view of William F. Knowland's behavior.

We are grateful to the University of Arizona's Social and Behavioral Sciences Research Institute and to Nancy Henkle for assistance with grants that helped finance travel. Jim Patten, head of the university journalism department, also provided travel money and found time to listen and offer support. Our good friend Bob Seward, with the help of Karla Loyd Elston, spent hundreds of hours going over rough drafts to point out the weaknesses we had to overcome and the strengths on which we could build. Professor Don Carson, Johnson's colleague at the University of Arizona, provided a great deal of the moral support and encouragement to stay with the project. And certainly we owe our special thanks to our project editor, Sue Heinemann, and our copy editor, Alice Falk, who made this a far better book than we could have ever hoped.

1

Footprints to Nowhere

On Saturday morning, February 23, 1974, former U.S.
Senator William F. Knowland was up early, and had coffee alone in his
luxurious Oakland home. He left a note to his wife, saying, "Dear Ann,
I will be back in a short time. Bill." He left two cups and the instant
coffee on a table in their Wayne Avenue apartment.

Knowland, publisher of the highly successful *Oakland Tribune*, drove
slowly down Valdez Street; a few minutes later, at about 9 A.M., he
guided his two-year-old Cadillac sedan into the company garage. He
had a lot to think about. Two days earlier he had been at the right hand
of California governor Ronald Reagan as they celebrated his family
newspaper's hundredth anniversary. He liked Reagan personally and
agreed with his political views. He had told his political editor that day
that Reagan would make a good president, and he would like to work
toward that goal. But on this February day, he had a different mission.

He told the attendant at the *Tribune* garage to put only five gallons
of gasoline in the gas tank. Pragmatic. Conservative. Practical. They
were all adjectives that had been used often with his name over his lifetime. He didn't need a full tank. He wasn't coming back.

The senator eased his bulk back into the Cadillac and drove through
the streets of Oakland for the last time. This was the city that he and
his father before him had ruled. The *Oakland Tribune*. The Tower of
Power. He must have thought of the days when the mayor asked him
for advice before taking any action, when presidents and governors and
senators and those who hoped to be presidents and governors and

senators stood in line for an interview in the paneled board room on the twentieth floor of the *Tribune* Tower—the days when his endorsement could make or break a candidate. He must have remembered the glory days of the U.S. Senate.

But today, he traveled north from Oakland along the east shore of San Francisco Bay, across the Richmond–San Rafael Bridge to Highway 101, then north again, pointing toward the small town of Guerneville on the Russian River. Saturday morning traffic was light, and he drove quickly along the freeway.

The problems were insurmountable.

There were the women, the booze, and, yes, the gambling. That was what really finished him. The images of the tables in Las Vegas recently had filled his thoughts with the enormity of the problems he faced. His debts were huge and the payment date was near.

There was his reputation. All of his life, his reputation was the rock that had held everything in place—a political career that took him almost to the White House, his family, his newspaper, his civic life. Nothing else mattered as much as that reputation.

There was Ann, his new wife. She was part of the nightmare that was eroding that precious reputation, grinding him down, making him weak. To Knowland, lost in his thoughts, the eighty-mile trip to the family compound would have passed quickly.

As he drove westward along the Russian River, his speed increased— almost to a reckless level between Guerneville and the compound. The operator of the Northwood Lodge in the tiny hamlet of Monte Rio said he recognized Knowland in the blue Cadillac, looking "like he was on his way to a fire."

He turned in at the familiar driveway at 19663 Redwood Drive and shut off the engine. He went into the house, then returned to the car briefly, leaving the keys in the ignition. He wouldn't be needing them anymore.

He apparently had a last-minute thought, perhaps a change of heart. He tried to call the *Oakland Tribune* on his walkie-talkie radio, but the distance defeated the unit. He tossed the radio as far as he could. *Tribune* security did not receive any signals on the frequency of Knowland's transceiver that morning.

He walked deliberately into his bedroom in the compound. A .32-caliber automatic was in a closet. It was lighter than the .45 automatic he had been wearing as an army major in Paris on the day in 1945 when California governor Earl Warren had appointed him to the U.S. Senate.

But it would do the job. Perhaps his memory flickered back to Paris, to his reading about the appointment in *Stars and Stripes*. It must have seemed so long ago.

He took the gun and went into the backyard, then strode down the steps alongside the half-submerged pier into the cold February water on the north shore of the Russian River. At the edge of the swift-running river, he checked the clip, then fired one shot into the river to assure himself that the pistol was dependable. He fired the second shot into his right temple. The immediate pain was like a hammer, but the greater pain was erased.

It had rained that week, and in the soft ground his heavy steps left a one-way trail of footprints to the river.

2

Heading West

California in the mid-1800s was a big, brawling, get-rich-quick dream. Like many other young men, twenty-three-year-old Joseph Knowland, a bonded farmworker in Southampton, New York, couldn't stop thinking about the fortunes lying in gold fields and waiting to be made in commerce. In late 1856 he booked passage on a steamer, the *George Law*, for the sea voyage from New York to Panama. He then boarded a rickety train, making a harrowing trip through the jungle across the isthmus to meet up with a second ship, the *John L. Stephens*, bound for San Francisco. On February 14, 1857, Joseph Knowland sailed through the Golden Gate. His arrival marked the beginning of a powerful California family. Joseph's son, Joseph R. Knowland, would serve in the U.S. House of Representatives and his grandson, William F. Knowland, would become U.S. Senate majority leader and a possible presidential contender.

Soon after arriving in San Francisco, Joseph Knowland set off for Yankee Jim's, a gold mining camp in Placer County, to search for his fortune. But within two years, faced with an illness and "not having found mining either profitable or agreeable,"[1] he was back in San Francisco. Like many other disillusioned gold seekers, Knowland decided to take advantage of the numerous business opportunities in the Bay Area that arose with the influx of population during the Gold Rush.

After starting off selling oranges on the streets, Knowland worked at various jobs in the shipping and then the lumber industries. In 1863 he married Hannah Russell, originally from Maine. By 1867 he had saved enough money to form a partnership in a lumber company with a young acquaintance, Jason Springer. This partnership dissolved after three years, but his next lumber company, established with Charles Franklin Doe, proved highly successful.[2] In 1872 Knowland and his family moved across the bay to a cottage on the island of Alameda. Soon afterward, on August 5, 1873, his son Joseph Russell Knowland was born.

Just across the estuary from Alameda, Oakland was booming. The big push had come in 1869, when the transcontinental railroad was completed. Oakland was its western terminus, and from 1860 to 1870 the town's population more than tripled, to 12,000. New businesses popped up everywhere, some just to meet the needs of railroad travelers waiting to be ferried to San Francisco. Oakland had become, after San Francisco, the West Coast's second-largest city.

Oakland's boom helped Joseph Knowland, whose fame and fortune were growing. He became president and managing owner of the Gardiner Mill Company, which not only owned extensive forested property but also had its own fleet of ships to carry lumber. In 1882 he became part owner of Kerckhoff-Cuzner Mill and Lumber Company, where his lumber was sold. He bought a whaling ship, the *Amethyst*, and interests in silver mines in Tombstone, Arizona. He also served as vice president of the 300-worker Kennedy Mining and Milling Company of Jackson in Amador County, a stockholder in the Alameda Bank, and a trustee of the Gas Consumers Association.[3] In addition, Knowland took part in various civic affairs, becoming a trustee of the Old People's Home in Alameda, a thirty-third degree Mason, and a member of the Independent Order of Odd Fellows.

As Joseph Knowland was increasing his fortune, he was raising a son who showed more interest in newspapers and politics than in the lumber business. The Oakland *Daily Times* already had become one of the most influential Democratic papers in the state by the late 1860s and early 1870s. The *Oakland Transcript* also was being published at that time. A third rival, the *Oakland Tribune*, was conceived when Joseph R. Knowland was just three months old.

On a brisk November day, two businessmen sat down at a polished mahogany table in the quiet bar of Oakland's Grand Central Hotel. These two men, Benet A. Dewes and George B. Staniford, decided the town needed another voice: a Republican voice. The paper they visualized that day would reign over Oakland for more than a hundred years, long after the *Times* and *Transcript* had disappeared. On February 21,

1874, the *Oakland Daily Tribune* printed its first edition. It was described as "insignificant in size, but very respectable in its typographical appearance and editorial tone, being the joint production of two excellent printers and journalists."[4] The four-page edition, printed on flimsy letter-size paper, proclaimed, "The paper is small but—so was Goliath once."

Forty-two years later, J. R. Knowland would buy a half interest in the *Tribune* and turn it into one of the most politically and financially successful newspapers in the state.

3

Newspapers and Politics

J. R. Knowland was fascinated by the Civil War stories told to him by his mother and father. A "northern political belief" and the fact that the country had been Republican during his formative years led him to embrace Republican philosophy. He was particularly impressed by the slogan "As the Grand Old Army had saved the Union, the Grand Old Party would save the nation."[1] This line of thinking set the stage for his political and newspaper career. Already as a young boy, J.R. was interested in journalism, and he frequented local newspaper offices in Alameda and Oakland. During his teenage years, he wrote many stories for the local Alameda papers. He also started a paper at the private boys' school he attended in Oakland; during the summer, he worked in the offices of the *Alameda Argus* and the *Oakland Enquirer*.

He went on to write articles for San Jose newspapers while attending the College of the Pacific, then in San Jose. Still in college, J.R. met Ellie Fife, the daughter of a prominent Tacoma, Washington, family, and the couple married on April 2, 1894. Their first child, Eleanor, was born in 1895. Six years later, in 1901, their first son, J. R. (Russ) Knowland Jr., was born. Seven more years passed before William Fife Knowland was born, on June 26, 1908. That third and youngest child would be the Knowlands' favorite, and one day would become one of the nation's most powerful political figures.

After working for several years in the lumber business with his father, J. R. Knowland began making his move in politics. He joined the newly formed Alameda Good Government Club, which was open only to prominent citizens. Young, wealthy, idealistic, and intelligent, J. R. Knowland was a perfect choice for the club.[2] At age twenty-four, the politically ambitious Knowland was asked to speak before the Unitarian Club in Alameda about newspapers. Because newspapers are "our daily companions," he explained to the audience, "we are likely to feel that . . . we have a special license to criticize their policies and to offer suggestions as to what they should and should not publish. The average individual's knowledge of newspapers is but superficial and the reforms which many of us are so free in suggestion might be found inexpedient, if we were ever placed in the position to carry them out." Knowland added, "If we should pick out, indiscriminately, twenty citizens from this or any other locality and request their respective views of what a newspaper should publish, the result would undoubtedly be that what any one of the single twenty would publish the other nineteen would severely criticize."[3]

J. R. Knowland used his connections with the Alameda Good Government Club and a seat on the Alameda Library Board of Trustees to start his career as a politician. At the age of twenty-five, he became the youngest person ever elected to the state assembly, beating his Democratic opponent, E. A. Holman, by more than 1,500 votes. In 1902 Knowland was elected to the state senate and served as chairman of the committee on banking. A year later, at the age of thirty, he was nominated by Governor George Pardee, a former Oakland mayor, to fill out the unexpired term of U.S. Representative Victor H. Metcalf, who had been appointed secretary of commerce and labor.

In the next election, in 1904, J. R. Knowland won his seat by more than 17,000 votes. He was reelected four more times. While serving on the House Committee on Interstate and Foreign Commerce, he supported construction of the Panama Canal and sought exemptions from toll payments for intercoastal American shipping. He made four trips to the canal during its construction and, after a 1907 visit, wrote an article for *Overland Monthly* extolling the canal's virtues. A ship leaving the West Coast, he pointed out, could cut forty-six days off the trip to the Caribbean by going through the canal rather than around the Horn. "For the first time, California will have direct navigation between our Pacific ports and those on the Gulf and on the Atlantic," he declared. "No state is watching the progress of the canal with greater interest than California, and her people will support the present administration and future administrations until the project is finally completed."[4]

Knowland also led the fight to bring the 1915 Panama Pacific International Exposition to San Francisco, initiated appropriations for the Alaska railroad, and obtained funds for Oakland's first harbor development.

In 1914, however, Knowland passed up what would have been easy reelection to the House to try for the U.S. Senate. He was defeated as a direct result of a split in the Republican Party, caused by the formation of a strong Progressive movement in California headed by Governor Hiram Johnson. Fear and distrust of the railroads, specifically the power of the Southern Pacific Railroad, led many Californians to embrace the Progressive Republican cause. As Thomas Storke, a longtime publisher of the *Santa Barbara News-Press*, explained, Southern Pacific "extended its evil influence . . . to Sacramento and Los Angeles, up into Oregon, and as far East as Washington, D.C. . . . I saw the Octopus nominate and elect governors. . . . U.S. Senators, judges, and even town constables owed their jobs to the machine bosses."[5]

J. R. Knowland appeared to be untouched by the widespread corruption in California, with one exception. As a congressman he had attended the 1906 state Republican convention in Santa Cruz, where Southern Pacific favorite James Gillett was nominated over the sitting governor, former Oakland mayor George Pardee. Historian George Mowry later proclaimed, "Never in the history of California had the Southern Pacific been so brazen in dominating a state convention as it was at Santa Cruz, threatening the wavering, providing for the faithful."[6] After Southern Pacific bought the nomination for Gillett, a victory dinner was held and its attendees photographed. One picture— featuring Knowland along with Gillett, Justice Frederick W. Henshaw of the state supreme court, and Abe Reuf, the San Francisco political boss who was in Southern Pacific's pocket—was published in the *San Francisco Call*. Headlined "The Shame of California," the picture proved to be a political embarrassment to Knowland for years. Every reform paper in the state and even some national magazines reproduced the notorious photograph.

The 1914 race marked the first popular election of U.S. senators, who previously had been appointed. Knowland, with almost six terms in the House, was the dean of the California congressional delegation, and he seemed a likely candidate to move up to the Senate. His opponents in the race were Francis J. Heney, the Progressive candidate, and former San Francisco mayor James D. Phelan, who was supported by the Democratic administration of Woodrow Wilson. Knowland stood for free tolls, higher tariffs, "and a return to the safe-and-sane business methods of the good old GOP."[7] In contrast, Phelan backed repeal of free tolls and low tariffs, and Heney campaigned for a steeply graduated income tax, an inheritance tax, and government ownership of utilities and natural resources. Phelan backers were confident of victory, claiming that old-line Republicans would reject Knowland's "standpattism" and, rather than see Heney elected, would switch over to Phelan.

Both nationally and in California, the Progressive candidates fared poorly, although Hiram Johnson was reelected. The biggest setback came with Phelan's victory over Heney and, of course, J. R. Knowland. Phelan received 279,000 votes to Heney's 255,000 and Knowland's 254,000. This fatal blow to Knowland's political ambitions touched off a bitter political dispute with Hiram Johnson, whom he blamed for causing his defeat. When Johnson gave up the governor's office in 1916 to make his own run for the U.S. Senate, Knowland remarked that it would be better to elect a Democrat than Johnson. But Johnson won anyway, and held that seat until his death in 1945.

Despite his dislike for Johnson, J.R. later would put his personal views aside in the interests of party solidarity. In 1920, when Johnson sought the GOP's presidential nomination, Knowland supported him at the party convention to show the nation that the Old Guard Republicans and the "Bull Moose" Republicans were joined in loyalty to their party.

.   .   .

William Fife Knowland was born during his father's third term in the House of Representatives. A month later, his mother died of an embolism and influenza. At the time William's brother, Russ, was just seven and his sister, Eleanor, twelve.

The death of a mother with young children is always hard, but J.R.'s marriage a year later caused a long-lasting division in the family. It was in a boardinghouse in Washington, D.C., that thirty-six-year-old J.R. met and fell in love with Emelyn S. West, the daughter of the boardinghouse owner. The couple was a study in contrasts—he a wealthy, urbane politician; she a woman from the back roads of Virginia, with little education.

Family members described her as a "Marjorie Main in furs," referring to the woman who played Ma Kettle in the popular 1950s movies. In the words of her grandson, Joseph W. Knowland, Emelyn "could easily give you the shirt off her back as well as cut you right down to the knees." A flamboyant character, she dominated the family and all those around her. She would often push her chauffeur aside and drive the family limousine from her four-story mansion in Piedmont, a rich enclave surrounded by Oakland, to go shopping. She would race from market to market, haggling over prices, buying clothes at thrift shops and inexpensive jewelry at dime stores. She then would drive to poor sections of town and dispense bags of groceries.[8]

When the newlyweds returned to California, Emelyn—later called "Mamoo" by her grandchildren (who called J.R. "Papoo")—took Billy, as he was called, to her heart. He was less than a year old. In adopting Billy as her own child, Emelyn virtually shunned Eleanor and Russ. Billy became the pride of Emelyn and his father. He emulated his father, and his father in turn had high expectations for this special son. "He was spoiled," said Bill Knowland's own son, Joe, in an interview. "This motherless child was taken to the bosom of his strong stepmother, who declared him as *her son* at the expense of shared parental love and attention to his older sister and brother." Billy only learned Emelyn was not his mother when he was seven years old. While delivering newspapers in Alameda, he dropped off a paper at a local pharmacy, and the pharmacist asked him, "How's your fine stepmother today?" He was devastated to learn that the woman he had called Mom was not his birth mother.

Years later J.R. often forgot Russ and Eleanor when introducing his family at public gatherings. Not surprisingly, Russ became jealous of his little brother and they were never close, although they were always cordial toward each other. Nor was Russ particularly close to his father, although they worked side by side at the newspaper for years. Russ was the more social brother, the one who fraternized with *Tribune* reporters and rolled dice for drinks with friends in the neighborhood bars. Bill had a single interest—politics—and his father loved him for it. For J.R., the boys' father and family patriarch, Billy was the heir apparent.

When the Knowlands went back to Washington, they took their youngest child with them for the half-year sessions, leaving Russ and Eleanor with their grandparents. In the next few years Billy spent at least half of each year in the nation's capital. As soon as he could read, he began collecting autographs—of politicians. He managed, for example, to get Herbert Hoover's signature during a meeting between his father and Hoover, who was then secretary of commerce.[9] Bill Knowland would later take up a related hobby, creating scrapbooks of articles about his political career.

It's not surprising that Billy would grow into a politician, for talk around the dinner table in J.R. Knowland's Washington home centered on politics. Billy also became a familiar figure in the corridors of the Capitol, accompanying his father on his political rounds. "His idea of a game," J.R. said, "was to get a box to stand on and make a speech."[10] At age eight, a year after he returned to California from Washington, D.C., Billy met a young girl, Helen Davis Herrick. "Wepwesentative government ith the way we do thingth in thith country," he explained to her.[11] Eleven years later this girl became his wife.

.   .   .

J.R.'s father, Joseph, died November 13, 1912, after a long illness. A week before his death at the age of eighty, he summoned up the strength to get out of bed and go to the polls to vote for another term in Congress for his son. It was his last public appearance.

4

After Politics

J.R. Knowland's ill-fated try for a U.S. Senate seat ended his political career. He was looking for a new profession when Herminia Peralta Dargie, the widow of former *Tribune* owner William E. Dargie, approached him through her attorney, Stanley Moore. Would he like to purchase the Dargie interest in the paper? By paying $228,000 and settling Mrs. Dargie's debts, he could gain half interest and control of the *Tribune*. Knowland jumped at the chance. He would use that base for more than fifty years to advance the conservative cause of the Republican Party in California and the nation. To Knowland, the *Tribune* was more than a newspaper; it was also a molder of public opinion. After serving for seventeen years in the state legislature and Congress, it was difficult for him to be objective. Knowland was deliberately buying a voice when he took over the *Tribune:* it was his chance to continue to exert power in the political process.[1]

Knowland gained control of the *Tribune* on November 3, 1915. Eleven days later, the *Tribune* ran an editorial proclaiming that "a great newspaper has both personality and character. It functions not only to inform, not only to reflect opinion, but to lead it and to be identified with the best interests of its community." Within a year after the purchase, he began asserting his new power. Despite his dislike for Hiram Johnson, Knowland wanted to establish the *Tribune* as a Republican power, so he gave Johnson a lukewarm endorsement as the Progressive candidate for Senate on the Republican ticket. The *Tribune* waited until the day before the election to publish its editorial stating that it was a Republican newspaper and it endorsed Republican candidates. Years later, when Bill Knowland sat in the *Tribune* publisher's seat, he made it clear that he, too, with rare exception, endorsed only Republican candidates.

In the same 1916 election, the *Tribune* successfully campaigned to save City Hall Plaza over the objections of the Oakland Board of Parks directors, who wanted to eliminate it. With its considerable muscle, the newspaper then embarked on a decade-long campaign to provide adequate hospitals for the city's inhabitants. The *Tribune's* support led the county to purchase Highland Hospital, which is still in operation. The paper's growing influence reflected its growing circulation, which hit 50,000 by 1920, climbed to 66,000 in 1930, and reached 80,000 by 1939.

Though J. R. Knowland had lost the political pull he had enjoyed as a congressman, he found new clout in the pages of his newspaper. As early as 1922, he began exerting that power statewide, joining with Harry Chandler of the *Los Angeles Times* and Michael de Young of the *San Francisco Chronicle*. The three newspapers demonstrated their combined powers when they joined forces to defeat Governor William Stephens, a Progressive. The *Tribune/Times/Chronicle* triumvirate backed former state treasurer Friend Richardson for governor and he won. The conservatives were back in power and the Progressive Party was on the wane.

Under Knowland, the *Tribune* quickly prospered. It moved from Eighth and Franklin in the old Golden West Hotel to the former Bruener Furniture Company store at Thirteenth and Franklin on March 25, 1918. A year later the twenty-one-story, 310-foot landmark Tribune Tower, with its four 15-foot-diameter clocks, was completed at a cost of $500,000. The architect was Edward T. Foulkes, designer of the Woodminster Theater in Oakland's Joaquin Miller Park. A 500,000-candlepower searchlight flashed across the Oakland skies on its completion. The newspaper would remain in this building for more than seventy years. In 1921 the *Tribune* opened radio station KLX in the Tribune Tower. The station's signal reached 150 miles, but the bulk of the listeners fell within a 50-mile radius. After city hall, the tower was the tallest building in Oakland, and it remained so until completion of the Kaiser Center in 1958. The tower "was meant to typify not only the home of the *Tribune* organization, but also the achievement of the East Bay Community," standing up as "a lantern of a metropolitan commonwealth that has developed within the span of a human lifetime".

and as a "battlement in the great empire which has risen from the dust of the West."[2]

One of J. R. Knowland's earliest fights in Oakland came during a proposal to consolidate city and county governments. Knowland feared that the charter proposal was framed in such a way that Alameda County, with Oakland as the county seat, would be balkanized into four or more parts, promoting Eastern-style ward politics. He set out to defeat the proposal, in one of his most concerted attempts to influence Oakland voters. There is little question that Knowland used the news columns to slant the news in favor of his own beliefs. Three weeks before the election, the *Tribune* ran one to three stories a day about the measure. Knowland's speeches also were treated as news stories.[3] Rarely was the other side of the story given in the *Tribune*.

The rival newspaper, William Randolph Hearst's *Oakland Enquirer*, also opposed the consolidation, but its coverage was more balanced. The measure went down to resounding defeat, no doubt because of *Tribune* and *Enquirer* opposition. Knowland said his newspaper "always tried to select the side that was right for the community."[4]

·   ·   ·

During the affluent 1920s, Knowland ran the paper and shared dividends with Mrs. Dargie. She was happy with the highly profitable arrangement and traveled extensively in Europe.

On one of those trips, she met thirty-one-year-old Captain Antonio Rodriguez Martin in Spain. She returned to California with Martin, who begin to delve into newspaper records to see if her interests at the *Tribune* were being protected.[5] Martin, an engineer, became especially interested in the costs of building the Tribune Tower. The relationship between Knowland and Mrs. Dargie began to cool. Then in September 1929, Mrs. Dargie became ill and was taken to the hospital, where Martin visited her faithfully. Her partner Knowland did not. On December 8, 1929, at age seventy-six, Mrs. Dargie died, touching off a battle over her estate. Martin began questioning Knowland's original half-interest purchase of the newspaper.

Those who believed that Knowland had used skullduggery to get control of the paper claimed that contrary to his recollection that she had first approached him, it was Knowland who went to a naive Mrs. Dargie in 1915 and reminded her of his long-standing friendship, political and social, and worked out a deal to buy the paper. Both versions were plausible. Her late husband had been a longtime booster of Knowland, and Mrs. Dargie had told friends she did not want to see the paper fall into the hands of newspaper magnate William Randolph Hearst.

Questions about how the money may have changed hands for the original purchase lent further controversy to the issue. Almost twenty-five years after Knowland secured control of the *Tribune*, Harold L. Ickes, then secretary of the interior under President Franklin D. Roosevelt, stepped into the fray. In his book *America's House of Lords*, published in 1939, Ickes devoted a chapter to "The Strange Case of the *Oakland Tribune*," indicting Knowland for spiriting the newspaper away from a poor helpless widow.[6] *Time* magazine also weighed in, asserting that Knowland had lent Mrs. Dargie $65,000, in return for which she temporarily assigned her half interest in the *Tribune* to him.[7]

Claiming Ickes's chapter on the *Tribune* was full of flagrant errors, Knowland sent a three-page letter to fellow newspaper publishers around the country whom he thought might print a review of Ickes's book. In it, he pointed out that he bought a half interest not from Mrs. Dargie but from her husband's estate. In addition to paying the estate $228,000 in cash, he lent Mrs. Dargie money to pay debts totaling $117,000. "Had I failed to purchase the estate's interest at that time and advance money for her pressing debts," he insisted, "Mrs. Dargie would have been compelled to sell all her *Tribune* stock."[8]

None of this dispute came out at the time Knowland secured controlling ownership in the *Tribune*. Only after Mrs. Dargie's death in 1929, when the other half interest was in question, did the dispute surface. It would continue for ten years as Knowland sought to gain full ownership of the newspaper, and as the courts sifted through the charges and countercharges. Eventually, in September 1937, Leo E. Owens of the *St. Paul Pioneer Press and Dispatch* offered $1,070,000 for the Dargie estate's half interest in the *Tribune*. Superior Court Judge John J. Allen rejected the offer, saying that outside ownership would result in disharmony.[9] Seven months later, Allen approved Knowland's much lower bid of $311,200. The Knowland ownership was complete and Alameda County's court system was in harmonious accord.

Critics charged that Knowland was forever indebted to Judge Allen and that Allen's son, a Republican, was richly rewarded by the Knowlands. He was supported in his bid for the Oakland school board, where he served a number of years, and his law practice flourished because of Knowland's aid. In addition, the *Tribune* backed young Allen for Congress, where he served six terms in the seat once held by J.R. Knowland. Judge Allen's decision, however, was upheld by an appellate court, and the Supreme Court refused to hear an appeal of the lower court's ruling. The Knowlands were free to concentrate their efforts on making the paper highly profitable as well as a political power.

.   .   .

The extent of J. R. Knowland's influence was evident in the push to develop the Port of Oakland, which by the 1990s would handle about 93 percent of the cargo ships operating out of San Francisco Bay ports. As a congressman, Knowland had already secured appropriations of several million dollars for harbor improvements and fought to allow ships to pass toll free through the Panama Canal on their way to West Coast ports. He had always maintained that the Oakland side of the bay, not San Francisco, was the best place for a port, and he hoped that Oakland would become the mercantile center of the West. In 1925 he led the effort to secure a $9.6 million bond issue for more improvements to the harbor, claiming that it would provide hundreds of jobs for East Bay residents. With the power of his newspaper behind him, he went against city hall and successfully urged voters to approve an independent Board of Port Commissioners. After voters approved the independent board, the fight over the waterfront ended.

"Knowland's influence was magnified many times because of his behind-the-scenes political activity," according to John A. Gothberg, a journalism professor who was a longtime observer of J. R. Knowland's career. "When he decided to back any issue or candidate, he had assuredly ascertained in advance the local political leaders he could count on for support. With the leaders behind him, the battle for public support was virtually won."[10]

The *Tribune* also exerted its influence over appointments to the Oakland City Council. Only five candidates between 1941 and 1965 won election to city council more than once without *Tribune* support. Almost 50 percent of the new councilmen acquired office through appointment, and incumbents were virtually assured of reelection, winning well over two-thirds of all races for council seats. "The record of numerous appointments to council, high victory ratio of incumbents and the failure of non-*Tribune*-endorsed candidates to reach office indicates a pattern of elitism in local politics in Oakland," political scientist Edward C. Hayes noted.[11]

With his hold on Oakland firmly in place, J. R. Knowland began exerting his influence and power throughout California. From the time he gained the newspaper in 1915 until his death in 1966, he was involved in a wide array of civic activities. "You would see Mr. Knowland in attendance at events ranging from the opening of a Safeway Store to a national political convention," recalled *Tribune* reporter Elinor Hayes in 1968. *Tribune* political writer Dave Hope agreed. "The list of organizations to which Knowland belonged seemed countless and yet he was active in all of them."[12] He was a member of the state park commission from 1932 to 1960 and was chairman the last twenty-three years of his service. Knowland's main interest outside of the *Tribune* was preserving historic sites, and he left his mark on hundreds of them throughout the state. His seemingly obscure position as state park commission chairman allowed him to wield enormous power all over California. The commission received millions of dollars a year in tideland-oil revenues paid by petroleum producers for drilling rights. The funds were used for civic improvements throughout the state. Eventually, those revenues reached almost $40 million annually. Knowland greatly influenced the distribution of those funds, and local politicians often were eager to carry out his wishes in return for those much-needed dollars. The friends he made through revenue distribution would provide help for his son Bill as he moved up through the political ranks in California.

In Oakland, he headed the Red Cross, the Community Chest, the March of Dimes, the Downtown Property Owners Association, and the Chamber of Commerce, and he was active in numerous other groups. He thought other businessmen should do the same. "It is a deplorable fact that in every community there are comparatively few who are willing to sacrifice time and give of their talents to public welfare," he said in a 1923 speech. "Many men and women of ability and ample means declare they find it impossible due to lack of inclination and fear of financial loss, to devote time to civic affairs. The result is the responsibility falls upon the shoulders of a few, which makes the burden heavy." He added, "In regard to being public oriented, it is only natural as an American citizen to believe you owe something to your community."[13]

.   .   .

J. R. Knowland's years in politics served him well as a newspaper man. In 1930 he noted that on the one hand, "Public life teaches one to become more tolerant. In long hours spent in community hearings it is found that there are two sides to every question. The politician is trained to move cautiously, and he gets an insight into legislation, world affairs and into human nature that is most valuable." On the other hand, it was difficult to go from a journalistic career to politics. "The publisher who later seeks to enter politics is at a disadvantage," he added. "He cannot give the proper attention to his paper. He learns to compromise and his paper loses a portion of its independence."[14]

His son Bill said in a 1968 interview that his father was not a political boss in the usual sense of the word. "People did, however, like to discuss certain issues with him from time to time because of his depth of understanding, knowledge and experience."[15] In most cases, such discussions ended with those individuals coming around to J.R.'s point of view, and not simply because of the force of his arguments. It was generally believed that he kept a "little black book" in his mind containing the names of those who disagreed with him over substantial issues.

5

"That Look in His Eyes"

At the beginning of the Roaring Twenties, J. R. Knowland's twelve-year-old son, Billy, was already putting his interest in politics to work. He was campaigning for the Harding-Coolidge ticket. His sixth-grade yearbook describes him this way: "Appearance—politics. Besetting sin—politics."

Despite his rather rugged physique, Knowland shunned athletics in high school. Instead, he devoted his efforts to school politics. His grades were average, but he organized a student Conservative Party and became student body president. He was elected on a platform of improving the content of the school newspaper, the *Acorn;* upholding the honor system; and financially supporting girls' athletics as well as boys'. The rival candidate, who described himself as "an athlete and a popular guy," credited Billy with knowing "how to make other kids take him seriously."[1] Once elected, Billy helped revise the school constitution.

During high school Billy participated in Republican precinct work, and his interest in his father's paper, the *Tribune*, sharpened as well. And it was as a teenager that young Bill began his long friendship with Earl Warren, a man seventeen years his senior, who would become a major player in his future. The two would trade political favors that would put one in the U.S. Senate and one on the Supreme Court. Young Knowland also began attending Republican committee meetings with his father. One story has it that when he was sixteen, Knowland sat in for his father as chairman of a committee to organize the Coolidge-Dawes campaign in Alameda County. The other committee members, much older than Billy, kept going off on tangents. Billy reportedly rapped his gavel and said, "Well, gentlemen, I thought we were here to try to elect Calvin Coolidge."[2]

Knowland enrolled at the University of California at Berkeley in 1925 to study political science. He ran for freshman class president, an election he lost. But he studied hard, worked in his father's office, and joined the Zeta Psi fraternity (rejecting another when he discovered that William Randolph Hearst Jr., the son of the rival newspaper publisher, was a member). It was at the university in Berkeley that the young Knowland had his first real break with his father. On New Year's Eve 1926, during his sophomore year, he eloped with his grade school sweetheart, Helen Davis Herrick. After obtaining a marriage license, they set out from Berkeley for a fraternity party in Monterey, about a hundred miles south. Halfway there, in Hollister, California, they found a minister who agreed to marry them. The same day, Bill's older brother, Russ, read the vital statistics being prepared for the paper and noticed that his brother and Helen had been issued a marriage license. He immediately called Bill's stepmother, who was enraged. She had envisioned her son marrying a governor's daughter, not Helen Herrick, the daughter of a divorced schoolteacher. She quickly phoned the police to prevent the marriage, but it was too late.

Eventually, J.R. and his wife went to see Helen's mother, Estelle Herrick. Emelyn was livid, but J.R. was much calmer and after several hours of talking they decided not to contest the marriage. Mrs. Herrick wasn't too happy, either; she liked Billy, but felt he and her daughter were too young to marry. Bill was eighteen, Helen nineteen. Helen later remarked: "I had to be a year older to catch up with him. He's always been so smart. . . . I always say if I hadn't gotten him then, when he was young, I never would have had a chance."[3]

Bill Knowland was graduated from Berkeley in three and a half years, in 1929, with a B– average. Both California governor Clement C. Young and University of California president William W. Campbell praised Knowland's political activities at his commencement. As president of the Oakland Young Republicans, Bill Knowland had led support for the Hoover-Curtis ticket in 1928. He attended the Republican National Convention as a guest that year in Kansas City, where he watched his father and Earl Warren nominate their fellow Californian, Herbert Hoover.

After graduation, Bill went to work full time in his father's *Oakland Tribune* office at $12,000 a year. Like every business, the *Tribune* was feeling the effects of the 1929 stock market crash, but nevertheless it continued to prosper. Bill was also ready to start his political career. "He was a young man with that look in his eyes," recollected Geraldine McConnell, a longtime acquaintance of the Knowland family. "He liked politics and politics liked him."[4]

In 1930 Bill Knowland was appointed to the California State Republican Central Committee. From this position, he began his campaign for a state assembly seat. Although Republicans had dominated the lower house since 1894, "it was a rough year for a young Republican to get started in public life," as Knowland remarked years later.[5] He not only had to unseat the Republican incumbent, Federal Bishop, but he had to buck what would prove to be a Roosevelt landslide to beat the Democratic nominee, Michael A. McInnis. Knowland won by 1,000 votes, even though Roosevelt carried the same district by 7,000 votes. Tough old J.R. had tears in his eyes when he boasted to friends, "Billy's done it."[6]

In 1932, at age twenty-four, Bill Knowland became the state's youngest assemblyman—younger even than his father had been when he first was appointed in 1899. Ironically for a man whose name one day would be anathema to organized labor, he was elected with the help of the State Federation of Labor, which was unhappy with his opponent's antilabor record. In his first term, Bill Knowland showed that he was an up-and-coming lawmaker by helping to cut the budget, raising corporation taxes, and backing a sales tax. Herbert L. Phillips, longtime political editor of the *Sacramento Bee*, called Knowland "an engaging, exceptionally able, straightforward and conservatively inclined young man." According to Phillips, Knowland "was forging smoothly toward the top at an age when most youngsters are just getting their careers fairly in motion."[7]

Assemblyman Bill Knowland introduced ninety-three bills that session, fifteen of which passed. At the urging of *Tribune* reporter Delilah L. Beasley, a noted figure within the Bay Area black community, he joined Fred Roberts, a black assemblyman from Los Angeles, as a co-sponsor of an antilynching bill. He helped make sure the bill passed in a state that had fifty-nine lynchings—more than any other state (outside of the South)—between 1875 and 1934.[8]

Those early years in the assembly were good ones for Knowland and his growing family. The California legislature still met only on a part-time basis, and Bill Knowland was able to devote time to his children. Longtime *Tribune* librarian Arthur Hakel still remembers seeing

Knowland several times a week at an ice rink in downtown Oakland, patiently teaching young Joe how to skate. Soon, however, Knowland would become more engrossed in his political ambitions, and his children would have too little of his attention.

In 1934 Assemblyman Knowland surprised his father by announcing he was going to seek a four-year term in the state senate. The election that year was complicated by a governor's race pitting socialist Upton Sinclair, as the Democratic candidate, against incumbent Republican Frank Merriam (the former lieutenant governor, who had acceded to the governorship only at the start of the 1934 election campaign, when Governor "Sunny Jim" Rolph died) and a third-party candidate, Raymond Haight of Hiram Johnson's Progressives. Sinclair, the muckraking author of such books as *The Jungle* (1906), which condemned conditions in the Chicago meatpacking industry, had already swept the Democratic primary for governor, defeating eight other candidates.

Sinclair's primary landslide stunned and scared an already worried Republican leadership. They knew the anti-Republican mood was strong in California: the Roosevelt tide was carrying candidates with it as voters sought change to counteract the poverty of the Great Depression. As Greg Mitchell declares in *Campaign of the Century,* "The prospect of a socialist governing the nation's most volatile state sparked nothing less than a revolution in American politics."[9] Sinclair quickly became the target of a massive Republican offensive. Directing the Republican assault were the *Oakland Tribune, Los Angeles Times,* and *San Francisco Chronicle.* Although it was always the posture of the Knowland family to downplay its influence and that of its paper, there was no doubt who was trying to run the state. Bill Knowland said innocently that during the gubernatorial campaign the *Tribune* simply quoted from Sinclair's writings and speeches. Yet Mitchell claims that J. R. Knowland "took the extraordinary step of ordering his attorneys to research the question of how badly the *Tribune* could lie about [Sinclair] and legally get away with it."[10] The Republicans unleashed what was to become one of the first modern negative campaigning efforts, led by the duo of Clem Whitaker and Leone Baxter, names that would be associated with Republican campaigns for years to come. Sinclair complained in vain that words from his books were being taken out of context. Billboards popped up showing a huge, ugly, bewhiskered figure holding a red flag while stomping on California. That kind of campaigning and a split in the more liberal vote between the Democrats and the Progressives handed the election to the rather lackluster Merriam. (The Democrats had learned their lesson, and four years later they united behind Culbert Olson, who soundly trounced Merriam to become California's first Democratic governor of the twentieth century.)

In addition to supporting Merriam in 1934, J. R. Knowland of course helped with his son's state senate campaign, but even with the *Tribune* behind him, Bill Knowland barely squeaked past his Democratic challenger, James R. Agee, a Sinclair supporter. The election was so close that young Bill Knowland wondered if any Republican would be returned to office the next time. The Democrats increased their representation in the assembly from 25 to 37 and in the senate from 5 to 8.

In the state senate Knowland promptly became floor manager for California's first unemployment insurance bill. "I think most responsible legislators recognized that some form of unemployment insurance was coming," he recalled almost forty years later. "There was opposition to it, of course, as there is to all this legislation."[11] The bill eventually became law.

During his senate term Bill Knowland was formulating his views on the labor problems that had troubled California businesses since the late 1890s. He often recalled how distressed he was when he had heard *Los Angeles Times* publisher Harry Chandler describe a labor-related bomb explosion in 1910 that killed twenty men and injured seventeen others at the *Times*. In 1937 he helped block the pardon of radical labor agitator Thomas J. Mooney, who had been convicted of murdering ten people and wounding forty in a bomb explosion during the San Francisco Preparedness Day Parade on July 22, 1916. Knowland was one of thirty-four senators who voted against the pardon; only five voted for it. He spoke out vigorously on the senate floor, arguing that not only did the senate have no power to grant a pardon, but the evidence was overwhelming that Mooney had committed the crime, and indeed all of the courts had upheld the conviction. Knowland went so far as to read the names of the dead victims—five of them from Alameda County—calling them the forgotten ones in the bombing.

By most accounts, however, Mooney was convicted by fabricated evidence. He was sentenced to be executed, but the sentence was commuted to life in prison. For twenty-one years, his lawyers—Clarence Darrow, labor lawyer Austin Lewis, and San Francisco trial lawyer George Davis—and an array of writers and actors worked to free Mooney, but it wasn't until 1938 that newly elected Governor Culbert Olson, a Democrat, freed him.

In one of Knowland's most important acts as a lawmaker, he led a

1938 campaign to place on the ballot a constitutional amendment that would require highway funds to be used for building, maintaining, and administering highways. It was an important step in providing an interconnected highway system in California. That year $700 million of the $1 billion in highway-designated revenues was set aside for roads.[12]

Knowland made an astute political move while he was in the state senate when he agreed to handle legislation relating to Los Angeles County school matters. Because its own senator had alienated some of his colleagues from smaller counties, Los Angeles often could not get fair hearings on school legislation. Los Angeles teachers talked Knowland into handling their cases, particularly pension legislation. Years later, when Knowland was campaigning for a full term in the U.S. Senate, he earned a disproportionate share of his votes in Southern California, a fact he attributed to his willingness to help L.A. schools.[13]

.   .   .

Soon after Earl Warren entered Alameda County politics in 1925 as a young assistant district attorney, he became a beneficiary of the Knowland influence. When his boss, District Attorney Ezra Decoto, accepted an appointment to the state Railroad Commission, Warren and Frank Shay, the other top assistant, vied for Decoto's job. Shay had the backing of the county's Democratic political machine, headed by Mike Kelly, but Warren knew that J. R. Knowland was not politically friendly with the Kelly organization. As Warren later described, "Without any acquaintance with [J. R. Knowland], I went to his office, told him the situation and asked if I could not get a fair break on the news from the courthouse. Knowland (who in print referred to Kelly and his aides as bosses) said yes and I believe that was the beginning of his interest in me."[14] Warren said Knowland used his influence on his behalf, and Warren was appointed by a 3–2 vote of the Alameda County Board of Supervisors.

Later, in 1932, Knowland shocked the California GOP by boosting Earl Warren as the party's new state chairman. Knowland was unhappy with Governor Frank Merriam and he disliked Merriam's candidate for state chairman, John McNab. "Earl represents the younger group and is a man of splendid character and the kind of leader we could well put to the front this year," J.R. said.[15] McNab pulled out of the contest at the urging of Kyle Palmer, the political editor and kingmaker of the *Los Angeles Times.*

J. R. Knowland downplayed his influence over Warren. "No one ever told Warren what to do in the line of duty, at least not more than once," he said. "I lost several friends who asked me to intervene in some important matter with Warren, and [they] wouldn't believe me when I told them I couldn't influence Warren, and that if I tried to interfere it would only hurt them or their friends. . . . He sought advice from his friends on every legitimate subject, but when he had a job to perform he went ahead on his own responsibility."[16] Warren's attitude toward Bill Knowland was similar. Even though Warren eventually appointed Knowland to the U.S. Senate, Warren confidant Oscar Jahnsen claimed that Warren never told Knowland what to do. "I think Warren felt that he could trust Bill," Jahnsen explained. "He admired Bill's ability and appreciated Bill's views. They had many conferences. What they discussed and what went on between them was between Mr. Warren and Bill."[17]

In 1936 Bill Knowland and Earl Warren were among the "Young Turks" who helped found the California Republican Assembly. It was that year, Knowland later said, that the CRA "had really won its spurs."[18] As Knowland told the story, Kansas governor Alf Landon had gotten off to a quick start in locking up the nomination even before the California primary was held. Knowland said that some of the CRA members got in touch with the Landon people, urging them to keep him out of the California primary. They said they wanted an "uninstructed delegation" to go to the convention. A committee, called the Carnahan committee, was set up to propose a list of delegates that would be broadly representative of the Republican Party from California.[19]

Since, under California law, even an uninstructed delegation had to run under someone's name in the primary, the Carnahan committee asked Warren to head the delegation. Warren, of course, had the support of the "triumvirate"—the *Oakland Tribune, Los Angeles Times,* and *San Francisco Chronicle.* Most Republicans were surprised when the Warren delegates won the contest, given Landon's lead in gaining the nomination and the support from Hearst. "We explained that the delegation was not prejudiced against Landon; [we] just felt that the party should not commit itself too soon and should have a look at the field at the convention," Bill Knowland said. Warren's delegates went to the national convention, which helped to spread his reputation nationally. "It gave him a degree of recognition throughout the country," Knowland recalled.[20]

In addition to serving as state chairman for the Republican Party,

Warren was a member of the Republican National Committee. When he decided in 1938 to run for California attorney general (with the Knowlands' strong backing, of course), he resigned as a national committeeman. He said he was seeking the endorsement of the Democrats as well as the Republicans, so remaining on the committee would be inappropriate.[21] Bill Knowland wanted to succeed Warren on the Republican National Committee and needed Herbert Hoover's help. Knowland approached Charles W. Fisher, the Northern California executive director for California Circles, a group trying to get Hoover nominated for president in 1940. Knowland asked Fisher to persuade Hoover to swing seventeen votes on the Pro-America delegation to the state Republican Central Committee over to him. After three attempts, Fisher got Hoover to agree, reluctantly.[22]

Apparently it worked. On April 9, 1938, the executive committee of the state Republican Central Committee met at the Palace Hotel in San Francisco to choose Warren's replacement. Lawrence Cobb, the committee's secretary, nominated Bill Knowland for the vacant seat, and the nomination was seconded by Agnes Morely Cleaveland of Berkeley and Sol Abrams of San Francisco. The vote was unanimous. At the age of thirty, Bill Knowland became the Republican National Committee's youngest member. He was even being mentioned as a possible candidate for lieutenant governor. There was also speculation in the press that he might run for the U.S. Senate.

In mid-1938 Knowland was optimistic about the West Coast Republicans' chances in the elections. "The New Deal recently lost considerable ground in the Pacific Coast states," he told John Hamilton, chairman of the Republican National Committee. "The business depression has given a severe jolt to those who believed the New Deal possessed some magical power of creating prosperity out of thin air by spending far more than it solicited in tax receipts and encouraging every one to work and produce less. Our people in California are commencing to realize that the money which the Roosevelt Administration is pouring out must eventually be paid by them, with interest."[23]

Knowland himself decided against seeking reelection to the state senate, but that did not signal a lessening of his political goals. Instead, he concentrated on his duties as a Republican National Committee member and, in two years, became the youngest chairman of its executive committee. Determined to bring the party back to a commanding position, Knowland described the 1938 campaign as "a prelude" to the 1940 presidential campaign, and he insisted that "there is much work to be done." He stressed "the importance of . . . California with its 22 electoral votes . . . in the National political picture. There have been five times in the Nation's history when a change of electoral votes would have resulted in [a] different President being placed in the White House. The Republican National organization is no stronger than its state and county organizations, and it will be my purpose to help build the party in California."[24]

At the end of July 1938, Knowland wrote a three-page article for a newsletter put out by the California Republican Assembly. "There is no excuse for a defeatist attitude on the part of any Republican in this state," he emphasized. "Our job is to face realities. . . . I am satisfied that Republicans will once again command majority support if they will present a constructive alternative to the government by hunch that exists in Washington today. We will not receive widespread support merely on a program of carping criticism. . . . We cannot arouse the interest of the people of this state merely on a narrow issue of the outs wanting to get in." Knowland urged Republicans to unite and "to have the courage to stand firm and fight," pointing out, "Less than a year remains before the Republican National Convention will nominate the next president of the United States. California must be prepared to play its part in that result."[25] These were savvy words coming from an upstart politician who was just turning thirty-one.

Bill Knowland also knew the value of party loyalty. In a July 16, 1938, letter to Henry S. McKee, the budget chairman of the Republican State Committee, Knowland bitterly opposed allowing money raised by the Republican National Committee to be used to finance one candidate over another. That, he said, would "result in serious consequences to the future of the party in California." He argued that the "Republican party is larger and more important than any organization, group of organizations, individual or group of individuals. The future of the party must be considered on this broad basis rather than from the angle of any single unit. We must not concentrate on the metropolitan areas to the exclusion of the balance of the state, nor must we support one organization to the exclusion of others. Of course, judgment has to be used in the allocation of funds so that the money will be wisely and economically administered."[26]

But one person who questioned Knowland's loyalty was Charles Fisher. After urging Herbert Hoover to support Knowland for the national committee job, he was upset when Knowland failed to help him in return. As he put it, "Bill Knowland did stab me in the back."[27] The incident occurred in 1940, when Fisher was approached to become chairman of the Alameda County Republican Central Committee. As he told the story, when Knowland learned that Fisher had the support of thirty-eight of the forty-six members, he told him that he shouldn't be the chairman, that John Allen was the better choice. (Allen was the son of the judge who had handed down the decision that enabled the Knowlands to acquire full title to the *Tribune*.) Surprised, Fisher replied, "'Bill, have you forgotten what I did with Mr. Hoover and the National Committee?' He didn't answer me. . . . Mr. Knowland and his little group went to every member of the central committee. . . . And one by one, they dropped me because the power was in Knowland's hands."

Young Bill Knowland had his eye on bigger things. He used the Republican national office to travel the state, getting to know people and letting them know him better. He posed with all the leading Republican candidates when they visited California. He supported Tom Dewey, even helping coordinate his visit to California during the 1940 campaign. He also got to know such future colleagues in the Senate as Arthur Vandenberg and Robert Taft. Wendell Willkie won the nomination, but Knowland noted that "most of those who had worked in the Republican vineyards for years were something less than enthusiastic" about his candidacy.[28]

Meanwhile, Earl Warren was making his move. In 1938 he was elected California attorney general, one of the state's most powerful constitutional offices. About eighteen months before the California gubernatorial election of 1942, the *Los Angeles Times* ran a story written by Kyle Palmer under the headline "Gubernatorial Whispers Fill the Air," predicting that Warren would seek the seat held by Democrat Culbert Olson.[29] Kyle Palmer wrote with more authority than the headline implied, for his source was apparently another Republican strategist, Murray Chotiner, later a major player in Richard Nixon's rise to the presidency. Chotiner was passing along information to Palmer that he had received from Warren's friend, Bill Knowland.[30] There was no doubt that Warren as governor would be in a position to advance Bill Knowland's political goals.

In a later interview with Jim Bassett, a *Los Angeles Times* editor, Bill Knowland was asked if he was the whisperer responsible for the Warren rumor. He replied, "I don't think I was the decisive figure by any manner of means, in Mr. Warren's determination . . . because he made up his own mind." Knowland pointed out that with the exceptions of Secretary of State Frank Jordan and the attorney general, the Democrats had swept the state elections in 1938. "It did seem to me that Warren was by far the outstanding potential candidate, with the capability of defeating Olson, who undoubtedly would be a candidate for reelection."

Knowland admitted that without any consultation he had floated Warren's name because he knew the high regard other Republicans had for the attorney general. Knowland said, "I pointed out to him that he was the one man in my judgment who could defeat Olson, and otherwise he'd be faced with the problem of being attorney general—I didn't think there was any doubt he would be re-elected attorney general—but he would then be faced with four more years of the Olson administration. I cited what this might do for the state."[31] He added that he was certain that the attorney general talked to several other top Republicans before he made his decision. One of them undoubtedly was Bill's father, J. R. Knowland. Warren certainly respected the elder Knowland's power and would not have taken such a step without his approval. He announced his candidacy on April 10, 1942.

After all, as Assemblyman Gardiner Johnson later said, "[J. R. Knowland] was a very experienced, very able, very assertive man. His opinion was valued; many people realized that he knew the political techniques. He knew what was going on; he knew who the people were and where they came from, and his judgment was good. To have him solidly for you was a very important thing."[32]

Although the plan had been for Bill Knowland to take an active role in Warren's campaign for governor, international events would take precedence. Germany was on the move in Europe and Japan was acting aggressively in the Pacific. The world was on the brink of war.

.   .   .

On the morning of December 7, 1941, Bill and Helen Knowland were eating a breakfast of scrambled eggs and coffee in bed when the *Tribune*'s city editor, Al Reck, telephoned to tell him of the Japanese bombing of Pearl Harbor. Knowland listened for a moment, then bolted out of bed, crying out, "It's come." He grabbed his clothes and was out the door before Helen knew what was happening. It was only later that she found out about the bombing, long after Knowland was at the *Tribune* office that Sunday morning helping to get out the next day's paper.[33]

Even though he knew he might be drafted, Knowland stayed active in Republican politics. On April 23, 1942, he wrote to Wendell Willkie urging him to support Tom Dewey's candidacy for president in 1944: "I share with you the deep conviction that the Republican Party is very likely the only agency left in the world today that can save those things in which we both believe. If this be so, then there is no question of a doubt that the party can best be directed by leadership from within the fold rather than by preaching from without." Willkie replied, "You are a tower of strength both in action and in advice. I shall never forget all you did."[34]

The following June 13, Knowland received his draft notice. He hurried over to Earl and Nina Warren's house on Vernon Street in Oakland to tell them. Ten days later William F. Knowland, at the ripe age of thirty-four, was inducted into the U.S. Army.

6

Billy Goes Off to War

It was unusual for a thirty-four-year-old father of three to be drafted, but Bill Knowland didn't complain. He loved his country, and he wanted to serve. He probably could have used his political connections to avoid the draft, or at the very least gotten a commission as an officer, but he did not want special privileges. Private William F. Knowland was ready to join ranks with men ten to twelve years younger than he.

In a letter to former president Herbert Hoover, Knowland explained: "The *Tribune*, as you know, has supported the original Selective Service Act and its extension, and as one who is responsible in part for the editorial policy of this newspaper, I was, of course, not going to be put into the position of advocating something for the other fellow which we would not be willing to do ourselves. Therefore, I made no effort to get a deferment nor would I permit any effort to be made along this line." Hoover, however, was depressed by Knowland's letter and replied: "I just cannot see how men with families are taken into the Army when there now is a surplus of men with no family ties, especially when it comes to men who, like yourself, are holding up the whole world."[1]

After just a few days at Fort Ord in Monterey, California, Knowland boarded a train to another training center in Texas. He described the trip to his father: "Soldiers do not travel in the best Pullmans! We have been assigned to two old pre-airconditioning cars which were hot yesterday crossing Arizona." He added that he was with "a nice bunch of fellows," mostly in their thirties, some married. In July 1942 Knowland arrived at Camp Wallace, between Houston and Galveston. There, he said, the weather was "10 degrees warmer than Hades." The drills caused him to shed weight, and his tan became "just a shade or two lighter than my Army shoes." In his opinion, the drills bad enough for the younger soldiers, but "for us old bucks [they were] a super dooper." On one obstacle course he described, trainees had to jump trenches, swing on ropes over water, climb walls, and crawl through pipes.

Knowland told his father that he had no regrets about joining the army, although he did miss his family. As time passed, he became used to the climate and built up his endurance. Yet he did have one complaint—he and the other soldiers were chafing under the "petty tyranny of small individuals given power (noncommissioned officers) who cannot assume authority without making themselves obnoxious." He was especially irritated by a corporal at Fort Ord, whom he described as "cocky, foul-mouthed, illiterate and a first class so and so." If that corporal had talked to anyone like that in civilian life, Knowland indicated, "he would have had his block knocked off."

A prolific writer, Knowland cranked out at least one letter—and sometimes two—a day to his wife, children, and father. He also wrote to friends and political leaders. He told Helen, "I have decided, since being in the Army, that mail is a great institution." And he admitted to his father that he had penned more letters longhand while at the camp than in his previous thirty-four years. Knowland's frequent letters to his father and his wife were concerned mainly with family matters, events at the *Tribune*, and, of course, politics. They tended to be more intellectual than intimate, but he did express affection, especially toward his wife. He wrote, for example, that he looked at Helen's picture several times a day and thought of her constantly. And when he received a letter from her, he claimed, "My morale goes sky high."

In Texas, Knowland began training in an anti-aircraft unit and was soon promoted to corporal. One thing he told his father he was learning was "a much higher appreciation of the dollar." He added, "I would sure like to be on a negotiating committee right now where time and a half and double time was being demanded."

By the beginning of August 1942 Knowland had been promoted to first sergeant and had filed an application for Officer Candidate School (OCS). When he appeared before the army review board, its members, two majors and a lieutenant, kidded him about being one of the "vanishing Republicans." They also remarked on how unusual his case was, given that he was married with children and had such a varied career. They didn't understand why he wanted to transfer from the relative safety of stateside anti-aircraft forces to go to OCS for an almost certain overseas assignment. Accepted into OCS, Knowland passed his physical. In a few days he was on his way to Fort Benning, Georgia. He wrote Helen that he hoped to get a two-week leave in another three or four months, and in the meantime he promised a photograph of her now physically fit "re-modeled husband."

While Knowland was living on his army salary, Helen was trying to get his father to increase her husband's salary so she could make ends meet. In a six-page letter to her father-in-law, she worried that they were spending some $15,000 more than their income from the *Tribune*. She herself was making $2,548 and her husband about $5,200 a year from the *Tribune*, but they had expenses of almost $23,000 for 1943. To help them out, she suggested that her father-in-law, whom she usually addressed as Mr. Knowland, consider redistributing income property among the children and grandchildren. It is not known how J.R. reacted to her request, although it is doubtful he would have allowed his favorite son to continue to operate in the red. J.R would help him financially several times over the years.

Even as he went through OCS at Fort Benning, Sergeant Knowland still found time to be concerned with politics. He expressed pleasure, for example, that Earl Warren had handily defeated Democrat Culbert Olson in the governor's race. "Glad Earl's margin was so large as it will give weight when he makes recommendations to the legislature," he wrote his father.

For the most part, however, his letters from this period reflect family concerns. In a rare display of affection, he wrote his father: "While I may not have expressed it in so many words, I think you know that my feeling has always been that no son ever had a finer father than I have." Knowland was worried about the separation from his family, and he was especially glad the family could all be together around Christmas. "Don't like to break up the family unit," he wrote. "After all it is the basis of our American way of life." That Christmas season he penned a poem for Helen called "A Soldier's Christmas—1942":

> The place was dark and the room was small
> But I didn't mind these things at all
> For she had come far alone
> To give this soldier a glimpse of home.
>
> The too few days have now passed by
> A clock ticks minutes now as I

Seek to fathom as night comes fast
If this farewell may be our last.

As she sleeps beside me in troubled rest
I think of our home when I was a boy
In a world at peace and full of joy.

And now the war clouds are here
We must fight for the things that we hold dear
For God, for country and for home
In great crusade in which we are not alone.

We should get down on our knees to pray
That at some not too distant day
Humanity freed from blood and pain
May learn His teachings once again.

Perhaps if we must die by steel or blast
Civilized nations may learn at last
To solve their problems without war or guns
and without drenching their soils with the blood of their sons.

For as my dearest has come this Christmas Day
I realize far more than words can say
That soldiers are here and then we are gone
But our women at home must bravely fight on.

In early January 1943, Bill Knowland received a letter from his father informing him that J.R. had received a tip that the newly appointed brigadier general in charge of Fort Lewis, Washington, was going to request young Knowland be assigned as his aide. J.R. insisted: "This comes without a solicitation on my part whatever or any member of your family." He urged his son to take the appointment, pointing out, "you are entitled to the best assignment possible." In addition, he underlined the advantage of "the fact that the general will come to California on an average of twice a month, bringing you with him." In this way, "you can keep in contact with your office and your family." Besides, J.R. continued, "I understand that men of your age and rank would not be sent [overseas], so that you would have to be somewhere in the United States for the time being."

By mid-1943, Knowland was on the West Coast, as an aide to General Marcellus Stockton, just as his father had predicted. He was stationed at Fort Lewis, the headquarters for the Northwestern Sector, Western Defense Command. There he not only served as the general's aide but became the general's hunting and fishing partner as well.

During this period two of Knowland's lifelong problems surfaced: his difficulties with money and with women. Apparently Knowland owed significant back taxes for 1942, and he worried that these would eat up his entire army salary for the year. To his relief, he received notice that he had been promoted from second lieutenant to first lieutenant. His pay jumped from $252 a month to $296.17, which included a $75 rent allowance and $12.50 for acting as an aide-de-camp.

The long separation from his family and loneliness were changing Knowland. Like many men of his wartime generation who were thrust back into a role of virtual bachelorhood, he began to seek other companionship. Evidently jealous to learn from one of Helen's letters that she found Henry Luce, founder of *Time* magazine, "most attractive," he retaliated, "If I could find myself a good looking nurse I would take her out to dinner today and dancing tonight. Getting a little fed up with this hermit life and in need of a little feminine companionship. . . . Perhaps I will just have to wait around until you arrive in August before I do much stepping out. Can't tell what the week may bring, however." Helen underlined the words "nurse" and "much" (referring to his stepping out) and attached her own note to the letter: "Wonder what's gotten into Billy! He's never written me a letter like this before in his life! Why a 'nurse'? Maybe he didn't approve of Mr. Luce." She signed the note HK and drew a sad face next to her initials.

Such references were scattered through his letters to Helen. In one, he wrote that he had $110 on hand, "which if I don't lose or squander on some blonde babe, should carry me through the month." In another, Knowland lamented not being able to take her to the Northwestern Sector officers' dance. Then, without explanation, he mentioned, "Barbara is going elsewhere with some of her friends and I will 'stag' it again as usual." (It is unclear who Barbara was.) In yet another letter he noted, "All the gals are either married or too young for me to enjoy the evening with. . . . The trouble is that after 16 years of Helen my standards for feminine beauty plus intelligence are so darn high that there are few if any in your class." Just how lonely he was is evident in his response on learning that Helen was coming for a visit: "Feel like a boy waiting for his girl to come so they can be married and go on their honeymoon!! I love you so much that it hurts."

Occasionally Lieutenant Knowland wrote Helen about his political concerns. He predicted that in 1944 the GOP would nominate New York governor Tom Dewey for president and Earl Warren for vice president. Dewey was nominated for president, but Warren wouldn't be nominated for vice president until 1948. "If Earl did not land on the ticket he might later be offered a cabinet position (attorney general as an example). . . . The situation seemed so clear to me that things would start to shape up this way. That is why I believed the time for Earl to be governor was now (when the contrast with Olson would be so great and the national significance of a change from Democratic to GOP would make news) rather than 4 or 8 years from now."

Knowland's letters reflect a sense of a growing distance from his former life. To be sure, he gave Helen constant advice on how to handle the sale of their house in Alameda and the purchase of a new one in Piedmont. When she complained about this overload of advice, he responded, "I am still part of the family and should be presumed to have some interest at least in such a transaction." Because Helen was replacing him on several boards of directors while he was in the army, he wrote, "I shall expect to offer advice from time to time to you. I don't want to feel that it is not welcome. . . . Don't count your Bill out of the picture. These things are one of the *very few* threads I have connecting me with my old life and I don't want it severed any sooner than necessary." But in reality, Knowland's connections with his old life already had been irreversibly severed. Like many World War II servicemen, he never would recapture the ease of the old prewar life.

He complained, "Your letter to me and this one to you seem more than any of our others like one business partner to the other rather than between a husband and wife who have just arranged to purchase a new home." Knowland claimed he wanted their marriage to work, not just for his own sake but because of their children's future. He told Helen she enjoyed a much better life than most wives. "Now I am not denying that your husband has liabilities but he probably has some assets and his liabilities are probably no greater than lots of other guys though they may be of a different type." He said that he wasn't feeling sorry for himself, but noted that he was far removed from his family and friends. "Yet this would be tolerable even though perhaps not pleasant if I felt I was a real part of the war against the Japs and other Axis powers but here in the Northwest I can't even get that stimulation." He concluded, "Well, put this down to a cold rainy day's influence on a husband who is many hundreds of miles away from the wife he adores."

In a letter to Helen written October 17, 1943, he was sentimental over his family and worried about their welfare should he be killed in the war. "My own mind will be at rest knowing you and the children are in our new home and that I have provided substantial protection in case I should not come back. This in itself would not be sufficient if I were not certain that you had the capacity and common sense to look after your own and the children's interests. . . . No man ever had a better reason to want to live through this conflict and come home again." Still, Knowland was getting restless about his assignment in the Northwest and was seeking a transfer to Europe. "Perhaps some will wonder why in such circumstances I should want to leave the Northwest and go elsewhere," he wrote Helen. "It is some inner urge that convinces me that I am not yet contributing my full share to the winning of this war which is a prerequisite of guaranteeing the peace to follow for Joey's generation and those that will come after."

Five days later, writing on a paper towel because he had no writing paper, Knowland told Helen he was close to being sent overseas and might be sent on short notice without getting a chance for a leave. Then he wrote, "What this separation caused by the war may do to your feelings toward me I, of course, cannot say. As for mine, they have made me love and respect you more than ever and to want to strive and do those things that will make your life a most contented one." Knowland apologized to Helen for having let his public life and civic activities interfere with their family life. "I realize now, too late, that it ate into the hours, days, weeks and months that a husband should have been giving to his wife and a father to his children. How changed my perspective is now on the things that are important." He told Helen that if he didn't return from the war, "I would expect that in due time you would find some man who would devote himself to doing all the things to make you happy that I shall pray it may be my privilege to return and do myself."

Knowland's letters to his wife expressed, however stiffly, his deep love for her, and she returned this affection:

There is no one comparable to you whom I have ever met, and I doubt if there is among those whom I do not know. You have the looks, the brains, the background, the ability, and above all a human understanding of what makes people tick—including your little girl, Helen.

I want you to come back to me and my prayer is that we may spend the rest of our lives together, working toward our goal which is to make even sounder than your Dad and Grandfather before so ably started the business of the family, and to raise three beautiful children into adults and, perhaps even have much to do with the destinies of their children, too. It will be a good life together.

It was not just in his letters to Helen that Knowland was preparing for combat. He specifically asked General Stockton to write a letter to his commanding officer urging that he be sent overseas as an officer on military government assignment. Stockton complied with a highly laudatory letter, describing Knowland as "preeminently qualified for the job he seeks." Stockton went on: "He has been modest in listing his experiences in the interest of brevity, and there could well be included many other activities in which he has participated with credit. Knowland is a man of high principle, unimpeachable integrity, excellent judgment, and possesses a keen analytical mind. He is highly attentive to duty, tireless, painstaking, and unusually alert, both mentally and physically. He is personable, tactful, loyal, and highly intelligent."

It wouldn't be long before Knowland got his wish.

.   .   .

While Knowland was getting ready to go overseas, back home in Oakland the *Tribune* was prospering, fueled by the "Second Gold Rush," a prosperity brought to the East Bay by World War II.

Construction of the Alameda Naval Air Station, Oakland Army Base, and the Naval Supply Base came with the war. Other military facilities also were being put up in the East Bay at a total cost of $60 million. Thousands of military and civil workers were hired at the bases. The federal government provided more jobs in the East Bay than the state and local governments combined. Those military bases would be key elements in Oakland's economy well into the 1990s.[2]

Fed by $5 billion in federal contracts, the East Bay became the top shipbuilding center in the country. The shipbuilding industry employed more than 150,000, or 80 percent, of the workers in the East Bay's heavy industries. Those high-paying jobs attracted thousands of migrants from the South, Midwest, and East Coast. The civilian population in the Bay Area grew by a half million people, or almost 26 percent, from 1940 to 1945. Half of those newcomers were in the East Bay and North Bay. Shipbuilding magnate Henry Kaiser called the East Bay "the coming industrial empire in the West."[3] Several major manufacturing and transportation corporations established headquarters or major branches in Oakland, including Kaiser Industries, Owens-Illinois Glass Company, Montgomery Ward and Company, Sears Roebuck and Company, Bank of America, Standard Oil Company of California, and the Santa Fe, Southern Pacific, and Western Pacific railroads.

To meet the housing needs of defense workers, home construction became big business. Before World War II, individuals built most of the homes in Oakland, but by the end of the war larger builders were putting up 35 percent of all houses there. The Oakland metropolitan area had almost 400,000 residents by 1945. With the increased population came the need for hundreds of businesses to serve their needs. The *Tribune* was to reap the benefits in increased circulation and advertising linage.

These were boom years for the aging J. R. Knowland as well. In a financial statement of April 1, 1941, it was revealed that his personal and separate property had a net worth of $562,310.

While at Fort Lewis, Bill Knowland received a report from the *Tribune* that ad linage for the first eight months of the year was more than two million higher than the previous year. While all newspapers in Northern California were showing gains in advertising, the *Tribune*'s were substantially higher.

7

From Major to Senator

On December 1, 1943, First Lieutenant Bill Knowland arrived in Washington, D.C., on his way to the School of Military Government at the University of Virginia in Charlottesville. There he paid respects to Senators Robert Taft of Ohio and Hiram Johnson of California. Both would play an important role in his future. "Johnson," he wrote to his wife on December 1, "is very feeble and for the first time looks like a very, very old man with hands trembling, etc. We had a very nice chat, and he seemed very pleased to see me."

On December 2 Knowland was promoted to captain and soon he began attending classes. He was being schooled in army history in preparation for a European assignment. While his classmates were writing home about personal events, Knowland was writing to Helen about his broader vision of the war and his convictions about the virtues of the American way of life. On January 19, 1944, he wrote:

Our way of life is a beacon light to a war torn world. In the "dark ages" of this century that are to come we must keep it burning brightly. By this I do not mean to force our ways (economic, political or social) on the other nations. This would be unwise and impossible.

Rather by making our free institutions work and by showing through precept and example that Catholic, Protestant and Jew, white, brown and black, labor and capital, rural and urban, Republicans and Democrats (as well as other minority groups) can work together for the improvement of our common weal, we will furnish hope and courage to those elsewhere who strive to bring order and tolerance to a disorderly and bigoted world.

41

Yet with all this we have the will to fight and die to guard that heritage. We are not the lazy and decadent people that Hitler, Mussolini [or] Tojo tries to make out.

At the same time we must be on guard against those who would squander our resources in attempting to "buy our way into the hearts of other peoples." My own belief is that such a policy will make international suckers of us. They will take our money and question our sanity, as well they might. [Years later he would bitterly oppose giving U.S. dollars to Communist countries.]

I have great fear that we will end up by having our people pay the war costs that in the normal course of events the defeated enemy would be called on to pay. Our people will of necessity carry a great debt to win the war and destroy the enemy in the process. If, then, there is added to this an international WPA at American expense we will be saddled with a double debt that may destroy our economy and open the door for political and social disorders that will put Americans to a greater test than they have yet to experience.

To me the safety of our political system is dependent upon the soundness of our economy. Twelve million unemployed could be fertile ground in which demagogues could work and perhaps pull down about the ears of 123 million the vast structure that has carried our people to great heights.

We must strive as a matter of policy to encourage home and farm ownership by our people. We must advance the process of education to the distant out of the way corners of our country. A wide ownership in our large and small corporations must be accelerated. We must prevent a Marxian cleavage between workers and capitalists through savings accounts, ownership of home, insurance, bonds and personal goods. This necessitates the payment of not only living wages but saving wages as well.

At the same time the common sense of Benjamin Franklin must once again become popular. Thrift and a desire to build for the future should be made a part of our life. Many who are making high war industry salaries are buying bonds and saving for the inevitable "rainy day." However, many others are not and they are so to speak on an economic "champagne binge" that will leave them down and out when the slack period comes. Out of this self same group will come leaders of the "world owes me a living" philosophy. They will then want to share the wealth with those who have been frugal and farsighted.

With it all we must encourage forthrightness in public life. Legislators and administrators must be willing to stand up and be counted. How else will we ever know if people of common sense or the "lunatic fringe" is in control.

While the pendulum will swing back and forth in political campaigns we need not fear for the Republic as long as the integrity of our election machinery is maintained. In the long run, given courageous leadership, the people will find the right solutions. It is only when through apathy or cowardice the press and those who should know better stand aside until too late that the Hitlers are able to fasten their systems upon a great people.

Knowland was writing more than a letter to a wife; it was as if he was preparing for his political campaigns and speeches on the U.S. Senate floor.

As Knowland reflected on the international war overseas, Helen expressed concerns about some family battles closer to home. She was struggling to meet the needs of her family while working as an assistant to her demanding father-in-law. From virtually the day her husband went into the army, Helen had moved into his office, taking over many of his duties, and she now felt increasing anxiety. Helen complained to her father- and mother-in-law that she had little social life. Although she attended political affairs because her husband expected her to, she wished she could instead "turn what little extra time I have in other directions which would give me more relaxation and personal pleasure." She did not believe her father-in-law understood all that was involved in working full-time and at the same time meeting the needs of her home and her children. Even with "a laundress to come in and iron," she explained, "in order for her to get it done . . . I have to wash much of it in advance myself, get it starched and dampened so that she is ready to go with no time wasted upon arrival." What with housework, shopping, and caring for the children's illnesses, she felt it was unjust that she was criticized for leaving early each day. Specifically, she said, "You mention that my leaving at varied hours in the afternoon is bad for the morale of the girl at the desk and, I supposed you meant, others. I would say that depends entirely upon the position which I am holding. If I am in the same category as the girl at the desk or Miss White, then it is, I suppose, true. But if I am representing Billy, then certainly it could not be so, for neither Billy nor Russell ever spent such regular hours here as I am and have been spending."

Much more disturbing to Helen than the disagreement over flexible work hours was the ongoing conflict with Mamoo. In a letter to her husband, Helen reported repeated run-ins with her mother-in-law: "She has attacked me daily, verbally, made terrible threats, called me everything under the sun, the worst and repeatedly, alone and before people." At one point, she said, Mamoo took a knife to the furniture and venetian blinds in J.R.'s office and threw the phone on the floor, yelling at the top of her lungs. Mamoo told Helen not to tell her husband what she had done to J.R.'s office, but Helen refused to make a promise. "She shook her fist at me and said I'd regret it the rest of my life if I told, that 'she'd get me,' that in three days I'd 'no longer have that pretty face,' etc. . . . She's unbalanced, dangerous. If she comes to this house and tries to get me alone, I'm going to call for police protection."

Rages at the office were commonplace. Once, Helen said, Mamoo drew blood when she struck J.R., and she attacked the paper's managing editor, Leo Levy, and others on the staff. Levy threatened to quit if Mamoo remained at the paper. "I have received her blows in silence for months on end, said nothing, and slowly I have come to the conclusion which I am now acting upon. I am sure I am right in this. . . . Dad is in such a state that he cannot reason wisely from a broad point of view. All he sees is the moment, it has passed before and will pass again. But he is wrong there, it does not pass." She was also worried about the effect the attacks would have on the children. "All three of them have seen their mother attacked and accused, all three have been devastated with grief and tears and it shall never happen again. God bless you, darling, we're both at war now, aren't we?"

.   .   .

On February 21, 1944, Knowland left New York on the French liner *Pasteur*, reaching England eight days later. He said the troops made the trip without a convoy or any escort vessels. "Theory was we could outrun any submarine," he wrote his father. "Good theory except that one night we had engine trouble and had to wallow standing still for several hours which was not so good." He arrived in Liverpool, and there boarded a train to Shrivenham, where he stayed until April at the American School Center for Military Government. Two days after his arrival, he found time to rent a bicycle and pedal around the countryside. "It was a grand day and I enjoyed it very much."

During his brief assignment in Shrivenham, he received orders appointing him chief of the historical section of the Forward Echelon Communications zone in London. He was greeted in London by German bombings that went on daily for several months. Several bombs came very close; one landed within a half a block of his flat, knocking out many of the building's windows. During his new assignment, he roomed with Dudley Frost, who became a close friend. Later, helped by the influence of the Knowlands, Frost would become executive director of the Port of Oakland.

In one of the oddities of war and danger, things that might be considered trivial in normal times became extremely meaningful. Knowland developed a craving for marshmallows. On July 3, Knowland wrote a short letter to his wife with one plea: "Please send me a *large box* of marshmallows. They are not available here and would be much appreciated. Find out the largest package you can send within the weight limit." He also asked for dental floss. "It will be your fault if I have to have a lot of fillings put in when I return merely for the lack of this request!" His concerns about his teeth notwithstanding, he made repeated pleas for marshmallows during his remaining tour in Europe. There never seemed to be enough of them and they always were too slow in coming.

On July 13, Knowland's group left England at Southampton and crossed the English Channel. It landed at Utah Beach on the Normandy peninsula the next day, just five weeks after D-Day. During the fall Knowland moved with units throughout Europe, living in tents and often sleeping on the ground during the rainy season. This man of wealth and privilege found himself without a wash basin; instead, he had to use his steel helmet for bathing, shaving, and washing socks and underwear. Sometimes he wrote letters to Helen by kerosene lamplight. But he said he was not really bothered by any of this:

It is interesting to note how quickly a new tent can become "home." You move into one that has just been put up, clear out (if there is any) any evidence that the field had been a pasture for sheep, horses or cows, put up your army cot, spread out your bed roll, set up your change (if you are lucky enough to have one), put down a piece of cardboard as a mat, put down a couple of boards on which to place your Valpack and Duffle Bag. Presto! Just like that, it's home and you look forward to getting back to it at night. You of course add some additional luxuries such as a wooden box as a dresser and perhaps a wash-stand out back in which to put your steel helmet so it won't tip over when filled with water.

Eventually he was able to rent a 9-by-13-foot attic room of a small fourth-rate hotel outside of Paris, where there was no heat and there were five flights of stairs to climb. "Rather run down place, but the bed is soft," he noted. "Almost getting to like the joint!" he cheerfully added later.

But Knowland was not always in good spirits. On one of his lower days, he wrote to Helen about his unhappiness at Franklin D. Roosevelt's reelection and his general wartime weariness. He also was feeling hurt that his children hadn't written to him. "It does seem to me that if I had a father overseas I could manage the time to write at least once a week," he complained. "I doubt if any of them . . . averaged once every two months! . . . Makes me feel that I have fallen down somewhere along the line, as perhaps I have." He then added, "Probably should have let this day pass without writing. However, daily letter writing is now a habit and furthermore you are far too smart a girl to be fooled into thinking that things look bright all the time."

On December 8, Knowland was ordered to Paris with the Fifteenth Army. There he was housed in an attic billet on the seventh floor, again with no elevator. He noted that "you get your hot bath Sunday morning or not at all." He enjoyed Paris life, taking in the Folies-Bergère, Napoleon's tomb, the Arc d'Triomphe, and the opera *Faust*. He came down with a bad cold, however, and spent two weeks, including Christmas and New Year's, in a Red Cross army hospital with an ear infection.

From his hospital bed he relived his eighteen years of married life. He specifically remembered the night he took back his fraternity pin, although he could not remember the exact reason. "Perhaps," he wrote Helen, "[it was] just for the pleasure of giving it to you again. . . . That I love you with all my heart you must know. More than anything else I long to be with you and hold you in my arms and tell you all that is waiting to be told. I need the soft touch of your hands, the warmth of your lips, the companionship of your intellect and the tranquillity that only comes to this restless—now more than ever—husband of yours when we are together." He enclosed a portion of a poem written by a Russian soldier to his sweetheart printed in the *Red Star*, a Soviet army newspaper:

Await me and I shall return!
But you must await me with your whole heart!
Await me when the yellow rain makes you sad.
Await me when the snow is falling.
Await me when the heat is stifling.
Await me when those who wait for others have ceased to wait.
Await me and I shall return and cheat Death.

While in the hospital, Knowland also thought about the future of world politics. "I want to see a better world," he wrote Helen. "I know that misery in Europe leads to war and twice in my generation our nation has become involved. But in taking on our responsibilities and in lending a helping hand we should not weaken ourselves. Once we allow ourselves to grow soft there will be fangs ready to sink themselves into the throat of Uncle Sam. Never forget it." They were words he would come to live by.

On January 8, 1945, finally out of the hospital, Knowland left Paris for Suippes, France, where the Fifteenth Army was located. The troops then moved to Dinant, Belgium; in April, they were sent to Germany. His work basically was that of a historian, gathering records and preparing for the occupation forces to come when the war ended. Shortly after arriving in Germany, he received word that he had been promoted to major. He was based for a month in a small town near the Rhine River that had suffered little damage, in contrast to the extensive bombing damage he had seen farther north. Cologne, once a city of 700,000 people, now only had 110,000 living among its ruins. Many of the fleeing Cologne residents were roaming Europe looking for shelter. Knowland described that city to his father: "Factories, hotels, public buildings, homes and stores are rubble or empty shells. At night, with the curfew, the streets are empty and it is like driving through a graveyard with nothing but broken headstones as landmarks. . . . Yes, the German people are going to pay a heavy price for the 'luxury' of 12 years of Hitler and his gang."

Some of Knowland's thoughts about politics at this time can be gleaned from his letters to his wife. He pointed out that "few people yet realize what a great void has been created by the destruction of Germany as a great economic and political factor in the world. Never before in history has a modern industrial nation had its back broken in such a manner." Although he greatly miscalculated Russia's intentions, stating, "I do not believe Russia is bent on the military conquest of the other European states," he was correct in insisting that the United States had "come of age." He underlined the statesmanship needed "to steer the course in the uncharted seas of the future. . . . It will not be a perfect world or a just world for a long time to come. Americans will be respected, feared, loved and despised in turn by various nations. . . . Just think of what could be done, given a century free from war and strife, with all the intelligence and effort and just a fraction of the cost devoted to those things that go to make up a more perfect life."

Knowland retained a keen interest in U.S. political leadership. The *Tribune* was being airmailed to him every day, and although the editions arrived about two weeks after they were published, they kept him informed about events at home. He expressed satisfaction, for example, with President Truman's appointment of the Republican John Foster Dulles as an undersecretary of state. "Dulles is a very able man," Knowland told Helen. "I am sure his interests are in finding a way to avoid war, but he has his feet on the ground and realizes there are many pitfalls in the path of this idea." Later, as a senator, Knowland would deal extensively with Dulles, who would become President Eisenhower's secretary of state.

In contrast, Knowland was not impressed with newly elected Congresswoman Claire Booth Luce. "She is an able woman, a quick wit and a facile tongue," Knowland wrote. "However, she is more apt to create a stir with a 'clever' speech that will amuse an audience rather than to lay out a sound policy upon which the future of the nation could be safely based." She was married to Henry Luce, and perhaps Knowland was still irritated by the interest Helen had shown in the publisher.

.   .   .

A glimpse into Knowland's character is provided by one of his roommates in Europe, Major Martin Hayden, who became the Washington correspondent for the *Detroit News* after the war. At one point Hayden and Knowland sat on a court-martial together. "We'd get back to quarters," Hayden said, "and I'd start talking about the day's court session, and he would shut me up. He said the regulations forbade discussion of a case outside the court. My roommate! He wouldn't even talk about the case with me, in our own room. It wasn't human nature, but it was Bill Knowland."[1]

Hayden also related a story about the two men taking a walk around Bad Neuenahr, where they were stationed. The army had a rule against fraternizing with the Germans, but few heeded it. When Hayden threw candy bars and gum to the children, Knowland objected. But when the ban was ended, Knowland wrote his wife for gift packages, which he handed out to the children.

.   .   .

While Bill Knowland was observing the devastation in Germany, Helen was caught up in the frenetic activity of San Francisco in early 1945. The war was winding down, but much of the Pacific Fleet action was still funneled through the Bay Area. Market Street was a carnival of energy awash in uniforms of every branch of the allied services. From the Ferry Building up Market Street to Van Ness Avenue, a continuous stretch of "beer-and-a-shot" bars, movie houses, and arcades attracted the young servicemen. Yet just up the hill from Market, at Powell and Geary, the dignified Hotel St. Francis was a gathering place for the diplomats, translators, volunteers, staff, and members of the press gathered for the conference that would establish the United Nations.

Helen Knowland, young, intelligent, and extremely attractive, found time to do volunteer work for this conference. At the St. Francis, she met Blair Moody, a reporter from the *Detroit News,* and she was quickly charmed by the witty and entertaining newsman. She liked music—he played the piano like a professional. She had grown up in newspapers and politics—so had he. She was lonely and bored by the deprivations of the wartime Bay Area—he was away from home in an exciting city. Bill Knowland was a world away in Europe. Moody, well-educated and athletic, told captivating stories of his life as a *Detroit News* reporter in Washington and as a war correspondent in Africa, Italy, Iran, and Britain.

Moody covered the convention by day and entertained Helen Knowland at night. By the time the United Nations Charter was signed on June 26, they were much more than friends. Moody returned to Washington after the United Nations conference ended, and although neither could have foreseen it, slightly more than two months later, Helen would follow.

·   ·   ·

Already at the start of 1945, speculation abounded on the West Coast about Bill Knowland's high political ambitions. *San Francisco News* columnist Arthur Caylor was predicting that even though Hiram Johnson had announced he would seek reelection, Knowland might enter the race. Caylor noted that "extremely powerful" Republicans were trying to get Johnson to change his mind so that Knowland could run for the office.[2] But fate made their efforts unnecessary.

On August 6, 1945, Hiram Johnson died; he had served thirty years in the Senate. Immediately, speculation began on who would fill the remaining year and a half of his term. Among the names bandied about were Governor Earl Warren; former president Herbert Hoover; Lieutenant Governor Frederick Houser; Philip Bancroft, a Walnut Creek farmer who was the Republican Party's nominee against Johnson in 1938; and . . . William F. Knowland. One rumor had it that Warren would resign, and Houser would become governor and then appoint him. That had happened in neighboring Nevada, when Senator James G. Scrugham died and Governor E. P. Carville resigned so he could be appointed to the seat. Warren ruled that out because he had promised to serve out his full term when elected. He had already turned down the vice presidential nomination in 1944 to keep that promise. Not much serious thought was given to Hoover, although he lobbied heavily for the job. Houser was seen as a likely candidate because he had been the Republican nominee for the Senate four years earlier. Houser had also said that he would run for Hiram Johnson's seat if the incumbent retired.[3] Most experts, however, bet that Knowland would get the appointment based on "political obligations and personal friendship" with Warren.[4] At least one report had it that Warren offered the Senate seat to Knowland's father, who had lost it to Johnson thirty years earlier, but J.R. declined because of his age.[5] If so, it seems likely that Warren really believed J.R. would not accept and that he was acting out of courtesy.

Warren quickly ended the guessing by appointing Bill Knowland to the Senate on August 14, although his formal telegram announcing it didn't reach Paris for four days. It seems likely that J. R. Knowland conferred with Warren beforehand, although Bill Knowland always contended that he was surprised by the appointment. Warren probably had promised Bill Knowland the seat if an opportunity should arise. Certainly both Knowland and the governor had known that Johnson was elderly and growing feeble.

In a two-page press release announcing Knowland's appointment, Warren asserted that "it was not an easy task to choose between the many fine men who have been recommended by their friends." But, he said, he could only make one selection so he drew up a list of necessary criteria. Not surprisingly, they fit Bill Knowland perfectly. He had to be a World War II veteran, be young, know government intimately, have a record of public service that was without blemish, have supported the war effort, and have a record of service to his party. In addition to supporting the defense and war program, Warren said that the candidate also "must believe in world cooperation as our greatest opportunity for preserving the peace which has been won at such great sacrifice." Senator Johnson, of course, had been just the opposite—an outspoken isolationist throughout his career. In appointing Knowland, Warren noted that he had known him all of his adult life and he vouched for "his integrity, his ability and his fairness."

Warren denied ever discussing the possibility of the appointment with Knowland, but he was sure of its reception: "knowing his aptitude for and interest in the public service, I am certain that he will accept," he said in the news release. In his memoirs published in 1977, Warren made no mention of the appointment of his lifelong friend. He did, however, acknowledge that the *Tribune* had thrown its weight to him in his bid to become district attorney. For all he owed the Knowlands, Warren didn't seem to feel he had to acknowledge that debt in words; his deeds spoke for him. With Knowland's appointment, Warren ensured that the Senate seat would remain Republican, as it had been since senators were first elected in 1914. The other Senate seat was in Republican hands half the time.

Just how Knowland heard of his appointment and how he responded are not entirely clear. As Hollis Alpert, a fellow officer in Paris, remembers it, he and Knowland were sharing a small office just outside Paris when an orderly brought in a telegram. Upon opening it, Knowland looked startled and with a trembling voice said, "I'm . . . very surprised. . . . Would you care to take a look at this?" he said, handing it to Alpert. The telegraph was from Warren informing Knowland of his appointment.

"Didn't you expect this?" Alpert asked.

"No, not at all," he said.

The next day while walking to their office, Alpert said he tried to talk to Knowland more seriously. "This may be a little early, but have you thought much about your policies, things you'll stand for?" Alpert asked.

"Yes, I've given it a bit of thought," Knowland replied. "Naturally, the main thing is to represent my constituents as best I know how. But I wouldn't want to commit myself at this point—not until I arrive in Washington and have a chance to assess the situation at firsthand." About the Russians, Knowland told Alpert, "If they can convince us of their sincerity, then I would say we might be able to work out our problems to our mutual satisfaction. On the other hand, there is the question of the atomic bomb. How will our unquestionable superiority there . . . "

Good God, Alpert thought, he's already talking like a senator.[6]

Alpert's account, however, seems questionable, given Knowland's letters to his wife. In a letter written August 15, Knowland discussed the probable appointment, but cautioned her that she shouldn't get her hopes too high. The next day he wrote that there was no news of his appointment in the morning in the international edition of the *Herald-Tribune*, which was filled with news of Japan's acceptance of President Truman's terms of unconditional surrender, but that he found a small article in *Stars and Stripes*, the army newspaper. "I did not feel I could ask for transportation home based on this article," he said. "Until I get some official word there is nothing much that can be done on this end." Two days later he received a cable from Warren that said, "You are appointed to Senate to replace Johnson. Hurry home." Only then did he arrange for a flight home, leaving Paris on August 21. He returned to the United States without seeing combat duty.

"Needless to say I am very pleased to have the opportunity of going to the Senate, the place where except for a three cornered fight you would have gone 31 years ago with qualifications far greater that I possess," he wrote to his father. "I can assure [you] I feel very humble at the moment with the responsibilities that go with the job in the face of the great problems that affect the nation and the world."

Knowland's father had already anticipated his son's response. He told the *New York Times* that Warren had "placed the utmost confidence in the boy and I'm sure he will feel duty-bound to accept."[7] With Johnson's death, the long war that J. R. Knowland had waged against the old Progressive was at an end. And he had secured a final victory—his son's appointment to Johnson's seat, with the aid of J.R.'s protégé, Earl Warren.

The elder Knowland celebrated his son's appointment the day of its announcement with a small dinner party at his co-op apartment house on Lake Merritt. Among the guests were Dr. James E. McConnell, who had helped to establish Columbia State Park, and his wife, Geraldine. The elder Knowland announced to his dinner guests, "Now we are celebrating tonight." In walked the butler with a large silver tray. When the butler took the cover off, each of the guests—despite the war-induced food rationing—had a hamburger patty about four inches across.[8]

Public reactions to the appointment were varied, ranging from best wishes from the *Los Angeles Times* (despite regrets that someone from Southern California had not been appointed) to claims that it was a payoff by Warren for the Knowlands' support over the years.

"Most Californians smiled," an article in *Time* said. "It had been understood that [J. R. Knowland's] boy . . . would get the next Senate vacancy. While Republicans complained that they had been given a slow horse for a fast race, Democrats prepared to fight Bill Knowland next year."[9] But the Democrats would find out that Knowland was no plow horse.

Newsweek accused Warren of drawing up specifications for California's next senator to fit one description, that of Major Bill Knowland, 6,000 miles away in Paris. The correspondent noted that Warren had passed over such contenders as Lieutenant Governor Houser, Mayor Roger D. Lapham of San Francisco, and Dr. Robert G. Sproul, president of the University of California. At thirty-seven, *Newsweek* noted, Knowland would be the youngest member of the Senate.[10]

Biographer Leo Katcher described Warren's obviously political appointment of Knowland as "the only one of that type he ever made. But if he had not made it, he would have been [an] ingrate. Whatever J. R. Knowland might have felt about Warren's policies, he never publicly attacked Warren and William F. Knowland never stopped being personally loyal to Warren. Warren might well have believed that the war and time might cause Knowland to alter some of his views."[11] In contrast, Knowland's friend McIntyre Faries disputed such criticism of the appointment. Noting Warren's and Knowland's close relationship, he insisted that the appointment "was not primarily" a repayment of a debt to J. R. Knowland. "Now it is true that he did owe a debt to Bill's father, but Warren recognized the potential ability and the abilities and the strength of Bill Knowland."[12]

A more lighthearted reaction came from one of Knowland's commanding officers. He asked if Knowland would take a letter back to the War Department (later to become the Department of Defense). It said, "For the past several years you people in the War Department have sent over a number of Congressional representatives that we have taken care of. Herewith we are sending you your first replacement."[13]

.   .   .

When Knowland arrived in Washington, he was still wearing his army uniform, his trousers tucked into his combat boots. He paid a call on Leslie Biffle, the Democratic secretary of the Senate, and then returned to California, where he called on Warren to thank him. He also received his honorable discharge from the army.

In California, he declared himself a "liberal Republican pointed toward national social programs and business stability and international cooperation based on a non-partisan approach to foreign policy." He said his army service would "strengthen my conviction that America can no more turn back to isolationism than a man can return to childhood. The atomic bomb may change the requirements for the size of a peacetime Army and Navy, but never should our defenses become as weak as they were in the years after World War I. We need a shotgun in the closet."[14]

After a short stay on the West Coast, Bill returned to the East Coast with Helen, who was delighted with her husband's Senate appointment. Before going back to Washington, he had to buy two new tailored suits. Suits that were tight-fitting before he went into the army were far too big now. They left their children in Oakland until they rented a house in Bethesda, Maryland. Bill wanted to be sworn in quickly to add to his seniority.

On September 6, the day that the Senate adjourned in memory of the late Senator Johnson's thirty years of service, Knowland was sworn in.

8

A Freshman Senator

Knowland came home from the war to find a country dominated by two fundamental beliefs: that the social and economic reforms of the New Deal ought to be preserved and that the United States should take a more active role in world affairs. Knowland himself opposed continuation of New Deal policies but agreed with the turn from isolationism. Taking office just six months after President Franklin D. Roosevelt had died, he entered a Senate that was controlled 57–38 by Democrats. The country had given the Democrats control of the Senate by heeding Roosevelt's words that the nation "shouldn't change horses in the middle of a stream." However, the Congress that Knowland joined was slower to reflect the national consensus on major issues than was the executive branch.

The Senate had ratified the United Nations Charter on July 28, about six weeks before Knowland was sworn in, but Congress was slow to accept President Harry S Truman's proposed major new domestic programs. The day that Knowland became a senator, Truman sent a 16,000-word message to Congress, presenting a twenty-one-point domestic agenda that included increased unemployment compensation, an immediate minimum wage increase, a permanent Fair Employment Practices Committee, tax reform, farm crop insurance, and a full year's extension of the War Powers and Stabilization Act, which would keep the government in control over business and federal aid to housing.[1] Congress's reluctance to take action can be traced to its committee seniority system and restrictive legislative rules. Committees were headed by conservative southern Democrats and midwestern Republicans. Even when legislation made it through the Senate, it was often blocked in the House, which was far more conservative.

According to *Time* magazine, Knowland "cut little ice in his first few months in the Senate." If, indeed, he had made little impact during his first six months that was not surprising, considering the makeup and traditions of the Senate: seniority ruled and newcomers were expected to serve an "unobtrusive apprenticeship."[2] Freshman members received the committee assignments that other senators rejected. Knowland's office was modest and his seat in the Senate chambers reflected his status. He was asked to do menial tasks and to do so without protest. He was expected to listen and learn. "Like children," one freshman once said, "we should be seen and not be heard." Tradition held that freshmen were supposed to avoid appearing overly aggressive.[3] Those unwritten rules rankled the ambitious Knowland, but he followed them. In addition to keeping quiet, freshmen were urged to work hard. That Knowland did. He would remain a freshman for only eighteen months.

From his first weeks in office Bill Knowland received a great deal of mail, enough to keep five stenographers working full time. He recognized that it was important to answer constituents' letters. "When a person writes, that is an important thing as far as he is concerned," Knowland commented to his father.

During his more than twelve years in the Senate, Knowland would be called a lot of names, many of them derogatory because of his stubbornness. One positive label stuck with him during those years that even his detractors could not discredit: the nickname "Mr. Integrity." No matter what his opponents thought of him, they would not question his honesty or integrity. They knew where he stood, and they knew he would be true to those beliefs. He was a man of his word regardless of whether he agreed with his opponent's position. Curiously, both the American public and political colleagues set different standards for professional integrity and integrity in personal affairs, and Knowland was able to keep the two separate throughout his life. His professional integrity manifested itself early in his Senate career, although those who knew him from his earlier political career were not surprised by his stands. Frank H. Kuest, a reporter who covered Knowland for the Copley newspapers, said of him, "I've never know him to lie to anybody, to double-cross anybody or to give anybody a wrong steer."[4]

Knowland's willingness to stand up for his convictions was evident from his first months in office. Unlike some Republicans, for example, he supported the "Full Employment" bill (S. 380), which virtually guaranteed that the government would provide jobs for all. As he explained to his father, "I think it is poor policy to have the GOP take a negative attitude on everything the President [Truman] has proposed because it came from that source. If we don't get some cooperation soon between capital, labor and management, the administration and Congress we will be heading for an economic tailspin that will produce a real swing to the left such as took place in England." While that bill failed to pass, a considerably weaker one was enacted. It urged the federal government to promote maximum employment, production, and purchasing power, and it established the President's Council of Economic Advisers and the Joint (congressional) Economic Committee.

On August 29, 1945, Knowland gave his first major speech in California as a senator. Addressing the Commonwealth Club in San Francisco, he claimed that he was not opposed to workers sharing in the profits of capitalism—a statement that would have surprised his later detractors. He insisted, however, that sharing profits was not the same as forced unionism. In his words: "If the American system is to maintain its place in the world in which vast changes are taking place it is highly desirable that a greater percentage of the profits of industry go to the employees who are giving their lives in the building of such industry or business. In maintaining the profit system it is vital that an ever-increasing number of our people have an interest in the maintenance of that system."

Knowland was beginning to assert himself in labor issues. When the leader of the coal miners, John L. Lewis, called a strike in May 1946, Knowland told President Truman that he planned to ask the Senate to consider antistrike legislation unless the strike was settled within a specific time. Unions already were accusing him of being antilabor for backing earlier legislation subjecting unions to suits for violations of contracts and other restrictions on labor activity. He also favored industrywide bargaining and union control of health and welfare funds. Knowland voted against a $25 increase in the weekly federal unemployment compensation and for the Taft-Hartley Labor Law. But he also voted to raise the minimum wage from 40 cents an hour to 65 cents an hour.

In February 1946, Knowland supported bills to establish a permanent Fair Employment Practice Commission, and he voted for cloture to end the filibuster on the bills. "I will vote for cloture on this and any other issues when a minority blocks the will of the majority of the representatives of the American people," he said. He also voted for limiting debate on anti–poll tax legislation and initiated the cloture petition on the debate on labor issues. In 1947 he introduced a measure, later killed by the Senate Rules Committee, to limit debate by a majority vote rather than by the traditional two-thirds margin. The importance of this effort was demonstrated later during the 1957 civil rights legislation battle, when southern Democrats frustrated Knowland, then Republican minority leader, with their filibusters. The senator also seized on an old theme that raised the hackles of some southern colleagues. Over their objections, he was successful in inserting a newspaper account of lynchings in the *Congressional Record*.

But Knowland was a strong supporter of states' rights. Thus, he criticized the Office of Price Administration (OPA); among other duties, it regulated rents, which he believed should be under the control of the states. When his idea failed to gather enough support, he voted for continuation of the rent ceilings under the existing system. Moreover, he voted in July 1946 for a tidelands oil bill, which would have given state governments control of lands covered by water within the three-mile limit of the United States. The bill was vetoed by President Truman.

Knowland's first committee assignment was on the Special Committee to Investigate the National Defense Program (originally known as the Truman Committee and then as the Mead Committee). In December 1945, Knowland joined Senators James M. Tunnell and Hugh B. Mitchell on a 30,000-mile, round-the-world investigation of the disposal of army and navy surplus property. Knowland missed Christmas at home because of his Mead Committee travel, but he believed that the committee had an important job to do. As he wrote to his father: "Not only are billions of dollars of the U.S. people involved, but also matters relating to our future security in a way of military and commercial air bases. . . . Information we gather will play its part in helping to determine a wise and constructive policy" toward foreign loans. He added, "I am convinced that 1946 is the critical period in history. Decisions on the Atomic Bomb, World Organization and Domestic Reconversion will be made. They are all tied together in one big web."

Knowland's father apparently thought Knowland should be working on his election campaign rather than traveling. But Knowland firmly stated the position that would long be his philosophy: that he would be making tough decisions in the best interests of the nation rather than for their political implications. "If I lose on this basis," he wrote, "I will finish my service with a clearer conscience than if I try to figure the political angles on every decision I must make."

Nevertheless, within ten days after being sworn in, Knowland began setting up his own election machinery. His appointment had come very late in a six-year term, and he had to face a primary election the following June. On September 15, 1945, Knowland wrote to a friend, Clarence A. Rogers in Santa Barbara, California, that he intended to be a candidate for a full term: "I rather feel like a fire horse that has been out to pasture and am taking a keen interest in and looking forward to the campaign next year as you will recall I always enjoyed a good political contest." He told Rogers he was pleased with the "splendid support" his appointment had received, particularly from Southern California. "During my service in the legislature, I never recognized sectional differences and it was my privilege to handle a great deal of legislation for many communities down your way."

While his son was learning the ropes in Washington, J. R. Knowland was setting up campaign machinery in California. Political strategist Murray Chotiner got his start with the Knowland election bid that year. The man often called the Machiavelli of California politics once famously remarked that "nice guys and sissies don't win elections."[5] Although he did help both Bill Knowland and Earl Warren, neither used him as Richard Nixon did, in ways that revealed his true genius for negative campaigning. From the time Chotiner began advising Nixon on a part-time basis in Nixon's 1946 congressional campaign until his death in a 1973 auto accident, his name would be anathema to Democrats and many Republicans.

Knowland also told his father that he planned to discuss the timing of his election announcement with Earl Warren. Although there is little doubt that Warren played an important role behind the scenes in Knowland's campaign, he did not endorse the new senator's candidacy until the very end. Warren was up for reelection and his opponent, Democrat Robert Kenny, was claiming that Knowland's appointment was the repayment of a debt. Warren's low-key approach concerning the endorsement was an attempt to distance himself from the Knowlands publicly. He also didn't want to alienate the supporters of the senator's opponent, Will Rogers Jr.; he had received strong crossover support from Democrats in his two earlier elections. As Chotiner described it, "We were happy to get Warren's endorsement when it came in September. We knew there wasn't a chance of running a joint campaign. That wasn't Warren's way."⁶

Just before the June primary in California, Knowland wrote to J.R. that he appreciated his father's help in the campaign "win, lose or draw." He expressed concern for the burden that it placed on his father, who was then seventy-two years old and still running the *Tribune*. "However," he noted, "an election campaign to you is probably like a bell to the fire horse out at pasture." Knowland was hoping to win both the Democratic and Republican nominations and thereby avoid a November contest. Even if he didn't, he hoped his total vote in the primary would be higher than that of Will Rogers Jr. "The psychological effect would be good as was the case of Warren vs. Olson four years ago," Knowland said. Republican Earl Warren almost won the Democratic nomination for governor as well as the Republican nomination in 1942. He had polled 404,000 votes to Governor Culbert Olson's 514,000 by cross-filing in the Democratic primary. Cross-filing was a strategy devised by the Progressives in 1913 to take some of the partisan politics out of elections. It allowed any aspirant for office to compete for nomination in the primary elections of as many parties as he wanted at the same time; no mention of political party would appear on the ballot.

Knowland had two obstacles to overcome: the long shadow of Hiram Johnson and the popularity of his opponent, Representative Will Rogers Jr., son of the famous humorist. Knowland found himself being compared unfavorably with Johnson. While he had no experience in national affairs, Johnson had been a colorful and powerful world figure for more than thirty years. And Will Rogers was capitalizing on his famous father's name, starting off the race with a two-to-one margin in the polls. Knowland also had to overcome a margin of 900,000 more Democrats than Republicans registered to vote.

Both Rogers and Knowland cross-filed in the June primary election. Rogers won the Democratic nomination over Lieutenant Governor Ellis Patterson in a bitter primary, while Knowland handily captured the Republican nomination. The Democratic Party was badly split by its liberal and conservative factions, and Rogers was thought to be the unity candidate. He also had the backing of both wings of the labor movement. But in the cross-filing there was no contest. Rogers drew only 90,723 Republican votes, but Knowland picked up 425,253 Democratic votes in the primary.

Knowland traveled up and down the state, giving more than 250 speeches in one month. He showed tireless energy and he raced from meeting to meeting with voters. Knowland was aided in his campaign by the astute political consultants Clem Whitaker and Leone Baxter as well as by Murray Chotiner. It was Chotiner's strategy not to try to change the candidate. Several members of Knowland's campaign told him, "Bill, you have just got to change. You have got to change your personality. You are too serious." Knowland good-naturedly took it all in, and when they were through, he told them, "Well, you know, you may be right. But that is the way I happen to be. If you start changing me, you are apt to get a worse product than when you started." Chotiner supported this approach and was also pleased that there were few weaknesses about Knowland that could be exploited.

Knowland told Chotiner explicitly that he was to avoid negative campaigning: "If I am going to be elected, I am going to be elected on what I stand for, and not on any attack on my opponent."[7] About the only advice that Knowland followed was to use the phrase "We will not surrender."[8] Chotiner was trying to plant the idea that surrender would be Rogers's path. Meanwhile, behind the scenes and apparently without Knowland's knowledge, he began to use negative campaigning. Throughout his career he believed that people voted against candidates, not for them. Therefore, the focus should be on attacking the opponent. To this end, Chotiner and his associates dug into Will Rogers Jr.'s record. He knew that Rogers had better name recognition than his candidate and they would have to come up with something to swing the vote toward Knowland. They found what they were looking for among Rogers's many activities—a contribution to a newspaper in Los Angeles considered to be the voice of the Communist Party.

It didn't help Rogers any that John S. Gibbons, a former member of the Los Angeles County Democratic Central Committee, was circulating a three-page letter that said the "communistic press shows sympathetic interest in Junior William Rogers." Gibbons recited from issues of the *People's World*, the Communist daily, dating back to 1936, showing an interest in Rogers's politics. Chotiner pointed out that the newspaper had boasted in a front-page editorial that Rogers had contributed to its sustaining fund. The attack worked, as several leading Democrats pulled away from Rogers's campaign. As an article in the *Nation* pointed out, "there is nothing to indicate that [Knowland] knew of the low attack on his opponent. Knowland had repeatedly expressed himself as opposed to mud-slinging of all kinds."[9] But soon, to some people in California, Rogers was "a Communist, fellow traveler and a crackpot," reported *Fortnight* magazine, which also described Knowland as having moved from being a middle-of-the-roader to being the "safe shelter of the right."[10]

Knowland avoided using his opponent's name except on one occasion, when he directly called on Rogers to express his opinion. Former vice president Henry Wallace had given a speech calling for appeasement with the Soviet Union. The Los Angeles County Democratic Central Committee passed a resolution agreeing with Wallace. At that point, Knowland said it was time for Rogers to state his opinion on the matter. "I felt that the time had come for our country to deal firmly, but fairly, with the Russians. Appeasement of the Russians is a deadly mistake," Knowland said. That, he said, was "the road that led to and from Munich [and] we are very apt to have the same results."[11] It was the first time Knowland publicly used the "road to Munich" allusion, but certainly not the last during his long career.

Rogers declined to comment on the issue. That might have been the turning point in the campaign for Knowland. Rogers's personal habits also were hurting his campaign and driving his backers to distraction. "I liked Will personally," said Oliver J. Carter, who managed Rogers's northern campaign. "He was quite a guy, except that his metabolism didn't start to work until after 7 P.M. He was a night-time guy and he didn't seem to wake up during the day. You couldn't get him to steam up at all. . . . Will didn't like to get up before noon, if he liked to get up then; and he liked to work way into the night. . . . I don't mean to say he was lazy or a sluggard, but he just worked a different hour schedule. . . . I always kind of felt that politics was not made for him, really, that he wasn't tough enough for it. He wasn't, maybe, interested enough."[12]

Two points, the need for a strong stand against communism and the need for change, were hammered home again and again throughout the national Republican campaign in 1946. Republican National Chairman B. Carroll Reece, a U.S. representative from Tennessee, promised that a Republican Congress would restore "orderly, capable and honest government in Washington and replace controls, confusion, corruption and communism." Knowland beat Rogers by a vote of 1,428,067 to 1,167,161, surprising even California Republican leaders. Nationally, the GOP gained 13 Senate seats and 56 House seats. Knowland was to be included in the so-called Class of 1946, despite his having been appointed to the post before the new class took office. Warren also was reelected, giving old J.R.'s Oakland protégés the two top political jobs in the state. Among those elected to the U.S. Senate that year were former Ohio governor John W. Bricker, George Malone of Nevada, Arthur Watkins of Utah, John Williams of Delaware, William E. Jenner of Indiana, and Joseph McCarthy of Wisconsin. Richard M. Nixon was elected to the House. Styles Bridges, the New Hampshire conservative with whom Knowland would team up again and again, proclaimed, "The United States is now a Republican country."

"They were determined to rid the government of Communists, perverts and New Dealers, get tough with Joe Stalin, crack down on labor unions and dismantle the Office of Price Administration," observed David M. Oshinsky. "Some compared them to small-town Rotarians; others joked about the resurrection of Calvin Coolidge. But all agreed that it was quite some time since this many like-minded conservatives had massed at the Capitol gates."[13] Surely, the civic joiner Knowland must have felt comfortable with a group of "Rotarians."

.   .   .

No sooner had J. R. Knowland finished with his son's election campaign than he was confronted with a general strike in Oakland. With the war over, employees were returning to the workforce in greater numbers, only to find jobs difficult to come by. Unemployment had risen from 1.2 percent in 1944 to 3.9 percent in 1946. Employees were looking for a living wage and job stability, and unions were growing in popularity and power.

East Bay businesses, too, were banding together. They formed the United Employers, a group of 6,000 members. Retail merchants countywide had their own association, which represented twenty-eight large Alameda County retail establishments. The general strike was over efforts to unionize Kahn's, a major department store. At 5 A.M. on December 3, 1946, the American Federation of Labor trade unions of Alameda County struck. An estimated 100,000 union members from 142 unions went off the job—and the city came to a virtual standstill. Businessmen asked for police protection. Three hours before the general strike was called, police cleared the streets of pickets and blocked access to Broadway in the center of Oakland. When police escorted the first "scab" truck to Kahn's, the labor leaders called the strike.

Among the first victims of the walkout were newspapers. Historian Philip J. Wolman described the metropolitan papers as antilabor propaganda vehicles. "Unions had not forgotten the distortions and adverse publicity that plagued the San Francisco Waterfront–general strike of 1934."[14]

Newspaper unions shut down the *Tribune*, the *Post-Enquirer*, the *Berkeley Daily Gazette*, and the *Alameda Times-Star*. No San Francisco papers were allowed into the East Bay. The only paper that was delivered to Oakland was the *Daily People's World*.

A side of J. R. Knowland rarely seen became visible during that strike. When several businessmen and union representatives were meeting to discuss the strike, Knowland was told that some business owners were refusing to negotiate even if most of their employees signed with the union. "Now wait a minute," Knowland said, chiding his associates. "Anybody, any union that comes into the newspaper and tells them that they represented the majority of the employees in any department and they could prove it, I'm going to negotiate a contract with them." Paul St. Sure, a lawyer who was representing the business interests, called a quick recess. After a long break, the meeting resumed, but J. R. Knowland was no longer at the table. He was not pro-union, but he would have nothing to do with stonewalling against negotiations. He never came back.[15] Despite his hard-nosed attitude against unions, Knowland believed in bargaining, and the *Tribune* would never again be shut down by a strike while the Knowlands were in control.

Although the general strike only lasted two days, it set off the most important political revolt the city had seen. All the city's unions united in opposition to the way city government was being operated. They put up five candidates for seats on the nine-member council in an effort to give labor control of the city council. The ensuing fight pitted the unions against the *Tribune*'s political coalition of downtown merchants. The labor candidates won in the April primary. The *Tribune* trumpeted in its top headline, "Oakland Primary Hailed as Communist Victory." The *Tribune* continued its red-baiting techniques to cast doubt on the labor candidates, running the following editorial the day before the general runoff, May 12, 1947: "Briefly, these are the facts. The Communist Party of the United States announced a program of concentrating on school boards and city council campaigns. Oakland has been selected as one of the cities. At a May Day Communistic mass meeting recently held in Oakland, one of the chief speakers, who was a Communistic registered primary candidate for the school board, and who in filing her expense account as required by law, acknowledged that her expenses had been paid by the Alameda County Communist Party, urged the election of the five left-wing candidates for the City Council."

The "Doubtful Five," as the *Tribune* dubbed the labor candidates, sensed victory. The unions staged a giant torchlight parade featuring a float that showed AFL and CIO workers lowering a casket labeled "The Machine" into the ground. It also portrayed the gloved fist of Oakland voters knocking the *Tribune* Tower in half. The slogan on the float read, "Let's finish the job—take the power out of the Tower." Four of the five union members were elected. Nonetheless, the establishment managed to keep control of five of the nine seats on the council. By 1951 the labor coalition collapsed, and the business community regained its dominance.

9

Making His Mark

While the nation was trying to shake off the remaining wartime economic controls, Americans also were beginning to realize that the postwar period would be one of continuing international tensions rather than any return to normalcy. Civil war in Greece, the Communist presence in Turkey, the ouster of non-Communists from the Hungarian government, the Communist coup in Czechoslovakia, growing animosity between North and South Korea, and the beginning of the Soviet blockade of Berlin would lead the list of troubles overseas.

When the 80th Congress opened on January 6, 1947, it contained three future presidents of the United States: John F. Kennedy, Richard M. Nixon, and Lyndon B. Johnson. At least one other highly ambitious member had his eyes on the White House—William F. Knowland.

Knowland was part of a Congress that would write laws that would guide domestic and foreign policy for many years to come. He was also among the Republican newcomers who were eager to gain some power. Senate Minority Leader Bob Taft was in control, no doubt about that, but he did promise the younger Republicans two posts on the Republican Policy Committee. During the remaining seven years of his leadership, he would be confronted by these ambitious young Turks again and again.[1] Before Congress convened, Knowland was named to the Republican Committee on Committees, where he handled assignments of Republican colleagues. He was also named to the Senate Appropriations (his first choice) and Rules and Administration Committees, as well as to the Permanent Joint Congressional Committee on Atomic Energy.

Although *Time* dismissed Knowland in his first few months in Congress as cutting little ice, the same magazine told quite a different story after he was elected to a full term: "He sailed into Washington with the enthusiasm of a man determined to stay. He was an attentive, fairminded and active member of the Atomic Energy Committee. He startled the party sages who expected him merely to sit tight, learn the ropes and follow the leaders."[2] The new class of senators was coming out of World War II with a sense of urgency, and its members were chafing at Senate rules that told them to be patient and wait their turns. Knowland certainly was one of the brashest young senators on the scene. The Senate usually paid little attention to such upstarts, but Knowland was impressing his colleagues with his integrity and his energy.

The junior California senator was becoming known as a man of principles; some said he was stubborn. His colleagues found him fearless, willing to stand up to anyone. Although he would bitterly fight someone over an issue, he almost never held a grudge or took anything personally. They knew when he was angry. They could see the ropey veins in his thick neck bulge out and they watched his face turn red. Bill Knowland told you what he thought and his colleagues knew where they stood with him. There would be no going behind their backs. He found compromise difficult; he was used to getting his way. His determination was clear as he moved with long, quick, powerful strides.

One early skirmish was with Bob Taft, and this may have helped cement a long relationship that would pay off handsomely for the young senator from California. Taft wanted to slash $6 billion from the budget. Knowland was determined to have $3 billion of that money set aside for reduction of the national debt. Taft responded, "My own feeling is that tax reduction is more important than a reduction in the debt," but he agreed to go along with a $1 billion debt reduction.[3]

Knowland replied that at that rate, it would take 259 years to wipe out the debt, and insisted that the Senate needed to do it faster. He had made the effort to line up maverick Republicans, and he knew that some Democrats would join him if for no other reason than to embarrass Taft. Finally, Colorado's Eugene Millikin proposed that $2 billion be set aside to reduce the debt, but Taft stuck to his position. So did Knowland, arguing that the Senate ought to be willing to reduce the debt by 1 percent, or $2.6 billion. Taft recognized that Knowland had the votes and eventually went over to his side. The Knowland amendment passed 82–0.

Today's annual budget deficits of hundreds of billions of dollars have proved Knowland's words to be prophetic. But few people listened to him when he addressed the Congress on February 26, 1947, thundering, "I do not believe the Congress of the United States will be faced with a more serious problem during the entire period of our service here. Certainly it is essential that we maintain a solvent Federal Government and a sound fiscal policy. The future of the American people is wrapped up in our doing this, for if we fail the entire national economy can be undermined."[4]

He was right, of course, but an interesting split was developing in the "public" Senator Knowland and the "private" Knowland. Although he pushed for the federal government to cut spending and lower taxes to keep its budget in balance, his private spending always increased, and he continually strove to raise his own revenues. Instead of trimming his own spending, he repeatedly went to his father for more dividends from the *Oakland Tribune*.

.   .   .

Knowland's tour of duty in Europe and his foreign travel with the Mead Committee had broadened his views on international relations. He was worried about the civil war in Greece and Communist pressure on Turkey. In a confidential letter to his father, written March 17, 1947, the senator mused on the foreign policy decisions the Senate faced, which he called "the most important decisions made in this generation." The United States, he felt, had two alternatives: to let the Middle East fall into the Soviet orbit or to bolster the strategically located nations outside the Iron Curtain until they were able to take care of themselves. "Either course . . . could lead to war," he admitted.

Knowland insisted that the United States should learn from its mistakes before World War II, when it stood by while Japan and Germany began their aggression: the United States instead should have taken a firm stand against Japan, Germany, and Italy. He accused the Western powers of surrendering at Munich in 1938, when British Prime Minister Neville Chamberlain notoriously promised that his agreement with Germany's Adolf Hitler would bring "peace in our time." If the Middle East were to fall to the Communists, he warned, China and the rest of the Far East would be next. That fear that would gain credence, and Joseph Alsop would name it the "domino theory" in 1954. President Eisenhower would use the metaphor in explaining his decision to send aid to South Vietnam. Knowland worried that if the Soviet Union were to gain control of that area, the result would be an atomic war that would mean "destruction of the world as we know it."

Congress had to change its foreign policy so that it was consistent throughout the world, Knowland said. But, he warned, the United States could not do everything for the rest of the world: "In my opinion even as rich and powerful as is the United States, we are not in a position to spread ourselves thin in all sections of the world. . . . Whenever we establish a policy this country must be prepared to back it, if necessary with our full power, economic and military. Any other course will destroy our influence abroad and lead the World to disaster."

In April 1947, Knowland resigned from the Mead Committee, which was winding down its investigation of war contracts, use of surplus property, and conditions in the European occupation zones. It was during the Mead Committee assignment that he became involved in the plight of the Nationalist Chinese in what he believed was their struggle to defend their homeland against Communist aggression. What he learned would have a major effect on his political views for the next decade.

Just after Congress adjourned, Knowland and three colleagues requested visas for an October trip to visit Russia as part of a European fact-finding mission. Knowland wrote to his father that he was not optimistic about the international outlook: "Not only does Europe need help but it should be apparent to everyone that the help that they get (or do not get) will have repercussions upon our own economy. . . . I strongly believe that the cause of world peace, our own national security and our American economy will be better served by a rehabilitated Europe. We must constantly keep in mind that the United States is the last great stabilizing force among the nations of the world." The four senators wanted to look over the U.S. embassy in Moscow and see the Soviet capital during their five-week European tour. The Soviets denied them their visas the morning they were to leave the United States. Knowland was furious. A half hour before he had to leave to catch his plane, Knowland sat down at his typewriter to write President Truman a letter of outrage. He suggested that the United States limit the number of Russians entering the country to the number of Americans entering the Soviet Union.

On October 1, 1947, Knowland left Washington, D.C.; after stops in Bermuda and the Azores, he reached Frankfurt at 3 A.M. two days later. On his trip he and Senators Guy Gordon of Oregon, Milton R. Young of North Dakota, and Theodore F. Green of Rhode Island would visit not only Germany but also Poland, Czechoslovakia, Romania, Bulgaria, Yugoslavia, Greece, Turkey, Italy, France, and England. Knowland once more was struck by the destructiveness of the war and by the difficult life of the Germans who were trying to get back on their feet. On seeing Berlin, 75 percent of which had been destroyed, he said, "This once great and proud city stands as a monumental tomb to man's folly." He wished every American could see what he had in Berlin. "Here but for the grace of God might be America," he wrote.

Knowland also described a 500-mile automobile trip through Poland, calling Warsaw the most damaged city he had seen. He was stunned by the ghetto in Warsaw where 400,000 Jews had lived and had been murdered. "The people there say that there are probably still 40,000 buried beneath the ruins 2½ years after the war had ended." (Twenty years later, after he took control of the *Tribune*, Knowland forbade the use of the word *ghetto* to refer to the black area of East Oakland. He felt that nothing in Oakland should be compared with what he had seen in Poland.) He noted that the Polish government was dominated by Communists and that the "iron curtain" had descended about 75 percent of the way in Eastern Europe. Knowland said he told Polish leaders that the United States did not want to see a Germany "that could again set out on a program of world conquest." In order to prevent that, Knowland said he foresaw up to forty years of Soviet rule in Germany. His prediction was right on target: almost forty-two years after his letter, the Berlin Wall, which became a symbol when it was built by Communist East Germany to stop a flow of refugees to the West in 1961, came down.

While on the trip, the senators visited Pope Pius XII at the Vatican. In a private audience, the pope told the senators that he hoped statesmen might reach an agreement that would eliminate future wars. He apparently made his appeal with the forthcoming conference of the Big Four foreign ministers in mind.

This European tour seems to have convinced Knowland to support the Marshall Plan and the Truman Doctrine, although most of his Republican colleagues in the Senate opposed both. Before he went to Europe, Knowland had written Marshall that he was in general agreement that the United States needed to furnish dollars as long as doing so didn't undermine the country's economy. He observed that it was in the best interest of world peace to bring economic stability to Europe. "However," he cautioned, "it does seem to me that if this nation disrupts its own economy through a runaway inflation or bankrupts the Federal Treasury through over-extending its resources and we head down the road that Great Britain appears to be now taking, we can neither be of service to the rest of the world nor to our own people."[5] Having gone so far as to note that U.S. reserves in such strategic resources as tungsten, lead, mercury, and petroleum were running low, he recommended that the United States trade its dollars to countries with large supplies of those raw materials and then stockpile them. "The difference between having abundant stockpiles of all types of raw materials . . . might be the difference between victory and defeat should we be so unfortunate as to again become involved in a war wherein we were cut off from world supplies." This dollars-for-resources deal, he said, "would command more respect than if we endeavor to run an international WPA. Not even this nation, as rich and powerful as we are, is in a position to do that."

Wherever he turned in Europe, Knowland was dismayed by the effects of the war on people. In particular, he was appalled by the difficulty American soldiers had adopting war orphans. He cabled his office, and by the time he returned to Washington a bill was ready for him to introduce in the Senate that would make it possible for Americans to adopt war orphans and bring them to the United States without waiting for a quota number. Knowland detested red tape.

Knowland returned to the states in time for the special session of Congress, which he believed ended on a satisfactory note. As he wrote to his father on December 21, the session ratified the Inter American Defense pact, adopted the Emergency Aid Program, and made "a start on a program to level off the inflationary spiral without placing the nation under a government controlled economy."

The California senator's international knowledge was increasing, his policies were developing, and his skills in the upper house were being refined. He also was framing a complex and sometimes pompous code of respect and courtesies that he believed belonged in government. Senator Arthur H. Vandenberg of Michigan and Knowland were becoming close working colleagues. Several times during the session, Vandenberg, one of the ranking Republicans as chairman of the Senate Foreign Relations Committee, asked Knowland to preside over the Senate as president pro tem. Once while sitting in, Knowland turned red-faced when Senator Glen Taylor (D-Idaho) compared President Truman to Benito Mussolini as a warmonger. Knowland stepped down from his chair and took the floor, where he ripped into Taylor. "As long as he sits in the White House," Knowland said, "President Truman is my president."

.   .   .

Knowland's letters to his father, once filled with the personal side of his life, now focused on the politics of Washington. On February 29, 1948, he got the first taste of what his future would be like, when for a week he acted as the majority leader. "While I had sat in for short periods before this, it was the first extended tour of duty in the front seat. It was interesting and the boys seemed to approve of the way the job was handled." In calling his colleagues "the boys," Knowland was using the language of the Senate, at that point an exclusive all-male club.

Knowland was also learning about hardball politics. He complained to his father that the Democrats were blocking the nomination of a Republican for a judgeship. "Downey [U.S. Sen. Sheridan Downey (D.-Calif.)] and I are going to the White House this week. If they do [block the nomination] I shall ask the Republican policy committee to hold up confirmation on all California patronage (customs, internal revenue, U.S. Attorney, Marshal, etc.). If they want to play rough they will find that two can play that way."

.   .   .

Knowland was becoming more and more concerned with the Soviet Union's forays into Eastern Europe. The Soviets began their blockade of Berlin in April 1948.

"The chips are down," he wrote his father on March 28, "and anything can happen. I do not think that the Russians want to provoke a war now but they did want to get all they could by finding soft spots into which to move. There are no more soft spots left. The real danger is that something may start in Yugoslavia or Bulgaria and the fuze [sic] will be burning before the Kremlin realizes it's so close to the powder keg." Knowland saw other danger spots in Iran, Turkey, Berlin, Trieste, Sweden, and Norway. He also feared a Communist attempt to overthrow the governments of France and Italy.

On April 2, 1948, Congress approved the European Recovery Program (the Marshall Plan) on a 69–17 vote. Knowland voted for it. Knowland earlier had tried to tie aid to the Nationalist Chinese to the plan, but his effort failed.

Knowland was convinced that the Democrats would lose the presidency in the 1948 elections. "The Democrats are in a blue funk," he wrote his father. "Never saw such a change in such a short period of time. Between Wallace and the South, the President will be left with no head or no tail to his donkey." Knowland himself was in close contact with one potential presidential candidate, California governor Earl Warren. On his frequent visits to Washington, Warren's first stop was usually Knowland's office, and he sometimes held news conferences there. The talk was that if Warren were to be elected president or vice president, Knowland would earn a cabinet seat as secretary of defense, but Knowland downplayed that possibility. "I like being a senator," he said. "I wouldn't trade it for any other job."[6]

Already in late 1947, Knowland was projecting New York governor Thomas Dewey as the front-runner and Bob Taft in the second spot on the Republican presidential ticket. Knowland praised Dewey's "courage and intellectual honesty," but he cautioned that "his chief drawback is a strong hunch that he can't be elected, on the part of the state and national leaders." Minnesota governor Harold Stassen would enter the Republican National Convention in third place, Knowland predicted. Of Warren, he said, "Earl, I believe is in a very good position. Hardly an article or cartoon is published in the east wherein candidates are mentioned that his name is not given a prominent position."

However astute Knowland may have been in his predictions, he made a bad mistake during the 1948 Republican convention, when his poor timing lost a major bargaining chip for Earl Warren. Knowland was chairman of the California delegation, and as such, he was expected to help California's favorite son, Warren, in his first bid for the presidency. The battle for the nomination came down to Tom Dewey and Bob Taft, with Warren a distant third. After two ballots, Dewey was just 28 votes short of securing the nomination. During a dinner break before the third ballot, Warren wrote out a statement releasing his delegation to Dewey, telling Knowland to get on the rostrum with the message. This, Warren believed, would put him in a position to bargain with the New York governor.

Warren and Merrill F. Small, the governor's traveling secretary, went back to their hotel room to watch the convention on television. "And then towards 9 o'clock, the California delegation went into the famous huddle . . . Knowland in the middle and all the delegates who'd arrived there . . . leaning over and listening to him as he read this statement the governor had written for him," Small described the scene. "This was the first they knew that they were being released, although, of course, they could figure it out, many of them, but you could see Margy Benedict crying, and you could see one of the men going like this as if he were cussing his lungs out, you know." The television cameras focused on Knowland, who was trying to fight his way to the platform. "He should have gotten there long before they called the convention to order—he should have been up there. They watched him, literally, just trying to shove his way through. Then they trained on John Bricker, and this became a marathon."

The Ohioan Bricker got there first and released his delegation, which put Dewey over the top. "And Knowland had become an also-ran, and a second-guesser, and unimportant," Small said, "and California just didn't have the bargaining position that Warren wanted them to have." Dewey then gained the nomination, to which Warren raised his glass and said, "Well, that's that. You can't win them all."[7] Despite Knowland's convention blunder, the size and power of California made Warren the choice for second place on the ticket. Dewey noted that "no other candidate could muster even a majority." Although Warren had previously said that he would never consider the vice presidency, he accepted Dewey's offer.[8] Apparently, Knowland's failure to switch the California delegation to Dewey hadn't hurt Warren after all.

As the presidential campaign began, the Republicans saw a chance to regain the White House for the first time since 1930. But Governors Tom Dewey and Earl Warren failed to hold the early lead they had built over Truman. And although Knowland was confident Warren would put California on the plus side for Dewey, Warren was unable to deliver his state.

At Warren's headquarters at the St. Francis Hotel in San Francisco on election night, Knowland told CBS, "I firmly believe California is going to be in the Republican column. The returns which we have from various sections of the state so far indicate, I believe, that Governor Dewey and Governor Warren will carry California by at least a 250,000 [vote] margin." Late returns from Ohio, Illinois, Wisconsin, and Minnesota indicated that Truman was pulling ahead. Then California began to slip. Knowland was still confident: "I am still convinced that California is going to end up in the Republican column by more than 100,000—maybe between 100,000 and 175,000 would be a good estimate at the present time." Knowland was wrong again, and Truman triumphed. He won despite two other candidates in the race who were predicted to draw off his votes: southern Democrat Strom Thurmond, running on the States' Rights Party ticket, and Henry Wallace, the Progressive Party candidate. Between them they could only poll 2.3 million votes; Harry Truman confounded all predictions, recapturing the presidency by 2.1 million votes out of relatively light turnout of 48.7 million voters.

Truman's victory also helped sweep in new Democratic senators who would be major players for years to come, including Lyndon B. Johnson of Texas, Hubert Humphrey of Minnesota, Paul Douglas of Illinois, Estes Kefauver of Tennessee, and Robert Kerr of Oklahoma. When it was over, the Democrats controlled the Senate, 54–42.

.   .   .

Nationally, and especially on the East Coast, attention was fixed on Europe, while those on the West Coast focused on the Far East, because of its war-making and trade potential. As a Californian, Knowland naturally reflected that "Pacific Rim" view, but he also was genuinely concerned about the fall of the world's most populous nation to the Communists; that concern was to set the tone for his foreign policy interests for the remainder of his years in the Senate. He had his own misgivings about Chiang Kai-shek's competence, but Chiang's army was the only one standing between the Communists and the rest of Asia. Although Knowland was not a lone voice in the Senate for the Nationalist Chinese, no one else fought for them with such energy or will.

The Communist movement in China had been growing stronger during and following the war. Encouraged by the Soviet Union, the Communists stepped up their attacks on the Nationalists. In 1945 President Truman had sent General George Marshall to China to seek a truce between them, but after a year he gave up, condemning both sides for their lack of effort. Nonetheless, Truman supplied the Nationalists with $2 billion in equipment and economic aid to battle Mao Tse-tung's forces.

In 1947 a full-scale civil war broke out in China. In 1948 Congress appropriated $400 million more to the Nationalists, despite Marshall's warning that nothing would save them. Knowland was the leader of a small but determined group of Republicans who threatened to block the appropriation for the Marshall Plan unless the Nationalists were given the funds. He was convinced that Chiang Kai-shek had not received "sufficient support, both moral and material, from the U.S."[9]

Leery of information he was receiving from the State Department, the California senator was relying on his own sources for information about China. One of those sources was a letter from Allen Griffin, the publisher of the Monterey, California, *Peninsula-Herald*, who was serving on the U.S. Economic Cooperation Administration in China. According to Griffin, the State Department was "dragging its feet" on China affairs. "No one in China can tell us what State Department policy is, since the latter appears to be chiefly negative. We have been confidentially informed that there is a lack of common purpose and harmony on the part of the State Department with the Joint Chiefs of Staff."

Unlike Knowland, Griffin worried about the fitness of the Nationalists, and he suggested that the feeling in China was that when Dewey won the presidency, "the floodgates will be opened and American money and materiel will flow into this country to bolster the Nanking regime regardless of the competence it shows or its coordination with essential American interests." The Chinese were told all they had to do was hold on until January and that all would be well. "The result is a negative influence on efforts . . . to bring about improvements here that are necessary if the Central Government is not to collapse." Reforms are necessary, he wrote, "unless China is to be a veritable rat hole down which we fruitlessly pour American money. In fact there won't be any central government except in name unless drastic changes are invoked to win back the confidence of the people and to cause an improvement in the deplorable military situation and the daily economic deterioration." Knowland sent a copy of the confidential letter to Arthur Vandenberg, chairman of the Senate Foreign Relations Committee.[10]

In a letter of December 8, 1948, Knowland asked if Senator Vandenberg had seen a 1947 report prepared by General Albert Wedemeyer, commander of U.S. forces in China. It suggested that because Nationalist troops were demoralized, the Nationalists should seek a coalition government with the Communists. Knowland, who had a hunch that the State Department was behind the report, felt that it would be "of vital interest to the nation's security to know if some of those who were active in disclosing the secrets of their own government to a foreign power had any hand in the lower levels in helping to initiate a policy which has played so tragically into the hands of the communists in China." Stressing that his concerns transcended partisan politics, Knowland urged that Republicans and Democrats "should be interested in working out a constructive American China–Far East policy with adequate safeguards against departmental sabotage."[11]

Vandenberg replied that he had not seen the Wedemeyer report but that General George Marshall had briefed him on it. Although he believed that no one other than Wedemeyer had written the report, "I can understand your suspicions about some of the men in the lower echelons of the [State] department at that time in respect to China," Vandenberg wrote. "I always shared those suspicions."[12]

10

Moving Up in the Senate

Knowland was beginning to attract more attention at the start of the 81st Congress. *Fortnight* magazine columnist Frank Rogers wrote that "some Republican strategists are known to be keeping an eye or two on him as a possible candidate for the type of new leadership they say is necessary if the Republican party is ever to have a New Look." Old Capitol hands questioned his leadership skills, but Knowland paid them little attention. "He was smart enough to realize the old adage youngsters should be seen and not heard need not apply to young Senators who know what they are talking about, who don't act like smarty alecs and who are not unwilling to listen to an occasional word of advice and counsel from the seniority boys," Rogers observed.[1]

Senate Republicans weren't sure yet what to make of young Knowland. He proved during the 80th Congress that he wouldn't just fall in line with the party, although he voted with a majority of the Republicans 70 percent of the time. But he also voted the same as his Democratic colleague from California, Sheridan Downey, on six of the ten most important issues before Congress.

"Unlike many newcomers who are always on the make for ways and means to escape the plague of obscurity which politicians fear, Knowland has refrained from indulging in the headline-hunting opportunities offered by Congressional investigations—and not because he hasn't had plenty of chances to get in on those actions," Rogers wrote. "Three years is too short a time to show whether Knowland will grow up enough to fill the shoes of Hiram W. Johnson. But the opportunity is there for him to measure himself, some day, alongside the career of a man who is still remembered in Washington as one of the great independents."

As a junior senator, Knowland was reluctant to challenge the more senior senators. "Most new members, and I think this would be true of Senator [Lyndon] Johnson on his side of the aisle and myself on my side, had a respect and a regard for the senators who served there for many years," Knowland recalled later. But at the same time, he pointed out, a junior senator was not doing his job if he "merely sits back and has the senior senator carry the Senate along with [him] when maybe that isn't the right way to go."[2]

On the opening of the 81st Congress in 1949, Knowland wrote to his father that the Democrats, who were in the majority, were taking greater control of committees than had the Republicans when they were in power. "Of course, they have the power to do this, however, the precedent established may rise to plague them later when the control again shifts, as it inevitably will." He also had concerns on the other side of the aisle: Knowland was among thirteen Republican senators who met in Washington before the opening of Congress to seek a revision of the GOP leadership, although they were aware that they were on the "short end of the fight." But, Knowland said, "if the group surrenders before a contest there never would be an opportunity for ultimate modification of the leadership."

Among those attending the gathering were Irving Ives of New York, Henry Cabot Lodge of Massachusetts, Leverett Saltonstall of Massachusetts, Kenneth Younger of North Dakota, Wayne Morse of Oregon, George Aiken of Vermont, Charles Tobey of New Hampshire, Raymond Baldwin of Connecticut, Ralph Flanders of Vermont, and H. Alexander Smith of New Jersey. A notable name missing from the meeting was that of crafty old Robert Taft of Ohio. The senators wanted Lodge for chairman of the Republican's Policy Committee, as the GOP rules forbade Taft from holding the post again. The majority leader, however, simply got the rules changed and defeated Lodge by a vote of 28–14. The group then decided to challenge the floor leadership of the party and nominated Knowland for the job. He was defeated by Senator Kenneth Wherry by the same vote. For Knowland it was a good lesson, which increased his respect for Taft. The older senator apparently viewed Knowland's move merely as a sign of restlessness.

As Knowland moved up in Senate seniority he also moved into better quarters. From suite 355 in the old Senate building he moved to suite 215, near the main entrance of the new Senate Office Building.

The new offices had a view of the Capitol and the inauguration stand where one day he hoped to be sworn in as president. One advantage of his new offices was that it was more convenient for him to attend Senate sessions. When the roll call bell rang for a vote, Knowland would barrel down the Senate Office Building hallways, arms pumping so hard in his determination that one observer remarked, "Put a pile of books under each arm, and you stop him dead in his tracks."[3] His elephantine walk on other occasions was described "as if into heavy surf or as hurrying reluctantly to his own execution."[4]

The new offices also allowed him to spend more time with the public, but he didn't take advantage of it. Helen Knowland often took his visiting constituents to lunch because the senator allowed them just a brief audience in his office. Knowland was uncomfortable in close contact with people. When he did spend time with constituents, it was rarely more than fifteen minutes. He would ease them out of the office by walking to his window, remarking on the beauty of the Capitol grounds. When they came to look, he would shake their hands and escort them out the door.

Although he could mesmerize a room full of admirers with his speeches, a one-on-one talk with the senator was painful for both parties. His son, Joe, said once, "The hardest thing I have to do is carry on a conversation with my father. Everything has to be just right or he won't talk."[5] One of his friends remarked, "He has more integrity than any politician I've ever known, but I wish he wouldn't talk to me as though he were making a speech on the radio." Another said, "He's the rudest man I know. I often wonder why I like him so much, but I do."[6]

.   .   .

In mid-March, some of Knowland's supporters were beginning to worry that his stands on labor-related issues might be too pro-union. His thinking on the Truman administration's proposed changes in the Taft-Hartley Law was of concern to the Northern California Employers Association, which was formed to deal with labor relations problems.

When asked directly about his position by Rudy Thumann, president of the United Employers of Oakland, Knowland indicated that he did not want to be pinned down; each piece of legislation had to be considered on its merit, and he would not be bound by what he might have said at a previous time. He did write that he would vote against

Truman's proposal, "which in effect repeals the Taft-Hartley bill in full. . . . It is my belief that the bill that is passed will be one that is written on the floor of the Senate and not the committee version. It shall be my objective to support a bill which will be in the public interest and equitable to labor, management and to the general public."

Later in the year, Knowland put his energies into supporting California's Central Valley Project, a massive federal plan to transport Northern California water to thirsty Southern California. The state originally had proposed the project but did not have enough money to continue it during the Depression, and the U.S. Bureau of Reclamation took over. The federal project delivered water only as far as the San Joaquin Valley near Fresno, and a parallel state project would be designed in the 1950s to get water to Los Angeles. That water made possible California's massive growth in the second half of the twentieth century.

.   .   .

The year 1949 was the pivotal year of Knowland's career in foreign policy. It was the year that he would obtain the unflattering nickname of the "senator from Formosa" because he believed that America's destiny hinged on the fate of Chiang Kai-shek and his government-in-exile on the island of Formosa (now Taiwan). The label was hung on him by Owen Lattimore, a Far East specialist at Johns Hopkins University. In addition, Knowland would be dubbed by his critics an "Asia First" member. What Knowland and other Chiang supporters could not understand was how the Truman administration could take so many steps to rebuild Western Europe and fight communism in the Middle East, but then let the largest country in Asia fall to the Communists. Knowland said he never maintained that the United States ought to concentrate primarily on the Far East. But, he said, it ought to give more than the token attention being paid to the situation.

At the time Congress was getting ready for its 81st session, Chiang was losing his war. On January 1, 1949, fearing the worst, he sought negotiations with the Communists, whose troops were advancing swiftly through the countryside. But with victory so close, the Communists saw no reason to negotiate. By mid-January, after sixty-five days of heavy fighting that took the lives of a half million of Chiang's troops, the Nationalists were all but defeated.

On January 20, 1949, President Truman was sworn in for a second term and Dean Acheson became his secretary of state. Knowland vigorously opposed the nomination, in most part because as undersecretary of state Acheson had helped set the U.S. policy that pressured Chiang to seek peace with the Communists: "I had felt that the handling of the policies in regard to the Republic of China had left much to be desired and that he was at least one of the architects of that policy."[7] Knowland was one of only six senators to vote against confirmation.

Those who opposed Acheson complained that he was too close to Alger Hiss and that his appointment was tantamount to nominating Hiss. Republicans in the era took great delight in linking Acheson and his State Department to Hiss, whom they believed had influenced the 1945 meeting of the three chief Allied leaders at Yalta. They also claimed that Acheson was part of a "pro-Soviet" bloc in the State Department that had helped draft the Yalta agreements. Knowland would refer to the Yalta Conference repeatedly in the years to come, likening it to England's appeasement of Nazi Germany at Munich. Yalta critics said that the Soviet Union failed to keep its promise of free elections in what were to become the Iron Curtain countries of Eastern Europe, installing Communist leadership instead. And so in the 1952 presidential campaign, Richard Nixon called the State Department Acheson's "Cowardly College of Communist Containment" and compared "khaki-clad" Dwight Eisenhower to "State Department pinks."[8]

Within a month after Acheson took office, fifty-one Republican Senate and House members, Knowland among them, sent President Truman a letter protesting the administration's inaction in China. It said a Communist victory in China would be "a historic defeat" for the United States and would pose "a grave threat to our national security." Acheson met with thirty of the Republicans and told them that the next step by the United States could not be foreseen "until some of the dust and smoke of the disaster clears away."[9] The Republicans seized on that statement as defeatist and stepped up their attacks on Acheson. And the secretary of state didn't help himself when he came out against a $1.5 billion appropriation for the Nationalists, arguing that the Nationalists' position was hopeless and the money would only prolong the hostilities and suffering of the Chinese people. The only answer, he said, was to commit U.S. troops to the fight, and he wasn't about to do that. He was successful in keeping the issue from reaching the Senate floor.

Knowland immediately went on the offensive against Acheson's policies. He introduced a concurrent resolution on April 21 calling for an investigation of U.S. foreign policy in the Far East by a bipartisan committee of five senators and five representatives. The resolution was ignored by the Senate Foreign Relations Committee. Knowland was convinced that the United States was losing the standing in the Pacific that it had won during World War II and blamed officials in the Far Eastern Division of the State Department for "frittering away" respect for the United States. He wanted a "fresh start on what has long been a bankrupt policy" and called for General Douglas MacArthur to play a bigger role in Far East affairs.[10] On June 24, Knowland released a letter signed by sixteen Republican and six Democratic senators asking President Truman to make it clear that the United States had no intention of recognizing Red China. That letter also was ignored. The Truman administration had no plans to deny itself the right to recognize another government if it chose.

In August 1949 American aid to the Nationalists was cut off and in a "white paper" Acheson noted that the United States had given $3 billion to the Nationalists and had little to show for it. The State Department blamed the Nationalists' defeat not on lack of money but on the Nationalist soldiers, who "did not have to be defeated; they disintegrated."[11] According to Acheson, the only alternative left for the United States was to intervene with troops, an option that was quickly quashed. Knowland joined Senators Kenneth Wherry, Patrick McCarran, and Styles Bridges in attacking the white paper as a "1,054 page whitewash of a wishful, do-nothing policy which has succeeded only in placing Asia in danger of Soviet conquest." Bridges charged, "China asked for a sword and we gave her a dull paring knife."[12] The United States was the only major power that refused to recognize the new government in China, a policy that would last until Richard Nixon opened diplomatic doors in the 1970s.

On August 12, Knowland urged a joint committee of the Armed Services (of which he was a member) and the Foreign Relations Committees to invite the testimony of General Douglas MacArthur and of Oscar Badger, commander of U.S. naval forces in the Western Pacific. It was an effort by Knowland to discredit Dean Acheson's white paper. His proposal was approved 13–12, but MacArthur declined to testify. Badger testified, however, pointing out the threat to U.S. security if Formosa was not supported. Even though the Democrat-dominated Senate turned down Knowland's resolution calling for an investigation of U.S. foreign policy, it recognized the need for Republican votes if it was to ensure assistance to its European program. It voted $75 million to "the general area of China." The wording carefully avoided any mention of Chiang.

.   .   .

Nanking fell to Mao's forces, and in October the Communists proclaimed China the "People's Republic" under Mao Tse-tung as president and Chou En-lai as premier.

Knowland and his wife, Helen, were to make many trips to the Far East. One of them, a Senate fact-finding tour in 1949, lasted for more than a month; during it the Knowlands were treated like royalty. They stopped off in Korea, where they wore borrowed wool underwear to ward off the bitter cold. Helen wrote to her mother that they were greeted at the Seoul airport with a nine-gun salute and a band that played the "Star-Spangled Banner." As they drove through the streets escorted by tanks and jeeps ("all well armed mind you"), they saw a big sign saying "Welcome Senator K." The streets were lined with South Koreans cheering the Knowlands. They stayed at the home of the U.S. ambassador, a house built by the Japanese during their occupation of Korea. Knowland met with South Korean president Syngman Rhee and his top advisers, who showed him the defensive lines maintained by the Republic of Korea's army at the Thirty-eighth Parallel, the dividing line between North and South Korea. He also interviewed five refugees who had escaped from the north. After the trip, Knowland came back to the Senate convinced that "there was every indication that within not too great a distance of time they [South Korea] might be subject to aggression from the north."[13] He was right, of course.

While he was on his fact-finding trip, the Chinese Communists jailed U.S. Consul General Angus Ward and four of his associates on charges of assaulting a Chinese employee. The arrests became a cause célèbre, with President Truman expressing his outrage. It appeared that the Chinese were trying to embarrass the United States by defying international law concerning consular immunity. If it accomplished anything, it discouraged the Truman administration from recognizing Red China. On November 29, while in Taipei, Formosa, Knowland cabled Truman that he had filed a formal protest against the arrests. He urged Truman to set up a sea and air blockade along the Chinese coast unless the five men were freed. He also called on Truman to seek UN approval and help from other nations. "If we continue to let Ward and others to be held as hostages by international blackmailers without more than words on our part," he said, "we will lose what standing we have left in this important part of the world and our own self respect as well."[14] Truman had no intention of blockading China, however, and Ward and the others remained in Chinese custody for more than a year before being released.

In late November, Bill and Helen Knowland flew to mainland China to investigate the rapidly deteriorating situation. They met with Chiang Kai-shek and other officials in Chungking as the Communist troops of Mao Tse-tung closed in on the city. As they were saying their good-byes, Madame Chiang gave Helen Knowland a ring identical to one she was wearing, and told her to show it if she ever needed help from the Chinese. (Helen never put the ring to the test, and it eventually was stolen in a burglary of the Knowland home.)

On December 7, Knowland and his wife slipped out of the city to a twin-engine airplane being held for them by the famous aviator Claire Chennault, leader of the World War II Flying Tigers. Chennault warned Knowland they might not make it off the ground. As they taxied down the runway of the old airport in Chunking, gunfire from the encircling troops flashed around the aircraft. They flew low through the bullets and were out of China before the red flag was raised over the city the following morning. It was a bitter day for Knowland, and it solidified his resolve to fight to contain what he considered a major threat to U.S. security. If the narrow escape bothered the senator, he hid it well. Later, he spoke of their departure in an offhand manner: "As a matter of fact, General Chennault was not quite sure we were going to get off at the airport, because firing could be heard in the general proximity of the airport and the Communists were closing in."[15]

The siege prompted Knowland to demand angrily that MacArthur be named high commissioner for Asia and that America set up an air and sea blockade of the China coast. He felt that MacArthur was the only general who understood the situation in Asia and the only man who could do the job. When he returned to Washington, he found new friends waiting for him, right-wing Republicans who embraced him as their new darling. No longer was he a middle-of-the-roader; he was now casting his politics with the right wing of the Republican Party.

While the fighting was going on, the State Department was continuing to encourage Chiang to set up a coalition with the Communists. Knowland was bitterly opposed to this policy. He noted that coalitions with Communists had never worked before. "The Communists never enter a government for the purpose of making it function," he said.

"They enter it for the purpose of ultimately destroying it and taking it over." Knowland said that while he was in Chungking, a high-ranking official told him, "Senator, I do not understand the policy of your government. Coalition hasn't worked. . . . We have an old expression in China, that you don't have coalition with a tiger unless you're inside the tiger. This is why we oppose coalition, and it would never work in our judgment." Knowland also realized that the Truman administration's policy toward the Far East had all but cut off aid to the Chinese Nationalists.

The takeover of China by the Communists left Americans bewildered and angry, political scientists Dumas Malone and Basil Rauch later wrote. "They would not believe that the United States could not have somehow influenced events—short of war—and obtained an outcome more favorable to American interests."[16] People began to visualize a worldwide Communist conspiracy headed by the Soviet Union. "I do not say our State Department is under Communist control," said Republican Senator Owen D. Brewster of Maine. "I do say that if Stalin had been in charge of our State Department, he could not have done a better job to secure the Communist penetration in China."[17]

Knowland was among those most critical of U.S. policy toward the Communist takeover. In the booming voice that became his trademark, Knowland hammered away on the Senate floor at Acheson, who, he said, sold off Formosa and South Korea. He was also highly critical when he learned that the State Department was distributing copies of the *Reporter*, which carried articles and editorials sympathetic to Red China, to U.S. embassies and consulates in the Far East. Knowland saw this as a sign that the United States was going to recognize the Communist government in China. In 1950 alone, he made 115 speeches on the Senate floor on Far East policy. His authoritative voice and well-researched speeches (all of which he wrote himself) rallied more and more Republican senators to his call.

Knowland never allowed himself to stoop to a personal level in his often bitter feud with the secretary of state. It was a trait that characterized Knowland throughout his dozen years in the Senate. No matter how adamant he was about an issue, he held no personal animosity toward his adversaries. As Acheson noted in his memoirs, "Senator William F. Knowland, who later criticized and opposed me strongly, in private always remained most courteous and friendly."[18] That was typical of the senator, according to Ed Salzman, a political writer who worked for the *Oakland Tribune* for several years. "Bill Knowland never attacked another individual, politician or otherwise, personally," Salzman said. "Every public statement he ever made was addressed to the issues of the day—but not because Knowland didn't have strong feelings about politicians. He simply played the game as fairly as it could be played."[19]

On April 23, 1947, as the Communists were moving on the Nationalist capital of Nanking, Knowland introduced an amendment to a foreign aid bill that would have granted an additional $125 million to Chiang and set up an American military mission to advise his government. Knowland introduced the amendment despite advice from two staunch Republicans who were members of the U.S. economic aid mission to China. Roger Lapham, who had been chief of the Economic Cooperation Administration mission in China, and newspaper publisher Allen Griffin, who had once accused the State Department of dragging its feet on China, bluntly told Knowland the facts of life about the Chiang regime. They said there was little hope it would win out in the long run. "The senator recognized the accuracy of their views," recalled then-Ambassador to China Philip S. Sprouse. "He knew they were correct, but he went right along with the line he had been taking earlier, because politically it paid off. This was one of the ways the Republicans could lambaste the Democrats."[20] It also was a way he could keep Truman from recognizing Red China. Said Griffin, "I thought Bill was misguided in many ways with his ideas and I several times tried to set him straight. But he was a determined man, [a] very strong character." He said Knowland, McCarthy, and others "thought they knew how to run the State Department better than they did."[21]

The amendment was battled fiercely along party lines. When Knowland asked that Congress not abandon Chiang, Senator Tom Connally of Texas said Chiang had "already deserted his people in going to Formosa with $138 million in gold in his pocket." It was one of the many times that Knowland and Connally tangled on the Senate floor.

·   ·   ·

While her husband had been fighting Mao's troops in China, Madame Chiang Kai-shek had established offices in Washington, D.C. She stayed for about fourteen months, until late 1949, during which time she attracted the top Chinese leaders in the United States to marshal American support. Out of that effort came the so-called China Lobby, with which Knowland was closely aligned. Although Knowland was not officially a member of the group, he was a focal point of the lobby's efforts on behalf of the Chinese; he was allied with other supporters of the Nationalist Chinese such as publisher Henry R. Luce, Republican Congressman Walter H. Judd, and importer Alfred Kohlberg. Knowland denied any knowledge of a lobby as such, remarking to Judd at one time, "Say Walter, what's this China Lobby we're supposed to be mixed up with?" "I don't know," Judd said with a laugh, "unless it's us—we seem to do most of the talking about China around here."[22] Knowland and others surely were influenced by those interested in restoring the Nationalist government on the mainland. At dinner parties sponsored by the Chinese, it was common practice for Knowland and others to rise in a toast, saying, "Back to the Mainland."

For his efforts, Knowland was chided by his critics. The ultraliberal *Nation* magazine, for example, called him the "noisiest and often the silliest" member of the China bloc,[23] which included Senators Styles Bridges of New Hampshire and Pat McCarren of Nevada, as well as Representatives John Varys of Ohio and Judd. But as the scholar Foster Rhea Dulles, a cousin of John Foster Dulles, noted, Knowland "was by no means as irresponsible as this allegation suggests. He was neither reactionary nor as isolationist as many of his fellow senators in this group, yet throughout his political career he held to his position with undoubted sincerity. No one more consistently stood up for Chiang Kai-shek or resisted more strenuously any move that might strengthen the regime of Mao Tse-tung."[24] Knowland's insistent questioning of State Department policy made a bipartisan approach toward Asia virtually impossible. Still, Knowland bristled when critics called him an "Asia Firster." He noted that he had supported economic and military aid to Western Europe to combat the Soviet efforts. "You can't close the door to communism in Europe and leave it open in Asia. There have been a number of those in the Administration who failed clearly to understand that communism is a global menace—what the men in the Kremlin understood two decades ago when Lenin pointed out that 'the road to Paris is through Peiping.'"[25] The California senator said that his support of Formosa was well known but his reasons "are not always taken into account by those who would write off this great island as though it were merely the estate of Generalissimo Chiang Kai-shek." He agreed that the Nationalists were not without fault but argued that they had served as loyal allies throughout World War II against the Japanese. "Our choice is not between 'Chiang and his crowd' or something better," Knowland said. "It is between a free republic of China on Formosa, with its present and potential value, or nothing at all."[26]

The China Lobby was credited with forcing a reluctant Truman administration to continue aid to the Nationalists, to prevent recognition of the People's Republic of China, and to keep Red China out of the United Nations. Knowland personally would long fight the efforts of Communist China to gain admission to the United Nations. He was worried that the State Department would side with Great Britain to open diplomatic relations with China. In a message pointedly aimed at the British, Knowland called the U.S. failed effort in China "as great a betrayal of human freedom as the Munich pact." He warned the British that by recognizing the Communist Chinese, they would lose their private property in China. He even went so far as to suggest cutting off aid to Britain if it persisted in seeking China's admission to the United Nations. Knowland also called on businesses to stop trading with the Communist Chinese, accusing them of putting short-term profits ahead of long-term national policy.

In truth, the lobby had broad-based support in the United States, primarily because of the widespread distaste for communism after the war. The support for Chiang might have dwindled rather quickly after he fled to Formosa had not the Red Chinese intervened in the Korean War. Once the Nationalists were on Formosa, Knowland's objective was to protect that island from attack by the mainland Chinese. He said if Formosa fell, Japan, Okinawa and the Philippines would not be far behind, warning that the U.S. defense line might have to be drawn back to California's Pacific Coast.

11

Formosa and Korea

Knowland had exploded in late 1949 when a State Department "guidance" paper was inadvertently released; intended for press and public affairs officers, it minimized the significance and damage if Formosa should fall to the Communists. The new year of 1950 started with the leaking of a telegram from the State Department to all Far Eastern posts stating its belief that Formosa would soon fall to the Communist Chinese and declaring that U.S. policy was to keep hands off. The telegram, dated December 23 and made public on January 3, outraged Knowland, Taft, and Herbert Hoover. The two Californians wielded considerable power in Asian policy—Hoover as a former president and GOP "elder statesman" and Knowland as a leader of the new breed in the Senate, tempered by war and impatient for a place in the decision-making process. They demanded that the U.S. Navy defend Formosa against an invasion. The Truman administration refused.

Hoover wrote his own seven-point plan for the Far East, which Knowland supported; it called for building a wall against communism in the Pacific, providing defense for Japan and the Philippines, preventing spy infiltration into Chinese consulates in America, keeping Communist China out of the United Nations, opposing Communist Chinese participation in formulating peace with Japan, and, finally, "maintaining at least a symbol of resistance" in southeastern Asia and "turning China in the paths of freedom again." Knowland released the Hoover plan to the press.

Senator H. Alexander Smith, a New Jersey Republican who had just returned from the Far East, suggested that the United States occupy Formosa but not with troops. It should be made a trusteeship area, he said. Democratic Senator Tom Connally ridiculed the idea, asking, "Does it mean occupation by a few tourists and U.S. senators? . . . senators who . . . at the firing of the first gun would go into a hole somewhere."[1] Knowland went a step further than Smith, arguing that a military mission should be sent to the island. Other senators joined in his call for intervention.

At the urging of Dean Acheson, Truman then announced that the United States would support the Cairo Declaration of December 1, 1943, and the Potsdam Declaration of July 26, 1945, which promised the restoration of Formosa to China. But the president rejected any military action, stating that he did not want to involve the United States in a Chinese civil war: "The United States Government will not pursue a course which will lead to involvement in the civil conflict in China. Similarly, the United States Government will not provide military aid or advice to Chinese forces in Formosa."[2] Such a declaration was necessary, according to Acheson, because the Communist Chinese were concluding from the proposals by Knowland and others that the United States was ready to send troops to Formosa.

At the same time, Smith and Knowland were meeting with Acheson to demand that the Formosa policy be rescinded. Acheson said the United States had only two alternatives: fight to save the island or accept the fact that Formosa might collapse. He told Knowland and Smith that the United States was not ready to send troops to defend the island. Acheson said the Joint Chiefs of Staff told him that Formosa was not vital to U.S. security.

Knowland was livid at the administration's "spirit of defeatism." In defending the policy, Acheson told Knowland to face up to the fact that Formosa might fall. Knowland countered by saying that if the United States pursued such a policy, Acheson would live to regret it. And, he said, he was just the person to give the American public that message. The same day, Acheson and Knowland went public with their positions—Acheson with a news conference, Knowland on the floor of the Senate.

Acheson stated the reasons the United States should not get involved with Formosa, which had to do "with the fundamental integrity of the United States and with maintaining in the world the belief that when the United States takes a position it sticks to that position and does not change it by reason of transitory expediency or advantage on its part."[3] For his part, Knowland bitterly denounced the administration's policy and again urged the appointment of General Douglas MacArthur as the coordinator of U.S. policy in the Far East. MacArthur believed that Formosa's seventy Japanese-built airstrips and its small but modern ports might go over to Russia if the Communists gained control of Formosa. That, MacArthur feared, would prove a real threat to the arc of U.S. defenses in the Pacific.

Many senators were adamantly opposed to sending American troops to battle in Asia. The Democrats seized this opening and challenged Republicans to say whether they wanted to commit troops to the defense of Formosa. Knowland protested that he had never advocated sending in U.S. troops. His position was that "for us to move in and occupy [Formosa would be the same as] Russia did in Poland. It would be a stab in the back."[4]

The California senator continued to distrust Acheson, as did other backers of the Nationalist Chinese. Their greatest fear was that Acheson would move to recognize the People's Republic of China without seeking Congress's advice. In a heated debate on the floor of the Senate, Knowland made clear his doubts that Acheson had any intentions of keeping his pledge to consult with Congress, suggesting that the secretary of state would come before the Senate Foreign Relations Committee and say, "We have determined to recognize the Communist regime in China; we wanted to notify you before the statement was given to the press." It is clear that Acheson wanted to recognize the Communist regime, but he was not able to accomplish it while he was in office, mostly because of the efforts of Knowland and his supporters.

On January 12, just a few days after Knowland's Senate statement—he was to make 115 speeches on the Senate floor about the Far East that year—Acheson delivered one of his most important speeches on Far Eastern policy before the National Press Club, titled "Crisis in China." Acheson drew a line in the Pacific that the United States was willing to defend, and Formosa fell outside that line. Knowland and other critics said that Acheson's statement encouraged the Communists to attack Formosa and Korea. It surprised no one that Knowland called for Acheson's resignation.

The Communists did indeed attack, forcing the United States to deploy troops to the Far East, but not to Formosa. Seven months later North Korea invaded South Korea, and American soldiers once again would be dying in Asia.

Writers for the magazine *U.S. News and World Report*, wondering why Knowland was so vociferous in his support of the Nationalist Chinese, suggested that Knowland was "simply expressing the dominant West Coast viewpoint. Businessmen there and particularly the vigorous shipping industry of the Pacific ports look to the Far East as the only promising area for an expansion of their trade."[5] But patriotic pride seems a more likely motive than a desire to help the Port of Oakland, as Knowland no doubt remembered too well the fears during World War II that the Japanese might invade the West Coast. The *U.S. News* article also speculated that the Republicans saw the China issue as a political weapon to defeat the Democrats. It was easy to suspect deviousness in Knowland's championing of the Chinese Nationalists, but it probably was not there. Once he made up his mind, he was impossible to sway, and he had decided that the Communist takeover in China was a threat to the world. Knowland did not parry and feint as a Nixon or Acheson might do; he plowed into battle, preferring the ax to the rapier.

Knowland kept up his attack on the Truman administration's policy toward Formosa. In a speech reprinted in the *Congressional Record*, he said that Acheson was treating the eight million people of Formosa and other nearby islands "as though they were ships which had been sunk beneath the waves of the China Sea and the Pacific. Since Formosa alone has more people than either Australia or Greece, this is hardly realistic. It is hardly conceivable that this Government can view with unconcern the moving of international communism off the Asiatic land mass on its first major island-hopping venture." Knowland insisted that the United States must not allow an invasion of Formosa: "In the hands of international communism the many Japanese-built air strips and the excellent harbors would drive a wedge into our Pacific defense line that runs from Japan through Okinawa to the Philippines. In unfriendly hands it would be a strategic loss that no competent military, naval or air commander would or has overlooked."[6]

.   .   .

On January 21, 1950, a New York jury convicted Alger Hiss of perjury for denying to a grand jury that he had been a spy. "Conviction of Alger Hiss is significant," Knowland wrote to his father the next day. "He was in Far Eastern Division of State Department. He and his brother are old time friends of Acheson. Brother is now law partner in Acheson firm."

Knowland's personal opposition to Acheson once again rose to the surface because of the secretary's somewhat tenuous link to Hiss and his refusal to turn his back on Hiss. "A roar of indignation rose from Capitol Hill and echoed across many of the nation's editorial pages. . . . Knowland said he would move to withhold State Department appropriations," *Time* magazine reported.[7]

The Hiss case gave a major boost to a young congressman from California, Richard M. Nixon. Nixon had pursued the Hiss case with all of his resources, thereby establishing himself as a frontline fighter against Communists. The door now was wide open in Congress for demagogic attacks on communism. Nixon made his decision to seek a more powerful office.

During his two years in the House in the late 1940s, Richard Nixon was well aware of who ran Republican politics in California. His attitude toward Governor Earl Warren and Senator Bill Knowland was almost subservient. At the cautious urging of his longtime mentor, Herman Perry, an influential Whittier banker, Nixon was considering a run for the Senate in 1950 against Democrat Sheridan Downey. The way was cleared for him when Downey decided against reelection, citing ill health. Before he could run, Nixon knew he had to have the backing of Warren and both Knowland and his father, J.R. On June 25, 1949, Nixon met with the senator, whose support was critical. He wasn't sure he could receive a strong commitment from Earl Warren, who also was up for reelection and who traditionally withheld early support from other candidates.

Knowland was cautious in his assessment of Nixon's campaign, saying he would endorse him if he was convinced that Nixon had "the best chance to win." The Democratic nominee, Congresswoman Helen Gahagan Douglas, was extremely vulnerable to Nixon's negative type of campaigning, and she was unpopular with many Democrats because of her liberal voting record. Nixon wrote in his memoirs that even Congressman Jack Kennedy personally delivered to him a $1,000 campaign contribution from his father, Joseph Kennedy.[8] Eventually Knowland, always the loyal Republican, supported Nixon's efforts and he campaigned vigorously for him. He may not have supported Nixon's tactics, but Nixon was the Republican nominee and Knowland would back him. Yet Nixon never seemed to feel any sense of debt, despite the full support not only of Bill Knowland but of the *Oakland Tribune* as well.

Bill Knowland's father kept his finger on the pulse of politics in California, and the *Oakland Tribune, San Francisco Chronicle*, and *Los Angeles Times* were setting the Republican agenda. In a September 27 letter to Herbert Hoover, J. R. Knowland commented on the Nixon-Douglas Senate campaign: "I think it looks quite well for Nixon for U.S. Senator. His opponent is a vote-getter, particularly among the women, but now that we are involved in a war with Communists in Korea her attitude on that issue is certainly not helping her. She has voted frequently [as a U.S. representative] with the small minority headed by Marcantonio of New York and the whole psychology is not very helpful for her. Nixon is making a very good campaign and he makes a fine impression wherever he goes. His record on the Communist issue is so outstanding that no one can doubt it."[9]

.   .   .

On June 24, 1950, Communist North Korean troops attacked South Korea. The United Nations ordered an immediate cease-fire, but the demand was ignored. The following day, Truman attended Sunday church services in Missouri, then flew to Washington for a meeting with Acheson and other advisors. While the White House was being remodeled, President Truman was living in Blair House across the street. There, the decision was made to commit U.S. troops to repel the invasion.

Knowland took the floor of the Senate the next day and said, "Korea today stands in the same position as did Manchuria, Ethiopia, Austria and Czechoslovakia of an earlier date. In each of those instances a firm stand by the law-abiding nations of the world might have saved the peace. . . . The destruction of the Republic of Korea would be catastrophic. . . . If this nation is allowed to succumb to an overt invasion of this kind, there is little chance of stopping communism anywhere on the continent of Asia."[10]

Knowland thought that Truman might not need Senate approval to send troops to Korea, but that he should have at least asked for a congressional resolution in support of his policies. "I think had he done that it would have saved him a lot of trouble in later years, where the sharp-shooting of those after the fact always takes place," Knowland said.[11] The California senator was especially unhappy that Truman cut out the Republicans from the decision making. He recalled that no Republican members of the Senate were invited to the Blair House conference during which the president and Democratic leaders discussed the Korean situation. "They [the Republicans] were told what decision had been arrived at at the Blair House conference on the Sunday night the hostilities broke out," Knowland said. "I think the president made a bad mistake in that."[12]

But he also came to Truman's defense. On the Senate floor, Knowland declared, "I believe that in the very important steps the president of the United States has taken to uphold . . . the United Nations and the free people of the world should have the overwhelming support of all Americans regardless of their party affiliation. The action this government is taking is a police action against a violator of the law of nations under the charter of the United Nations."[13] Knowland had coined the phrase "police action," which would become the euphemistic justification for an undeclared war. A reporter left the Senate after Knowland's speech and went to a presidential press conference, where Truman was saying, "We are not at war." The reporter asked whether it would be accurate to call the Korean intervention a "police action" under the United Nations. "Yes," Truman replied, "that is exactly what it amounts to."[14] On June 27, two days after the North Koreans attacked, Knowland remarked, "If Korea is not supported and maintained, there is no place on the continent of Asia that can be ultimately supported and maintained."[15] That day, Truman ordered General MacArthur to lead the stand against the North Korean aggression.

Knowland took his Senate responsibilities on the Korean situation very seriously, for he was a deadly serious man. He worked hard and he expected others to do the same. His aide Jim Gleason remembered that Knowland was in his office on a Saturday afternoon when he tried to get someone from the Defense Department on the telephone, but there was no answer. He slammed the telephone down and shouted, "Goddamnit, don't they know there's a war going on?" A few days later, Knowland wrote his father that Washington was very tense over the possibility of war in Korea. "War is neither inevitable nor impossible and I believe it is now very much touch and go. . . . The situation in Korea may get worse before it gets better. With ample warning signs and with pleas for help from the Government of Korea we got caught short again. The American people are being spoon fed. I think the people are more realistic than the government. They should be told the truth, i.e. that the draft will have to be used quickly if we are not to endanger the security of the whole free world."

As the Korean "police action" expanded, Knowland was concerned that Truman initially had limited the U.S. involvement to below the Thirty-eighth Parallel, the line drawn at the end of World War II separating the two Koreas. On September 27, 1950, after MacArthur's strikingly successful invasion at Inchon, Truman allowed him to move north, but not beyond the Yalu River at the North Korean border with China.

Later in the fall, Knowland traveled to Korea, where he visited U.S. forces. He met with some of the combat troops who had been sent to the Yalu River area to blow up bridges so that Chinese supplies could not be delivered. He said he was appalled that the troops were told they had to do their job entirely on the south side. Truman refused to budge from the position that U.S. forces could not cross the Yalu River, fearing that drawing Communist China into a full-scale war inevitably would draw in the Soviet Union and bring on World War III. In a speech of December 4, 1950, Knowland told his colleagues in the Senate that these restrictions endangered the soldiers: "I talked to some of the men who had had many casualties in their crews. They could see the anti-aircraft guns firing on them from the north side of the Yalu River. Yet the limitations imposed upon them prevented their 'taking out' that anti-aircraft fire." Although soldiers could see fighter planes rising from the airfield north of the river to attack, inflicting casualties, U.S. planes were not allowed to pursue the fighters. "I think it is rather tough to ask men to fight and perhaps to die under those conditions, when they know that day by day there are concentrations of tanks and vehicles carrying gasoline and ammunition which are being supplied to the Communist troops south of the Yalu River." Knowland came home from that trip raging about U.S. troops being forced to fight with one hand tied behind their backs.

On the Senate floor, Knowland railed against Communist aggression, urging President Truman to take steps to head off the "fanatical foe" and thundering that "all of Asia hangs in the balance. If the manpower and the natural resources of Asia fall into the orbit of international communism there will exist the greatest aggregation of power the world has ever known." Although he did not coin the phrase the "domino theory," Knowland in this speech was clearly referring to other nations falling, one after the other. "If the free people of China on Formosa are sacrificed, where do you draw the line? Cannot the same argument apply to Korea? To Japan? To the Philippines? To Indonesia? To Indochina? To Burma? To Siam? To Pakistan? And to India? Where do you draw the line? Is it now approved doctrine that small nations can be sacrificed to expediency or does this doctrine apply only to the Asiatic area? If so, is it the color of a man's skin or his geographic location that determines his right to live in a free world of free men?"

Stopping just short of calling on Truman to drop the atomic bomb on China, Knowland urged the president to use more conventional bombs on supply lines from China. He said Truman should make it clear to British prime minister Clement Attlee, who earlier had in person sought assurances that the United States would not drop the bomb without consulting with its allies, that the United States had no intention of "giving him or anyone else a veto over the use of the atomic weapon. We are not going to be destroyed as a Nation, or permit a free world of free men to be destroyed while someone else is passing judgment on whether or not aggression is really aggression."

Knowland ended his speech by saying that if the United States were to cringe before Communist aggression, "countless men who are now free may be bending their backs in the slave-labor camps of Siberia a year or two from now. Stand up to Communist aggression today, and millions who are now enslaved in Poland, the Soviet Union, Czechoslovakia, Bulgaria, Romania, Hungary, Latvia, Lithuania, Estonia and China will gain new hope that they too may some day be free from the most godless tyranny man has ever known."

12

"Bill, You Don't Kiss Babies"

When the 82nd Congress opened in early January 1951, the Korean War was on America's mind. So preoccupied was Congress with the war that little was accomplished other than foreign and military affairs. Defense spending in Korea rose to $56.9 billion for fiscal 1952 and $46.6 billion in fiscal 1953, all appropriated by this Congress.

Because of efforts of Knowland and other conservatives, popular liberal programs desired by the Truman administration such as national health insurance, aid to education, and increased public health benefits fell by the wayside. The Senate Republicans were aided by a strong new class elected in November, including Richard Nixon of California, Everett McKinley Dirksen of Illinois, and James H. Duff of Pennsylvania. The Democrats also added some formidable new senators, including George Smathers of Florida and Mike Monroney of Oklahoma.

Knowland continued to strike a balance between his roles as a domestic conservative and an internationalist. He took issue with the neo-isolationists in Congress who wanted to prevent American troops from going to Europe as the North Atlantic Treaty Organization agreement required. A resolution by Senator Kenneth S. Wherry of Nebraska to bar the sending of any troops to Europe brought heated debate. "If Communism is a global menace, which it is, then it must be met on a global basis," Knowland argued. "We cannot expect [Western Europe] to build an army that would make Europe impregnable to Communist aggression before we place an additional man or dollar on the continent." His solution was to send one American division for every six European divisions until there were a total of seventy.

Knowland also spoke out strongly in defense of Douglas MacArthur and accused hatchetmen in the Truman administration of trying to undermine MacArthur's position in Korea. "Our Armed Forces in Korea are entitled to all-out support," Knowland said. "The Nation is now confronted with the choice between the far eastern policies of the Secretary of State, Dean Acheson, or Gen. Douglas MacArthur. Both cannot be right." He demanded that Acheson be removed, not MacArthur: by giving full support to MacArthur, the United States would be saying that it would no longer be "playing footsie" with the enemy.[1]

On April 11, 1951, President Truman fired General Douglas MacArthur. To his father, Knowland wrote that he believed Truman's excuse for firing the general to be a letter from MacArthur to House Republican Leader Joseph Martin calling for all-out war in Korea. The general declared, "There is no substitute for victory." Martin thought that MacArthur's popularity at home would sway Truman to step up the war in Korea, but Truman, who had told MacArthur that his job was to hold the defensive line in Korea near the Thirty-eighth Parallel, removed the general from his commands in Japan and Korea and called him home. Knowland thought that MacArthur's firing would have come anyway: "My deduction based on present available facts is that the President was preparing a March public proposal in the name of the UN for a cease fire. The deal had been worked out with most of the UN members. It was to be advertised as 'no appeasement' when in fact it would have opened the door for a Far Eastern Munich. MacArthur had shown sufficient independence that they feared he would let go with a blast when the facts became known. It was necessary to get rid of MacArthur before the proposal was made. The Martin letter gave the excuse for the administration to hang its hat on."

The general came home to address a joint session in Congress, where he reiterated his demand that the United States fight the Communists to win. In that speech, MacArthur asserted, "War's very object is victory—not prolonged indecision."[2] That statement, which both reflected and fed the deep discontent with Truman's handling of the "police action" in Korea, ultimately would hurt Democrats in the 1952 election. Not only had Knowland strongly supported MacArthur's military judgments since first meeting him in 1946, but he too believed the United States should opt for all-out war, even if it meant risking the intervention of the Soviet Union. Knowland joined Styles Bridges and Bob Taft in helping MacArthur prepare for his testimony before Congress about the Truman administration's actions in the Far East.

In another letter to his father, Knowland complained that the administration had usurped the powers of Congress by declaring war in Korea. "The constitutional power for a declaration of war, of course, rests with the Congress," he noted and pointed out that when a member of Congress speaks on the subject of war, his statements are recorded in the *Congressional Record:*

The public is thereby able under our constitutional system to hold him responsible for his actions and to remove him if they do not agree.

We have now passed into a constitutional twilight stage. We are now engaged in the fourth most costly war in all of our history. [One hundred forty thousand Americans would die in Korea.] We were placed in that war by the action of the President and his advisors and without the approval of Congress.

If this country can be placed in a war en camera and the Congress can be foreclosed from inquiring as to what stand was taken by several individuals present, we have a situation then where anonymous advisors to the President without their views or their votes ever being a matter of public record or even available to a Congressional committee will be able to deprive the public and the Congress of knowledge to which I believe they have a basic right when it involves their lives, their property and their future.

That same day he delivered a speech on the Senate floor echoing the letter to his father. Indeed, his argument that the president must seek Congress's approval before entering a war would be heard again and again, long after he was out of office. Senators complained long and hard, also to no avail, that Lyndon Johnson usurped their power to decide whether the nation was to send troops to Vietnam. The same argument would be made later over U.S. intervention in Panama, Grenada, the Persian Gulf, Somalia, and Bosnia. "This has nothing to do with the desirability or lack of desirability of our becoming involved there; but I merely state as a fact that under those circumstances—with the public not present and with the press not present—a decision was reached which put this nation into a war," he roared.

Before the year was through, Knowland would make another hundred speeches in the Senate about U.S. support for Nationalist China.

.   .   .

President Truman's popularity in 1951 was clearly on the wane; his problems with foreign policy, the charges of communism at home, and several scandals within his administration continued unabated. Knowland, now the senior senator from California, was continuing his ascent as a rising star in the Republican Party. On March 29, 1952, Truman announced he would not seek another term. But Republicans were already lining up for a shot at the presidency, with Bill Knowland and Earl Warren right in the middle of the political action.

Nixon advisor Herman Perry had been concerned early that Representative Chet Holifield, a Southern California Democrat, might be a candidate for Knowland's Senate seat. Perry feared Holifield because the congressman was "highly regarded by liberal and conservative Demócrats. He tries to play both sides of the fence. I think it is high time that Bill Knowland should definitely get busy about his campaign."[3]

During the Republican primary, Knowland's opponent, Robert D. Adams of Los Angeles, accused him of unfair campaign practices. In a May 17, 1952, letter to the U.S. Senate, Adams asked for an investigation of Knowland's "mis-conduct" in the campaign. He charged that the money came from the notorious liquor lobbyist Artie Samish, Standard Oil Company of California, Union Oil, and General Petroleum. He also claimed that the contributions to Knowland's campaign were being carried on the books as advertising expense and that Knowland knew it. Furthermore, Adams accused the press of a conspiracy "to suppress and withhold the news about the illegality of Knowland's campaign" and claimed that Knowland directed and controlled a "press ring" in California: "The tentacles of this invalid ring reach to the source of all media of public communication, thus withholding news that would be published were it not shut off at the place of its origination. The power to suppress public information that emanates from the Tower of the OAKLAND TRIBUNE would indeed have made Boss Tweed blush for his want of temerity." He complained that earlier charges that he brought against Knowland "were treated with thundering silence" by the state's biggest newspapers, which thus provided proof of a conspiracy.[4]

The Senate had no intention of getting involved in one state's election, and Adams's complaints were ignored. When Holifield decided not to enter the Senate race, Knowland's 1952 political problems evaporated. Yet many Republicans in California were more concerned about getting Knowland reelected than they were about any presidential bid by Earl Warren. From the Nixon camp, Herman Perry wrote to a colleague on April 21 that he thought it was "more essential for California to re-elect Bill Knowland than it was to have a presidential candidate from California. . . . Unless you have been 'out in the sticks' and 'below the tracks' you have no idea as to the feeling of some people with reference to Earl's present [attitude] towards certain trends of our government. . . . I can assure you that some of the people who . . . furnish a lot of do-re-mi also have opinions on the subject which should not be overlooked." He closed his letter by saying that Knowland and Nixon more clearly represented the thinking of the Republican voter than did Warren.[5]

On June 2, the day before the California primary, Knowland delivered a particularly harsh attack on President Truman at a campaign rally in his hometown of Oakland. He charged that the president's "vacillating policies" had "encouraged our enemies and discouraged many of our friends," noting that since the end of World War II, the number of people behind the Iron Curtain had increased from 200 million to 800 million. "An evil and ruthless force has expanded its totalitarian power at the rate of almost 100,000,000 people a year," he told the cheering crowd. He accused the Truman administration of a "catastrophic 'waiting for the dust to settle' policy in China while looking upon the Chinese Communists as agrarian reformers and which ignored the clear signal of danger in the statement of Lenin many years ago that 'the road to Paris is through Peking.' "[6] (Knowland repeated that statement, putatively by Lenin, in almost every foreign policy speech he ever made.)

This assault on national policy was typical of Knowland's campaign. When Republican leaders complained that he was focusing too much on Asia and not enough on California, Knowland declared, "Maybe I am doing the wrong things. But I believe I am concentrating on the overriding issue of our time. Boys are dying in Korea and if we're asking them to sacrifice their lives, I can risk sacrificing my political career."[7] Indeed, Knowland was enthusiastically received when he questioned the Truman administration's policy of a limited war in Korea. "I do not believe this government or the United Nations has the right to ask Americans to fight and die and then deny them the right to win," he insisted. The speech was one of three he used during his campaign. One took five minutes, one took fifteen, and one took half an hour, but they all harped on the same topic: the Truman-Acheson Far Eastern policy was catastrophic.[8]

Knowland's reelection was assured when he won both the Republican and Democratic nominations by cross-filing in the June primary.

His name went on the ballot of each party, and thus only astute voters knew for sure the candidate's real party affiliation. This was a common tactic in California elections; from 1914 to 1952, as many as 90 percent of candidates for the state legislature and for Congress who cross-filed and won both party nominations were victorious in the general election.[9] Knowland's Democratic opponent in the primary was Representative Clinton McKinnon, who repeatedly labeled Knowland the "senator from Formosa." But it didn't seem to hurt the forty-four-year-old incumbent. He won 2.5 million votes in both primaries while McKinnon was only able to scratch up 750,000 votes. In November, Knowland was reelected with 3.9 million votes, the most ever received by a public official in California. He carried fifty-seven of the state's fifty-eight counties.

The margin of victory came even though Knowland was not a particularly good campaigner. Although he professed to like campaigning, he was shy; his efforts to meet people were often awkward, and his speeches were filled with too much bluster. One of his supporters said, "Bill, you don't kiss babies." Another said, "You don't slap backs." Yet another said, "You don't see enough people personally." Asked to comment on his success, despite his awkwardness, one Republican Party official said, "Bill Knowland is a straight-thinking, forward-looking, hard-working, sincere kind of guy. What the hell more do you want in politics?"[10]

13

Betrayed Loyalty

At the same time Knowland was running his own 1952 reelection campaign, he was working to help Earl Warren's last-gasp bid
for the presidency. Warren, the GOP vice presidential nominee in 1948,
had won the party nomination for president in California in the primary. He knew he was in no position to go head to head with either
Robert Taft or Dwight Eisenhower, who was widely regarded as a possible candidate even though he had not publicly announced his decision to run for the office. However, with the support of California's big
delegation Warren hoped to be a compromise candidate if neither Eisenhower nor Taft could grab the nomination in early ballots. Warren's
efforts set off one of the most intriguing stories of backroom politics,
loyalties, and betrayed loyalties in election history. The political maneuvering turned Californian against Californian, thwarted Warren's own
White House bid, and perhaps even kept Bill Knowland from becoming
president the following year.

For Warren's plans to have any chance, he had to have help from
Knowland, his fellow Californian. As head of the 1948 California delegation, Knowland had helped the governor become Thomas Dewey's
GOP running mate, and he was Warren's choice to spearhead the 1952
attempt. Thus Knowland began working to set up the machinery for
California Republicans to choose a delegation pledged to Earl Warren
at the national convention in July. On November 7, 1951, he sent a telegram to prominent California Republicans, urging them to ask Warren to run and praising Warren for his vision and for his leadership:

"We know you to be exceptionally qualified to discharge the duties and to meet the obligations of the president of the United States. We know that you have to an exceptional degree won not only the respect and confidence of the people of your own state, but that you enjoy the respect and confidence of your fellow citizens throughout the nation."[1] The telegram concluded by calling on Warren to submit a slate of delegates in the California Republican primary the following June. Also signing the telegram were such powerful state Republicans as State Comptroller Tom Kuchel, who would later replace Richard Nixon as California's junior senator, and Nixon himself.

Although he signed the telegram, Nixon was never a Warren man. As one who long carried grudges, Nixon remembered well Warren's less-than-enthusiastic support of him when he ran for senator in 1950. Knowland talked the reluctant Nixon into backing Warren, pointing out that it would be a slap in the face to Warren if the junior senator from California declined to be a delegate. And though he pledged to support Warren, Nixon had let it be known to his close associates long before the primary that he favored Eisenhower. But he realized early that it would be in his best interests to be a delegate at the convention, even if he had to pledge fealty to Warren. He agreed to join the Warren delegation only if he could have a voice in selecting delegates.

Nixon told close associates that in early 1952 he had met with Taft, who asked for his support. Nixon's response was to make clear his respect for Taft's leadership in the Senate but to stress his belief that in the next few years foreign affairs would be crucial; he told Taft that he thought Eisenhower was better qualified for the job. He said that he was supporting Eisenhower and that he had informed Warren and Knowland of his support, a statement both later disputed. Indeed, Nixon never openly declared any such turn away from Warren. In a radio broadcast just before the June primary, Nixon insisted, "I have constantly stated that the Republican convention should select the very strongest possible nominee at Chicago." Warren was the best candidate, but "if the convention does not turn to Governor Warren, our delegation will be in a position to throw our vote to the candidate who will be selected."[2]

That Nixon's arm had to be twisted to induce him to join the delegation should have been a clear warning to Warren. One of Knowland and Warren's closest associates, Republican National Committeeman McIntyre Faries, said the governor trusted Nixon. "He [Warren] was a bit like Bill, a bit naive," Faries said. "He thought if a man gave his word in writing he would stand by it."[3] Nixon knew if he could name some of the members of the California delegation, he would be in a position to broker support at the convention. One of those Nixon suggested as a delegate was his old friend Murray Chotiner. Warren disliked Chotiner intensely but finally agreed, to avoid a split with Nixon. "In an attempt to be fair, he gave his approval," said a Warren supporter. "We knew from [that] . . . time we had to watch Nixon."[4] Knowland was given that assignment. Others named as delegates were Ray Arbuthnot, Pat Hillings, Frank Jorgensen, Roy Day, Jack Drown, and Roy Crocker, all longtime Nixon supporters who would do what he wanted. Knowland already was becoming suspicious of Nixon, but he wanted the junior senator where he could watch him. As Keith McCormac, chairman of the Kern County Republican Central Committee in California, remembered it, Knowland "didn't grasp the situation as to what Nixon was going to do to him. See, he believed that Nixon was an honorable man."[5]

Like all others who were on the primary ballot to serve as delegates, Nixon signed an oath that he would support Warren unless released by the governor. The pledge said, "I personally prefer Earl Warren as nominee of my political party for President of the United States, and hereby declare to the voters of my party in the State of California that if elected as delegate to their national party convention, I shall, to the best of my judgment and ability, support Earl Warren as nominee of my party for President of the United States."[6] To Knowland, that pledge was sacred. Nixon signed it, but he didn't mean it and he didn't follow it.

Friendship to Warren aside, Knowland would have preferred Taft as the party nominee. He had grown to admire Taft during their service together in the Senate, and his philosophy was closer to Taft's conservatism than to Warren's increasing liberalism. Knowland, too, wanted to stack the delegation with his people in case Warren faltered. He wanted some delegates who supported Taft as well, should Warren decide to release his delegation at the convention before the first ballot. But he would not make a move until Warren gave the word.

Both Eisenhower and Taft thought it wise to stay out of California in deference to Warren's power, and neither was on the state's primary ballot. Although Warren was still enormously popular in California, a great deal of that popularity came from across party lines. The Democrats held the edge in registration, and Republicans needed a strong crossover vote to gain election. Indeed, many Old Guard Republicans in California were becoming disenchanted with Warren because he was promoting government-supported health care and favoring labor unions. "Creeping socialism," they called it.

Right-wingers decided to put up a slate of delegates pledged to "anyone except Warren." It was headed by U.S. Representative Tom Werdel of Bakersfield. Werdel believed that the governor had abandoned Republican tenets and had embraced Franklin Roosevelt's New Deal philosophy. Those who supported the anti-Warren slate said the governor was a Republican by registration only, arguing that he didn't really want to be president but was merely trying to work a deal for a place in a Republican administration. The theme of Werdel's supporters was "real Republicanism versus Warren's Trumanism." They also charged that Warren headed a "captive delegation." Knowland tried to ward off the attacks. In a December 15, 1951, speech in Werdel's backyard, Knowland told a Bakersfield audience that Warren "does not have an ounce of socialism in his makeup. He would make an excellent president."

Anti-Warren forces spent between $500,000 and $600,000; some estimates put the figure as high as $1 million. Warren backers spent no more than $150,000. In the June primary, the governor easily won the contest to represent California's seventy delegates to the Republican National Convention that July, winning twice as many votes as Werdel. Yet a half million California Republicans voted against the incumbent governor, a sign that his support at home was slipping among conservatives. And Warren fared poorly in other states' primaries. While he had a lot of scattered support from Republicans throughout the nation, he only had six other pledged delegates, elected from Wisconsin.

The governor had said during the delegate vote in California that he would not attempt to swing the delegation one way or another if he no longer had a chance to be nominated. Privately, he was telling acquaintances that he would support Eisenhower if he failed to get the nomination. Because he had so few delegates, there were rumors of a possible deal with either Taft or Eisenhower that would land Warren a Supreme Court seat or a cabinet post if he released his delegates to them. But he denied them: "There is nothing, I hope, that I have ever said or done that would indicate anything of the kind. There is no basis in fact for those assumptions." Warren claimed to be hopeful of lining up more delegates once the convention began. "I think I'll have a few more than 76," he said in late June.[7]

Werdel had drawn enough votes in the California primary to weaken Warren, and his chances as a compromise candidate were fading while

Knowland was becoming more powerful. The senator was even talked about as one of the top vice presidential contenders, though he dismissed such talk. He was going to the convention as chairman of the governor's delegation and he would not put his ambitions before Warren's. There is little doubt, however, that if Warren were to release the delegation early, Knowland would quickly jump to Taft. "I was very friendly with Bob Taft . . . I had a high regard for him, but I was [a] senator from California. I didn't feel I could or should participate in advancing the candidacy of someone else while Earl Warren's name was before the convention," Knowland would say later.[8]

Nevertheless, talk on the convention floor was that if Knowland threw his support to Taft he could have the vice presidential nomination. He would have been a perfect fit for Taft: he was conservative, young, a huge vote getter, a veteran, a Westerner. Knowland could not have foreseen that if he had accepted such an offer and Taft had won the presidency, Taft's sudden death would have made Knowland president within a year. But even if he had, the fiercely loyal Knowland would not have abandoned Warren without the governor's blessings.

Richard Nixon had no such qualms. Despite his pledge, he continued to work for Eisenhower and to undermine Warren, an effort that eventually would get him the vice presidential nomination. His maneuvering touched off a political storm that forever soured Warren's and Knowland's relationships with Nixon.

On July 1, six days before the convention began, Nixon told reporters it was anyone's guess who the presidential nominee would be.

Just before the eighteen-car Warren Special left the Western Pacific Station in Sacramento for Chicago on July 3, Knowland was chosen as the delegation's chairman. All delegates were aboard, except Nixon. As Warren remembered in his memoirs, Nixon "sent word that he had conflicting engagements in the East."[9] "The East" was New York, where Nixon was the principal speaker at the annual state GOP fund-raising dinner. After the speech, former New York governor Tom Dewey invited him to his hotel room for a drink. Eisenhower backers Lucius Clay and Herbert Brownell were there. When Dewey broached the subject of the vice presidential nomination, Nixon said he would be delighted to accept it. It wouldn't hurt his chances, he was told, if he helped swing the California delegation to Eisenhower.

After the New York meeting, Nixon traveled to Chicago, where he joined the committee that was writing platform resolutions; it was meeting before the start of the convention. Warren had appointed him to it at Knowland's urging. "I told [Nixon] that you were desirous of him taking on this assignment," Knowland wrote Warren. "He said he will be glad to serve in that capacity."[10] Knowland and Warren might have thought the committee work would keep the junior senator out of trouble and away from the California delegation, but the ever-shrewd Nixon knew that the assignment would put him in an excellent position to look for disputed delegates when the fight over credentials began. He provided Eisenhower with inside information and maneuvered convention rules to help the general.

Knowland, meanwhile, was holding the California delegation together on the train ride to Chicago. It turned into one big mobile party. The governor's daughters danced in the aisles to the pounding beat of a piano while fireworks were shot out of the train's windows. The mood changed, however, at least for Knowland and Warren, when Nixon boarded the train in Denver. He wasted no time in trying to persuade delegates to switch to Eisenhower. On Nixon's instructions, his delegate Roy Day began going through the train, repeating, "Isn't it too bad that Taft is such a wonderful person, but he's just not electable. It's just a shame." He would tell that to anyone who would listen.[11] Rumors were flying throughout the train within minutes. Knowland moved quickly to counter Nixon, who was telling delegates that Warren could not win the nomination and that they should think about switching to Ike. To some, he even admitted his interest in the vice presidency. Nixon said that if California failed to swing to Eisenhower early, Ike might be unable to reward California as the state deserved—with the vice presidency. And he was the one who should be Ike's running mate.

As Warren remembered it,

Nixon paid his respects to me and said if any of his friends got out of line to let him know. He then visited throughout the train. I do not remember if I saw him again before he left us prior to our arriving in Chicago. Anyway, during the night, the Nixon delegates—but not the [junior] senator as far as I know—held caucuses and urged other delegates to vote for General Eisenhower on the first ballot.

Some of those who were importuned came to me and asked what the situation was. I told them what I had told the voters: that the delegation was not a front for anyone, and that no matter what happened it was obligated to vote for me on the first ballot at least.

During his meeting with Warren on the train, Nixon told the governor that he supported him 100 percent and that the rumors of his

interest in the vice presidency were ridiculous. Warren knew otherwise and called Nixon a traitor. "I wish you would tell General Eisenhower," he told an Eisenhower aide, "that we resent his people infil-
trating, through Nixon, into our delegation and ask him to have it
stopped."[12]

Eisenhower denied any knowledge of Nixon's activities and told
Warren that if the convention deadlocked he hoped Warren would win
the nomination. "If anything happens to Warren's candidacy then the
nomination might fall to [Gen. Douglas] MacArthur and that would
be a calamity," Eisenhower told associates.[13] In his memoirs, Nixon denied working secretly for Eisenhower while pledged to Warren. "I had
already informed Knowland and Warren as to my decision [to support
Ike]."[14]

But Knowland flatly disputed Nixon's spin on the events. "There was
no doubt about it, in my judgment, that Senator Nixon's secondary
choice was clearly Eisenhower, and it's my personal belief that he had
indicated that to the Eisenhower people." He said Nixon was, at the
very least, letting the delegation know he was behind Eisenhower. "I
remember the governor was particularly annoyed . . . when Nixon sent
out some kind of a poll to see how the state stood, in the event that
Warren was eliminated. I don't know just how the question was put,
but the governor felt that this was undercutting him."[15]

After the primary election, Nixon had sent a June 11 letter to 23,000
California Republicans asking them who would be the strongest candidate the Republicans could nominate for president. It asked nothing about whom they preferred if Warren bowed out. When Warren
found out about the letter, he asked Nixon supporter Bernie Brennan to intercede to block release of the results. "I was deeply troubled
about the way Nixon and some of his closest associates were working
for Eisenhower long before we left for Chicago," Brennan said later.
"I warned Nixon that if this group did bolt, he would be finished as a
man of honor."[16] Warren was especially upset because California Republican voters had just chosen him as their candidate for president,
and the delegation was pledged to him. Nixon promised not to release
the results, which favored Eisenhower; but they were leaked to the
press within twenty-four hours of tabulation.

Thomas J. Mellon, a member of the California delegation, told a different story about Nixon's role. Mellon, who later went on to become
the chief administrative officer for the city and county of San Francisco,
said several delegates pledged to Warren were working on Nixon "to
cut Warren up." Mellon said he had a bedroom on the train across the

aisle from a group of delegates who were meeting with Nixon. Among them were Jack Drown of Long Beach, a close friend of Nixon's, and Frank Jorgensen, a Los Angeles insurance man:

They sat up there that night. They didn't even know I was there, but I was right across the hall and the door happened to be open. . . . I was going to bed and about to close the door when I heard this big discussion going on. I just sat there for about two hours and let these guys talk.

They really put the heat on Nixon. I think he was making an effort to live up to his commitment to Warren, but they were really putting the heat on him. Every possible way. At one point, he said, "Well, after all, I am a United States Senator." And they said, "We don't give a damn what you are." So he was pressured actually by a lot of people in our own delegation. . . . He wasn't pressuring them that night. But where he really fell down, he didn't have quite the courage to meet the commitment he had made.[17]

Fifteen minutes before the train arrived in Chicago, Nixon slipped off at a suburban station. He was not in the photograph showing the "united" delegation arriving in Chicago.

Later that day the California delegation held a caucus at the Knickerbocker Hotel. Knowland opened the meeting by saying that he had reports there were scattered delegates across the country who would be voting for Warren when the convention began polling delegates. In an attempt to offset Nixon's efforts, he urged the California delegates to hold their ground and to "approach the job prayerfully and not take action on unfounded rumor" that Warren didn't have a chance for the nomination. The senator was shaking with anger. "I just want everyone in this room to know," he said, "that never in history has any delegate ever violated his pledge and been respected again." Nixon sat quietly on the platform, without expression. Knowland said that while he could not offer assurances Warren would win, "we have the opportunity to nominate Earl Warren as president of the United States." Even if Warren were to release the delegates, he said, "California will act solely in the interest of the Republican Party and the nation, and not engage in any type of deal whatsoever." He also told the delegation he was not interested in being a "bandwagon jumper."[18] When California's senior senator was through speaking, it was Warren's turn. He praised and thanked the delegation for sticking by him; then he turned to Knowland, saying that he wouldn't trade him "for any six chairmen of other delegations."[19]

Knowland refused to tell anyone who his fallback choice would be if

Warren released the delegation: "If I told somebody in the Taft camp or the Eisenhower camp that California might be for them, or I might be for them on the second ballot, they have to tell their immediate people. That's no longer a secret. Pretty soon it's appearing in a [newspaper] column. My own delegation would be upset, because nobody could have delivered that delegation en bloc, not even Governor Warren, to someone else."[20]

The pressure on Warren to release the delegates would prove to be enormous even before the Twenty-fifth Republican National Convention opened on July 7. A week before the convention, Eisenhower strategists, meeting over coffee and sweet rolls, had spent eight hours at San Francisco's Palace Hotel—the same hotel where President Warren G. Harding had died on August 2, 1923—designing a plan to lure Warren's delegates to Ike. But they underestimated Warren and his backers. They were not open to political approaches and held the line going into the convention. Taft's troops also were trying to buttonhole the Warren delegates, saying that their man had a good chance of winning and that the California delegates should throw in their support early. But Taft's supporters weren't any more successful than Eisenhower's: Knowland was keeping the delegation in line.

The Eisenhower camp was dangling the vice presidency in front of Nixon in the hope that he could get the delegation to switch to Ike or, at the very least, prevent its switch to Taft. "It was Nixon's role to keep California from going to Taft," said Senator Henry Cabot Lodge, Eisenhower's preconvention campaign manager. "I approached him on the Senate floor well before the convention, and asked him if he would be interested in the vice presidency. 'Who wouldn't?' he said. Not very elegant, but that's what he said."[21]

As the convention opened, speculation centered on Knowland, Representative Walter Judd of Minnesota, Governor Dan Thornton of Colorado, and Nixon as possible running mates for Eisenhower. Nixon's reputation as an anticommunist crusader, particularly his work on the Alger Hiss case, gave him the edge, some observers said. "I knew that some of Eisenhower's more liberal advisers had preferred Earl Warren [for vice president] to me, and that some of his more conservative advisers had preferred Bill Knowland, or even Bob Taft if he would accept," Nixon wrote in his memoirs.[22] Nixon, too, credited the Hiss case with swinging the tide for him. Newspaper columnist Drew Pearson said that Knowland was clearly "peeved with Nixon and the rumors of his vice presidential nomination."[23]

All the while, Nixon was working behind the scenes to help Eisenhower get the nomination. At one point he confessed to Knowland that he was going to try to deliver the delegation to Eisenhower. Knowland was appalled. Helen Knowland said she found her husband in his hotel room looking stunned. She asked him, "Do you think Nixon double-crossed you?" "Yes, I think so," Knowland replied.[24]

While Nixon was lobbying the delegates for Eisenhower, Taft was trying to persuade Warren to turn the California delegates over to him, stressing that this was his last chance at the presidency. Warren said he held his own share of the delegates, but Taft insisted that only he and Eisenhower had a chance. That might be true, Warren told Taft, "but I had told the people of California how my delegation would vote, and that would be done." Taft asked if there was any position he would like in his administration in exchange for his delegation and mentioned the attorney general's job. Warren told him no, that he would be happy to return to California as governor. "Well," Taft said, "Bill Knowland can have anything he wants." But Warren again rebuffed Taft. "No, Senator, we will go ahead as we promised."[25] Despite the rumors that Taft and Eisenhower were trying to work a deal with Warren to give him a cabinet post or judgeship in their administration, political pundits were saying that Warren was the only man in the United States who could be offered a job no matter which party won the White House.

Taft's floor managers approached Knowland several times during the convention, promising him the vice presidency if he would deliver the California delegation to Taft. "Why no, I wouldn't do that," Knowland said. "As long as Earl Warren is in the picture, I will support Earl Warren." Afterward, an aide who overheard the conversation told Warren about it. "I knew Bill would be that way and that is it," Warren said.[26] Warren pointed out that Knowland "was perfectly loyal to me" and that "he held the delegation together as a solid unit throughout," though he often wondered if Taft had offered the vice presidency to Knowland. "Being senator from California, the only thing Knowland possibly could have been interested in was the vice presidency. Had he accepted such an offer and been elected, he would have become President of the United States, because within a year Senator Taft died. I mention this because thereafter my relations with Knowland, political and otherwise, cooled markedly—not to the breaking point, but noticeably."[27]

Knowland was upset with Warren for refusing to release the delegation despite the odds against his getting the nomination, but while Nixon openly shopped for the vice presidency, Knowland stood by his pledge to support Warren in his increasingly futile quest for the presidency. Publicly, Knowland said he had told both the Eisenhower and Taft camps that he wasn't interested in the vice presidency. "I enjoyed the Senate, and I was not interested in discussing the vice presidency," Knowland said years later. "After the nomination was made, that would then be for whoever the nominee would be to make the decision."[28] Yet Knowland was also realistic. He owed Warren his loyalty for one ballot and no more. If Warren had released the delegation after the first ballot, there is little doubt that Knowland would have jumped to Taft.

Paul Manolis, Knowland's longtime aide and confidant, confirmed that Knowland would have accepted the second spot on the ticket with Taft. Knowland had spoken to him a number of times about how Hiram Johnson had turned down the chance to be Warren Harding's vice president and that he would have been president when Harding died. "So I don't think the senator ever lost sight of that lesson," Manolis said.[29] But as Knowland's older daughter, Emelyn, emphasized with some regret, her father "would have never made a deal to do something that went back on his word and his integrity in order to further his own career. He should have—I mean in my judgment, I think he should have done it because nobody else was watching out for his interest. Why shouldn't he have, because it was the thing he wanted in life. That man wanted to be president of the United States. He never admitted it publicly, but that's where his whole career was shooting for. That's where he wanted to be."[30]

In an issue published just before the convention, *Time* magazine suggested that the chances of Warren becoming a compromise candidate were poor. The shift in his fortunes forced politicians "to revise their thinking about California. . . . California's most promising figure now is Knowland, who has the bark and grain of vice presidential timber."[31] No mention was made of Nixon. *Time* publisher Henry Luce, who had been closely associated with Knowland on the China issue for several years, often used his magazine to further his political interests, and Nixon was not one of those interests. Theodore White, writing in *Collier's* magazine, observed that Knowland "could play the part of a Roman senator with no coaching at all. His enormous outer self-possession may make visitors squirm and fidget . . . but . . . [he is] a man of solid, obstinate honesty."[32]

Herbert Brownell, who would become attorney general in the Eisenhower administration, approached Murray Chotiner about which senator from California would make a better vice presidential candidate.

Chotiner recalled their conversation: "I had worked with both men and I gave him my opinion that Nixon had it over Knowland as a campaigner and also had a wider appeal. He wanted to know what Knowland's reaction would be. I told him that Dick was willing to stand down to Knowland, if the choice narrowed down to the two of them." When Brownell asked Chotiner how Warren would react to Nixon's nomination, Chotiner said he didn't know, but there "had not been any warmth between the two." He also told Brownell Helen Knowland's reaction to Nixon's possible nomination: "Helen said, 'You tell Dick not to think anything of it [about him being chosen over Knowland], to go right ahead and if it is awfully close not to think for a moment how Bill would feel about it.' I reported that to Brownell, and he said, 'Well, if Bill Knowland's wife feels that way about it, why that must be it.'"[33]

At home, the *Los Angeles Times*'s political editor Kyle Palmer was writing, "Some of the eager beavers who are so busily engaged in conjecturing how many ballots Warren will expect [the delegates] to stay hitched [for] might ponder the significance of Knowland's position and attitude. When Earl Warren's status has been determined one way or the other, Bill Knowland will regard himself as a free agent and not before. Why am I so sure? Do you know Bill Knowland? If not, I can let you in on an important fact: he is an honorable man. He didn't make the pledge to support Earl Warren for President with any shabby reservations. Honorable men don't stab their friends—or enemies—in the back."[34]

Warren later recalled that at the convention, Knowland's father was adamant that his son not accept the number two spot on the ticket, from either presidential contender. J. R. Knowland was heard muttering, "I hope Bill don't accept that vice presidency. I hope Bill don't accept that vice presidency." The elder Knowland apparently believed that Eisenhower would only serve one term and that his son would be ready for the presidency in 1956.[35] Longtime Republican Party worker Frank Jorgensen remembered riding to the convention with Senator Knowland, his wife, and his family. "I remember his father pleading with Bill not to let himself become a candidate for vice president," Jorgensen said. He believed that J.R. wanted his son to be closer to home to take care of family affairs.[36]

Even Bill Knowland sometimes wondered whether he wanted the second spot. He liked being a senator, and he served on the powerful Appropriations, Foreign Relations, and Atomic Energy Committees. He had more voice on the Senate floor than he would playing second fiddle to either Taft or Eisenhower. The odds were, however, that mindful of how many presidents had died in office, Knowland would have accepted the vice presidential nomination.

Nixon also was seeking advice from his advisors about whether to accept the vice presidency. "Dick, you're a junior senator from California," Chotiner told him. "Knowland is young and he's healthy, and unless something should happen to him, you will always be second man in California. The junior senator from California doesn't amount to anything. There comes a time when you have to go up or out. Suppose you are the candidate and we lose. You're still the junior senator and you haven't lost anything. If you win and are elected vice president and out at the end of four years, you become all washed up, you could open a law office in Whittier and have all the business you want. Any man who quits political life as vice president as young as you are in years certainly hasn't lost a thing."[37]

.   .   .

If Earl Warren ever had even an outside chance for the presidential nomination, that was all but lost during a battle over seating contested delegates at the convention. Bill Knowland, of course, was right in the middle of it.

Even though Eisenhower enjoyed tremendous popularity after World War II, much of his support was from Democrats. Taft headed into the convention far ahead of Eisenhower in delegates, although he did not have the nomination sewn up. Among pro-Eisenhower southern delegates chosen at state and local party conventions were many independents and ex-Democrats who had entered Republican politics because they supported Eisenhower. The Democrat-dominated South was just beginning what would become a trend over the rest of the century—a move toward the Republican Party in name as well as in conservative vote. But the Taft-controlled state Republican organizations in the South began disqualifying Eisenhower's delegates, leading to charges by the Eisenhower forces that Taft was trying to steal the convention. Ike began attacking the old-line party hacks backing Taft, claiming they were guilty of "a betrayal of the whole Republican Party and its principles" when they "deliberately and ruthlessly disenfranchised" those who had voted for Eisenhower delegates. He said no party "can tolerate a rigged convention and hope to win."[38]

At the start of the convention, the delegate question was the first major issue to be decided. Some of Taft's strength lay in the disputed delegations of Texas, Georgia, and Louisiana. The credentials committee approved 68 of the contested pro-Taft delegates, but Eisenhower asked for a convention vote on a "Fair Play Amendment" that would block them from voting on the remaining delegates in question. Those delegates would go to Ike if the convention voted for the amendment.

The vote was expected to be extremely close and California would be a key state in the voting. If all 70 California delegates voted for the amendment, Eisenhower would win the contested delegates and would be a shoo-in for the nomination. If the delegates were split, Ike's chances for a first-ballot victory would be considerably reduced. A deadlocked convention then might turn to Warren as a compromise candidate; at the least, such a vote would have aided Taft and boosted Knowland's stock in the Taft camp. In meetings throughout the night, Knowland argued that members of the California delegation should split their 70 evenly and thereby defeat the amendment. Just before the vote, Nixon rushed to the microphone, where he told the delegation, "I feel that any candidate who is nominated for President of the United States would have far greater difficulty in winning in November with those contested Taft delegates than otherwise."[39] Warren urged that the delegation vote in caucus to either support or defeat the amendment. The final vote, 61–9 for the Fair Play Amendment, meant that California would vote as a bloc to seat Eisenhower's delegates.

Knowland noted that when California's 70 votes went for the amendment during the roll call "there was a kind of rumble of 'Oh' through the convention floor. Many people assumed that the same vote would be cast for the presidential candidates as was cast on the rules," Knowland said. "But that was not the case." All 70 delegates stood by Warren on the first ballot.[40] Nevertheless, the Fair Play Amendment started Eisenhower on the road to victory and sealed Warren's fate.

When it appeared, then, that Taft would fall short of the nomination, some of his supporters urged him to switch to General Douglas MacArthur as the presidential candidate. But Taft refused, he said, because he felt he owed it to his friends to go through one ballot. That was a waste of time, Knowland concluded; Eisenhower could not be defeated. "Look," he said, "there won't be a second ballot; he'll win on the first ballot."

As the first ballot approached, Eisenhower was nine votes short of the nomination. Minnesota governor Harold Stassen sent his aide, Warren Burger (the future U.S. chief justice), to Knowland, urging him to switch to Eisenhower "as a means of healing party wounds." Knowland replied, "We don't want any credit or any responsibility for that nomination." But then Knowland reconsidered. "I've got to go and phone Earl right away to get his [wishes] and see what I can do." But he soon returned, reporting, "I can't get Earl, can't find him, can't get hold of him." Finally Stassen turned his 12 delegates over to Ike, securing the nomination. Warren was to say later that even if Knowland had asked he wouldn't have released his delegation.[41]

Eisenhower supporters were confident of victory after New York cast 92 of its 96 votes for Eisenhower. But they were still worried about California's 70 delegates. They wanted Warren to stay in the race, more to deny the votes to Taft than to get them to switch to Eisenhower. If Warren refused to release his delegates on the first ballot, they believed, Eisenhower could win the nomination. They were right. After the vote Knowland was told that Nixon had said his second choice after Warren for the nomination was Eisenhower. In his typically gruff manner, Knowland replied, "I was for Governor Warren, period. I didn't have a second or third choice." But according to one estimate, had Warren released his delegation earlier, as many as 57 to 60 of the 70 delegates would have cast their votes for Eisenhower.

With Eisenhower chosen as the nominee, the convention then turned to the question of who would be the vice presidential nominee. The choice, of course, was Eisenhower's. It didn't take much to persuade him to go for Nixon, who had been at the head of Ike's short list. Nixon had also come through strongly for him at the convention.

At a meeting of staffers at the Conrad Hilton Hotel the afternoon after the nomination, the choice was fairly clear. It would be Dick Nixon, a man Tom Dewey famously called "a respectable McCarthy." The choice was acceptable to Eisenhower.

Publicly, Warren and Knowland supported the choice of Nixon as the nominee; Warren called it a great honor for California while Knowland called Nixon an excellent choice. But Nixon's actions during the convention had forever turned his two fellow Californians against him.

An ecstatic Nixon called Knowland right after he was told he would be the nominee. Knowland said he then got another call from someone on Nixon's staff asking if he would place Nixon's name in nomination. "I was told by someone whose name I don't recollect . . . that Dick would like to talk to me," Knowland said. "Dick came to the phone and asked whether I would be prepared to place his name in nomination. I had already at that time been informed that he was the choice as the nominee for vice president. I forgot whether it was Brownell or someone else who informed me."[42] The California senator didn't know that he was Nixon's second choice to give the nominating speech. McIntyre Faries later said that at Nixon's request, they had gone together to ask Senator John Bricker of Ohio to give the speech in the interest of harmony. Bricker, Taft's top man, said he would have to get approval from his delegation. He returned to say that they did not approve.

Knowland didn't answer Nixon immediately. He returned to his hotel and ran into Faries and Tony DeLap, a California state senator from Richmond. "This is going to be awful rough on Bill," DeLap said. "Let's get him out of here, take him around town and take him to lunch." Taking Knowland by the arms, they said, "Let's go out and get a little air." According to Faries, they drove all over Chicago "and we talked about kings and cabbages, and so on." The purpose of the ride was not to persuade Knowland to nominate Nixon but "to give him a chance to react, a chance to think and take his mind off a lot of things." Faries said he was sure Knowland was disappointed that Taft had not won the nomination and that it cost him the vice presidency. "Bill's shirt was as wet as the sheet before you put it in the dryer. He goes back to the [hotel] apartment. He comes back in a clean shirt and makes the nomination of Dick for vice presidential candidate"[43]

Nixon remembered it this way: "I found Bill Knowland and asked him if he would do me the honor of placing my name in nomination. Knowland was not only a personal friend, but also the man whom Bob Taft probably would have chosen as his running mate. Knowland said he would be proud and happy to nominate me."[44]

Knowland proceeded to deliver a particularly lukewarm speech. "I could tell he would have rather had a beating than had to do that," said Keith McCormac, a close Knowland associate who was watching the speech on TV. "You could tell by looking at him. Knowing Knowland like I did, you could tell that he would rather have been anywhere but there, nominating Nixon. I remember the look on his face. He looked like a fellow with egg on his face, you know, when he was making the speech."[45] In his prepared 600-word address, Knowland praised Nixon's "bulldog determination" that enabled "the government to hunt down and unravel the Alger Hiss case." He also praised him as a campaigner "who puts forth more of his heart into a campaign . . . and a young man who gives to the Republican ticket an appeal to the young men and women of this nation."

Two months later, Nixon was in trouble. He had to scramble to rebut charges that he maintained an $18,000 "secret fund" supported by wealthy Republicans. On September 18, 1952, the liberal *New York Post* ran a story about Nixon's fund with the headline "Secret Rich Men's Trust Fund Keeps Nixon in Style Far Beyond His Salary." It totaled $18,235—a large amount of money in the days when a home could be bought for $10,000. Nixon went on national television to defend himself with the famous "Checkers" speech.

This scandal almost put Knowland back in the running for vice president. The indications were that a couple of Warren backers, still angry about the way Nixon had treated their candidate, had leaked the story to the press in an effort to destroy Nixon and deprive Eisenhower of the election. Many agreed that the fund was neither secret nor illegal, but it suggested that Nixon was in the pockets of the nation's most wealthy men. This image led several of Eisenhower's advisors to urge that Ike dump Nixon from the ticket. Newspaper editorials began to run heavily against him.

On September 20, Ike summoned Knowland from his vacation in Hawaii to stand by as a possible replacement for the beleaguered Nixon. As Eisenhower advisor Sherman Adams remembered it, Knowland was a "valuable liaison man" between Eisenhower and Nixon. "He was a great help in smoothing over this difficult misunderstanding because he knew Nixon privately much better than either Eisenhower or I did at the time," Adams said.[46] On leaving Hawaii, Knowland told reporters that the crisis "will be overcome," but he thought that the Democrats would take advantage of it. When he caught up with the Eisenhower campaign train—the "Look Ahead, Neighbor," special—he immediately went to see Eisenhower. Nixon fund-raiser Earl C. Adams gave a second-hand report of their conversation: "I know from what Bill Knowland told me that Knowland . . . stood up for Nixon and said 'It's no go. You leave him alone and he stays on the ticket.' "[47] Knowland was motivated more by worries about the effect of Nixon's removal from the ticket on Republican chances in November than by any sort of loyalty to Nixon. Eisenhower looked to be the Republicans' first real chance in twenty years to return to the White House.

Three days later Knowland met with several Eisenhower aides at the Statler Hotel in St. Louis. There they developed plans for a coast-to-coast radio hookup for Nixon's rebuttal speech, which was to be televised as well. Harold Stassen was urging Nixon to drop out and be replaced by Earl Warren. Eisenhower was leaving it up to Nixon to decide what to do. Nixon told Ike, "General, a time comes in politics when you have to shit or get off the pot." To which Eisenhower replied, "Keep your chin up."[48]

In his speech, Nixon spoke about his humble upbringing, his wife's "Republican cloth coat," and the Texan who had given his family the cocker spaniel named Checkers. He described how important the dog was to his two young daughters, with a catch in his voice, and said, "We're going to keep it." The speech was widely derided as demeaning and corny, "one of the most sickening, disgusting, maudlin performances ever experienced."[49] Nevertheless, it worked; Nixon saved his spot on the ticket, and another chance for the vice presidency dissolved for Knowland.

Always the loyal Republican, Knowland stated publicly that he had "full confidence" in Nixon. The next day Nixon left to campaign in Montana, while Eisenhower, with Knowland aboard his train, headed for Wheeling, West Virginia. While there, Eisenhower decided to keep Nixon on the ticket, summoning him to Wheeling. When Nixon got off the plane, Eisenhower and Knowland were there to meet him. Ike said to Nixon, "You're my boy." Knowland told him, "That was a great speech, Dick." Nixon then buried his head on Knowland's shoulder and wept, a scene that was photographed and displayed in virtually every newspaper in the United States the next day. "It was quite a tense and emotional situation," Knowland recalled. "I said, 'Everything is going to be all right, Dick,' and he came over and said, 'Good old Bill.'"[50]

It was not surprising that Knowland was there for Nixon to lean on; he always put the party first. It was true that Knowland didn't trust Nixon, but as his daughter Emelyn Jewett said, "I think it's a fair statement that he never publicly washed that linen, but he watched very carefully what Nixon was up to. I think they had a good working relationship as far as the business activities . . . were concerned," she said. "Dad did some things that were contrary to this thing that I say was a lack of trust in Nixon. But again, you have to understand Dad and his sense of morality—that even if you don't like or trust someone, if they're getting a bad rap they're not responsible for, Dad doesn't feel they should be hung on that issue; hang them on the issues that they're really responsible for."

Jewett said Knowland comforted Nixon after the speech "because he didn't believe this was an issue upon which Nixon should be thrown out and that the man deserved support at this time on that issue. But that did not mean that there was a lasting close friendship and alliance there. . . . Dad was straightforward and honest and candid, and when he made a statement it was based upon his true beliefs. Nixon was a political expedient. I think my dad saw through him and didn't admire him because of that, because Nixon would take sides on issues based upon what was going to help Nixon. Dad took an issue based on what he felt was right whether it would hurt him or not. That was the difference in the two men, and it wasn't easily reconcilable."[51]

The 1952 campaign was Earl Warren's last hurrah in elective politics. Although Knowland was his own man now, he had one piece of unfinished work to do. Despite the coolness that had settled in over their relationship, Knowland felt he had a debt to repay Warren. While traveling with Eisenhower on his campaign train, Knowland persuaded Eisenhower to promise that Warren would be named to fill the next vacancy on the Supreme Court. Knowland traveled to thirty-four states campaigning for Eisenhower. He was able to spend the time on the presidential campaign because he had locked up his Senate race at home by winning both the Democratic and Republican nominations.

GOP National Committeeman McIntyre Faries said that after Knowland's return to California, they discussed the Supreme Court deal, calling it "just a friendship deal that Bill put through."[52] Nevertheless, Knowland always would deny publicly that any deal was made to assure a seat on the Supreme Court for Warren. "I can personally knock down any story of a deal, because a deal could not have been made without me having knowledge of it," Knowland told an interviewer in 1967.[53]

Eisenhower kept his promise to Knowland, although he later would regret the day he made that appointment. Faries may have called it a friendship deal, but Knowland knew that he had to get Warren out of the picture in California: otherwise, he would continue to live in Warren's shadow. With Nixon on his way to the vice presidency and Warren soon to sit on the Supreme Court, Knowland was at the top of Republican politics in California.

14

The Republicans Take Over

Despite Dwight D. Eisenhower's landslide victory over Adlai Stevenson, the Republicans were able to win only a slim majority in the Congress. In the Senate, they had a one-seat edge, with 48 Republicans, 47 Democrats, and maverick Senator Wayne Morse of Oregon, the Republican turned independent. Some future leaders joined the Senate, including Democrat John F. Kennedy, who defeated Eisenhower advisor Henry Cabot Lodge; Barry Goldwater, an Arizona Republican; and Democrats Stuart Symington of Missouri, Mike Mansfield of Montana, Henry Jackson of Washington, and Albert Gore of Tennessee. In the House, the Republicans gained twenty-two seats, putting them just three over the total needed to give them control. But despite the slim margins, the Republicans controlled Congress and their man was in the White House.

Bill Knowland wanted to be majority leader when the Senate session opened in January, but Robert Taft had his own agenda. He could have denied Knowland any position of significance, but he saw promise in the brash Californian. He also knew that the Republicans had to develop new leadership and naturally was predisposed to favor Knowland, who really had been a Taft man during the 1952 Republican convention. "Besides," observed veteran Associated Press writer Jack Bell, "Taft had no taste at that point for intra-squad fighting when he wasn't sure how hard he would have to battle the man in the White House to get his way."[1]

The two strong-willed men managed to avoid any real confronta-

124

THE REPUBLICANS TAKE OVER   125

tion over the job. Taft liked Knowland's stand on the Far East. After all, no one had worked harder than the California Republican to oppose the Communists in Asia. Taft had no trouble persuading Knowland to step in as chairman of the Republican Policy Committee, making him second in command of the Senate Republicans. Knowland was satisfied, because the job would allow him to attend the weekly meetings of Senate leaders with Eisenhower.

The Republicans were in power, but they had to deal with an unknown in the White House. Taft had the political experience, and Eisenhower had virtually none. Most presidents had moved up to the job through the governor's office or Congress. Eisenhower had never been elected to political office before. That worried Republican leaders; and according to Knowland, that lack of political experience made it difficult for them to deal with the president.

In the week before Eisenhower's inauguration, Knowland, together with Taft and Gene Milliken, chairman of the Republican conference, met with Eisenhower in New York. Knowland said he was chosen as a spokesman for the group because he knew Eisenhower best, having traveled with him extensively during the campaign. The group asked the president-elect to recommend that the top policy positions in several departments be removed from the civil service. Because of his landslide victory and Republican control of both houses of Congress, they assured Eisenhower, the Democrats would let the legislation be passed. Knowland, Taft, and Milliken told Eisenhower that they were not suggesting a return to the spoils system or the abolition of civil service; but unless they could remove the top people in some departments and appoint their own people, the Republican cabinet would be "flanked by the same people who had flanked the Cabinet under the Truman administration."[2]

While Eisenhower understood the significance of such an act, he was concerned that it might look like the spoils system was returning. The group continued to argue their position, and Eisenhower agreed to consider the recommendation. A few weeks later, he turned down the suggestion, saying it would appear to be an attack on the merit system. After the next congressional election, Knowland said, Eisenhower admitted that he had made a mistake, but by then it was too late. The honeymoon was over and the Democrats' voice in Congress was stronger. Knowland recalled, "it was quite clear to [Eisenhower] that even some of his own Cabinet officials and their undersecretaries had been hamstrung."[3]

With the Republicans in charge, all should have gone smoothly, but it did not. Taft immediately was "flabbergasted" when Eisenhower presented his first budget, which was far higher than Republicans in Congress had expected. After all, the Korean War was winding down; now was a good time to substantially reduce the budget. "Taft, I won't say lost his temper, but he certainly expressed himself in no uncertain terms as to how he felt this was letting the Republican voters down, and the Democrats who had voted for Eisenhower because they felt a change was needed, with this kind of budget," Knowland said. "It was quite a tense scene there, in the Cabinet Room that day." Eisenhower flushed a little but maintained his composure.[4]

As unhappy as Taft was, Knowland said the majority leader had enough political experience to know "that the party couldn't survive if, in the first few months of a new president's term, his leadership in the Senate or House broke with him on this kind of issue." Moreover, Eisenhower also realized that he needed Taft's help. "So I think it was reason triumphing over what may have been some very strong feelings on both of their parts, right at that time."[5] Knowland also observed, "I think he envisioned himself . . . as being more the 'father of his country' in the Washington tradition, than he did as a rough-and-tumble party presidential leader." Even so, he added, Eisenhower "very rapidly . . . learned the cold hard facts of political life in Washington and on Capitol Hill. . . . Eisenhower made it clear from the inception that while, as far as the administration was concerned, the ultimate decision had to be his, that he respected the judgment of the party leaders, he wanted them to deal frankly and lay it on the line."[6]

One savvy step by the new administration was its choice for secretary of state: John Foster Dulles, who had worked in the field of foreign affairs for half a century as a public servant and as an international lawyer. Early on, Dulles's strategy was never to oppose the will of Congress. He believed that the main reason the Truman administration's foreign policy failed was its inability to gain the confidence of Congress. One of the first senators Dulles wanted to pacify and bring into the Eisenhower camp was Knowland. As a gesture of goodwill toward Knowland, Dulles convinced Eisenhower to include in his State of the Union speech to Congress on February 2 the statement that because the "Red Chinese" had intervened in the Korean War he had no problem with sending Nationalist Chinese troops to Korea to fight the Communists.[7]

Knowland was delighted with Eisenhower's speech. But even though Dulles was more to his liking than Acheson, he still badgered the secretary of state about the nation's foreign policy. The so-called China

Lobby had faded somewhat by 1953, but the efforts to protect Formosa from Communist incursion had not. Now they centered in the Committee of One Million against the Admission of Communist China into the United Nations. Former president Herbert Hoover, Congressman Walter Judd of Minnesota, and, of course, Bill Knowland were major forces on the committee. In nine months, the committee succeeded in gaining one million anticommunist signatures. The committee later became known just as the Committee of One Million.

·   ·   ·

Knowland found himself in the middle of one of Eisenhower's first controversies when on February 27 the president nominated Charles E. "Chip" Bohlen as ambassador to the Soviet Union. Bohlen, who came from a wealthy family, was a lifelong diplomat described as a tough, seasoned, trained, authentic authority on the Soviet Union. The nomination went to the Senate Foreign Relations Committee, where Knowland was a ranking member.

In early March the security chief for the State Department, Scott McLeod, learned that the FBI had found some derogatory information about Bohlen. The information was rumored to indicate that Bohlen had several close friends and intimate associates who were known homosexuals, though the FBI found no "direct" evidence that Bohlen had engaged in homosexual activities.[8] McLeod told Dulles and Senator Joe McCarthy of Wisconsin. McCarthy complained that Bohlen had been at the disastrous Yalta Conference when President Roosevelt "gave away" Eastern Europe to the Soviet Union.[9] Bohlen didn't particularly help his cause when he praised the conference, where he had served as a Russian translator. He also denied that Alger Hiss had any role at Yalta.

Knowland announced that Dulles had given him, in confidence, a classified document proving that three senior Foreign Service officers had recommended Bohlen for the job, just as Dulles had said. McCarthy then asked that Senator Everett Dirksen be allowed to see the document. Knowland, the back of his neck a bright crimson, angrily replied, "When a letter comes to the Senate from the Department of State, I do not want to have to call in a handwriting expert to determine whether a forgery has been committed. . . . God help us if that is the basis upon which we have to operate."[10] When Dulles testified, Knowland and others grilled him on Bohlen's role at Yalta. The secretary of state assured them that Bohlen was beyond reproach, and the committee approved Bohlen's nomination, 15–0.

That was not the end of it. McCarthy insisted on seeing the raw data that the FBI had collected on Bohlen. Knowland argued that no one should be allowed to see the files and that Congress should trust Eisenhower and Dulles rather than relying on rumors. The FBI's L. B. Nichols summarized the agency's role as follows:[11] Dulles had earlier told FBI Director J. Edgar Hoover that Eisenhower wanted the director's views on Bohlen. Hoover pointed out that it was against policy to make such judgments, but he would honor the request because it came from the president. Hoover told Dulles that he could not give Bohlen a complete clearance because of his homosexual friends. When CIA Director Allen Dulles, John Foster Dulles's brother, suggested that Bohlen be given a lie detector test, Hoover recommended against it. Hoover warned Allen Dulles not to reveal the contents of their private conversation to the Foreign Relations Committee.

Four days later, on March 21, Knowland met with Hoover at Attorney General Herbert Brownell's office. The California senator had asked Hoover if one or two members of the Senate committee could review the FBI report, an action that would dissipate the opposition to Bohlen. Hoover refused, and then Knowland asked whether a committee made up of Vice President Richard Nixon and a cabinet officer or two could examine the report. Hoover said that would be up to Brownell, who disapproved of the proposal. The meeting adjourned with Hoover holding fast to his opinion that the report should not be made available to any senator.

Three days later Hoover received a call from Deputy Attorney General William Rogers, who asked if he had heard that the Senate Foreign Relations Committee had assigned Bob Taft and Democrat John Sparkman of Alabama, who had been Adlai Stevenson's running mate, to look at the FBI report. Rogers told him that to refuse to allow such prominent senators to view the files would put the department in a bad light. After reading the raw data, Taft and Sparkman announced that the report contained no suggestion of any tolerance toward communism. If there was anything in the data about Bohlen's homosexual friends, it was not revealed by Taft or Sparkman. On March 25, the Senate confirmed Bohlen as ambassador to the Soviet Union by a vote of 74 to 13.

· · ·

Senator Joseph R. McCarthy, the Wisconsin Republican, had first claimed that Communists were working in the State Department in a speech

made in Wheeling, West Virginia, in 1950. Although he had continued his charges of communist influence throughout the government,
he didn't really gain center stage until early 1953, when he was named
chairman of the Senate Government Operations Committee. There, he
investigated the State Department, the Voice of America, the Department of the Army, and other departments and organizations. Early on,
he had a willing ally in Bill Knowland.

As McCarthy's biographer William Ewald Jr. put it, "Knowland
would have stood shoulder to shoulder with McCarthy at every turn
but for one thing: McCarthy's carelessness with fact. Sure, the State
Department contained Communists. No doubt about that. But get the
names and addresses straight. On the imperative of accuracy, McCarthy
and Knowland parted company."[12] McCarthy's liability, Knowland said,
"was a tendency to overstate his case. . . . He offended a lot of Republican senators by some of the statements he made. . . . I really resented
when McCarthy got up on the floor and referred to [Sen. J. William
Fulbright as] Senator Halfbright. I mean, it was this kind of thing, you
know, that just isn't done. . . . To make references of this kind, I felt,
cost McCarthy a lot of support that otherwise he might have had." To
be sure, he had no doubt that there were Communists trying to infiltrate the government: "Just know the communist animal as it is, I think
this is the thing that they try to do in every country of the world. . . .
To the extent that he was trying to expose this and get them out, I
think McCarthy commanded the support of a lot of Democrats as well
as Republicans."[13]

Still, Knowland found himself backing away from McCarthy. While
Knowland was staunchly anticommunist, he played by the rules. In
addition, he wasn't sure those people in the State Department that
McCarthy branded Communists really were Communists. "There are
a lot of people who may play into the Communist hands who think
they're as patriotic and in their own mind perhaps are, as anyone else,"
he said. "But their weakness is the fact that they haven't seen the menace and they haven't realized that they may have added at least one bit
to the Chinese jigsaw puzzle of Communist intelligence which helped
the Communists get the whole picture. The government employee may
have done it inadvertently by just dropping something in the niche which
did not seem too important at the time. Others knew they were betray-
ing our country."[14]

Critics of Knowland's leadership in the Senate would later accuse
him of doing little to control McCarthy. Knowland chose to remain

silent, neither encouraging McCarthy openly nor condoning his conduct—but taking no action to curb his excesses. McCarthy obviously
was a dangerous man who posed a real threat to those who might wish
to take him on. Most—including President Eisenhower—chose to protect their own prestige by doing nothing.

.   .   .

Knowland was appalled at what was going on in the Far East, writing
angrily to his father on May 10, 1953: "I believe we are getting mouse-
trapped on the Korean cease fire. On the P.O.W. issue the Communist
proposal for supervision by five 'neutrals' is stacked against us. Two of
the five (Poland and Czechoslovakia) are Communist nations. One (India) has voted with the Communists about 80% of the time in the U.N.
since the Korean war started. Two of them (Sweden and Switzerland)
while neutral have recognized Communist China. This means that all
five consider the Communist Chinese the legal government of China."
He predicted a cease-fire on the present battle line in Korea and the
admission of Communist China into the United Nations within six
months. "I am disgusted and shocked. We will lose all of Asia within
four years and the balance of power will have overwhelmingly shifted
to the Soviet Union and their satellites. It is my intention to speak in
the Senate within the next ten days to lay out the implications of what
is being done. The American people should not get sugar coated cya-
nide without at least knowing the cold hard facts." Knowland opposed
any truce that failed to restore Korea as one nation and that didn't send
the Communist Chinese home.

As a fear grew among senators that Communist China might be admitted to the United Nations, they prepared to fight. On May 28, 1953,
the Senate Appropriations Committee approved a bill rider that would
prohibit financial aid to the United Nations if Communist China were
given membership. The committee chairman, Styles Bridges, told Eisenhower that all Republicans supported the bill. On June 2, Eisenhower
met with Knowland, Styles Bridges, Leverett Saltonstall, and House
Speaker Joe Martin, among others. He came right to the point. "I oppose [the rider] because I believe that the United States cannot properly serve notice on the United Nations in such a manner, and more
fundamentally, that the United States cannot live alone," the president
said.[15] Bridges told Eisenhower that he, Knowland, and Saltonstall approved the rider because they thought that laying down the rules before

a crisis began would strengthen the president's hand. They didn't want to embarrass the president, he said, but they wanted the world to know what they thought of admitting Red China to the United Nations.

Knowland made his views clear. "The admission of Red China," he said, "would violate every one of my basic beliefs. Already rumors are rampant that the British will start pushing for admission of Red China soon after the negotiation of the cease fire in Korea. Under ordinary procedures the United States could not possibly come out on top in this issue if it came to a United Nations vote; therefore, we have to take an active and aggressive stand now." Eisenhower disagreed, saying that the United States could not be expected to win every battle in the UN and that if the UN failed, NATO would fail—"and where would we be then, how could we then maintain our own security?" Knowland then backed off, saying the senators might find another way to make their point without putting the president in such a bind. With that, Eisenhower said he would let the leaders of other countries know the attitude of Congress and tell them that they should be wary of admitting Red China because he "could not answer for the response of the United States."[16]

Although Knowland's main interest was the growing presence of the Communists in the Far East, the next few months would provide him with a new and greater challenge much closer to home.

15

Nobody Can Push
Him Around

In early May 1953, Majority Leader Robert Taft was stricken with a bone lesion in his hip; it would bring Senator Knowland to another major turning point in his life. Taft was a very sick man. Whether he knew how close to death he was is uncertain, but he did begin to heed his doctors' advice to stay off his feet. Even then, he refused a wheelchair, choosing instead to use crutches. Realizing that he couldn't continue all his duties, Taft decided that Knowland should replace him temporarily as Republican floor leader. He thought the California senator courageous and able to stand up to the "Eastern internationalists." In addition, the Ohio senator liked the way Knowland had handled himself during the Republican convention. Although Knowland would not help him, he hadn't sold out Warren, and Taft admired that loyalty. Taft had been infuriated with the Dewey people who were running Eisenhower's campaign, and Knowland had refused to be taken in by them. So no bitterness had been left over from the convention when the congressional session started in 1953.

The ailing Republican leader hobbled onto the Senate floor, where he called Bill Knowland to his side. He looked pale and drawn. "Bill," he said, "I have to stay off my feet a good deal for the rest of the session. I'd like you to act as floor leader." Knowland immediately agreed. Taft then met with reporters and told them, "I have asked Bill Knowland to go on as the acting floor leader. I will continue, however, to be at the presidential meetings, policy committee meetings and so on— unless some specific treatment should prevent that on some specific day." He simply said, "I appoint him," deliberately letting it be known that Knowland was his hand-picked successor. If he had totally abdicated his position, other Republicans would have demanded an election to choose their new leader. This way, Knowland could work into the job, and when the time came for him to take over permanently he would have already proven his worth. Finally, Taft limped over to see Styles Bridges, the president pro tempore of the Senate. "I'm going away and I've asked Bill to carry on for me. Nobody can push him around," he said.[1]

Although there were major political differences between Taft and Knowland, he was the best compromise Taft could find in a badly divided Senate. Knowland was conservative, but not like Joe McCarthy or some of the other right-wingers. Neither was he pro-Eisenhower, like Leverett Saltonstall of Massachusetts, the party whip, who was technically next in line. Knowland was a "safe" Republican. "Here was a typical 'Senate man,'" New York Times reporter William S. White said. "Here was a man of strength and stubbornness—not a brilliant man and not, one gathered, accepted by Taft as an intellectual equal, but a man who would not in any circumstance panic in the face of any internal Republican trouble and who certainly would not deal with the Democratic minority any more gently than the circumstances might require."[2] Knowland later said that he had no idea Taft was gravely ill. "Whether Bob Taft knew it at the time or not, I just don't quite know," Knowland recalled. "I rather believe he did have an inkling that he might not be back in the Senate."[3]

Helen Knowland predicted difficulty for her husband in his new job. "He's never had to compromise," she said, "but he'll have to now, and that will be hard work. Billy will need a new technique."[4] Indeed, he tried compromise, but he was more successful when he bulled his way through. He was hampered by his desire to control everything and everyone. Bill Knowland told people what to do: he always had and he always would. One Senate colleague grumbled, "He treats us like kids."[5] Not everyone in the Republican Party was happy with Taft's selection. He hadn't bothered to confer with them and they were irritated. But Knowland was up to the task. His major job was to steer legislation, particularly appropriations, through the Senate, and he had strong help from his colleague Styles Bridges. The New Hampshire senator was chairman of the Appropriations Committee.

Knowland gleefully took over the assignment of remaining on the Senate floor at all times to see that Taft's work was done. Taft would continue to handle high policy matters and attend White House meetings. Knowland would have no trouble stepping in; as one of the top Senate Republicans, he knew what was going on with Taft and other leaders of the party in the Senate. But Knowland would be acting floor leader for just two months. On July 31, 1953, Taft died of leukemia.

Lyndon Johnson was the first in the Senate to hear about Taft's death. "Clint! Clint!" Johnson called out to Senator Clinton P. Anderson, the New Mexico Democrat. "Bob Taft has just died."[6] Knowland summoned absent members to the floor. Johnson had tears in his eyes. Trying to compose himself, Knowland looked almost angry. On the floor, senators were bowing their heads, silent in their grief. Eisenhower was devastated by Taft's death. "I don't know what I'll do without him. I don't know what I'll do without him," Ike said.[7]

On August 4, the day Taft was buried, Knowland was unanimously elected as majority leader for the remainder of the congressional session. Thirty-nine of the forty-six Republican senators attended the session to elect Knowland. Those who stayed away did so rather than vote against him. At the last minute, right-wingers and isolationists had attempted to delay the election until January, but the effort collapsed and no one challenged the burly Californian. Among those seven senators who stayed away were Styles Bridges, the party's dean in terms of service, Everett Dirksen of Illinois, Herman Welker of Idaho, Joseph R. McCarthy of Wisconsin, and John W. Bricker of Ohio. Of the remaining forty-six Republican senators, thirteen had more seniority than Knowland, a fact that often would make his job more difficult.

Although Eisenhower could have intervened in the selection of a new majority leader, he refused to become involved. "I want to say with all emphasis at my command that the administration has absolutely no personal choice for new majority leader. We are not going to get into [the Senate's] business."[8] Several of Eisenhower's advisors urged him to favor a man of their choice, using patronage as a coercive method of getting his way. "Under other circumstances this might have been the thing to do," the president said. "But what my friends did not appreciate was that the parties were so evenly balanced that we needed the vote of every one of our Republican senators to put through the legislation in which we believed." Moreover, Eisenhower recognized that Taft had gone out of his way to preserve party unity; to ignore his choice of Knowland as majority leader might rankle some of the senators Taft had been able to hold in line.[9]

Knowland himself thought Eisenhower handled the selection of the majority leader the right way. He noted that the Senate "is very touchy on the subject" of the president interfering with the selection of its leader. He also said the president knew him fairly well. "So I'm sure my selection was not objectionable to him, though I don't say he might not have had somebody else he'd have preferred to have in that position."[10]

When Knowland took over for Taft, it became immediately clear that he was his own man. He let it be known that he was not an administrative cabinet official who could be appointed and dismissed at will by the president. Neither, Knowland said, was he "an Army officer who can be disciplined by the commanding general," an obvious reference to Eisenhower. "There is no question but that we are going to have a united Republican Party in the Senate," Knowland said in a written statement. "No one, of course, in the real sense, can replace Bob Taft. There will be cooperation in this team under the leadership of Dwight Eisenhower. Again I should like to express my appreciation for the cooperation of the Democratic leadership. Without that cooperation in so closely divided a Senate, this legislative body could not function."[11]

Knowland became Senate majority leader by the narrowest of margins. With two seats vacant because of the deaths of Taft and Charles W. Tobey (R-N.H.), the Senate was made up of 47 Democrats, 46 Republicans, and the independent Wayne Morse of Oregon. Morse sided with Knowland, leaving him tied with Lyndon Johnson in the race for majority leader. Richard Nixon, as presiding officer of the Senate, cast the tie-breaking vote. Knowland was fond of saying that he was the only majority leader in history to be elected without a majority. "Had the Democrats at that point wanted to take over control of the Senate, they could have done so merely by moving to depose [Republican] Senator Styles Bridges from New Hampshire as president pro tem and take control of the Senate committees," Knowland said. But Democrats feared such action might throw the Senate into a turmoil.[12]

The *New York Times* took note of Knowland's unusual position in an editorial, remarking that he

starts off with a considerable handicap in that he is a majority leader of a party that does not have a majority. . . . Senator Knowland's position is a delicate one. In addition to helping determine Republican policy at both ends of Pennsylvania Avenue, he also has the responsibility of seeing it enacted into law. This means that in the present situation he will necessarily work in close collaboration with the Democratic leadership.

In so narrowly divided a Senate the Administration has to rely on some Democratic support for anything it proposes. Thus far that support has been freely given. Mr. Knowland is therefore at the same time a principal Republican spokesman on Capitol Hill and a principal negotiator with the Democrats. He has a big job and we wish him the luck he will need.[13]

Knowland had to walk a politically tight line in serving the president, the Senate as a whole (particularly in dealing with Johnson), the Senate Republicans, the right-wing majority within the Senate GOP, and his own political ambitions. The area that caused the most controversy was his often contentious relationship with Eisenhower.

When he took over as majority leader, Knowland expected no conflict between himself and the president. He let it be known again, however, that he served the Senate first and then the White House: "I would like to make this clear at this point. In all of the sessions that I have attended . . . [Eisenhower] has made it very clear that he recognizes the constitutional responsibilities of the Congress as a coequal branch of the Government, and at no time at any of those meetings has he ever taken the position that the Congress had to rubber-stamp a particular Administration recommendation in the specific way in which it has come up to the Hill from either the White House or from some of the other administrative agencies of the Federal Government."[14] Recognizing that the public perceived him as a spokesman for the administration, Knowland often tried to separate his personal views from those of his post as majority leader.

Knowland was willing to work with Eisenhower and foresaw no problem that couldn't be worked out between the Senate and the president. "Frankly, I cannot at the moment conceive, in the way that we have been working, because the president is a great team player and is very sincerely interested in getting the points of view of his leadership in both the House and the Senate, that type of situation would prevail."[15] But Eisenhower's chief of staff, Sherman Adams, said that Knowland made the weekly meetings of the party leaders (including House Speaker Joe Martin) an ordeal for Eisenhower.[16] Eisenhower harped on how much he disliked the meetings, which too frequently would end in disagreement. The conversation often ran like this: "Mr. President, I can't support that." "Well, Bill, that's your opinion, but I do."[17]

Eisenhower complained in a note to a friend that "it is a pity that his wisdom, his judgment, his tact and his sense of humor lag so far behind his ambition."[18] Even the *Washington Post* jumped in editorially: "Senator Knowland does not seem able to separate Administrative objectives from his own pet phobias." On another occasion after disagreement over domestic policy, Eisenhower said, "Don't the damn fools realize that the public thinks the dollar sign is the only respected symbol of the Republican Party?"[19]

Senator Barry Goldwater played down the rift between Eisenhower and Knowland: "I've never known [anyone] as headstrong—I don't like the words stubborn or obstinate, but they would apply. He's a very determined man, and a very highly principled man, and as long as he and Eisenhower agreed on the legislation that Ike wanted, Bill would fight his head off for it. Bill had such high principles that he just couldn't work both sides of the street. But I'd say 98 percent of the time he was right there working with Ike and working hard for him, working the Republican side of the aisle towards Eisenhower's wishes."[20] In his autobiography, Goldwater remarked that Knowland was a great patriot, "but he was more inclined to tell people what they should do than he was to persuade them to follow a particular course."[21]

When Howard Baker took over as the Republican leader in the Senate twenty years later, he looked back on the way that Knowland held the position as "a disaster." "He tried to be president in a way. He was always griping and scrapping with Ike. . . . He was never happy, never cooperative and never really was sympathetic to the Eisenhower program. There are two roles of majority leader in the Senate. One is the president's spear carrier and the other is an independent force. And I chose to be a spear carrier," Baker said.[22]

Knowland certainly was an independent force. And he continually got under Eisenhower's skin, as he did on July 7, 1953, when his habit of shaking his head in disgust at proposed spending programs for foreign aid and national defense caused Ike to blurt out, "My God, you just can't sit back and assume the nation is safe from all harm because the Republicans won the last election."[23] Indeed, one of Knowland's first clashes with Eisenhower after he became majority leader came over funds for the Mutual Security Appropriation (MSA), which provided funds for European countries to help them defend themselves. There could be no clearer statement by Knowland that the Senate's wishes, in his mind, took precedence over the president's wishes, although he knew his role was to work for some form of compromise.

Knowland wanted to end the MSA, for which former President Truman had projected $7.6 billion in 1954. Eisenhower had agreed to reduce that figure to $5.5 billion, but he thought the program so important that he was willing to use all of his political clout to defend it.

Though it seemed to Knowland that Eisenhower was changing Truman's foreign policy too little, the president felt it was irrational to expect a revolution when the world itself changed only gradually. But Eisenhower's attempts were only partly successful; Congress cut the MSA funds to $4 billion.

Eisenhower Chief of Staff Sherman Adams would remember how the president would try to butter up Knowland, praising him for his work. "Then Knowland would knock over the apple cart, and Eisenhower would have to try all over again."[24] Ike told an aide of his frustrations: "I will spend hours here in the office staring out those windows, sometimes a little hopelessly, with Senators Dirksen or Millikin or Knowland here, to tell me what industries I have to protect with higher tariffs—or how the folks back home don't like these big bills for Mutual Security."[25] According to Jack Bell, the veteran Associated Press writer, "As Knowland saw his job, it was to translate to Eisenhower the view of other Republican senators and in turn to interpret the President's position to the senators. Having done this, Knowland considered that he had fulfilled his responsibilities. He then was free to attack any policies with which he disagreed. While he might cite a high percentage of support for Eisenhower's proposals, those he opposed often counted the most."[26]

The record shows that Knowland supported Eisenhower a vast majority of the time, mostly on domestic issues. Where they parted was on foreign policy, particularly in the Far East. Knowland repeatedly ran into trouble with the administration when he disagreed with one of Eisenhower's legislative proposals. Knowland sometimes would try to amend it as a compromise, but Eisenhower often refused to accept the amendments. "I would say my batting average was very good despite some of the columnists to the contrary," Knowland nevertheless recalled. "I had the highest percentage of support of the president of any member of the Senate for at least three or four of the sessions, and up among the top two or three in the balance of the time that I served as Senate Republican leader in Washington."[27]

With Knowland irritating Eisenhower on many occasions, the president often turned to Johnson to get key legislation passed. Eisenhower's press secretary, James C. Hagerty, was asked once by an interviewer if Eisenhower felt he could work better with Johnson than he could Knowland. "That's the understatement of the interview," Hagerty replied. "He worked much more closely with Mr. Johnson than he did with Senator Knowland."[28] Fifty-eight times in 1953 the Democrats provided the winning margin for Eisenhower's legislation.[29] Minority Leader Lyndon Johnson knew that even without control of the Senate he could control many votes. On a number of occasions, he helped push through an Eisenhower program that Republicans had stalled. "I cannot help but believe at least he was not completely unhappy with Eisenhower's election," Knowland said. He indicated that Johnson was not happy with Adlai Stevenson; furthermore, having a Republican president made Johnson the most powerful Democrat in Washington.[30]

Senator Hubert H. Humphrey, the Minnesota Democrat, noted that Johnson liked Eisenhower and that Eisenhower trusted Johnson. "I think actually Johnson decided that he wasn't going to let Knowland have more influence with Eisenhower than he had. He moved right in on him. You've just got to understand the personality of the man. He just made up his mind that, 'The president is over there and I've known him longer than Bill Knowland has, and I'm going over to see him.'"[31] Johnson aide Walter W. Rostow said he overheard Johnson, when he was president, thank Eisenhower for his support; "And I heard General Eisenhower respond by saying in effect, 'It's the very least I owe you. You were my strong right arm when I was president.' Then he explicitly referred to the fact that it was on Senator Johnson that he counted to bypass the disruptive stand of Bill Knowland. And it was Senator Johnson who made it possible for President Eisenhower to carry forward a foreign policy of the kind in which he believed."[32]

With their egos and divergent views, it is remarkable that the trio of Knowland, Eisenhower, and Johnson was able to accomplish anything. One of the reasons that Knowland and Johnson worked well together was that both believed the Senate had an obligation to serve the nation. At least one observer, the liberal Republican senator Clifford Case of New Jersey, said Johnson enjoyed the obligation but Knowland did not: "I always had the feeling that Johnson loved the work; I wasn't very sure that Bill liked the work at all. He liked to be the leader; he liked to be in the position, I think, of being the leader. But I don't think it was nearly as important to him in relation to his stand on issues as it was to Lyndon Johnson."[33]

Knowland recalled that he and Johnson had "a long and cordial relationship" while they were leaders of their parties in the Senate. "In the very operation of the Senate, unless there is a good relationship between the majority and minority leaders, the Senate can be tied up in knots. . . . We not only conferred across the center aisle, but generally once and sometimes several times a day we would either meet at his office or mine in the Capitol Building to go over the legislative program that was coming up." The two men learned to trust each other: "I will say that Senator Johnson . . . at no time broke his word to me . . . nor did I break my word to him."[34]

They often worked out their differences over a drink in one or the other's office. On one occasion, not long after Knowland became majority leader, Johnson came by for a drink. As was Johnson's way, he brushed past the secretaries and burst into Knowland's office without a word. Knowland drew the only bottle of whiskey he had out of the refrigerator, but he couldn't get the cap off because of its long disuse. Then he tried to pry out a tray of ice stuck in the freezer. After several futile minutes, Johnson ushered Knowland upstairs to his own office, "where we know how to open bottles." Knowland never let that happen again. From that day on, his office always had a well-stocked liquor cabinet.[35]

Longtime Johnson associate Walter Jenkins said that at first he thought Knowland lacked the background, the knowledge, and the ability to work closely with someone whose political beliefs might be different. He recalled that "Johnson had to whip him a few times before he really began to realize what the situation was." While Knowland and Johnson finally worked out a relationship similar to the one Johnson and Taft had, "it was only after a few months of working at cross purposes that that was accomplished."[36]

Johnson at times clearly outwitted Knowland. Once, for example, Knowland called a night session without notifying Johnson. The Democratic leader felt this was a violation of the rules "so he decided he would show him that he had better follow the rules. Johnson talked two Republican senators into joining the Democrats in halting the night session." Knowland was furious, Jenkins said, but the Texas senator "felt good about it, he felt like he had killed a bear. Knowland checked with him from then on on everything."[37] It was one of the worst indignities that can be imposed on a majority leader—the minority leader adjourning the Senate right out from under his nose.

As William S. White remarked: "Knowland was very inflexible and not one-tenth as bright as Johnson in maneuvers and so on. So Johnson took care that he always maintained a very close personal relationship with Knowland, so that he could approach him at any time. He really just sort of overwhelmed Knowland with his brilliance as a leader." And he clearly was more able to build support among the senators. "Oh, Knowland was always caught off guard, yes. Knowland, see, never did his homework the way Johnson did either. He never went around selling these people. Knowland was very standoffish." But, White also made clear, none of this meant that Johnson was a superior person to Knowland; "It only meant that he was a more intuitive man, operating with more freedom of motion in a more relaxed party. To put it another way, the stiffness of Knowland, an honorable and very downright man quite incapable of subtlety, had a kind of inevitability in the very nature of his party. The flexible, inventive, more volatile characteristics of Johnson were in a sense really the human characteristics of his party."[38]

Johnson liked to needle Knowland. He would lean across the aisle toward Knowland and say softly, "You don't have the votes, Bill." Knowland would give him a wry smile in agreement. Nor was Johnson above belittling Knowland on occasion. According to Booth Mooney, Johnson would mimic a number of his colleagues in the Senate, including Knowland. "He puffed out his cheeks and walked across the room with a slow, ponderous stride to show how Knowland approached a legislative problem."[39]

If Knowland felt that Johnson belittled him and dominated him, he never acknowledged it. Besides, Knowland sometimes needled Johnson. On an occasion when Johnson was responsible for getting several pieces of legislation passed in a single week, Knowland remarked, "It is only in the dictatorships of the world that legislation whizzes through."[40]

The two opposing leaders remained friends long after each left the Senate. When Johnson was president, Knowland wrote to him offering him support during the Vietnam War. Johnson wrote Knowland that "we did more than sit across the Senate aisle from each other. We also had frequent occasion to exchange counsel and profit by it. That much has not changed. You can be sure your views have been taken to heart and will weigh in my judgment of how the nation can best move toward an honorable settlement in Vietnam. . . . I am encouraged in every exploration by the knowledge that your skill and wisdom support us."[41]

.   .   .

On the Republican side, Knowland came to closely resemble Taft in many ways. Douglass Cater, a columnist for the *Reporter* magazine, even called Knowland "the man who wants to be Taft" because of the many similarities of their manners in the Senate and their pursuit of the presidency along conservative paths.[42] Other critics said that although

Taft was a hidebound conservative, Knowland's view was narrower. They even said he had an "agenda of cherished issues" that he favored much to the detriment of other conservative causes. White noted, "In the personal sense, too, Knowland embodied much that Taft had always approved—solidity and a certain stability, a gravity of approach that was sometimes very near to humorless."[43]

Knowland was able to keep his leadership role in the Senate, but not because he was the most liked man in the chamber. The aloof Knowland liked to make decisions by himself and rarely consulted with other members of the leadership or the other Republicans in the Senate. One journalist described his leadership as like that of the old-time cavalry colonel: "He takes his position well out in front of the troops, never looking back, lest he undermine morale."[44] The venerable senator Russell B. Long of Louisiana agreed with the military analogy. "Bill Knowland was a good, decent sort of fellow and a man dedicated on certain matters, but he was no general to lead his army any way except straight ahead."[45]

One explanation of Knowland's style of leadership can be attributed to his membership in the so-called Inner Club within the Senate, often called the most exclusive club in the world. In a perceptive analysis of the Senate, William S. White laid bare how the club functioned on a day-to-day basis. Whether a senator was "in" had nothing to do with party, seniority, or wealth; it had a great deal to do with stature, personality, and integrity, but not necessarily power. Arthur Vandenberg, the Michigan Republican, was a leader in foreign affairs but never a member of the Inner Club. John F. Kennedy, despite his Irish charm, never made it. Yet Bill Knowland belonged, even though he was, in White's words, "less than a relaxed social being." To those in the Inner Club "it was sheer nonsense to talk of Knowland as the president's leader; plainly he was the Senate's leader, on one side of the aisle." White noted that some Eisenhower backers—also known as Deweyites—tried to dump Knowland as their leader. This move, however, "died . . . in the throats of its utterers before the stern reproof [of the Inner Club]."[46]

Johnson, too, was a member of the Inner Club. He was able to hold the Democrats together by railing against the Republicans as the party of the rich. Johnson also held them together by the sheer force of his personality. He was once able to pass more than one hundred bills, some of them controversial, in about an hour. He could do this simply because "Lyndon wants it," it was said.[47]

So, while Knowland drew more attention for his forays against Eisenhower, he was not alone; Lyndon Johnson stood by him virtually every step of the way when the prerogatives of the Senate were concerned. Johnson also was trying to establish that not only could he fight against a Republican in the White House, he was against any White House if it tried to usurp the power of the Senate. Knowland and Johnson, White believed, "had between them struck an informal bargain to protect and defend the true faith." The styles of the two men were very different. "Where Knowland as a leader largely took up the aloof posture of the commanding general back at headquarters, leaving the details of field leadership to subordinates, Johnson went down to the very platoons," White said.[48] While Johnson was the back-slapping Texan, Knowland's demeanor was more that of a prison guard—he rarely smiled and was quick to anger.

Another writer described Knowland: "His frown of concentration creases great furrows upon his forehead and knots his brow like a constricted muscle. In anger, ropey veins push out; his brows appear to move together, kneading the fleshy area between as an ordinary man might clench his fist. His smile, while rarer, can be a pretty fearsome thing too. With all this, his colleagues attest that temperamentally Knowland is a shy man behind the awesome exterior and the booming voice, a politician who is profoundly uneasy in the personal relationships that are his daily burden."[49]

That shyness, often mistaken for aloofness, added to his appearance of being stubborn and lacking in personality. Nevertheless, he was able to maintain the respect of those he worked with. Their respect helped Knowland hold together his coalition of Taft Republicans over the Eisenhower moderates. He had just enough votes among the Taftites to keep the leadership. He also held on as leader through sheer determination. He may not have been the smartest or most politically savvy man in the Senate, but he was one of the hardest workers. He often was the first to arrive in the morning and last to leave at night, his briefcase always bulging with papers. "I don't know how intellectually bright he was, but I imagine he had to work pretty damn hard to get ahead of these things," former aide James Gleason told us.

·   ·   ·

In 1953, early in Knowland's days as majority leader, Senator John Bricker of Ohio introduced a constitutional amendment that would limit the powers of the president in the conduct of foreign affairs. Many senators, dating back to the Roosevelt and Truman administrations, were determined to prevent another Yalta: no unilateral decision by a president or any world government should undermine the sovereignty of the United States.

The Bricker Amendment was designed to take power from the executive branch of government and give it to the legislative branch, and it opened what *Time* magazine called "one of the basic constitutional debates of the century."[50] Sixty-four senators lined up behind the original amendment, more than the two-thirds necessary for approval; forty-five Republicans, including Bill Knowland, were joined by nineteen Democrats. Fifteen of those Democrats were Southerners who wanted to use the amendment to prevent a UN compact on human rights that might interfere with state laws regarding segregation.

Knowland clearly believed that some limits should be placed on presidential encroachment on congressional prerogatives, but he sought to work toward compromise, especially after Eisenhower announced his opposition to the amendment. The president warned that foreign leaders would regard such limits on his powers as a sign that the United States was retreating to the isolationism of the 1930s. The majority leader sought an accommodation for the sake of party unity.

On January 23, 1954, Bricker complained that President Eisenhower shouldn't be involved in a decision on the amendment because under the Constitution, the president had no role in the process. When Knowland challenged that assertion, Bricker agreed that Ike had a right to express his views but not to go against the spirit of the Constitution. Eisenhower said that he understood he had no role in the process but that when it came to an amendment that would change the balance of powers, "then the President clearly has the responsibility to make his views known to the nation."[51]

When the vote on the Bricker Amendment came after eight months of parliamentary wrangling and numerous proposed changes, Knowland left his leader's seat and walked to the back of the Senate chambers to register his vote in favor of it. He declared that he was voting as a senator, not a spear carrier for the administration: "I have left the desk of majority leader because I wish to make it very clear that what I say is not said as majority leader but is said in my capacity as an individual senator of the United States." He said the bitter and long debate over the amendment indicated that the executive branch's intrusion on the powers of the legislative branch needed to be halted.[52]

The measure would have passed the Senate but for the deciding vote, cast by a senator who had to be called in from a nearby tavern. Harley Kilgore, the West Virginia Democrat, was brought into the Senate chamber and propped up; and a vote of "nay" was heard. Whether it was Kilgore's voice remains uncertain, but his vote was recorded.[53] The final vote was 60 to 31, one vote short of the two-thirds majority required for a proposed constitutional amendment.

.   .   .

Chief Justice Fred Vinson died on September 8, 1953, giving Knowland his chance to repay his political debt to Earl Warren.

During his 1952 presidential campaign, Eisenhower had promised Knowland that Warren would be first in line for a seat on the Supreme Court, but not for that seat. Eisenhower said that "from the very beginning of my acquaintanceship with [Warren], I had him in mind for an appointment to the high court—although, of course, I never anticipated an early vacancy in the Chief Justice position."[54] Vinson was younger than several of the other justices.

Eisenhower really didn't want Warren to become chief justice, and by appointing an associate justice to the top seat, he would have two appointments to offer. Warren, however, was insisting on the top spot and called Knowland's aide Jim Gleason, trying to forestall the maneuver. The California governor desperately wanted to talk to Knowland so that he could lobby for the chief justice seat. It was protocol for the senior senator of the nominee's home state to sanction the nomination of any Supreme Court justice, but Knowland couldn't be reached immediately; he was on his way to visit Chiang Kai-shek on Formosa when Vinson died. Gleason spent hours tracking down Knowland, and when he reached him, the senator told him to call the White House and to recommend Warren for the top job.

Knowland cut short his Far East trip and immediately flew to Washington, where he met with Eisenhower and pressed for Warren's appointment. Ike had sent Attorney General Herbert Brownell to the governor's office in Sacramento, to talk to Warren and others. Brownell spent three hours with Warren. Brownell told the president that Warren "took the position that he was ready to accept the Chief Justiceship, . . . that he did feel that he had a commitment for the next vacancy, and that this was the next vacancy."[55] Brownell then flew to Los Angeles, where he met with other Republican leaders before returning to Washington to confer with Eisenhower. According to Brownell, although it was never intended that Warren would be the chief justice, there was in the end little choice. The court was made up entirely of old men like Felix Frankfurter and Hugo Black, who were eliminated from contention. The name of William J. Jackson came up, but he had led Roosevelt's fight to pack the Supreme Court in the late 1930s, so he was crossed off the list. There was nobody left but Warren.

Richard Nixon wanted Earl Warren as well, for very pragmatic political reasons. "You must get Warren out of California," Nixon told Eisenhower. "He has control of the Republican Party machinery and we can't do business with him."[56]

Three weeks after Vinson's death, Eisenhower made his decision, nominating Warren on September 30 as chief justice of the United States. The nomination was made during the fall recess, so it wasn't officially submitted to Congress until January 11, 1954. It then ran into trouble in the Senate Judiciary Committee, where Chairman William Langer, a North Dakota Republican, revealed that the committee had ten unsworn charges against Warren that had been filed by two hundred opponents. Knowland and others strongly protested these unsubstantiated charges, and the committee eventually approved Warren. The Senate then confirmed the California governor on March 1 by voice vote.

Both Nixon and Knowland disliked Warren's liberalism. But Nixon supported the governor to get him out of California politics and Knowland added to that motive his long personal loyalty. Knowland knew Warren would be happy on the court, and the appointment left Nixon and Knowland free to pursue their ambitions without his hindrance.

.   .   .

Throughout this period, Knowland continued to pound away at the communist threat throughout the world, urging that there be no conciliation with the Soviet Union or the Republic of China. In a speech to the Chicago Executives' Club on November 20, 1953, he argued it did no good to close the door to communism in Europe if the door to communism was going to be left open in Asia. "For a period of years we followed the fatal policy of waiting for the dust to settle in China. Well, the dust did settle in China and some 450 million people who had been our historic friends and our allies in two World Wars, were taken behind the Iron Curtain."[57]

Since his first six months as majority leader, Knowland had been a thorn in the side of the Eisenhower administration, particularly in foreign policy matters. That would not change much during the next five years. "I think," Eisenhower said, "my party ought to trust me a little bit more when I put not only my life's work, but my reputation and everything else on the line."[58]

Knowland, unlike Eisenhower, believed that communism would be the big issue in the 1954 congressional election and that the United States should get tough against allies seeking trade with the Republic of China; no trade should be allowed, "certainly until the Communists have agreed to sit down at a peace conference in Korea." He was sure that communism would be an issue not only in the 1954 election but in 1956 as well. "What good will it do to clean the situation up for four years . . . if we then are going to be faced with the same kind of people who were so naive and lax before?" he asked.[59] On the issue of whether China, known then as Red China, should be admitted to the United Nations, Knowland told a reporter for *World* magazine, "I have introduced a resolution in the Senate providing that if Communist China is admitted to the United Nations, the United States should withdraw. I shall press, in committee and on the floor of the Senate, for the adoption of this resolution if Communist China is admitted to membership."[60]

At the same time, he was taking a hard line against countries such as India that had remained neutral during the Korean War. "I do not believe that the neutralist nations which sat on the sidelines for three years of the Korean War should take part in a general conference on the basis of equality with three nations which supported collective security and suffered casualties. Perhaps, as a basis for agreement, the neutralist countries of Asia might be permitted to select one of their number to represent them at such a conference."[61] Eisenhower was worried about the way Knowland was interfering with the administration's foreign policy. He once remarked that Knowland's idea of foreign policy was to develop high blood pressure at the mention of China.

The president wanted foreign policy to be a bipartisan venture and spent a good deal of his time attempting to persuade Congress to that end. Eisenhower knew only too well that he had little power to remedy the situation, but he had no other choice but to try to compromise or bypass Knowland and work with other leading senators. He even considered trying to remove Knowland, but the risks were too great. Not only would he have run into opposition from Knowland's supporters among the Senate Republicans, but others might be protective of

Senate prerogatives. And while Knowland might have been the loudest voice in the Senate attacking the nation's policies toward Asia, he certainly wasn't the only one. Despite his grousing about Knowland, the president put on a good face publicly. "Not for one moment, I said, should anyone think that I was complaining against the leadership," Eisenhower wrote in his book about the White House years, *Mandate for Change.* "I just wanted all Republicans to keep working for every single item we, as a party, had promised to the nation."[62]

The California senator knew that as majority leader he was supposed to represent the Senate's views to the White House and the White House's views to the Senate. Occasionally, to present his own views on important issues, he left the speaker's podium during debate and with those long, loping strides would return to the Senate floor, where he would speak his mind. Often his views conflicted with those of the Eisenhower administration. "I did not abandon my responsibilities as a United States senator when I became majority leader," he was fond of saying.

At one point, Knowland complained to Eisenhower that it was difficult to put administration programs through a Senate that had only a one-vote margin. Even that margin was precarious. Ohio governor Frank Lausche had appointed Democrat Thomas A. Burke to replace Taft. That gave the Democrats 48 votes and the Republicans 47, with independent Wayne Morse of Oregon most of the time siding with the Republicans. In 1955, Morse switched over to the Democrats.

Even in 1953, the Republicans could expect no more than a 48–48 tie on votes that were along strict party lines. Vice President Richard Nixon then would cast the deciding vote. Knowland told Eisenhower it would be easier if the Senate had a margin similar to the one Franklin D. Roosevelt had enjoyed when he took office in 1933.

.   .   .

In September 1953, Knowland traveled to Formosa, Korea, and the three associated states of Indochina—Laos, Cambodia, and Vietnam. He said: "I felt with the changing developments taking place unless you go back at least every year or two you lose touch with the feel of the situation. . . . I had constantly felt that if the Chinese and North Koreans were ultimately stopped at some line . . . that they would move somewhere else. . . . I felt that in due time there would be problems in what had been the Indochina area. . . . It was a likely soft spot, and my general observation is that whenever communism finds a soft spot, why, they tend to penetrate and to move."[63]

On October 5, 1953, Knowland met with Secretary of State John Foster Dulles at Dulles's office on three matters of concern to the senator from California—Japan, Okinawa, and Indochina. Knowland urged continued pressure on Japan to build up its military forces, so that the United States could take its military out of Japan. He said he felt that U.S. troops on the Japanese mainland would become a subject of irritation in Japanese goodwill.

Knowland also urged a clear position on Okinawa; he firmly believed that the United States should continue to hold the Japanese island. Dulles responded that the administration had no intention of giving up Okinawa, but that there were several problems concerning civilian administration and relations with Japan. "I was reluctant to see us issue a statement on Okinawa," Dulles said, "until these matters had been agreed upon. I did not think that we could put Okinawa in a completely closed compartment without economic and social relations with neighboring islands and the acute problems of fishing, etc." Knowland agreed but insisted that the United States retain the civil administration and questioned the practicality of using Japanese currency.

Knowland also asked about the terms for delivery of U.S. military supplies to the French, who were fighting the Communists in Indochina. He wanted to be sure that the matériel did not fall into the hands of Ho Chi Minh if the French negotiated a deal with him.[64]

16

The McCarthy Era

Bill Knowland was optimistic as he began his first full term as Senate majority leader when the new session of Congress opened in 1954. But he also was realistic. "This will be an important and rugged session," he said in an interview with the Associated Press in December 1953.[1] That turned out to be a gross understatement.

One problem was that Eisenhower was getting even more fed up with Knowland. In his diary on January 18, he wrote, "Knowland means to be helpful and loyal, but he is cumbersome. He does not have the sharp mind and the great experience that Taft did. Consequently, he does not command the respect in the Senate that Senator Taft enjoyed."[2] Eisenhower was aware of Knowland's zealous guardianship of congressional prerogatives. "He always acted impulsively to any fancied slight by the liaison officers upon whom we so much depended in maintaining coordination between the White House and Republican Congressional leaders," Eisenhower said. "Naturally, when everyone in an entire organization is working at top speed and sometimes under high tension to further a common purpose, it is not always easy to keep sand from fouling the gears of cooperation. Though Senator Knowland was hypersensitive in such matters, he was an effective party leader in the Senate."[3]

With the bitter debate over the Bricker Amendment out of the way, it was time for the Senate to move onto other pressing matters, particularly the domestic program that would have an impact on the congressional elections later in the year. The country was also in the middle of a recession, which did not bode well for Republican candidates. In January 1954, unemployment nationwide rose to more than 3 million. Eisenhower's administration was being labeled the "millionaires' corporation" by Democrats, and he was trying to battle claims that only the Democrats represented the "little fellow."[4] The Eisenhower administration had been fighting a two-front war against both the Bricker Amendment and Joe McCarthy's increasing demagoguery on communism. McCarthy was clearly out of control, and the Republicans were spending too much time dealing with him. The president often found himself turning to the Democrats for support, telling them that his programs were a form of Roosevelt's New Deal.

On March 12, Knowland became incensed at what he thought was Eisenhower's failure to follow protocol. It stemmed from a claim by the Eisenhower administration that Senator McCarthy sought favored treatment for one of his friends who had been drafted into the army. This was a counterattack on McCarthy designed to offset attacks on Ike. When a long report on McCarthy's activities was finished, it was sent to select members of Congress and released to the press. By mistake, Knowland and several other influential senators didn't receive a copy. Knowland called the White House, threatening to resign as majority leader.

"According to the papers this morning," Knowland roared, "this report from the Defense Department was circulated to some 18 Senators over here. . . . As Majority Leader, I did not get a copy. . . . I don't know who the 18 Senators could have been unless they were on the Democratic side of the aisle." Eisenhower tried to bluff, saying he "didn't know a thing about it." Knowland responded, "I don't think you can operate a team this way."[5] But as Knowland raged on, Ike admitted his involvement, saying, "This is the first intimation I have had that you have not been cut in."[6] When Knowland threatened to resign again, Eisenhower calmly told him, "I can't talk about your operations down [there]. I can only say I will check up and find out what happened and get in touch with you. I think we have got to realize that blunders do occur and not all on the Executive side. . . . I know nothing about [this]. . . . There has been a blunder, and I am sorry."[7]

Later in the day Eisenhower's press secretary, James C. Hagerty, talked with the president, who remarked, "You know, Jim, I suppose that if those leaders had seen the report, it would never have gotten out in the papers. They always want to play everything the hard way—compromise, compromise. Nuts." Such confrontations with Knowland only seemed to confirm the observation Eisenhower had made a few days earlier: "I used to think Knowland was a good candidate for president, and now I know he isn't."[8]

Eisenhower's chief of staff, Sherman Adams, said that try as hard as he could, the president just was not able to win over the stubborn and principled Knowland to supporting all of the administration's policies in the Senate. On one occasion in a dispute over Red China, Eisenhower told Adams, "There's one thing I have learned not to do. There are times when you must never say 'never.'" Adams said he took that to mean "that the single-minded Senator had no room in his thinking for a 'maybe,' an 'if' or a 'perhaps.'" Although Eisenhower knew that most members of Congress weren't overly happy with his foreign policies, he had the backing of 34 million American voters and assumed members of his party would follow him. Not being a politician, Eisenhower hadn't reckoned with the independence of members of the U.S. Senate.[9]

·   ·   ·

On May 17, 1954, Chief Justice Earl Warren's Court handed down its historic decision *Brown v. Board of Education of Topeka, Kansas*, declaring racial segregation in public schools to be unconstitutional. Warren wrote the unanimous opinion, infuriating Eisenhower and other Republicans, including Knowland. Eisenhower had often said appointing Warren was the biggest mistake of his presidency.

Knowland was less vocal, but he was less than pleased with the decisions of the Warren Court. Years later, he told an interviewer that as governor, Warren

had shown no indications to my knowledge of some of these later court decisions. I don't think it's quite fair to blame Mr. Warren alone for it, because it takes five votes on the court and I don't know that he necessarily swayed five votes. But were it to be five or seven or nine votes on the situation, the facts speak for themselves. . . . I would be less than frank not to say that I was also [disconcerted] somewhat [by the decisions]. It hasn't changed personally my personal relationship and friendship with the chief justice, but I find it hard to understand what brought about some of these decisions.[10]

Knowland would be especially upset years later, when the Warren Court would declare that California's system of geographic representation in the state senate was unconstitutional, even though it was patterned after the federal system. The "one-man, one-vote" decision dramatically altered the balance of power in California, taking senate seats from the rural north and giving them to Southern California.

On another occasion, Knowland said there were a number of decisions that concerned him. "But I'm sure that there are a number of my votes in the Senate the then-governor had not been particularly happy with," and he noted that despite their philosophical differences, he and Warren remained on friendly terms.[11] After Knowland had left the Senate, the chief justice still would drop by the *Tribune* Tower to chat whenever he was in Oakland.

.   .   .

Early in 1954, Joe McCarthy's reign of terror over the country was continuing; as chairman of the Senate Government Operations Committee he had stepped up his activities and investigations.

Eisenhower met with Knowland, who assured the president that he would seek to curtail McCarthy's practices. Ike was unsure whether Knowland would actually carry through on his promise, however. "What's the use of trying to work with guys that aren't for you and are never going to be for you?" he asked.[12]

But in fact, McCarthy's support was eroding quickly. He was flailing about and attacking former friends. In the spring of 1954 he met his match when he charged that communists had even infiltrated the U.S. Army. The result was the lengthy Army-McCarthy hearings, which displayed the senator's rantings to a national television audience. On March 9, Senator Ralph Flanders, the Vermont Republican, spoke out against McCarthy in a Senate speech, comparing him with Hitler. "Were the junior senator from Wisconsin in the pay of the Communists he could not have done a better job for them," he said.[13] His face red—obviously angry—Knowland sat behind Flanders, powerless for the moment to do anything. He was being drawn reluctantly into a position against McCarthy. The Republicans didn't want to deal with the issue, but Flanders was forcing their hand and they resented it. Knowland himself took to the Senate floor to denounce McCarthy for saying that the Democrats had engaged in "twenty years of treason." In an appeal for bipartisan support of foreign policy, Knowland asserted that the Republicans did not have a monopoly on patriotism:

Republicans and Democrats alike should and do resent any reflection upon the patriotism and devotion to public service of our two great political parties and the lesser ones that now, and from time to time in the past, have played a part in our constitutional system.

Let us here and now . . . recognize the fact that there is only one group that can be properly charged with being the "party of treason" and that is the Communist Party and the underground conspirators who may in the interest of Communist conspiracy seek to infiltrate whichever party has the responsibility for determining national policies or has access to information which their espionage agents feel it essential to secure.[14]

While some believed that Eisenhower had put Knowland up to giving the speech in an effort to show that the Republican leadership was repudiating the senator from Wisconsin, his comments were consistent with his strong opposition to attacks on American institutions, especially the Senate and the presidency. Yet it was obviously painful for Knowland to turn against McCarthy. He had been holding back while other Republicans, including Senator Margaret Chase Smith, took the lead. Four years earlier, she had spoken out in her "Declaration of Conscience" speech: "The American people are sick and tired of being afraid to speak their minds lest they be politically smeared as 'communist' or 'fascist.' "[15]

Knowland now not only was worried about McCarthy's methods, but he believed that the senator might be censured. He sensed that Eisenhower was siding with Flanders and told the president so, comparing his interference to Roosevelt's efforts to get rid of senators he did not like. Eisenhower denied that he was meddling, insisting that he "would not be trapped into any purging action; the matter belonged in the Senate and, so far as I was concerned, there it would stay."[16]

Eisenhower was playing his hand carefully. Publicly he wouldn't attack McCarthy, for he was fully aware that the senator might still have more public admirers than detractors. But behind closed doors, he told Knowland and other Republican leaders that he was "considerably disturbed and embarrassed. The worst thing about this McCarthy business is that the newspapers are all saying that the leadership in the Republican Party has switched to McCarthy and that we are all dancing to his tune." Eisenhower also worried that too little was being accomplished in the Senate because the members were focused on the hearings McCarthy was conducting. Knowland jumped in to say that although McCarthy had "distracted attention on the Hill," not a single bill had been sidetracked.[17]

The McCarthy issue was particularly troublesome to Knowland. He complained to his father that Senator Flanders was going to bring up the McCarthy censure resolution even if it disrupted the flow of legislative matters. Although Flanders did not immediately introduce the resolution—Senate Resolution 301—when he did, on July 30, it set off a storm. The resolution read, "Resolved, that the conduct of the Senator from Wisconsin, Mr. McCarthy, is unbecoming a Member of the U.S. Senate, is contrary to Senatorial traditions, and tends to bring the Senate in disrepute, and such conduct is hereby condemned."

The majority leader was sitting at his desk on the Senate floor when Flanders strolled up and unceremoniously informed him that he was introducing the resolution. He told Knowland that he didn't have a copy of it, but Knowland looked at the full press gallery and observed that the reporters surely had copies—they clearly knew that something big was coming up in the Senate, and there was nothing scheduled of major importance. Knowland scolded Flanders for not consulting with anyone before introducing the resolution, but Flanders said he did so purposely, "because if I did consult them they might talk me out of it."[18]

Knowland was opposed to the resolution from the beginning. Although he and many other senators were often offended by McCarthy's actions, he was worried that the censure resolution would cause a bitter floor fight, further splitting the Republican ranks and endangering Eisenhower's legislative program. Knowland called the resolution "unfair and unprecedented" and predicted that it could not pass. He was joined by Vice President Nixon, who said the censure resolution would not pass "in its present form" and possibly in any form. Knowland continued to work at keeping Eisenhower out of the fight, announcing publicly, "It is the position, I understand, of the President that this is a problem for the Senate of the United States and that it would be improper for him to inject himself into it."[19] The president's liaison to the Senate, Jerry Persons, also was urging Eisenhower not to interfere in the process.

With the McCarthy battle looming, William S. White reported in the *New York Times* that Knowland saw his duty as negotiating between the Republicans and the president, not as attempting to tell the Republican Senate what actions the president said it must take. However, "he is, judging by the whispers one occasionally hears 'downtown,' a great deal more loyal to the administration than some in the administration are to him." White also criticized the administration for failing to grasp many of the fine points of dealing with the Senate.[20]

Knowland and Lyndon Johnson conferred about what they might do with the McCarthy censure resolution. Unfortunately, as Knowland conceded, "it couldn't be obviously ignored and it couldn't be tabled and it had to get some place." But they couldn't send it to the Government Operations Committee, whose chairman was Joe McCarthy. Knowland was beaten back by a massive lobbying effort when he tried to refer it to the Senate Rules Committee, where it would have been buried by William Jenner of Indiana, one of McCarthy's allies. So Knowland and Johnson agreed to appoint a special committee.[21]

By a vote of 75 to 12, the Senate referred the resolution to the special committee on August 2. Knowland and Johnson were to each appoint three members of each party to the committee. "I think we had both agreed that we would try to get what you would now term, I think, a moderate-type of a committee there, not one that would prejudge the case one way or the other on it," Knowland said. "For that reason I think that Senator Johnson discussed the names that he was considering [with me]. I don't mean by that he gave me a veto over them, but I think had I felt very strongly that one of them would be a mistake. . . . We each tried to agree with the other's selection."[22]

White later recalled that it was really Johnson who selected every member, although he and Knowland were supposed to split the number of appointees. White, who was in Johnson's office with Knowland when the appointments were made, described how Johnson "would fix on some Republican he knew Knowland detested. He'd say, 'Now, Bill, I'm sure you want so-and-so.' Knowland would say, 'Oh, no! Good God, no, I don't want so-and-so.' And he'd wind up naming the man Johnson wanted. He did it all the time."[23] Not one member of the committee was controversial or on record against McCarthy, and each got along well with his colleagues. None was up for reelection. Johnson had planned it that way.[24]

Knowland appointed Republicans Arthur Watkins of Utah, Frank Carlson of Kansas, and Francis Case of South Dakota, while Johnson's selections were Democrats Edwin C. Johnson of Colorado, John Stennis of Mississippi, and Sam Ervin of North Carolina. According to Watkins, who was named chairman of the committee, Knowland never indicated his personal preferences and did not instruct him "even to the slightest degree" to go easy on McCarthy. "Presumably the other Republicans on the newly appointed Select Committee were treated as respectfully by Senator Knowland," Watkins said.[25]

By now, the senator from Wisconsin was out of control. He was drinking heavily and railing against communists at every opportunity. On November 10, McCarthy issued a statement that said, "I would have the American people recognize the fact that the Communist party has now extended its tentacles to the United States Senate. It has made a committee of the Senate its unwitting handmaiden."[26]

Some Republicans, however, continued to take McCarthy's side, and they reacted angrily to any actions against him. "We had some people on my own side of the aisle . . . who were very bitter at me that I joined with Johnson and we jointly sponsored the appointment of a committee, because they felt that McCarthy could do no wrong," Knowland said. His own feelings about McCarthy were mixed: "I think there is no doubt about it that there were espionage agents that had infiltrated the government. I think he was really a dedicated man and hoped that by his efforts he would play a major part in eliminating them from whatever positions they may have gotten into. But I think he was loose with his figures."[27] The California senator may have based his beliefs that there were communists in the State Department on reports from his own inside source. George Wilson, who had been his commanding officer in Europe and then became his administrative assistant when he was appointed to the Senate, now worked for the State Department. The two of them kept in close contact over the years. It is likely that Wilson would have tipped off Knowland to what was going on in there.

Knowland said he knew a number of people who attempted to get McCarthy to temper his tactics, "but nobody seemed to have any real influence with him. . . . I think had McCarthy just toned down his methods and followed a more normal procedure, he might not have gotten the headlines that he got in the early stages, but I think might have performed a far more useful service than he ultimately was able to do." Everett Dirksen and Knowland himself met with McCarthy and tried to reason with him. "Joe," Knowland said, "look, there is enough evidence that you have or that is available, that if you just stick to the documented cases on it, and follow through on it, you've got a case. But when you fuzz it up and overstate your case on it, we think you're doing more harm to the cause you purport to be interested in, and are interested in, than otherwise."[28]

Knowland could not understand McCarthy's anger and vindictiveness. "I belonged to the school that, when the fight is over you shake hands and you're generous in offering your congratulations to the victor, and tried to have a humility when you were the victor," Knowland said. "You work and live and fight with people and it's almost like a family. . . . So many people who otherwise would have been more inclined to go along with McCarthy, I think felt offended."[29] Right up to the end, McCarthy offered no apologies for his behavior, although he said he had never meant to offend anyone. "I admit that at times I have been extremely blunt in expressing my opinions. I do not claim to be a master of words." But, he said, "In the facts and opinions that I held, I am unchanged."[30]

On September 27, the Watkins committee recommended that

McCarthy be censured. Watkins had received 30,000 letters; they ran two to one against censure.[31]

On December 2, the full Senate voted to censure. Bill Knowland was one of twenty-two senators, all Republicans, to oppose the measure. Knowland believed that the censure would inhibit free speech. He also objected that McCarthy's offenses had come before he was re-elected in 1952: "I do not believe the Senate should now, in an ex post facto sort of way, adopt a resolution of censure. . . . Mr. President, are we to have no statute of limitations at all?"[32] He said that he made his decision after "prayerful consideration." But by repudiating the committee he helped create, Knowland, his colleagues complained, "ran out on us." *Time* magazine predicted, however, that there would be no move to remove him as majority leader. "He will simply continue as the Republican non-leader in the Senate."[33]

That afternoon, Eisenhower wandered into press secretary James C. Hagerty's office with a ticker clipping that said Knowland had just announced he was against the censure of McCarthy because it would curtail the investigative powers of the Senate. "What's the guy trying to do?" Ike asked. "Here, he personally picked the committee to draw up the censure charges, he vouched for their honor and integrity and then he turns around and votes against them, using this phony reason of investigative curtailment. If I am asked about it at my press conference, I will say it is entirely a Senate matter and that no one in the executive branch had any idea of any curtailment of investigative powers." Hagerty told the president he thought Knowland was paying off right-wing support of his foreign policy statements. He recorded in his diary, "As far as I was concerned, this is just another instance of Knowland being taken up on the mountaintop by the right wing and promised a lot of things, and the President agreed with me." Hagerty urged Eisenhower to open his news conference by remaining firm, advising him to reject warlike acts.[34]

The next day he and two colleagues got into a heated argument over whether the president's opening statement would be construed as a slap at Knowland. "So what!!" Hagerty wrote in his diary. "If anyone has earned a crack from the President it has been Knowland with his break on foreign policy and his stand against McCarthy censure—and I know the President feels pretty much the same. Knowland can work with us if he chooses. If not, we will work with other more liberal and pro-Eisenhower members of the Senate once the session starts."[35]

This was one of the few times that the motives of "Mr. Integrity" were open to question. By voting against censure, Knowland ensured the continued support of the conservative Republicans. If he had voted for censure, it probably would have done little to put him in good standing with the Eisenhower Republicans while infuriating his conservative colleagues. As Robert Griffith put it, "The moderates were disorganized and leaderless. They were also less vindictive. In time they would forget [Knowland's] apostasy; the McCarthyites would not."[36] His vote thus may have reflected pure politics, being designed to help him keep his party leadership. He was in an unenviable position, to say the least. One historian identified Knowland's real reason for opposing the censure as his fear of "alienating conservative support for his principal political objective, a strong U.S. commitment to the defense of Formosa."[37]

That half the Republicans in the Senate voted against censure suggested that they either wanted him to continue his assaults or were afraid of curbing him. In either case McCarthy, although finished as a national figure, could continue to cause trouble in the Senate. Indeed, McCarthy himself appeared unconcerned about the censure. Following the vote he said simply, "I'm happy to have this circus ended so I can get back to the real work of digging out communism, crime and corruption. That job will start officially Monday morning after 10 months of inaction."[38]

17

Politics at Home

Many people viewed Knowland's stands against censur-
ing McCarthy and his attacks on the administration's foreign policy as
a prelude to running for the presidency in 1956 should Eisenhower bow
out. While the political jockeying between Knowland and Nixon continued to be analyzed, talk also turned to the possibility of Knowland
opposing Johnson in the 1956 presidential race.

"Neither seems to be exactly unhappy about [the talk]," observed
journalist Patrick McMahon. "They are both reasonably ambitious men.
However, thus far at least, neither has shown any trace of that dread
infection which has blighted so many promising political careers, a disease that becomes endemic in the Capital as a Presidential year approaches; the disease known as 'White House-itis.'"[1] As *Newsweek* magazine pointed out, "When [Knowland] talks about placing the good of
the country ahead of his own political welfare, none of his associates
smiles to himself about this political cliché. Knowland means it and his
associates know he means it. He has believed deeply in what some others might consider the bromides of democracy ever since he was in
knee pants."[2]

The portraits being painted of Knowland were sounding familiar.
"Knowland has little gift for repartee, either on the floor or in the
cloakroom," McMahon noted. "He has little time for those friendly,
backslapping chats with recalcitrant party members that his colleague,
Lyndon Johnson, finds so effective in picking up a vote here and there.
He simply comes directly to the point, says what he has to say, and

there it is. And while he is learning to temporize, as an essential part
of his job, he is still inclined to stand by his guns with adamant stubbornness, once he takes a position." Others called the forty-six-year-
old Knowland "a young fogy."³

How was Knowland reacting to all this criticism? "I long ago
learned that, if you're in public life, you have to have a hide that can be
harpooned, and so it hasn't bothered me too much," he said.⁴

.   .   .

While Knowland was the Senate Republican leader, his staff grew to
about thirty people. James Gleason, who later was defeated in his bid
from Maryland for a U.S. Senate seat, was the senator's administrative assistant. He had joined Nixon's staff in 1950 after graduating from
law school and stayed for two and a half years, including six months
while Nixon was vice president. When George Wilson left Knowland to
join the State Department, Gleason agreed to join Knowland's staff.
(Gleason later noted, "The difference in working with Senator Knowland and Nixon was like night and day. You weren't there a week or so
with Senator Knowland before he told you you were doing a good job,
which you never heard from Nixon.")

He would be the number two man behind Bill Jaeger, a former
Piedmont resident and attorney, whose family had known the Knowlands for years. When Jaeger left in 1954 to practice law in California,
Gleason moved up as Knowland's top aide. On December 29, Knowland added a young graduate of the University of California at Berkeley
to his staff. Paul G. Manolis was in Sigma Alpha Epsilon with Knowland's son, Joe. While Manolis was in graduate school studying history,
Joe Knowland had urged him to seek the job. Joe's fraternity brother
was to become the senator's closest friend and right-hand man, his confidant for the rest of his life. The senator even would name Manolis
as the executor of his estate. He was like a son to Knowland, in many
ways replacing his own son, Joe, and driving a wedge between the senator and his family. Manolis's relationship with Senator Knowland virtually ended his friendship with Joe.

With Knowland's increased responsibilities, he had little time to
spend in the Senate office. He left much of the day-to-day operations
to Gleason, Manolis, and his private secretary, Mary Beary. There was a
clear chain of command. The staff would read his mail carefully and
handle constituency problems. Seldom did he personally answer any

letters. Knowland was so remote from the daily operations that it was a joke among the staff that during the annual Christmas party, Knowland would say after greeting everyone, "See you next year." But as Gleason remembered it, Knowland "had a heavy responsibility in a Republican administration, which gets you in the White House every day. He was doing what he thought was important to do, which was running the affairs of the country and we were doing our jobs [i.e., running the office]."

Knowland also had reason to be concerned about politics at home. The Republican Party in California suffered a major political setback in 1954. For the first time in forty years, the Democrats were able to present a united party slate for every national and state office at the November 1954 general election. Because of potential Democratic gains, the fight for control of the Republican Party was, as Governor Goodwin Knight called it, "a fight to the finish."[5] The 1954 elections didn't finish the Republicans, but they were a forewarning of the divisions among Richard Nixon, Knight, and Knowland that would devastate the party in 1958. There was already plenty of political maneuvering among the three factions.

Part of the reason for the Democrats' 1954 resurgence was a modification in the rules governing cross-filing. For the first time since 1914, candidates had to state their party affiliations next to their names. With their 850,000-voter edge in registration, the Democrats now had a new advantage. In addition, in 1953 the Democrats had established the California Democratic Council, a volunteer group similar to the GOP's own California Republican Assembly. It was conceived by Attorney General Edmund G. "Pat" Brown and other Democratic leaders as a way to combat cross-filing. State senator George Miller Jr., the Democratic state chairman, called the first CDC convention. Alan Cranston, a Northern California property manager who one day would become a U.S. senator, was elected president. The CDC helped revive the party by endorsing a slate of candidates at the first preprimary convention of the California Democratic Party since the time of Hiram Johnson.

The Republicans also were faced with the post–Earl Warren era. Goodwin J. Knight, the Republican lieutenant governor under Warren, was now governor and titular head of the party. While the Democrats were unifying, the Republicans were battling among themselves. After the 1954 elections, Knowland joined Knight against Nixon to gain control over the California Republican Party. That served the governor and the senator well; Knight would solidify his hold on the governor's office and Knowland would move toward gaining control of the 70 delegates to the Republican National Convention in 1956.

Nixon put up a vigorous fight in his attempt to control the Republican State Central Committee. While Knight was on his honeymoon with his second wife, Virginia (his first wife had died two years earlier), Nixon was busily rounding up support through Murray Chotiner. When Knight found out what Nixon was doing, he canceled his honeymoon and returned to California. With Knowland's help, he was able to hold off Nixon's effort and retain control of the State Central Committee.

Then the infighting got nastier. It reached its peak in 1955 with a battle over who would officially lead the party in the 1956 California elections. Although the Nixon faction wanted state senator John McCarthy as GOP chairman, the Knight/Knowland candidate, Tom Caldecott of Berkeley, won easily. The real prize, however, was the vice chairmanship. Nixon wanted his man to win the second spot, because by tradition that person would automatically become chairman in 1956, a presidential election year. Knight put up his former campaign manager Howard Ahmanson and gained the support of Knowland and California's junior senator, Tom Kuchel. The Nixon contingent wanted Ray Arbuthnot, a Southern Californian.

It appeared that Arbuthnot had the job in hand, but then Knight put the pressure on, warning state legislators that they could not expect state patronage or the governor's signature on their favorite bills if they voted against Ahmanson. Arbuthnot, seeing his chances evaporating, pulled out of the race to avoid the impression that Nixon had again been defeated. The Nixon supporters asked Knight to state that the vice president was not personally involved in the race, but Knight refused. And he refused to let up. "I had to demonstrate to them that I keep my agreements and that I am the governor," he said.[6] As Los Angeles writer Martin Hall noted several years later, "It is hardly conceivable that Knight could have made those statements without the knowledge and full approval of Senator Knowland, without whose backing he would never have won. Knowland knew as well as did Nixon that control of the California delegation to the 1956 National Convention is an indispensable stepping stone towards the nomination for president and both men are determined to get that nomination."[7]

A veteran political observer said, "Nixon and Knowland can deny a split till hell freezes over, but it will still be there. Anything else wouldn't be natural. They're both from the same state. They both want to move to the White House. They can't both get there." In *Look* magazine, another observer predicted that Knowland would prevail over Nixon simply because of the power of his father's *Tribune*. "If Knowland ever decided to get rid of Nixon, he could murder him. One sound defeat could ruin Nixon in the state, but Knowland and the *Tribune* will be around for a long time. And the politicians know it. In a showdown, they'll go along with Knowland."[8]

On July 16, 1954, *U.S. News and World Report* was speculating on the futures of Knowland and Nixon: "In Washington and in California, many are watching this little-publicized contest between Vice President and Majority Leader. It is not to be brought into the open soon. But the split is there. California, a big State, may prove too small to accommodate the futures of two such men as Mr. Knowland and Mr. Nixon." That split would lead to a three-way division in California's delegation to the Republican National Convention in 1956.

While the Democrats were encouraged by their showing in the 1954 primary, the Republicans were apprehensive. President Eisenhower was brought in to rally the troops. In a speech in late September, Eisenhower warned of the dangers of party division and said that the "completion of this great [administration] program requires the election of a Republican Congress." The president, together with most of the Republican candidates, tied the party's hopes to his own coattails.

Nevertheless, the Democrats were hoping to hold the party line, as state chairwoman Elizabeth Snyder made clear: "our general and strongest appeal is for the registered Democrats to vote the Democratic ticket in November."[9] With their large advantage in registration, party loyalty could enable the Democrats to win the election. But the voters did not cooperate. With 70 percent of the registered voters going to the polls in 1954, the Republicans won every major race except that for attorney general, which was held by the incumbent, Democrat Pat Brown. The GOP also won most of the minor races.

The only solace to Democratic leaders was that their party polled the largest vote in its history. But an even greater consolation was soon to come: within four years, the Democrats would take control of California, as Knowland, Nixon, and Knight entered into a winner-take-all battle for control of the GOP.

.   .   .

The 1954 national election would seriously damage Knowland's career. In the Senate, the one-vote margin shifted in favor of the Democrats,

with such newcomers stepping into the chamber as Richard L. Neuberger of Oregon and former vice president Alben Barkley of Kentucky. The Democrats also gained the majority in the House.

When the Democrats gained control of the Senate, Knowland lost
his job as majority leader. Lyndon Johnson took over when the session
opened in January 1955, making Knowland's job that much more difficult. Knowland was simply no match for the shrewd Texan.

During the 1954 campaign, Eisenhower had warned that the election
of Democrats to Congress would stymie his efforts to get his programs
through, saying that it would be the start of a "cold war of partisan politics." Democratic leaders Lyndon Johnson and Sam Rayburn replied
that "there will be no cold war conducted against you by the Democrats" and accused the president of making an "unjust attack on the
many Democrats who have done so much to cooperate with your administration and to defend your program against attacks by members
of your own party."[10]

It was a not-so-subtle attack on the leadership of Bill Knowland.

18

Standing Up to Ike

The second half of 1954 would see Knowland distance himself further from Eisenhower by rejecting the president's statement that the nation needed "the courage to be patient" in Far East affairs.

While the internal battles over communism were going on in the Senate, Congress and the Eisenhower administration were struggling to deal with the Communists' action to regain Vietnam from the French. The United States had been giving financial aid to France since 1950 to help it fight the war. The Big Five nations were to meet in mid-1954 at Geneva to discuss the situation in Indochina.

The French intended to press for a truce, but Secretary of State John Foster Dulles protested that a truce would be handing victory to the Communists on a political platter. The French wanted to set up a coalition government in Indochina, but Dulles believed that the Communists would soon take over. But the French, pointing out that the United States had already accepted a truce in Korea which divided that country, argued that the same solution should be acceptable in Indochina.[1] Dulles also warned that the possible intervention of Chinese troops would lead to "grave consequences which might not be confined to Indochina." That was thought to be a veiled threat of using the atomic bomb.[2]

In keeping with the president's wishes, Dulles called a meeting of Senate and House leaders on April 13 to discuss U.S. involvement in Indochina. Dulles had in his pocket a proposed joint resolution of Congress calling for support for the president's effort to help the French (in language similar to that used ten years later in the Gulf of Tonkin Resolution, which led to a major expansion of the Vietnam War).[3] After a meeting lasting over two hours, the leaders joined in overwhelming opposition to sending troops to Indochina. Knowland, who had started out "hawkish," had changed his mind by the end of the meeting. Lyndon Johnson noted that the United States had fought the Korean War virtually alone and would not do so again. Neither Democrats nor Republicans were in a position to be involved in another war. The Republicans had labeled the Democrats the "war party," and the Republicans had campaigned on the premise of being for peace. They did agree that they might reconsider if U.S. allies would join in the fight.[4] Ironically, Johnson and John F. Kennedy, who also joined the senators denouncing U.S. intervention, in the 1960s would mire the United States in Vietnam.

Before the Geneva Conference began at the end of April, the United States asked Britain to join it in military intervention in Indochina, but the British refused. U.S. officials contended that had Britain agreed, the conflict could have ended early. Without the British commitment, the United States was a half-hearted participant in Geneva. The British and the French also were concerned that Dulles had destroyed the allies' unity by putting them in a position to disagree. That, they said, would hurt them in the talks with the Communists. But Dulles countered that the possibility of joint military action against them might make the Communists more cooperative during the talks.[5]

After meetings with the French and the British, the United States and the other powers agreed to establish a Pacific NATO, later to be called the Southeast Asian Treaty Organization, or SEATO. The enabling legislation was passed by Congress in 1955, but not before the pact drew Knowland's full fury because it failed to include Formosa or Korea. Admiral Arthur Radford, chairman of the Joint Chiefs of Staff, had told Knowland that Chinese Nationalist and Korean troops could be used to help fight in Indochina without weakening the defense of Formosa. According to Radford, the United States would only use sea and air power in Indochina, not ground troops; Knowland told him that Congress would be opposed to committing U.S. ground troops so long as there were Asian troops available. Thai and Philippine troops also were considered for the job.[6] But eventually it would be left to U.S. ground troops to take on the Communists in the ill-fated war.

As the Geneva Conference drew nearer, Dulles asked Knowland how the United States should approach the conference. "I told him that I did not believe that we should go as an active member . . . as a full-fledged delegate. We had not been a party to the conflict. I felt it was all right for us to send an observer, but I did not want to . . . be a party to what might turn out to be a Far Eastern Munich." And, he said, if the French lost, the Communists "were apt to lay down some fairly stiff terms and I did not want to see the United States become a signatory to this kind of an operation." The United States took precisely the role Knowland suggested, although he sought no credit for it, as others also were taking a similar stand.[7]

The California senator said he wasn't against intervention by the United States so long as it was joined by other countries. Knowland, who had flown over the Vietnamese countryside with French officers, said he would lead a fight to send U.S. troops to Vietnam if Eisenhower thought it necessary. Before the conference began, Knowland said the British and French were about to embark upon "another Far East Munich," leading the *Sacramento Bee* to editorialize, "he has so confused the idea of Munich with legitimate negotiations that he is all but closing the door to any solution short of military action."[8]

At the Geneva Conference, all countries except the United States and South Vietnam agreed to respect the sovereignty and independence of Cambodia, Laos, and Vietnam, with the demarcation line dividing Vietnam along the Seventeenth Parallel. They also stipulated that elections would be held in 1956 on Vietnam's national unification and agreed to a prohibition on foreign troops in Vietnam. The United States decided instead to "refrain from any threat or the use of force" in Indochina, while making clear that it would view any renewal of aggression in China "with grave concern and as seriously threatening international peace and security." Knowland wasted no time attacking the agreement, calling it "one of the greatest victories for communism in a decade."[9]

While the French were urging the Americans to intervene, the Eisenhower administration was sounding out the Republican and Democratic leadership in both houses. Ike wasn't going to take any action without deliberation with Congress. He remembered Congress's anger when Truman committed U.S. troops to Korea after consulting only with Democrats. Besides, in his campaign he had pledged to include the full Congress. Eisenhower told congressional leaders that the French wanted the United States to send in planes to help defend Dien Bien Phu, which was about to fall to the Communists. The only thing that might save the French was U.S. intervention. "But," Eisenhower said, "we are not going to be involved alone in a power move against the Russians." Knowland replied, "If we don't offer to do something, they'll say we're not facing up to the situation."[10] Knowland recalled that Republicans and Democrats were virtually united on keeping the United States out of Vietnam, and apparently he agreed "that it should only intervene in the event that our other allies interested in that area of the world would do it on a joint basis." Members of Congress also wanted a guarantee of independence for Indochina if the battle of Dien Bien Phu was won.[11]

On July 1 on the Senate floor, Knowland backed the "agonizing reappraisal" of the country's foreign policy toward Vietnam and China along the lines suggested by Dulles. His declaration came after Prime Minister Winston Churchill had warned Eisenhower that the British might lead a drive to admit Communist China into the United Nations if the United States pushed too hard. Still, Knowland worried that 10 million Vietnamese were going to fall under Communist control and said that the free world "seemed to be seized by inertia." He went on to ask, "Where is the line to be drawn? Alaska? Hawaii?" and reminded his listeners of the American lives lost in Korea. "Are the hundreds of American prisoners killed in cold blood with their hands tied behind their backs to become the forgotten men while the blood-stained hands of the Communist murderers are clasped in fraternal greetings by our allies in the United Nations' building in New York?"[12]

Although some Democratic senators rebuked Knowland for his stand, Johnson came to his defense. "The American people want no appeasement of Communists," Johnson said. "The American people will refuse to support the United Nations if Red China becomes a member."[13] Facing such formidable opposition, Churchill notified Eisenhower that the British would make no effort to seat Red China "at this time."

In a July 19 letter to his father, Knowland said that he had received "heavy mail" as a result of his speech, about 90 percent of it favorable. He noted, "The news from Geneva does not look good and the Communists are winning a tremendous victory which is going to cost the free world much in blood, sweat and tears in the years ahead." Knowland was as surprised as anyone when the French decided to cut their political, economic, and military ties to Indochina. The United States had expected that France would at least keep a system similar to the British Commonwealth, Knowland said. And when the French rejected even that system, there was no one willing to step in against the Communists.[14]

Around this time, Vice President Nixon put out a feeler at a press briefing to determine what public reaction might be to U.S. intervention in Vietnam. Knowland, whose policies were very similar to Nixon's, said he was not consulted about the trial balloon nor did he know who requested it. But, Knowland said, it proved to be a lead balloon—no one in the House or Senate would endorse such action. "There was not great enthusiasm . . . in this country on the general theory of colonialism," he observed. "The idea of supporting colonialism is just not a popular cause in the United States."[15] Indeed, the reaction to Nixon's briefing displayed by Senator Ed Johnson, the Colorado Democrat and one of the most senior members of Congress, confirmed Knowland's judgment: "I heard the vice president whooping it up for war in Indochina. . . . I am against sending American GIs into the mud and muck of Indochina on a blood-letting spree to perpetuate colonialism and white man's exploitation in Asia."[16]

At the same time, Knowland was giving speeches indicating that if Red China were admitted to the United Nations, he would resign his leadership post and spend the rest of his days in the Senate urging U.S. withdrawal from the United Nations. He said he would resign so as to not cause the administration embarrassment by his actions. *New York Times* columnist Arthur Krock saw Knowland's statement as a concession "that there are limits to the usefulness of a party leader in Congress who opposes a majority policy of a President of that party."[17] There was also a growing isolationist sentiment in the country that perhaps the United States ought to stay out of Indochina completely. "Such a step would, of course, be tragic and would be a complete repudiation by the United States of its world leadership," wrote James C. Hagerty, the president's press secretary, in his diary.[18]

Eisenhower was particularly concerned about Knowland's threat to resign from his Senate leadership role. "What the hell did he have to say that for?" Eisenhower asked. "That implies that we would favor the admission of Red China to the U.N." Just about that time, Knowland telephoned the White House asking to meet with the president, and Ike saw a chance to calm him down. Following two meetings that afternoon with Knowland, Eisenhower remarked, "He thinks he's Horatius at the bridge. All he wants is attention and he acts like a little boy at times."[19]

On July 8, Knowland hand-delivered to Eisenhower a rider calling on the president to inform Congress of the implications of any proposal to admit Communist China to the United Nations. In an "eyes only" memo to Dulles, Eisenhower said he had no objections to the language "because I could not detect in it any attempt on the part of

Congress to attempt to invade the rights and responsibilities of the Executive [branch]. I told [Knowland] that on no account did I want to be known as a sponsor of this kind of legislation."[20]

On July 17, Knowland spoke with Dulles on the telephone about the Communists' proposal for free elections in Vietnam. He told the secretary of state that the United States might go along with the elections under the watch of the United Nations as long as the Communists agreed to free elections in Korea. Dulles responded that Germany (then not a UN member) should be included, and Knowland agreed. However, none of this came to pass.[21]

Knowland's relationship with Eisenhower took a turn for the worse on September 5 when he released a telegram to the press before he sent it to the president. Knowland was criticizing Eisenhower's letter to the Soviet Union about a navy jet shot down over the Sea of Japan as too tame. "Just another note from our State Dept. to the Kremlin hierarchy will not impress these uncivilized rulers," he insisted. "The breaking of diplomatic relations is justified." In the telegram, he urged Eisenhower to expel the Soviet ambassador from the United States and recall the U.S. ambassador from Moscow.

Knowland was called to the White House to meet with Eisenhower over his demands. Before his arrival, Secretary of State Dulles said that reporters would be waiting after the meeting "on the Knowland foolishness" and it would be all right with him if Ike wanted to "slap Knowland's ears back."

When Knowland came into the room, Eisenhower turned on his secret tape recorder. Ike had explained to an associate his use of audiotapes: "It is a good thing when you're talking to someone you don't trust in Washington and I want to have myself protected so they can't later report that I said something else." The president then told Knowland that the plane might not have been innocent, revealing that it was possibly on a spy mission—something that Knowland could not have known.[22]

Two days later, on September 7, Eisenhower sent a "personal and confidential" letter to Knowland, although he wrote that he had never answered a message received under such circumstances. After asserting his belief that Knowland had not intended to embarrass him (though the senator clearly had), the president acknowledged that he was considering just such action. He added: "There is one point to be constantly borne in mind—namely, that any definite and irrevocable decision of the kind you suggest will advance American aims and objectives in the world only as it is based upon such reasons and circumstances as will unquestionably convince intelligent people among the free nations that we are defending the rights of freedom and our own self-respect."[23]

Sometimes Eisenhower's troubles with Knowland were more a matter of his perceptions than of actual disagreements between the two. During 1954 Eisenhower submitted 232 specific requests for legislation to Congress. Knowland voted with the administration on 91 percent of the requests. "Obviously it's not a pleasant thing to be in difference with your administration even 9 percent of the time," Knowland reflected.[24]

· · ·

In September 1954 the shelling of the island of Quemoy off Formosa by the Communist Chinese sparked heavy debate in the Eisenhower administration, particularly because of Knowland's demands that the United States protect the tiny, barbell-shaped island.

Knowland led the effort to pass the Formosa Resolution, which would give Eisenhower the authority to defend Formosa and "related positions and territories now in friendly hands"—referring, of course, to the two islands. Eisenhower was willing to pledge to defend Formosa, leaving to presidential discretion the defense of Quemoy and its neighbor, Matsu. Both islands were just a mile off the mainland. When Knowland told Eisenhower that the Senate would pass the resolution, although he expected some of the mavericks to object, the president interrupted him to remark, "You sure got some strange characters up there on our side in the Senate. I can pick my boys here in the White House, but you fellows have to take what comes along."[25]

Eisenhower could have said the same of his relationship with Knowland: he didn't elect him, but he had to deal with him. The feud between Eisenhower and Knowland was so intense that Democratic presidential nominee Adlai Stevenson once remarked that they should sign a nonaggression pact. Now, during the debate over the resolution, Knowland criticized the administration's position that it would only retaliate against a Communist attack of the offshore islands if it could determine what the intentions of the aggressors were. "What nonsense is this?" Knowland asked. "When the assault is under way, are we to inquire through the good offices of Mr. [UN Secretary General Dag] Hammarskjold, Mao Tse-tung and Chou En-lai in Peiping, as to whether their assault is only for possession of these outer ramparts?"[26] In early 1955, Democrats helped pass the resolution. Senator Wayne Morse of Oregon labeled it a "treaty with Knowland."

On October 1, 1954, *Collier's* magazine gave two full pages to Knowland's assertion that free nations must draw a line against further Communist encroachment in Asia, in an article titled "We Must Be Willing to Fight Now." It quoted the senator: "When I say fight, I don't mean fight in another little war. The free nations should let Red China know that if she invades—directly as in Korea, or indirectly as in Indochina—any territory we have undertaken to defend, she must take the consequences not only on the violated land, but on her own mainland. Hard, sane courage is the quality most likely to save us from war, or from defeat if war comes." Knowland claimed that the United States had made three major errors in dealing with the Communists: Yalta, accepting a stalemate in Korea, and allowing the French surrender in Indochina. He said that the U.S. failure to win the Korean War "may turn out to have been one of the worst mistakes of history."[27]

In its own story on the article, the *Reporter* magazine commented that it "stops just short of telling that farmer to send his son back to Korea or thereabouts. He wants the United States to draw a line somewhere, anywhere, in Asia and fight an all-out war if the Reds dare to cross it." The article even implied that Knowland made the statement in hopes of the Republicans losing the 1954 elections so that the old Republican Party could be buried and a "real" conservative party could be formed.[28]

It was at this time that an obscure academic journal, the *Review of Politics*, carried an article that would further shape Knowland's attitude toward the Communists quite markedly. The article was written by "Ferreus" (the Latin adjective meaning "iron"), the pen name of a European-born scholar who was an adviser to the Eisenhower government. In effect, Ferreus said that the United States should never abandon the pretense that it might start an atomic war, for "so long as the United States clings to the concept that under no possible circumstance will it initiate war, not even while the opponent is preparing to strike, so long will the initiative remain in Soviet hands." He added that "in an atomic conflict the force which plans to strike second may never be in the position to strike at all." Ferreus argued,

In the discharge of its security duties toward itself, its allies and the free world, the United States must seize the political initiative. Yet, this initiative cannot be seized so long as the opponent knows that the United States does not mean it seriously and will shrink away from the ultimate consequence. . . . I have nothing but contempt for those who are willing to surrender to Communists in order to avoid nuclear war and thus to assure the physical survival and the enslavement of the maximum number. If such a spirit were typical of the free society, our civilization would be dead by now. I do not believe that doom is near, let alone that it has come. But I am worried that the voices of cowardice are heard far more often than the voices of determination.

Knowland distributed the article to his Senate colleagues, and though he claimed not to endorse the concept in its entirety, he said he thought his colleagues "will find it challenging, and in due time and at an early date I believe they will want to explore some very basic questions raised, which vitally affect the security of the country."[29]

Knowland was telling all who would listen that the sooner and the more firmly the United States took a stand against the spread of communism, the easier the task would be and the greater the chance of forestalling atomic warfare.

.   .   .

Knowland's speeches on foreign policy were well written but unexciting. His aides said he refused their help, always writing his own speeches. They usually were about coexistence and atomic stalemate. He accurately predicted that by 1960, the Soviet Union and the United States would have stockpiled so many nuclear weapons that neither Moscow nor Washington would "dare to use or threaten to use its atomic power against the other."

Knowland said the Soviets would exploit the standoff, in which "the free world [would] become paralyzed and immobilized." That, he said, would lead the Soviets to bully and beguile "peripheral nations" into their orbit. "Operation Nibbling," he called it, and it would result in an "ultimate Communist victory." He said the Communists were advancing "the Trojan horse of coexistence" to gain time for an atomic stalemate: "We must face the fact that the Communist concept of peaceful coexistence means that the United States or other free nations of the world will be allowed to exist only until communism is able to subvert them from within or destroy them by aggression from without."[30]

Asked later what the alternatives were to peaceful coexistence, Knowland replied, "The Russians are using the plea for peaceful coexistence to gain time so they can take over country after country without risk. . . . I think we should resist any further Communist aggression either from without or by subversion from within and, at the same time, arouse the moral forces of the world." He told colleagues that the free world must choose between peace with honor and peace at any price. He believed that the term itself, which the Soviet Union had been using since Lenin's time, had no meaning, and he called on the free world to meet any new aggression by the Communists. But he was not advocating a military attack, further insisting, "I know of no one in a position of responsibility in the government who is advocating preventative war in the sense that you would start a contest without provocation other than the fear that at some future unknown date you might come out at the short end of a struggle."[31]

Knowland continued to defend Formosa and to make the point that Formosa was worth protecting. He pointed out that while somehow people had the impression it was like Catalina Island off the coast of California, there were 9.5 million people living there, a population equal to that of Australia. The Eisenhower administration, he insisted, must be prepared to back up any promise it made to defend Formosa: "We shouldn't talk unless we're ready to follow through. That only convinces the Communists, as it has in the past, that we won't act the next time. That made us what they call in the Orient a 'paper tiger.' Unless we are willing to sacrifice those people to Red slavery, we must have the will to stand." Knowland acknowledged that his saber rattling frightened many people in the United States, but "as a U.S. senator I have some facts available which are not available to the general public" about the situation in the Far East. And he wasn't precluding the use of atomic weapons in the event of war; they were a necessary deterrent, for the Soviets recognize the superiority of the United States in atomic weapons and "they won't precipitate war until they have the odds in their favor."[32]

In response to charges by Senator Estes Kefauver (D-Tenn.) that a group of "sinister" men, including Knowland, were trying to start a war between Red China and the United States, Knowland asked why Kefauver didn't also name George Meany, who was head of the American Federation of Labor, the national president of the American Legion, and others who were apprehensive about the "red menace." He continued, "I noticed that he also said we needed, in order to maintain peace, men like Wilson, Roosevelt and Truman running the country. Those were the presidents under whom we fought World Wars I and II and the Korean War. Our best chance for peace is to stand firm and not allow the Communists to get the edge."[33]

On November 15, Knowland gave the Eisenhower administration a slap in the face by calling for a congressional review of its policy in dealing with the "cold war." He took this extraordinary step right in the middle of the Senate's debate over the censure of McCarthy, again keeping both the administration and the Senate off balance and the political pundits guessing about his motives. In fact, they were simple: he believed that the foreign policy direction of the United States was far more important than any censure of McCarthy.

The joint chiefs were urging a bombing of the China mainland and they had the support of Secretary of State Dulles. Under pressure from Eisenhower, however, Dulles backed off and supported the president's position of trying to coexist with the Communists. Knowland didn't believe that such coexistence was possible; for him, "the possibility of a free world of free men [hung] in the balance." "The civilizations that flourished and died in the past," he contended, "had opportunities for a limited period of time to change the course of history. Sooner or later, however, they passed the 'point of no return' and the decisions were no longer theirs to make." Knowland darkly warned that time was running out, reminding the Senate that "in this day and age of the airplane and atomic weapons, time is not necessarily on the side of the free world."[34]

Lyndon Johnson and his fellow Democrats were surprised by Knowland's proposal to review cold war foreign policy. They didn't expect a Republican majority leader of the U.S. Senate to hint that his own party's administration was following foreign policies that were dangerous to the nation, and that committees headed by Democrats should investigate them. Naturally, they welcomed the suggestion; and as might be expected, Eisenhower and Dulles were livid. That anger was kept under control in the statement Ike released: "The president has always believed that any senator has a right to differing opinions from his own. [Senator Knowland] has often told me and said so publicly that he believes we have one of the wisest, most courageous and most dedicated men in our history as Secretary of State, John Foster Dulles." Eisenhower then chided Knowland, saying it was easy for him to take a "truculent, publicly bold and almost insulting attitude toward the unending harassments of the China Communists." And, he continued, "I want to make it quite clear that when one accepts the responsibilities of public office he can no longer give expression freely to such things; he has got to think of the results."[35]

Knowland wrote to his father on November 20 that his speech "created quite a stir, to say the least." Knowland said he had given a great deal of thought to where and when he gave the speech, recognizing that time-honored bromide that in politics timing is everything. He chose to make it on the Senate floor rather than at an outside meeting because he wanted to speak in an official capacity.

Knowland's attack on Eisenhower's foreign policy gave rise to speculation that he would either resign as majority leader or be removed by his Republican colleagues. In fact, neither would happen, and Knowland vowed to fight any effort to replace him. Eisenhower was advised not to undertake efforts to unseat Knowland. The Eisenhower Republicans in the Senate just didn't have the clout, he was told, and if an effort to remove the majority leader failed, it would vindicate Knowland and seriously weaken Eisenhower.

As *Los Angeles Times* columnist Holmes Alexander put it, "The fires of moral conviction burn so fiercely within that fullback chest and behind the dead-serious face that the question least likely to bother Bill Knowland is 'What will people say?' . . . Nobody can doubt that leadership is an instrument often forged under the strokes of ridicule and opposition. One sure test of the finished instrument is that it becomes impervious, like Knowland, to the hammers which beat it into shape."[36]

On November 22, China handed down prison terms for eleven U.S. airmen who were prisoners from the Korean War. Knowland took to the Senate floor to call again for a blockade of the China coast. Knowland said that he was aware that he was risking war, but "I am prepared to accept that risk. We have to do more than merely send a note in this instance." Knowland and the China Lobby put terrific pressure on Eisenhower, arguing that anything less than a blockade of the Yellow Sea would be tantamount to appeasement.

Sherman Adams said that Eisenhower was worried the United States "was being deliberately goaded by the Communists in the hope that they could provoke us into an impulsive action that would drive a wedge between us and our allies." Ike noted that because the airmen were prisoners from the Korean War, it was the responsibility of the United Nations to negotiate their release, and he called for "the courage to be patient."[37]

Knowland responded in a speech in Chicago by charging that the United Nations had failed to secure the airmen's release and demanding that the United States should take action to set them free. Eisenhower reacted with extreme annoyance: "I can't understand that fellow Knowland. He had a talk with Foster Dulles on Saturday about his speech but did not bring up any specific thing that he would say, other than that he expressed the opinion that he believed he should show objection to the failure to get our airmen released at this time. But as far as I'm concerned, this just confirms my opinion that Knowland is beyond the pale."[38]

On November 23, during a meeting in the White House, the president upbraided Knowland, saying, "you apparently think we are just sitting supinely and letting the people do as they please." That was not the case, Eisenhower said; he just couldn't talk openly about global situations. "I know so many things I am almost afraid to speak to my wife," he said. "Suppose one day we get in war. If too many people knew we had done something provocative—so what I'm asking is— take a long look at these things—I have never tried to make a rubber stamp out of Congress or anyone, and I realize there must be a close understanding between us, but I do try to spare other people some of the things I do."

Eisenhower cautioned Knowland that the Republican Party must be united—not in details, necessarily, but in general. "I just want to say that we might have to answer to charges of being too provocative, rather than being too sweet." Knowland did not appreciate a lecture on party unity from a man who had never been a Republican leader until he became the party's nominee for president, a man who had even considered running as a Democrat.

The president warned Knowland that a blockade of the China coast or a break in relations with the Soviet Union was "a step toward war; if you do that, then the next question is, are you ready to attack? Well, I am not ready to attack." According to a summary of the meeting, Knowland's answer was that he did not want to take the president's time to discuss it.[39]

Knowland later told the *New York Times* that he had always held that the majority leader should not be "muzzled or gagged in expressing what is a very deep and honest conviction. I feel it is entirely proper that we have a full discussion so that our people as well as our Congress thoroughly understand just what all the implications are."[40] Later, Knowland would add, "I don't intend to remain silent and have my grandchildren 10 or 20 years from now . . . say, 'You had some responsibility—you had more knowledge than perhaps the public had—why didn't you speak up at that time, when you saw this atomic stalemate, or Soviet superiority coming?'"[41] The *Sacramento Bee*, a Democratic newspaper, editorialized that no one was questioning Knowland's right to speak his mind "no matter how unworthy of good thinking and rudimentary caution his speaking may be." But, the *Bee* said, he should step down as majority leader before doing so.[42]

Knowland saw no reason to step down. After all, he believed that Congress was a coequal with the executive branch and that as leader of the legislative branch, he was well within his right to express his views. Republicans in both the conservative and moderate wings of the party were worried that the split between Eisenhower and Knowland would by exploited by the Democrats during the final two years of Eisenhower's first term: they needed to unify. The first step was to bring Knowland and Eisenhower together to develop a better working relationship. Despite their differences, it wasn't long before Eisenhower changed his tune of "peaceful coexistence" to one of "competitive coexistence." Knowland, through his pressure on the president, was largely responsible for the subtle change, although he still doubted that any kind of coexistence was possible.

But Eisenhower wanted to keep peace among the Republicans; this was his way of compromising. He admitted that peaceful coexistence is all right "beyond the condition of the Thanksgiving turkey, which coexists up until two days before Thanksgiving and then the ax falls on its neck. Now if that is what 'peaceful coexistence' means, I don't think the American people want to buy that. But I think that's precisely what the Communist world has in mind for us."[43]

While Knowland insisted that his differences with Eisenhower were exaggerated, Ike for his part acknowledged that Knowland had a right to speak out and that their disagreements were usually over method rather than principle. More embarrassing to Eisenhower was that his own Joint Chiefs of Staff agreed with Knowland. Some critics were saying that Knowland may even have been their spokesman in Congress.[44] But the California senator took offense at charges that he was opposed to the foreign policies of either the Truman or the Eisenhower administration. He agreed that he spent a great deal of time directing attention to problems he thought were of grave concern to the country, but firmly stated that since the day he set foot in the Senate he supported the general foreign policy of both administrations, including the Marshall Plan, the Greece-Turkey aid program, the legislation in support of NATO, and other particular programs.[45]

The differing views of the two powerful Republicans reflected their backgrounds. Knowland was a legislator, who expected to butt heads with his friends and foes, then go out and have a friendly drink with them afterward. Eisenhower was a military man who expected to issue orders and have them followed. Knowland did not accept orders easily.

Reaction to Knowland's stand predictably took either Eisenhower's or Knowland's side. The *Christian Century*, for example, supported the president, who was described as "stand[ing] for patience, restraint, negotiation through the U.N. and other channels, no war if there is any possible way of avoiding it." In contrast, "Senator Knowland stands for rashness, seizure of any incident as a cause for reprisal, action without regard to consequences. Between the two policies, if a showdown ever comes, we are confident the American people will have no difficulty in making their choice."[46]

The magazine *America*, however, said that Knowland had put his finger on a weak spot in the nation's defense policies: "His own solution seems not only dangerous but very inadequate. However, this does not mean that our national policy is therefore adequate. Our Asian policy, where the trouble mostly lies, calls for a full airing."[47]

19

Waiting in the Wings

From 1955 to 1956, the 84th Congress was concerned with tension in the Formosa Strait, de-Stalinization of the Soviet empire, revolt in Poland and Hungary, and war at the Suez Canal.

As the new year began, the *New York Times* named Bill Knowland one of the ten most influential members of Congress:

The hierarchic heir of the late Senator Taft, 46-year-old William F. Knowland of California is a man with an unquestionably sincere mission to harden our policy toward Asian communism—and one whose convictions have unquestionably damaged his mission as GOP leader. Without great flexibility, and without the seemingly indolent, casual grace in action of his opposite number, Senator Johnson, Knowland for all that retains great power in the Senate.

More nearly than not, he still articulates most of the basic views of the orthodox Republicans who still outnumber the "Eisenhower Republicans." His leadership is one of open thrust and parry; one of recurring, more or less ad lib accommodations with now one and now another of the Republican factions. Large, solid, stable and deeply courageous, he is a good "Senate man," regardless of whether he is a good Administration man.[1]

The new year also was to end his reign as majority leader. The balance of power had shifted to the Democrats, who now held a 49-to-47 edge in the Senate.

The shift did not silence but seemed to exacerbate the tirades of the now-discredited Joe McCarthy, who was bitter over the Republicans' loss of control of the Senate. While that doubtless upset Knowland, at least he didn't blame it on Eisenhower. Not so McCarthy; he complained that Eisenhower's failure to support Republican Herman Welker of Idaho, who lost to the young internationalist Frank Church, had cost the Republicans control of the Senate.

It had also cost McCarthy his bully pulpit—the chairmanship of the Senate Government Operations Committee, which he had used as an investigatory panel. He would not have at his disposal any weapon to attack those who voted to censure him. "This year, I believe for the first time in history," McCarthy raged on the Senate floor, "we saw the President trying to purge a member of his own party after the primary. . . . The control of the Senate today by the Democrats is the direct responsibility of a so-called Republican president. Eisenhower did not do it inadvertently. He did it deliberately. He knew what he was doing."

Bristling, Knowland hauled his large frame from his chair and rose to defend the president against the man he had tried to shield from censure. Knowland noted that Eisenhower had made speeches for Welker in Idaho and had written laudatory letters in support of Welker's reelection. No other senator defended the president. Later McCarthy stepped up the attack, claiming that "the White House palace guard encouraged the raising of money in New York to be sent into Idaho to defeat Welker and elect a Democrat." At that point, Knowland read from a letter Ike had written Welker, quoting Eisenhower's praise of his fellow Republican: "little recognition has been given to the many times you have wholeheartedly supported the Administration in advancing key parts of its program." Then he told McCarthy, "I don't want any unfairness to be implied to the President of the United States."

As Associated Press reporter Jack Bell put it, "This was the Knowland of responsibility, a grim-visaged mastodon with convictions and the courage to back them up. Here was Taft's unwanted legacy to the Eisenhower administration, a man who would be fair to friend and foe, but who was not more likely than Taft to wear any man's collar, including the President's. Armed with a fierce integrity and a deep devotion to his country, Knowland would plow his own furrow. If it ran parallel to administration efforts, well and good. If it did not, that was regrettable, but not something to worry about for long."[2]

· · ·

On the morning of January 18, 1955, Eisenhower and his press secretary, James C. Hagerty, met to discuss a speech Knowland had given the previous night in Chicago, during which he had ignored the president's admonition against attacking the United Nations. Knowland had lashed out at Dag Hammarskjold, the UN secretary general, for his failure to negotiate a return of the eleven airmen still held by the Chinese Communists, and had insisted that the United States ought to take action on its own to get them back. Knowland warned the president that any "appeasement of the Communists will be subjected to not only the most searching scrutiny by the American Congress but by a far more potent and solemn referendum of the American people in 1956."

Three days before he gave the speech, Knowland had met with Secretary of State John Foster Dulles over the fate of the airmen. "I assured him that no 'deal' was contemplated involving recognition, UN seat, trade or like subjects," Dulles wrote in a memorandum of his conversation with Knowland. "Senator Knowland expressed considerable dissatisfaction at developments, although he did not press for any drastic action." The California senator told Dulles he realized that military action might not free the airmen and could, in fact, harm them; but he was also worried about America's self-respect. "He said he agreed with me that we should be 'slow to anger' but that does not mean that we should never be angry," Dulles said. Knowland said that perhaps it was appropriate and would be helpful if he spoke out vigorously against the continued holding of the fliers. "I said I saw no serious objection to the expression of such a sentiment," Dulles said, "although I hoped that he would not urge specific drastic action, which, in fact, the Administration would not be disposed to take."[3] Thus while Eisenhower was angry with Knowland for attacking the United Nations, his own secretary of state did not object to Knowland's tirades, at least before the fact.

At the beginning of 1955, the Communist Chinese launched a number of offensives against a string of islands in the Formosa Strait, including the Tachen Islands and the little island of Yikiang, and the Joint Chiefs of Staff demanded that Eisenhower take some action. When the president argued that the islands were not strategically important, Knowland was incensed. However, Ike agreed that if the Chinese should launch an attack on Quemoy or Matsu, two strategic islands that were stepping-stones to Formosa, the United States would act. On January 24, the president delivered a message to Congress calling for passage of the Formosa Resolution, proposed a few months earlier, which would give him authority to protect the island that served as headquarters of the Nationalist Chinese. Although Eisenhower said he did not need this authority from Congress, he wanted to make it clear to the Communists that the full force of the U.S. government was behind his move.

At a meeting with Eisenhower on January 25, Knowland told him that the Senate Foreign Relations Committee was likely to report out the Formosa Resolution that day. Eisenhower told Knowland, "You know, Senator, sometimes we are captains of history. Formosa is a part of a great island barrier we have erected in the Pacific against Communist advance. We are not going to let it be broken. . . . We just can't permit the Nationalists to sit in Formosa and wait until they are attacked, and we just can't try to fight another war with handcuffs on as we did in Korea. If we see the Chinese Communists building up in their forces for an invasion of Formosa, we are going to have to go in and break it up." Knowland replied that he believed the president would have overwhelming Senate support for the resolution. He noted that William Langer of South Dakota would probably vote against it, but that while Estes Kefauver and Wayne Morse would make long speeches against it, they would vote for it.[4]

The resolution went so far as to give the president the authority to defend "related positions and territories now in friendly reference to Quemoy and Matsu." Some Democrats tried to get that provision stricken from the resolution, but they were beaten back. To quell their discontent, Eisenhower sent a dispatch to Democratic Senator Walter George of Georgia stating that the president and only the president would make the decision whether to commit American forces to any attack on the mainland. Senator George then declared, "I believe that President Eisenhower is a prudent man. I believe that he is dedicated to a peaceful world. I believe what he says, and I am willing to act on it."[5] With that, most opposition disappeared. The Senate passed the resolution 83–3, and on January 29 Eisenhower signed it. Senators Langer, Morse, and Herbert Lehman of New York were the three opposing votes.

It was a major victory for Knowland, who told *Newsweek* magazine that Quemoy and Matsu were the last areas of defense between the mainland and Formosa. "To use a football analogy, the defense cannot wait until the team with the ball crosses the line of scrimmage before resisting. By that time, it may be too late to stop the advance," he said. But the resolution, he thought, would also decrease the danger of war, "although it must be clearly recognized that the Communist world holds the key to the final answer."[6]

Reflecting on that resolution in 1967, Knowland would call it a necessary act to tell the Communist world that the United States was willing to draw the line. He believed that had the United States taken similar action it might have averted World Wars I and II as well as the Korean War. "We felt, to our national interest, it was better for any potential aggressor to understand thoroughly that if an attack was made upon Formosa that we considered to be vital to our Pacific line of defense which ran from Japan through Okinawa to the Philippines and anchored on Singapore and Australia, that a breach of that line would be contrary to our best national and international interests." The resolution proved successful, he noted, for the Communist Chinese had made no further attempt to breach that line.[7]

Hostilities in the Formosa Strait were heating up again, as the Communist Chinese were making threatening overtures toward Quemoy and Matsu while Eisenhower once more was trying to determine whether the United States should be put in a position to defend the Nationalists. In March 1955, Admiral Robert Carney leaked to the press a story that the Red Chinese were set to invade the strategic islands and that Eisenhower was going to order a bombing of mainland industries.

If that was Ike's plan, Knowland was all for it, but he wanted a clearer commitment from the White House. He launched a vigorous attack on the Eisenhower administration for seeking appeasement rather than risk war with the Chinese. At that point, Senator George leaned over to urge Lyndon Johnson to answer "that wild boy who is trying to force Ike into a flat commitment to defend Quemoy." Although Johnson agreed with Knowland, to keep harmony in the Democratic ranks he rose and attacked Knowland for proposing an "irresponsible adventure."[8]

Then in a surprise announcement on April 23, Chou En-lai said that his government was willing to negotiate peace with the United States. But John Foster Dulles, worried that the Chinese were "playing a propaganda game," put three conditions on the negotiations: that the Nationalists be included as equals in the talks, that all American prisoners in China be released, and that China accept the United Nations' offer to participate in the talks. Chou rejected the conditions, and on April 26 Dulles modified them. He said a cease-fire was necessary in the Formosa Strait and that the United States would not talk behind the Nationalists' back. Eisenhower was even more conciliatory.

On April 27, Knowland spoke with Dulles. The secretary had an aide listen in on all telephone conversations concerning State Department business and take notes of the conversation, and those notes record Knowland questioning how Dulles could back away from the three conditions he had set forth for negotiations to proceed: "He does not see how the Sec. can negotiate a cease-fire without affecting the Nationalists and realistically he does not think the Chinese Communists will be interested in negotiating without a down-payment of the offshore island. The Sec. said he does not think so either."

Although Dulles claimed that his follow-up statement was a restatement of his original policy, "K. was most upset. He is concerned and discouraged and shocked at what appears to be a reversal of the weekend. The Sec. said he did not think it was a reversal. . . . K. thinks once we get into this kind of a pow-wow he'll be surprised if we are not prepared to give not only our shirt but someone else's and we will be accused of running out." Knowland also expressed anger about being kept in the dark about the latest policy toward Communist China, which he had first read about in the *New York Times*. Dulles said "he would not take back what he said, but did not know the press conference would take the turn it did."[9]

That evening Dulles invited Knowland and colleagues Bourke Hickenlooper of Iowa and Alexander Smith of New Jersey to meet with him at 6 P.M. at his home. There, Dulles explained that the Communist Chinese were building up their airfields, which would give them air dominance of Quemoy and Matsu "in the absence of an all-out United States atomic attack." But the president was reluctant to allow the Nationalists to bomb the airfields with U.S.-made planes, because "this would seem in the nature of 'preventive' war and make us seem responsible for the hostilities which would doubtless ensue." He also said that Eisenhower was reluctant to use atomic weapons because they would cause heavy casualties. "This might alienate Asian opinion and ruin Chiang Kai-shek's hopes of ultimate welcome back to the mainland," Dulles warned.

The secretary of state said diplomacy, not force, should be used "to avoid a misfortune of considerable proportions in relation to the coastal positions which might either be lost or only held at prohibitive cost." He told the senators that friends of the United States had put pressure on Chou to seek the negotiations and that a "complete turn-down by the United States would alienate our Asian non-Communist friends and allies." Dulles pointed out that the Nationalists had already agreed under their defense pact with the United States not to attack the mainland unless they were attacked or unless the United States agreed. Therefore, he claimed, he only had to persuade the Communists to accept a cease-fire.[10]

The Republican Senate leader was not convinced; he did not trust the Communists. "I for one do not believe the Communist leopard has changed its spots," he said on May 5. "Their objective has been, is, and will continue to be the destruction of human freedom." Calling Dulles's three original conditions for the negotiations reasonable, he expressed particular disturbance at China's refusal to allow the Nationalists into the talks: "History teaches us that prior experience of great powers negotiating in the absence of small allies has not reflected great credit upon the large nations and has been disastrous to the small ones." Once again, he referred to Munich with its impact on Czechoslovakia and to Yalta with its impact on Poland and the Nationalist Chinese. "That we are at one of the great turning points of history I would not deny. Whether it is a turn for the better or for the worse only time will tell."[11]

In early August 1955, the Americans and the Chinese opened negotiations that were to last more than a year. Not long after the talks began, the Chinese freed the American fliers. It wasn't until January 21, 1956, that the State Department released a summary of what had taken place. About all that had been accomplished was an agreement not to use force in Sino-American relations. The Formosa Strait issue remained unsettled. On the one hand, the United States argued that the renunciation of force was meaningless so long as the Communists maintained their threat against Formosa; on the other hand, the Chinese insisted that Formosa belonged to the Chinese and was outside of the agreement. The stalemate led the Chinese to suggest that the talks continue at the foreign minister level, but Dulles refused, feeling this to be an implicit recognition of the People's Republic of China.

While the talks were going on, the hostilities in the strait had quieted and the immediate danger had passed. The talks had led to no firm agreements, but then no war had broken out either.

·   ·   ·

The friendship that Knowland and Lyndon Johnson shared would show its best side after July 2, 1955, when Johnson suffered a heart attack and was hospitalized at Bethesda Naval Hospital in Bethesda, Maryland. "I sent word to Senator Johnson as soon as I could that he need have no concern about any advantage being taken of his absence," Knowland said. "But I did no more really for Johnson than I would have expected he would have done for me had the situation been reversed."[12]

In a July 12 letter to the Senate majority leader, Knowland wrote that Johnson's stand-in, Senator Earle Clements of Kentucky, was doing a fine job and that he was pleased that Johnson's health was improving. "As your 'older' or is it 'younger' brother, I want to give a little gratuitous advice which I probably wouldn't take myself. Remember that the most important thing . . . is to give first priority to the complete restoration of your health. When one has been as active as you have, it is difficult not to get restless and worry about things which should or should not be done. Avoid doing this." Knowland then proceeded to fill Johnson in on legislative action and noted that he was going to meet with Clements to discuss bills before the Senate.

On September 27, Johnson wrote Knowland that his friendship had sustained him during his recovery. "I will never forget the long letters that kept me informed of what was going on in the Senate," Johnson said. "I will never forget the generosity with which you gave of your time and your abilities to finish the work we had started together. I will never forget your visits and how much they lifted my spirits. I could not thank you adequately at the time, but I want to say now that I have never known a man whose integrity I respected more or whose friendship I cherished to any greater degree. In the Senate we may sit on opposite sides of the aisle but in personal affection there will never be any dividing line."[13]

.   .   .

The political campaign began heating up in early 1955, primarily because Eisenhower was hinting that he might not run for office again. In fact, as early as mid-1954 he was considering ending his presidency after one term. In a letter to his brother Milton, the president wrote, "if ever . . . I should show any signs of yielding . . . please call in the psychiatrist—or even better the sheriff."[14]

Several prominent Republicans were suggesting that Eisenhower should be drafted to run in 1956, but Bill Knowland was not one of them. He told a panel of newspapermen that he had never believed in the doctrine of the indispensable man and that the party should not have a reluctant candidate. When pressured about whether he would be a candidate, Knowland said that he would decide only after Eisenhower declared he would not run. But Knowland disagreed with the conventional wisdom that Eisenhower was the only Republican candidate who could win in 1956. "I think the Republican nominee at the next convention will be elected," he said.[15]

Nevertheless, a poll taken on February 13, 1955, pitting Richard Nixon against Adlai Stevenson showed Stevenson favored by 61 percent to Nixon's 39 percent. An April poll had Earl Warren in a dead heat with Stevenson. On May 13 Knowland polled 40 percent of the vote against Stevenson's 60 percent. Even against Senator Estes Kefauver, Nixon was favored by only 41 percent of those polled; Kefauver, by 58 percent. The polls were a bad sign for any Republican other than Eisenhower. Nixon himself indicated that Ike was the only Republican who could win.

Pundits were suggesting that Earl Warren would seek the presidency one more time if Eisenhower were to back out. So persistent was the talk that Warren was forced to issue a statement expressing his embarrassment and trying to put an end to it. In mid-June, *New York Times* writer James Reston was speculating that Knowland had his eye on the vice presidential nomination. That, of course, would mean ousting Richard Nixon. Eisenhower, by selecting Knowland as his running mate, would remove him from his seat in the Senate to a job that a former vice president, John Nance Garner, had described as not worth a spittoon of warm spit.

Reston reported that Knowland and Goodwin Knight were forming a California coalition to take Nixon out of play at the Republican National Convention; the plan was to send Knight to the convention holding California's 70 delegates. "Mr. Knowland's supporters hope that Mr. Knight will not agree to cast the state's delegation for Mr. Nixon in the vice presidential balloting. They also hope they will be able to persuade the president that he should not insist on Mr. Nixon as his running mate if Mr. Nixon cannot even get the support of his own state delegation."[16] But the Knight/Knowland coalition was never formed, and the *Sacramento Bee*'s Washington correspondent, Gladstone Williams, discounted that scenario: according to him, Knowland really was looking to the presidency if Eisenhower decided against running.[17]

On September 24, Eisenhower suffered a heart attack—a coronary thrombosis that totally incapacitated him for several days and kept him hospitalized for almost two months. Nixon's name, of course, came up as a candidate to replace the sixty-four-year-old Eisenhower, but Knowland scoffed at the idea. "I do not consider a Pepsodent smile, a ready quip and an actor's perfection with lines, nor an ability to avoid issues, as qualifications for high office."[18] It was one of the few times that Knowland spoke publicly in a derogatory manner about Nixon.

Governor Knight's animosity toward Nixon can be traced back to 1950, when Nixon put up a candidate to oppose Knight's bid for reelection as lieutenant governor. After winning that race, he moved up to governor when Warren was appointed chief justice. Their relationship continued to sour, and on October 5, 1955, Knight said that if Eisenhower chose not to run again he would head up the California delegation to the Republican National Convention as a favorite-son candidate, even if it meant confronting Nixon directly. "The Republicans of California will want to be represented by a completely independent delegation devoted to the Republican Party and not to the ambitions of any one man," he declared.[19] The California governor said he would go ahead with his favorite-son slate regardless of what Nixon did, stressing that he was for Eisenhower "first and foremost" and that he would head the delegation to support the president if he chose to run again. Few sophisticated followers of politics in California were fooled. Favorite-son candidates almost always have their hearts set on the White House, hoping that somehow their long-shot run will succeed.

Knowland disputed Knight's position, saying that the Republican voters in California would determine whom the delegates would support. Representative Carl Hinshaw, chairman of the state's Republican delegation in the House of Representatives and a Nixon supporter, also jumped on Knight, who, he said, was seeking to position himself as a presidential candidate: "Except in the ambitious dreams of Mr. Knight, he is something of a joke in national politics and it will prove most unfortunate for the Republican Party of California and in the nation if this unseemly and almost indecent haste to exploit the unfortunate illness of President Eisenhower should result in creating a false impression of his real standing."

Knight responded sharply to the criticism. "Although I have been endorsed and supported by organized labor, still both in public and private utterances, I have made it clear I have the word 'Republican' blazoned across my chest. I have done nothing inimical to the Republican Party or the Republican platform. From 1932 to 1952 we were affected with creeping paralysis and couldn't talk to anyone but fellow Republicans. Let's not lose the contact we now enjoy."[20] But not long after, Knight said he doubted whether either Nixon or Knowland could be elected president.

While Nixon and Knight were sparring, Knowland was keeping out of the fight, even though he was thought to have joined Knight's camp in a "stop Nixon" effort. Knowland was urging that presidential aspirants proceed cautiously until it was determined whether Eisenhower was going to run again. Although Nixon was organizing his troops, Knowland was sitting quietly in the background in California. After all, there was plenty of time; the primary in California wasn't until June.

William L. Roper wrote for *Frontier* magazine that California could "become the battleground of one of the bitterest pre-primary fights in the history of the Grand Old Party. Even if does not commit suicide, it will never be the same."[21] (During the 1958 gubernatorial campaign, Roper would become Knowland's publicity director in Southern California.) After New York, California would have the largest bloc of delegates at the Republican convention and Knight, Knowland, and Nixon each wanted that bloc. There were proposals for a coalition delegation with votes split among Nixon, Knowland, and Knight. Knight dismissed them, saying that "bloc delegations are stupid, dangerous and inevitably disastrous."[22] But when Eisenhower decided to run again that's just what happened, with California's three most important political leaders sharing the delegation.

Knowland later recalled that there were serious doubts whether Eisenhower could or should run for president again because of his heart attack. Immediately the name of Eisenhower's brother Milton came up as a possible candidate to replace him. Knowland rejected the idea, saying there should be no "heir apparent" and that the president should do nothing to influence the choice of his successor; Knowland knew, of course, that Eisenhower would never choose him. "I don't think I need to point out . . . that this was greeted with something less than enthusiasm by not only what might be termed the Taft wing of the party, but by most of the people who had supported Eisenhower," Knowland said. "Had this happened, I think there would have been a major confrontation in the Republican Party, because they were not prepared to accept Milton Eisenhower in place of Dwight Eisenhower."[23] Members of Congress, cabinet officers, and other friends wanted to know before the 1956 primaries whether Milton was going to be substituted for the president. They didn't want the president coming into the Republican National Convention in August making known at the last minute his desire for his brother to succeed him.[24]

Eisenhower also was considering Tom Dewey as a possible replacement. "You know, boys," Eisenhower told Sherman Adams, Jim Hagerty, and others, "Tom Dewey has matured over the last few years and he might not be a bad presidential candidate. He certainly has the ability and if I'm not going to be in the picture, he represents my way of thinking." Hagerty and Adams were shocked. Hagerty said the president was asking for a revolt of the right wing of the party if Dewey were put forward again. They might even nominate Knowland, Adams protested. "I guess you're right," Eisenhower said and dropped the idea.[25]

It didn't matter, because Knowland had his own plans. He would be a "provisional" candidate for president. He would not run against Eisenhower, but if the president wasn't going to seek a second term, Knowland wanted to know as soon as possible so he could put his campaign into gear. He made it known that he would be "available" in case Eisenhower bowed out. Knowland already was planning to enter the California campaign in hopes of landing its 70 delegates, regardless of what Nixon or Knight might do. Knight still wanted to go to the convention as a favorite-son candidate, a position that would give him political leverage at the convention. In a three-way race, according to the political prognosticators, Nixon would win, but if Knight were to throw his weight to Knowland then Knowland would carry the delegation. No one saw Knight as having a chance of winning.

Toward the end of the year, Knowland had given four major speeches, in Boston, New York, Cleveland, and Peoria, Illinois. And he had scheduled at least thirty speeches outside of Washington in the months ahead. The *Sacramento Bee* editorialized, "It would be unreasonable to suppose he would be laying the foundation he is without some conviction [that Eisenhower wouldn't run again]. He may be right."[26]

On December 12, Hagerty asked Eisenhower if he was planning on running again in 1956. "Jim," Ike told his press secretary, "you've always known that I didn't particularly want to be President, and that I had always thought that while I was in the White House the Republicans would have an opportunity to build up men who could take my place and who could successfully keep out of that office the crackpot Democrats who were seeking it. I don't want to run again, but I am not so sure I will not do it. We have developed no one on our side within our political ranks who can be elected or run this country. I am talking about the strictly political men like Knowland. He would be impossible and so in answer to your question, I don't want to but I may have to."[27]

Eisenhower was worried that Knowland couldn't beat men like Adlai Stevenson, Estes Kefauver, and Averill Harriman. "I can't see Knowland from nothing. . . . Actually I can't see anyone in the Senate who impresses me at all on both sides of the aisle."[28] The president's dismissive statement reveals his remarkable distance from the upper house, which would in fact produce every presidential nominee for both parties for the next four elections.

The men closest to Eisenhower didn't like Knowland much either. They devised a scheme that Knowland resentfully called "a squeeze play." The plan was to get Eisenhower to withhold any announcement of his intentions until late March to keep Knowland and any other presidential hopeful from entering the early Republican primaries. Then if Eisenhower decided against running, the plan went, he could announce his chosen successor just before the convention opened. Knowland had other plans. He gave Eisenhower an ultimatum: if the president didn't announce by January 31, he was going to enter the primaries anyway. But one Eisenhower aide remarked, "Knowland can't alter our plans. He's the only man trying to force an early announcement, and one person can't make much of a stir. If you think about it a moment, you realize that it's almost miraculous that no one else in the party is insisting on an early announcement. No matter what he does, there will be no change in our present plans."[29]

On another front, an anonymous group was circulating posters seeking support for Knowland if Eisenhower decided against another term. Copies of the posters can be found among Nixon's papers in the National Archives, indicating the extent of his interest in his rivals. The poster was explicit that the efforts on Knowland's behalf were only to be made in the event Eisenhower decided against running again, and it was printed by the "Knowland for President . . . If . . . Committee." It listed no names—only a Glendale, California, address for anyone interested in receiving more copies of the poster: "Please do not attach any special importance to the personnel of this committee, or to the headquarters. We are busy people who will have no time for interviews. That is why we are using only a post office box." But the writers claimed, "If we do not take such steps, it is very possible that the next President of the United States will be named in a smoke-filled room occupied by an amazingly small number of people operating under the direction of political strategists whose choice for President would be very unsatisfactory to the Knowland-Taft-MacArthur elements."

Those who devised the poster said that Knowland knew nothing of the group's efforts. "If we had gone to him first, he would very likely have opposed it on the grounds that it might embarrass his position in the party. We believe that the situation is so fraught with danger in the light of the world crisis that a 'Draft Knowland' Movement should rise above even its own personal desires, to the end that the Republican Party be saved from the menace of appeasement, New Dealism, U.N. tyranny and a score of other threatening potentials that might mature if a last-minute decision had to be made by a handful of men who literally hate such statesmen as Knowland, Bricker, MacArthur, McCarthy, Jenner, Welker and their compatriots."[30]

Knowland was endearing himself to the growing conservative movement across the United States. The archconservative William Buckley Jr. began to publish a new magazine, the *National Review*, and Knowland wrote an article for its first issue on November 14, 1955. He warned against Soviet disarmament proposals and called for the Republicans to return to the 1952 platform pledge to seek the freedom of people enslaved by Communist dictators. Another article in the issue reported that "right wing organizations are trying to interest conservatives in the possibility of a coalition campaign for the presidency to start that fall. Senator Knowland, according to the plan, would act as the titular standard bearer on the understanding that the coalition's final selection will not be made until the convention. Knowland's immediate task will be to capture the all-important California primary, to enter the Oregon primary, and perhaps, Minnesota's."

The Knowlands: young Bill
(center) with, from left, J.R.
(father), Eleanor (sister),
Emelyn (stepmother), and
Russ (brother)

William F. Knowland in 1926

William F. and Helen
Knowland on a visit to
Washington, D.C., in 1936

Above
From left: Congressman Ralph Elste, William F. Knowland, Earl Warren, and Wendell Willkie in Oakland in 1940

Left
Major William F. Knowland in Paris in 1945

Right
The Knowlands during the Senate years: William F. (center) with, from left, Joseph (son), Emelyn (daughter), Helen (wife), and Estelle (daughter)

Below
From left: Senate Minority Leader William F. Knowland, House Speaker Sam Rayburn, Senate Majority Leader Lyndon B. Johnson, and House Minority Leader Joe Martin in 1957

Top
President Dwight D.
Eisenhower and Senator
William F. Knowland
(Courtesy United Press
International)

Above
Helen and William F.
Knowland reading early
results in 1958 gubernatorial
race (Photo: Lonnie Wilson)

Opposite (top)
Gubernatorial contenders
Pat Brown (left) and
William F. Knowland (right)
watch Lawrence Spivak toss
a coin to decide who will
be interviewed first on 1958
TV program (Courtesy
Los Angeles Times)

Opposite (bottom)
From left: Chiang Kai-shek
and Madame Chiang with
William F. Knowland in
Formosa in 1963 (Photo:
Wu Chung Yee)

Left
William F. Knowland amid
California delegates at 1964
Republican National
Convention in San Francisco
(Photo: Lonnie Wilson)

William F. Knowland at play
with one of his two St.
Bernards

William F. and Ann Knowland
on their honeymoon in 1972
(Courtesy Associated Press)

20

Stepping Aside

The Republican Party would be affected by two critical decisions in 1956: whether Eisenhower would run again and, if he did, whether Richard Nixon would again be his running mate.

On January 10, Knowland again announced that the Republican Party did not want a reluctant presidential candidate in 1956 and said he would not join a "draft Eisenhower movement." Reacting to Knowland's statement, Eisenhower wrote in his diary, "In his case, there seems to be no final answer to the question, 'How stupid can you get?' Why he has to talk about such things I wouldn't know unless he's determined to destroy the Republican Party."[1]

At home in California, Knowland's father was busy helping his son's campaign. J.R. wrote on January 27, 1956, that he had met with Governor Goodwin Knight and Clem Whitaker of the campaign consulting firm of Whitaker and Baxter. They said they wanted to avoid a fight in California that would put the senator, Vice President Nixon, and Knight on the June presidential primary ballot. If that happened, they told Knowland, "there would be a grave danger of Nixon winning out," primarily because Eisenhower would support him. "Frankly I have no trust in Nixon regardless of what he may say," J.R. Knowland observed. "When a man double crosses you twice and you give him a third chance we should have our heads examined. . . . I am satisfied that you can never expect a particle of help from him. He is not built that way. He will be for Nixon first, last and all the time."

When J.R. told Knight and Whitaker that the president's reluctance to declare his intentions was fouling up everyone's plans, "They both agreed that probably what was happening was that the immediate followers of the president in Washington were using every possible force to get him to delay. Of course, that delay would give them more chance to tie up the convention, which unquestionably is their aim." Knight was trying to strike a deal with the Knowlands to share the 70-member delegation to the Republican National Convention and cut Nixon out.

J.R. went on to offer his son a bit of advice: "Of course, if you lose out at the primary you are not even a delegate at the convention. It would be a tremendous humiliation, in my judgment. I guess the governor figures it would be the same for him." Knight wanted to meet with the senator sometime in early February, he reported, but not in Washington; "I really feel that you should talk with him, regardless of how you may feel, as he made the advances." The elder Knowland pointed out in his letter that a fight in the California primary would be very costly—upward of $50,000—and would be a long shot for his son. A primary contest "would split the party wide open in California," he said. "Business people would have an excuse to give to neither. I think you have the best chance of winning finally, but [it's] a long shot at best."

Senator Knowland's stock among the ultraconservatives rose in early February when James L. Wick, executive publisher of *Human Events*, made public his support for the senator's presidential bid. "Don't waste precious time, energy and money seeking to change left-wingers," Wick wrote. "In the first place, it's too late for that. In the second place, conservatives are already in the majority—in your state, in almost every state." In the February 4 edition of his magazine, he predicted that Knowland would become president "if conservatives . . . will work as hard for [him] in 1956 as Ohio conservatives worked for Taft in 1950." Wick described Knowland as "not only conservative, but what is more important—he is a trustworthy conservative. Because he has integrity, he is deeply respected by virtually every member of the Senate, Democrats and Republicans alike, regardless of their political convictions." He also printed a form for readers to join a Knowland for President Club, urging them to express their preference "for a GREAT man for President of the United States" in the April 10 primary in Illinois, which Knowland had entered in response to a "spontaneous demand by Republicans everywhere in the state."[2]

It didn't hurt Knowland's chances when in late February a *New Republic* article by William S. White reported that he was "unimpeachably respectable and for the qualities of courage and candor is without doubt one of the most honored of all men in the Senate—in both parties." To those Taft men to whom he appealed, White observed, he is "a man of the highest personal integrity, a man embodying the best rather than the mediocrity or the worst of their movement, and above all, a man so placed as to protect and forward their truly fundamental design."[3]

.   .   .

When Eisenhower aide Len Hall remarked to Sherman Adams that if Ike didn't run again it would come down to Nixon or Knowland, Adams snapped back, "Neither of 'em."[4]

On February 29, 1956, Eisenhower, who had gone through a thorough battery of tests to determine his fitness for office, announced that he was healthy enough to carry the "burdens of the presidency" and would seek a second term. Then on June 8, Eisenhower was hospitalized again, this time with ileitis, a digestive disorder. He underwent successful surgery in which a small section of his intestine was removed. No sooner had the operation ended than his surgeon announced that there was no reason why the president couldn't run again; indeed, according to the doctor, Eisenhower's life expectancy had actually improved. He was hospitalized for three weeks.

At a July 10 meeting with Republican leaders Bill Knowland, House Speaker Joseph W. Martin, and others at his Gettysburg farm, Eisenhower said he thought he would stand by his decision to run for a second term, but he wanted their opinions. Knowland was the first to speak up. "Mr. President, I think you should clarify the situation as to whether you're going to be a candidate for president, and if so, the Republican leadership and the country ought to be notified so that Eisenhower delegations can be put in the field and there's no uncertainty as to your position on the matter."[5] The senator said he felt the Republican Party would be united if Eisenhower decided to run again. Eisenhower replied, "Why shouldn't I run? . . . I am in better condition today than I was then [in February when he first announced he would run]. I have had a condition that has bothered me from time to time for years and my doctors say that I am better than I have ever been."[6]

"To the surprise and delight of everyone," Knowland recalled later, "he finally said he would be a candidate." Eisenhower asked the Senate minority leader to make the announcement: "Well, Senator Knowland, why don't we clarify this today." Knowland replied, "Fine, I think that would be delightful."[7] As they left the meeting, Knowland told a gathering of the press outside the Gettysburg home about the president's decision.

The first question from the press was whether there was any discussion of Eisenhower running again. "Yes, there was," Knowland said. "The president was in excellent spirits and good humor. He discussed with the legislative leaders the situation, and stated that he felt that he was in better shape—and we believe he is—than he was when he made his announcement of a second term in February. He and we are looking forward to a vigorous and active campaign under his leadership." The senator told the reporters that he had no doubts before the meeting that Eisenhower would run again. Asked if Eisenhower had authorized him to make the announcement, he replied, "No, the president did not, but he knew we were going to talk with the press. We try to make our reports as frankly as possible." They put the question slightly differently, asking if he had told Eisenhower that he was going to report to the press, and he answered, "No, we didn't tell him that."[8]

Knowland said he believed that he was chosen to make the announcement because he was the Republican leader in the Senate and it was important not to leave the impression that Eisenhower couldn't get along with the Republican leadership. He added that he had raised the question of whether Eisenhower would be a candidate and acknowledged his own interest in running if the president had chosen not to.

Then, three days later, Eisenhower nominated Knowland to the U.S. delegation to the UN General Assembly. Given his attacks on the United Nations, Knowland's nomination was something of a surprise. Knowland's name was sent to the Senate for confirmation, along with those of former UN ambassador Henry Cabot Lodge; Senator Hubert H. Humphrey; Paul G. Hoffman, chairman of the board of the Studebaker-Packard Corporation; and Ellsworth Bunker, president of the American Red Cross. Eisenhower's press secretary, James C. Hagerty, refused to comment on correspondents' questions about whether intraparty politics had figured into Knowland's appointment, but the UN nomination was seen as an effort to bring Knowland closer to the White House by ending the long bitterness over foreign policy. As the appointment came on the heels of Knowland's making the announcement that Eisenhower was going to run again, no other conclusion could be drawn. Knowland was to serve in the UN General Assembly for nearly three years, but he never let up on his criticism of the world body.

Because of Eisenhower's delayed decision to seek reelection, it was too late to remove Knowland's name from Republican primary ballots in Illinois, Minnesota, Pennsylvania, and the territory of Alaska; but his name was pulled off the ballot in New Hampshire. Even though he was not a candidate, Knowland drew 33,534 votes in Illinois, 3,209 in Minnesota, 43,508 in Pennsylvania, and 488 in Alaska, totaling more than 80,000 votes. Ike, who was on the ballot in twelve states and Alaska, received 4.9 million. Eisenhower's health would remain an issue right up until the day before the November 7 election. Democratic nominee Adlai Stevenson said repeatedly during the campaign that "every piece of scientific evidence we have" indicated that Eisenhower couldn't survive another term.

At the same time, rumors were rampant in the press that Eisenhower was going to dump his vice president. The stories were encouraged by Minnesota governor Harold Stassen, who had his eye on the second spot. Others mentioned as possible replacements for Nixon were Tom Dewey, Henry Cabot Lodge, Christian Herter, John Foster Dulles, Milton Eisenhower—and Bill Knowland.

Eisenhower thought long and hard about who would become president after him. He wanted not Knowland but Warren—indeed, he had even thought of Warren as his successor if he had decided not to run again because of his health. But he knew Warren wouldn't give up his seat on the Court. During this time, according to Knowland's daughter Emelyn, her father told her as they were driving from San Francisco to Oakland that Eisenhower had held out the possibility of the vice presidential nomination to him. She asked him if he would accept and he said he would consider it, but he never answered the question directly.[9]

What ultimately saved Nixon's job was a pivotal act in the California delegation. When Eisenhower was undecided as to whether to run again, the delegation split into three groups, each headed by one of the three most powerful men in California—Goodwin Knight, Dick Nixon, and Bill Knowland. None of the men wanted a delegation solely in one of the other's names, so they agreed on the three-way division, with each getting 23 delegates. The final delegate—number 70—was California's junior senator, Thomas H. Kuchel, a party moderate offensive to no one.

Governor Knight refused to issue an endorsement of Nixon for vice president, explaining that the decision was up to President Eisenhower and that if that was what Ike wanted, well, Knight would go along—not exactly enthusiastic support. Indeed, Knight clearly was opposed to Nixon and indicated that he might join the movement to dump the vice president. He may even have thought he had a chance of securing the second spot for himself. On August 14, he said he was "available" for the vice presidency, though he denied he was seeking it. But Knowland had other ideas. "It was at this point that I called Vice President Nixon and told him that as far as I was concerned I intended to support him for retention," Knowland later told an interviewer.[10] Knowland's third of the delegation and Nixon's third together would control the California delegation, effectively putting an end to the efforts to oust Nixon. On August 14, 1956, as Republicans prepared to open their national convention in San Francisco, Knowland said he didn't feel that anyone should be chairman of the California delegation who was not in sympathy with the sentiments of the entire delegation and the recommendation by the Republican State Committee. A day later Knight responded, stating that he was forming the three-way delegation at the direction of the Republican State Committee. "My purpose has constantly been to maintain harmony in the Republican Party in California," Knight said. "I have said many times that I will support the president, as I and the delegates chosen by me are pledged to do. I have said I will support whomever the president and the convention select as the vice presidential nominee." He denied that he had any aspirations to replace Nixon as the vice presidential nominee or that he had authorized anyone to organize a campaign on his behalf. Knight added that while he expected to head the delegation as recommended by the state committee, he refused to be steamrollered into supporting Nixon.

When Eisenhower said at the Republican National Convention that he would retain Nixon, Knight agreed to go along, although rather unenthusiastically. "This little episode drew quite a bit of public attention in an otherwise uneventful convention," later observed *Sacramento Bee* political writer Herbert L. Phillips, "and managed once more to spotlight California's manner of political life as being incomprehensibly odd."[11]

Much more important was the nomination of Eisenhower. With the Democrats renominating Adlai Stevenson, the stage was set for a repeat of the 1952 campaign. Although Eisenhower defeated Stevenson by 9.6 million votes in November, he failed to carry congressional Republicans on his coattails. For the first time in 108 years, the party of a victorious president had not won at least one chamber of Congress. In the House, the Democrats gained two seats; in the Senate, one seat. The Democrats would be clearly in charge when the 85th Congress opened in January 1957.

One of Knowland's last grasps at the majority leadership would come in 1957. Democrats held a 49-to-47 majority, but they were uncertain how Frank Lausche of Ohio would vote. Although Lausche was a Democrat, he acted more like a Republican, and Democrats worried that he might bolt Johnson's leadership. With a 48–48 tie, Knowland could regain his majority leadership, as Vice President Nixon would cast the tiebreaker. Lausche made no reply on the first roll call on whether Knowland should get the job. But on the second vote, Lausche bellowed out a "no" and Johnson was elected majority leader.[12]

Knowland would remain minority leader. At forty-nine, he was still young compared to his colleagues: 75 of the 96 senators were older than he.

21

The Suez Crisis

New world crises were erupting while the Republicans and Democrats were involved in their election year battles.

In early 1956, Knowland was a leader in a congressional effort to block a U.S. loan to help Egypt build the Aswan Dam on the Nile River. The dam was thought to be a crown jewel for Egypt's new leader, Gamal Abdel Nasser, and Israel was worried that a loan would mean that the United States was leaning toward Egypt and away from Israel. Knowland warned Secretary of State John Foster Dulles that Congress was against the loan and that the administration should "proceed at its peril." Dulles told Knowland he was "pretty sure we are not going ahead."[1] On July 19, President Eisenhower did indeed announce that the United States would not be participating in the dam project.

A week later, Egypt reacted by seizing the British-held Suez Canal and denouncing the Western powers. Nasser justified these actions as a response to the U.S. decision to pull out of the Aswan project, announcing that he planned to build the dam from revenues earned from the canal. Despite summer-long negotiations, Egypt rejected efforts to halt nationalization of the canal.

On September 8, Knowland met with Dulles and "expressed very strongly" that the country was not prepared to back the British and French in military action to take back the canal. Britain, he said, was an undependable ally. He said he hoped the British wouldn't start a war "which needs our help. I don't think public opinion would be ready to support that."[2] Knowland believed that the United Nations should step in and use its influence against armed aggression, and Dulles said that he had refused to assure the British and French that the United States would oppose a UN resolution calling for renunciation of force. That was the right thing to do, Knowland told Dulles.[3]

There were serious foreign policy concerns elsewhere in the world. In Europe, on October 23, 1956, the Hungarians revolted against Soviet domination of their affairs, but resistance was soon crushed by Soviet troops and tanks that rolled through their cities. No Western power rallied to Hungary's cause.

Less than a week later, Israel, whose ships had been denied passage through the Suez Canal since 1950, launched an invasion of Egypt, aided by the British and the French. The world once again was brought to the brink of war when the Soviet Union threatened to intervene with atomic weapons if the British and the French didn't pull out. Knowland, shocked by the British action, rushed to the White House to tell Eisenhower not to let the British "drag us into another one of their wars." Ike exclaimed later to one of his aides, Emmet Hughes, "If that isn't the silliest damn kind of talk."[4]

The United Nations, led by the United States, condemned the British, French, and Israelis, and a cease-fire was declared on November 7, 1956, the day after Eisenhower's reelection. The British and the French quickly withdrew their troops, but the Israelis remained in the Sinai Peninsula. That became a sore spot with the Eisenhower administration.

The new year of 1957 opened with the president introducing the Eisenhower Doctrine, a policy he would ask Congress to approve that would give him the power to protect the security of Middle East nations against communist aggression. Eisenhower had revealed the doctrine on New Year's Eve and met with congressional leaders the next day to discuss it. The proposal had gotten into the newspapers before Knowland was told about it; once again, the failure to inform him raised his ire. Eisenhower wanted the doctrine to be the first order of business when Congress convened. Indeed, he felt so strongly about the need for the doctrine that he made a special appearance before a joint session of Congress on January 5, 1957, to urge its passage. "If the nations of [the Middle East] should lose their independence," Eisenhower said, "if they were dominated by alien forces hostile to freedom, that would be a tragedy for the area. . . . Western Europe would be endangered just as though there had been no Marshall Plan, no North Atlantic Treaty Organization. The free nations of Asia and Africa, too, would be placed in serious jeopardy. All this would have the most adverse, if not disastrous, effect upon our own nation."[5] The doctrine called for use of U.S. troops in the Middle East if the countries attacked by Soviet forces requested help. Eisenhower also asked for approval of $100 million in economic aid in the Middle East.

Knowland's reaction was predictable. He would support a policy that would prevent Soviet aggression, so long as the details were worked out in Congress. The doctrine wound up passing in the Senate by a 72–19 vote.

John Foster Dulles noted that Israel was holding out. The Israelis wanted concessions from the Egyptians, including UN police occupation of the disputed Gaza Strip and free passage of ships through the Tiran Strait, which would give Israel access to the Red Sea and the Indian Ocean. Though Dulles did not disagree with Israel's position, he said that he could not support any concessions that were made at gunpoint. He urged Israel to pull back, allowing the United States to try to get the concessions through negotiations, but the Israelis refused.

Dulles then floated the idea of UN sanctions against Israel. It may have been no more than a feint, but Knowland would have none of it and he wasted little time making his views known. He telephoned Jack Bell, the Associated Press reporter in the press gallery. "Jack," he said, "if you want to come down to my office, I'd like to give you a statement I think you might be interested in." He wasn't waiting to find out what Eisenhower thought he should do or say: this proposed sanction had to be squelched right away. When Bell showed up in Knowland's office, the senator handed him the statement written in pencil. It called even the slightest consideration of sanctions immoral. Although Dulles contended he was bluffing, Knowland felt that even to intimate any such action was uncalled for, especially in light of the U.S. failure to do anything about the Soviet massacre of Hungarians.[6] Knowland received widespread coverage and reaction from around the world when his statement was carried by the Associated Press.

The senator followed up by saying he would resign as a delegate to the United Nations if sanctions were imposed on Israel. He had called Dulles on February 1, 1957, to plead Israel's case against sanctions. But Dulles replied, "If we cannot get the Israelis out of Egypt the Russians will get them out and in the process we will lose the whole of the Middle East. I don't see how we can have any influence with the Arab countries if we cannot get the Israelis out of Egypt. We have tried everything short of sanctions." Told that the president was endorsing the sanctions, Knowland warned, "I've gone along as far as I can and this will mean the parting of the ways."

"I think you should study this," Dulles said. "We can't have all our policies made in Jerusalem." Knowland replied, "I agree, but sanctions are pretty serious. I would like to know the timing. I want to send in my resignation [as a UN delegate] before the delegation votes on sanctions."

On the Senate floor on February 6, Knowland showed his obstreperous temper by becoming the first politician of national standing to lash out against the unfairness of the United States threatening sanctions against Israel while having done little about the Soviet Union's treatment of Hungary. Knowland drew on his sense of right and wrong to point out once more the incongruities of the Eisenhower administration's foreign policy. He said that to punish Israel while "sidestepping the larger aggression" of the Soviet Union would be "immoral and insupportable," a sign of a double standard.[7] His critics would argue in response that the standards were the same; but as a practical matter, they just couldn't be enforced against the Soviet Union.

On February 11, 1957, Knowland launched an attack on the United Nations that was widely interpreted by political reporters as the opening salvo in his 1960 campaign for the presidency. He told an audience at Georgetown University in Washington, D.C., that the United Nations had five defects in how it functioned: the abuse of veto power by the Soviet Union, a growing double standard of international morality, the increasing trend to bloc voting, an expanding tendency to interfere in the internal affairs of member nations, and the unwillingness of many of the eighty members to share the costs and other obligations of the United Nations.

Knowland complained that since the United Nations' inception, the Soviet Union had recorded seventy-nine vetoes in the Security Council while the United States had exercised none: "Unless the Soviet Union can be expelled from membership in the meantime, that Godless communist totalitarian dictatorship holds a veto in perpetuity on any charter amendment." He feared that if bloc voting continued, "preconceived viewpoints may act to prevent the United Nations from functioning on the facts presented."

Knowland pointed out that the United States paid nearly a third of the costs of UN operations. "It is going to be very difficult to expect the nations which are bearing the heavy burden of costs to continue to assume that burden if smaller nations under the sovereign equality section of the charter continue to insist on the voting of obligations without a willingness to assume their full share of the burdens." He also noted that in Korea the United States supplied more than 90 percent of the resources "used to gain the stalemated armistice. . . . Never before in all of our history have our field commanders been so handicapped or our men asked to die in a war they were not permitted to win."

The senator called for a reappraisal of the United Nations. "It is unfortunate for that organization that some of its friends oversold it to the people of the United States," he said. "Perhaps, because of that, we expected more than it was able to accomplish." In particular, he cited the example of the General Assembly's passing ten resolutions between October 27 and January 10 opposing Soviet repression in Hungary. "Nations can die while delegates talk," Knowland said. The United States should make it clear that American foreign policy "should not be tied as a tail to a United Nations kite." Based on the United Nation's record, he argued, "no nation, including our own, dare risk its security on the United Nations' ability to function effectively."[8]

In an unsigned memorandum prepared on February 14, 1957, for Majority Leader Lyndon Johnson by his staff, Knowland was accused of himself holding contradictory positions, at the same time wanting to restrict the veto power of the Security Council and criticizing the United Nations for invading the internal affairs of member nations. Regardless of whether his points were valid, the authors noted, the speech put Knowland "on a course which is bound to bring about increasing collisions with the administration." As they pointed out, "He is criticizing the United Nations for 'defects' which cannot be changed at the present time under any circumstances. Since they cannot be changed, he is bound to become more and more critical and more insistent that either the Soviet Union get out or we get out. It is inconceivable that this or any other administration would take the United States out of the United Nations or act to expel the Soviet Union from the United Nations. In other words, there is no middle group upon which both Senator Knowland and the Administration can stand." To a Democrat, this was not necessarily bad news, as the memo concluded: "Since Senator Knowland is a strong personality who is not likely to retreat from any position he believes is right, and since the Administration cannot retreat, the results should be interesting."[9]

In an interview in 1970, Knowland said, "I am sure that the State Department was a little unhappy about the statement. . . . I think it is maybe one of the few instances where a statement by a senator caused them to take a second look at the situation. I pointed out in a Senate speech and in a statement which I made that to impose sanctions on a small country, when they had lacked the courage to impose it on the Soviet Union for what was perhaps even a worse situation, was morally wrong, and what was morally wrong could never be politically right."[10]

On February 20, in a meeting with Johnson, Knowland, and about fifteen other congressional leaders, Eisenhower explained why he was considering UN sanctions against Israel. He believed that Egypt would allow no oil shipments through the Suez Canal unless Israel gave up its war gains. In addition, he said, the Arabs might seek Soviet aid. "And then the whole thing might end up in a general war," Eisenhower said.

According to Ike's chief of staff, Sherman Adams, Johnson's expression indicated that he was not going to budge in his opposition to the sanctions and Knowland "was wearing his classical toga of lofty defiance."[11] They argued again that Dulles was applying a double standard. "Nobody likes to impose sanctions," Eisenhower answered, "but how else can we induce Israel to withdraw to the line agreed on in the 1949 armistice? The Arabs refuse to discuss a permanent settlement until that move is made." Johnson told Eisenhower that he and Knowland agreed on their opposition to sanctions. "After all, there are times when Congress has to express its own views," Johnson said. "I certainly have no objection to that," Eisenhower replied. "Thank you," Johnson responded with a wry smile.

Knowland said if sanctions were not imposed, some other alternative had to be found to force the Israelis to leave the occupied territory. He suggested that a neutral zone be established between Israel and Egypt, but Henry Cabot Lodge pointed out that a similar solution had been before the United Nations three weeks earlier and had found no support. Finally, Knowland agreed that the United States could not avoid voting to sanction Israel, but only if sanctions were also applied to the Soviet Union. "How much support could be found for applying sanctions against Russia for its failure to comply with the UN resolution on Hungary?" Knowland asked. "The UN will never vote for sanctions against either Russia or the United States," Lodge replied.

When Johnson and Knowland left the meeting, Johnson told reporters, "Our views have not been changed."[12]

As it turned out, the threat of sanctions was enough to pressure Israel to withdraw. Nine days after Eisenhower had announced his willingness to take the issue to the United Nations, Prime Minister Golda Meir said that all Israeli troops would be withdrawn from the Gaza Strip. In the end, Nasser built his Aswan Dam with a $554 million loan from the Soviet Union. It also took the work of 35,000 Egyptian laborers and 2,000 Russian technicians. Nasser died in 1970, just a year before the massive dam was dedicated.

.   .   .

In late summer of 1957, Knowland led the fight to strike $4 billion from the administration's budget request and Eisenhower was clearly annoyed. During a press conference, he was asked if he intended to punish Republicans who did not support his spending plan. He answered by equivocating, "I don't think it is the function of a president of the United States to punish anybody for voting for what he believes." And, he said, referring to a possible change in leadership, the Senate's organization "is a matter for Senate decision."[13] But on August 29, when Eisenhower and Knowland had another of their frequent breakfast meetings, they discussed Republicanism and agreed that despite newspaper columnists' attempts to create a schism between conservative and liberal Republicans, they were in accord in much of their thinking.[14]

The next day, Eisenhower wrote to Republican National Chairman Meade Alcorn that Knowland stood among the first four or five senators who had supported measures the president had proposed. "With one or two exceptions over the five-year period, his differing vote has been based upon some detail or technical feature," Eisenhower said. "We have, at times, differed on applicable policy in foreign affairs—but in important administrative projects he has led the fights for approval." Eisenhower called the charge that he and Knowland were at opposite ends of the political spectrum a "gross exaggeration." The president undoubtedly was reacting to the Democrats who had slashed his budget, gutted his foreign aid, and played politics with civil rights. While not exactly putting himself in Knowland's camp, he told Alcorn, "He and I [agree] that we are conservatives."[15]

Later, Eisenhower was asked by a reporter if he planned to support those in Congress up for reelection during 1958 who opposed him on budget matters as strongly as those who did not. Knowland undoubtedly took note of the response. "I hope," Eisenhower said, "I am never accused of being so namby-pamby that I don't have degrees of enthusiasm about people who stand for me and who stand against me. I most earnestly believe that the Congress and the White House should be occupied and controlled by the same party, for the reason that you can then fix responsibility. . . . When it comes down to who I am for enthusiastically and who I am for because he is a Republican, there is a very wide difference."[16] (Knowland surely would remember that statement in 1958, when Eisenhower half-heartedly campaigned for him.)

To Alcorn, Eisenhower urged that the party should "hammer away continuously on the subject of unity." That unity, he said, should be based on a few common doctrines such as opposition to the trend of "increasing dependence of every citizen upon the Federal government," the equality of all citizens, and the practice of sound fiscal policies. The president called the policies "essentially conservative principles applied to 20th century conditions." With such a policy, he believed, "there are a thousand details and technicalities on which we can disagree and still not destroy the essential unity of the Republican Party."[17]

On that same day that Eisenhower was defending him, Knowland was meeting with Secretary of State Dulles concerning the possibilities of hostilities in the Middle East. As Dulles saw it, the situation was dangerous: the Soviets were trying to extend their orbit to Syria and then on to Jordan. And with Egypt on the other side, Israel would be surrounded by aggressive enemies. Dulles told Knowland that the United States "had to be ready, if necessary, to provide assurance against direct Soviet military intervention, assuming this was requested by our allies or under the Eisenhower Doctrine." While the possibility of hostilities was not so imminent as to justify any general discussion with Congress, Dulles "did not want [him] to go away without knowing that such a possibility, even though remote, did exist."

Knowland replied that he thought the American people would have been more willing to back action in Hungary than in the Middle East. But Dulles pointed out that "it was one thing to use United States military force to drive the Soviets out of a position where they were and another to interpose United States force between the Soviet Union and some new area which they might be intent upon attacking. The first would surely mean general war; the second probably not."[18]

. . .

On January 30, 1957, an incident in Japan centering on an American soldier drove another wedge between Knowland and Eisenhower.

Specialist 3rd Class William S. Girard of Ottawa, Illinois, accidentally killed a Japanese woman who was looking for brass casings on a firing range seventy-five miles north of Tokyo. Because Girard was not on official duty at the time, he was turned over to Japanese authorities for prosecution under the Status of Forces Treaty agreed to with nations where U.S. troops were stationed. That touched off a storm of protest in Congress; Knowland was among those arguing most adamantly that the United States should have jurisdiction over its soldiers on foreign soil. In the House, Representative Frank Bow of Ohio introduced a resolution calling for an end to the Status of Forces Treaty.

On investigating the workings of the treaty, Eisenhower found that in 14,000 other cases U.S. soldiers had been treated fairly by the Japanese having jurisdiction over them. He decided that the United States shouldn't go back on its word to its allies because of one such incident, and thus he said he had no choice but to fight the Bow resolution. But Knowland believed that turning the serviceman over to the Japanese violated the serviceman's basic rights and the rights of all other American soldiers stationed overseas.

On May 28, Knowland met with Dulles, who told him that the United States "had no practical alternative to allowing the Japanese to go ahead and exercise jurisdiction in the Girard case. I pointed out that this had already been agreed to and I saw no practical way of retracing our steps without throwing doubt upon the value of our agreements and raising a storm which might sweep us out of all the Western Pacific." While Knowland remarked that this would be "tough," he did not indicate approval or disapproval.[19]

On July 9 at a meeting in the White House, Eisenhower, who had originally helped draft the agreement, tried to explain its importance to Knowland. But the senator would not be persuaded. In what Eisenhower aide Sherman Adams called a "most angry scene," Knowland exploded. He demanded that Eisenhower issue an executive order ensuring an American trial for any American soldier accused of a crime on a military post or on military duty in any foreign country. He pounded the table and roared, "A young man drafted in peacetime, sent overseas against his will, assigned to a duty—by God, I don't think he ought to be turned over for trial. He's wearing the uniform of our country. I wouldn't want my son to be treated that way. We're being derelict toward them."[20]

Eisenhower assured Knowland that before Girard was turned over to the Japanese, the authorities promised the United States a light sentence if he were convicted. He was worried that passage of the Bow resolution could mean that a foreign country might refuse to allow American servicemen into their countries, because they would be in effect exempt from that nation's laws. Eisenhower told Knowland that he would not yield in his opposition to the Bow resolution. "If the Republicans desert me on this issue, I'll be more disappointed than I have been about anything that has happened to me since I've been in office." He said the amendment would threaten U.S. security, alienate its friends, and "give aid and comfort to those who want to destroy our way of life."[21]

The Democrats also were pushing for passage of the bill to embarrass the Republicans. That, coupled with the president's plea, led the Republicans to back off. Knowland's ire cooled somewhat when he learned that Girard, after being found guilty, received a suspended three-year sentence. The Bow resolution quietly died.

Such run-ins with the president were leading several columnists to call for Knowland's resignation as Republican minority leader. But Eisenhower publicly remained aloof and refused to be involved in any question of party leadership. "It has never even crossed my mind to ask the resignation of anybody," he said, "because they are not direct subordinates of mine." He agreed that Knowland had differed with him "on some very important points and I think some of them are critical and they represent real differences, but it does not mean that he is my enemy; it means that he has got some very strong convictions on the other side of the fence."

The president rejected going behind the backs of congressional leaders and said he would talk directly to them in his "quiet conversational way." "I am not one of the desk-pounding type that likes to stick out his jaw and look like he is bossing the show," Eisenhower said. "I would far rather get behind, and recognizing the frailties and requirements of human nature, I would rather try to persuade a man to go along, because once I have persuaded him, he will stick. If I scare him, he will stay just as long as he is scared and then he is gone."[22]

. . .

On October 4, 1957, the Soviet Union launched *Sputnik*, the satellite that sent shock waves around the world. Knowland went to Eisenhower, telling him that it was psychologically necessary to work quickly on a "lunar probe." But Ike said he was not interested in any glamour projects, especially reaching the moon. "We have no enemies on the moon," he said.[23]

Years later, Knowland recalled that there was a feeling of disbelief in both the House and the Senate that the Soviets could put a satellite in space while the United States had no similar capabilities. The senator disagreed with Sherman Adams, Eisenhower's chief of staff, who at the time downplayed the Soviet accomplishment. Knowland himself was not surprised by *Sputnik*, because he had sat on the Joint Atomic Committee for thirteen and a half years and he knew that the Soviets had the capability. But he suggested that the United States could have been first and should have been first, "for psychological reasons if not for any other reason."[24]

At a White House meeting of Republican leaders in February 1958, Knowland reiterated his plea to put up some kind of a rocket. "If we are anywhere near it, we ought to push it."[25] But again Eisenhower rejected his pleas, saying that the country should not make an all-out push without knowing the costs.

22

Civil Rights

At a time when Knowland was considering a future run
for president and dealing with the crisis in the Middle East, he was also
at the forefront of the first civil rights legislation to pass the Senate since
1875. Although he initially opposed any such legislation, in deference to
President Eisenhower he agreed to support the bill, which ultimately
became a watered-down version of what the president had originally
sought. By the time the legislation was enacted into law, Knowland had
come around to believing that perhaps passage of a civil rights bill was
the right thing to do—and also that it might help him in the race for the
governor's seat, given California's high number of black voters.

The civil rights bill originated three days after Christmas 1955, when
Attorney General Herbert Brownell told the Justice Department to
draw up general civil rights legislation, but to make it a bill that would
only be acted on well after Eisenhower's reelection. The proposed bill
reached the White House in mid-March 1956, but Eisenhower was not
willing to send it on to Congress. Although this was legislation that the
president favored, Knowland's strong opposition led him to withhold it
at first. Knowland had read about the bill in the *New York Times*, and he
didn't like what he read.

More than a month of negotiations between the Justice Department
and Eisenhower's cabinet led to amended legislation that seemed likely
to attract enough support to be considered by Congress. The revised
version called for creation of a bipartisan commission to investigate violations of civil rights, creation of a civil rights division within the Justice

Department, new laws to aid the enforcement of voting rights, and permission for the government to seek preventive relief from courts in civil rights cases.

Even with this version, Knowland saw little chance for success. He said that the commission and the civil rights division might be approved, but this was "as far as you can go this session."[1]

But Lyndon Johnson recognized an opportunity to embarrass the Republicans and grab some glory for himself. He and others in the Democratic leadership accepted the president's proposal, thereby undercutting any effort by the Republicans to oppose it. All that remained to fight the bill were the southern Democrats, a powerful group that planned to use delay to defeat it. They threatened filibusters that would effectively prevent the Senate from taking any action on the bill.

To forestall this tactic, early in the 1957 session of Congress Senator Clinton Anderson (D-N.M.) introduced his proposal to change Senate rules governing cloture, or limitation, of debate. Under Senate rules, to end a prolonged filibuster by a minority member that is designed to wear down the majority, the Senate must gain a two-thirds vote of the entire membership to limit debate. Getting 64 votes of the 96 members had been next to impossible. Since 1917, there had been twenty-two attempts to impose cloture, but only four cases had been successful, none of them on civil rights. Anderson and his liberal supporters believed that unless the Senate could block filibusters, civil rights legislation had little chance of passing.

Changing rules in a tradition-bound Senate would be far from easy. The conservative southern Democrats would never go along with an effort to change the only weapon they had to combat any civil rights movement. At least eighteen southern senators were expected to filibuster against the legislation. The Senate rules were drafted for just that reason, designed to prevent action unacceptable to a sectional minority. Some conservative Republicans, Knowland among them, and northern Democrats were also openly averse to any changes in the rules. In fact, they seemed to fear such change in procedures more than any extension of civil rights. Many senators didn't like changing the rules governing a continuing body, one that reelects only a third of its members at a time.

Anderson wanted the filibuster rule changed before the Senate's official work began. "If you want to change the rules, do it now," Anderson told his colleagues. Knowland worried that any delays would force the Senate to work with no rules, causing the Senate to be "plunged into a jungle." Anderson replied, "The House [which adopts new rules each session] walked through this jungle yesterday and in 30 seconds emerged intact."[2]

When the time came for a vote, the civil rights backers lost, 55–38, although 17 Republicans joined 21 Democrats in voting in their favor. Bill Knowland voted against any change. Anderson believed that Knowland "couldn't care less whether the [civil rights] bill passed or failed. Knowland after all, had lined up with the southerners to protect the filibuster. He seemed thoroughly willing to let the southerners filibuster the bill to death—an event which would permit him to blame the Democrats for its defeat and permit the Republicans, in future elections, to pose as defenders of the American Negro."[3]

Senator Joseph S. Clark of Pennsylvania expressed surprise over the number of senators he had thought were proponents of civil rights who voted against changing the rules. "It was some little time before I learned how the Establishment (i.e., those who really run the Senate) operated," he said.[4] By the time the House had passed its version of the legislation and sent it on to the Senate, it was mid-June 1957. Senate Majority Leader Lyndon Johnson predicted that debate would last well into September. And with the southerners' strongest weapon against the civil rights bill intact, few would say he was wrong.

Although Knowland had voted against changing the rules on cloture, it was not because he was against the civil rights bill. Knowland was to say thirteen years later that he and his colleagues in the Senate "generally agreed that something should be done [about civil rights], and of course in the Senate it's always the art of the possible, what can be done."[5] Indeed, the California senator was to take a gigantic step to ensure the chances of the bill being passed by the Senate.

The House version of the bill was destined for the Senate Judiciary Committee, which surely would have been its graveyard. The committee was loaded with southerners, including Chairman James O. Eastland (D-Miss.), Harry F. Byrd (D-Va.), and Strom Thurmond (D-S.C.). They would never allow the bill to leave the committee. The Senate Judiciary Committee already had a Senate version of the civil rights bill before it and was moving very slowly.

"We don't intend to wait until the closing days of the session for Senate action on the bill," Knowland said.[6] His strategy was to place the House bill on the Senate calendar, where it could be called up for consideration by a majority vote at any time, rather than wait for the Senate bill to emerge from committee. He had formed an unusual alliance in this attempt: liberal Democrats Hubert Humphrey of Minnesota and Paul Douglas of Illinois stood side by side with him in the move. Richard Nixon also helped uphold Knowland's position. As the Senate's presiding officer, Nixon ruled that the bill did not have to be referred to committee.

Knowland vowed at one point to keep the Senate in session all winter if necessary to secure passage of a civil rights bill. That led Majority Leader Johnson to take a shot at Knowland. Johnson warned Knowland against threats and insisted that an effective bill could be passed by appealing to the best in men. On July 5, noting that the southerners were working behind the scenes on a compromise, Eisenhower said some amendments would be acceptable. Three days later Knowland said he intended to bring the bill to the floor of the Senate.

The southerners were effectively using the threat of a filibuster to water down any civil rights bill; in fact, they had no desire to actually undertake that stalling tactic. They feared that if they used the filibuster, liberal senators again would try to change the rules on cloture, a change they very much wanted to avoid. In addition, if they did filibuster, they could unite the rest of the Senate against them and wind up being forced to accept an even stronger bill.

Knowland continued to keep the House bill on the Senate calendar and keep it away from the Judiciary Committee, where the Senate bill already was being held hostage. The southerners tried to force the bill into the committee but the floor vote was defeated, 45–39. Knowland later told an interviewer, "It's my personal opinion . . . that we would not have had a civil rights bill passed that year had this gone to the committee."[7] Although the southerners lost on this point, they still had the opportunity to filibuster, both when the bill was called up from the calendar for consideration and when the bill was debated or amended on the Senate floor; they continued to use that threat to negotiate changes in the bill.

Eight days of debate began, and sixty-six senators rose to speak. Finally, Johnson and Knowland joined forces to end the debate: the Senate agreed on July 17 by a 71–18 vote to consider the bill passed by the House. At that point, the two men leaned across the aisle and shook hands. The response of Democrat Richard Russell of Georgia was that the southern opposition forces were prepared to expend the greatest effort in history to prevent passage of the bill.

The Senate then found itself locked in twenty-four more days of debate. Southerners avoided filibusters, choosing instead to focus on passing an amendment that called for a jury trial for anyone cited for contempt of court in a civil rights case. Because virtually all juries in the

South were made up solely of whites, it would be almost impossible to get a conviction in such cases.

Knowland sponsored two bill amendments. One, cosponsored with Humphrey, would repeal an 1866 statue that gave the president power to use troops to enforce civil rights legislation. It passed by a 90–0 vote. The second amendment was to establish rules for the operation of the Civil Rights Commission. Oregon Democrat Richard Neuberger criticized the amendments for weakening the "extremely modest" civil rights bill and blamed President Eisenhower. He accused the president of spending too much time on the golf course rather than pushing for a stronger bill.

It was not Eisenhower's style to pressure Congress on issues. His philosophy was that the president proposed and the Congress disposed. At a news conference at the height of the civil rights debate, Eisenhower backed the rights of legislators to vote their consciences. "If [a member of Congress] is doing what he should, he is voting for what he thinks is right," Eisenhower said. "And I repeat, if these programs I suggest are not right for the United States then they [Congress] should oppose them. . . . I, as you know, never employ threats. I never try to hold up clubs of any kind. I just say, 'This is what I believe to be best for the United States,' and I try to convince the people of the logic of my position."[8]

In a strong show of party loyalty, Knowland defended Eisenhower against Neuberger's attack. "I do not believe any useful purpose is served by attempting at this time either to gain a partisan political advantage or to obtain a negative partisan political advantage by attacks upon the Office of the President of the United States," he said. "It is not his legislative responsibility. The details of the bill belong to this body and to the other body of Congress and then, finally, the bringing together of the points of view of the two houses of Congress." Eisenhower did appeal to Republicans to oppose the amendment concerning juries. Knowland said on the Senate floor that a vote for a jury trial "will be a vote to kill for this session . . . an effective voting rights bill." He pointed out that the bill would have to go to a conference committee of the House and Senate to work out differences in the two versions of the bill, and that "from that place . . . it will not likely emerge at this session, and perhaps not at the next. I appeal to Republicans . . . to support [Eisenhower]."[9]

When the Senate passed the amendment 51–42, some, including Richard Nixon, thought there was no hope for the legislation for that year. Eisenhower called the amendment one of the worst political losses of his career; even the normally unemotional Bill Knowland had tears of frustration after it appeared the bill was dead. Yet Knowland and Johnson were able to pull their troops back together, and within a week the entire bill came up for a vote.[10] It wasn't as bad as the Republican leadership had thought. In the end the Senate passed it by a 72–18 vote and returned the bill to the House for concurrence on amendments made in the Senate.

For the first time in eighty-two years, the Senate had passed a civil rights bill, which was called "incomparably the most significant domestic action of any Congress in this Century."[11] Lyndon Johnson's role should not be underemphasized. The Senate majority leader helped secure the bill's passage by telling liberals it was a strong bill and southern Democrats that it was as weak as possible.[12] The major provisions of the bill created a commission on civil rights, created a new assistant attorney general in a civil rights division of the Justice Department, repealed presidential authority to use troops to enforce civil rights laws, prohibited intimidation of people from voting, and required jury trials for criminal contempt cases. The jury trial amendment, Knowland believed, greatly weakened the bill but didn't destroy it. After Republican and Democratic leaders of both houses managed to work out a compromise on this issue, the bill had to go back to each house for ratification.

The battle still wasn't over. The Senate then had to withstand a marathon speech of twenty-four hours and eighteen minutes, the longest in Senate history, by Strom Thurmond. To show why federal voting laws were unnecessary, he read aloud the election statutes of every state, the Declaration of Independence, the Bill of Rights, and Washington's Farewell Address. The speech was labeled a "talkathon" rather than a filibuster. Because the southerners were worried about the reaction across the country to such tactics, many were angry with Thurmond.

At 6:30 in the morning, Knowland came onto the Senate floor to urge the South Carolina Democrat to drop his fight. The Senate was going to pass a civil rights bill before adjourning, he told him. The "talkathon" continued until 9:12 P.M. on August 29, when Thurmond finally gave up. Two hours later, the Senate approved the compromise bill, 60–15, and sent it to Eisenhower for his signature. He signed the bill on September 9, 1957, while vacationing in Newport, Rhode Island. Attorney General Brownell praised Knowland for his work on the bill. Knowland, he said, "was very helpful in getting the [civil rights] legislation passed. I think he carried a number of conservative Republican votes with him. So it was more a matter of individual voting than it was a bloc."[13] Eisenhower also was indebted to Knowland, praising him for his "courage, energy and idealism" and saying that his leadership in the fight "will be remembered gratefully by the American people long after the names of the opponents of the measure have been lost to memory."

Toward the end of this legislative struggle, the president added in the same letter to Knowland that his "great respect for your deep sense of responsibility, your integrity and your forcefulness in upholding your clear convictions was never higher than it is at this moment."[14]

23

The Private Man

During his years in Washington, Senator William F. Knowland's public life and private life were growing in strikingly different directions. While the public senator was becoming more conservative, the private man was living ever closer to the edge. He was in constant financial difficulties and he was involved in an intense romantic relationship outside his marriage. Publicly he was rigid, strict, and ponderous. Privately he played fast and loose.

Senator Knowland was "a very good man," Eisenhower's press secretary George Reedy said of the public Knowland, "but he was a mechanical thinker. Dick Russell once said about him, 'He walks like he thinks.' . . . If you've ever seen Knowland, boom, boom, boom, boom, boom, boom, walking down the street. You can almost hear the floor tremble under his feet. He was like a Sherman tank."[1] An Associated Press report described Knowland as a "ponderous truck powered by a racing engine."[2]

In private life, the senator liked dancing and ice skating, and he was competent at both. He liked good food—he liked any food—and although he had slimmed down with the rigors of army life, when he got to the Senate he quickly began to add on pounds. Weight problems would trouble Knowland for most of his later years, as he made the rounds of political dinners. But the extra weight only added to his strong presence and his often intimidating manner. During his early years in the Senate, he looked somewhat comical stuffed into his old suits brought for a smaller girth, and Helen finally saw to it that he bought new clothes.

Publicly, Knowland could debate and fend off attacks with ease. When caught off guard, however, he was shy and easily embarrassed. Not long after he was sworn in, a group dropped into Knowland's new office in suite 355 of the Senate Office Building. The office was a mess, with file drawers open, papers piled on desks, and telephones on window sills. When they walked into an inner office they found Knowland kneeling on the floor and speaking into a telephone. The embarrassed senator hung up, scrambled to his feet to greet his guests. "Where is Senator Knowland?" one asked. "Why . . . er . . . uh . . . I . . . he's me," Knowland replied.[3]

.   .   .

Soon after the Knowlands arrived in Washington, Helen introduced him to her friend Blair Moody. The two men couldn't have been more different. Whereas Knowland was seen as plodding, colleagues said being around Moody was "like trailing a meteor—your feet wear off and your tongue hangs out."[4] Nevertheless, the new senator and the seasoned Washington reporter hit it off immediately. Moody helped Knowland wend his way through the labyrinth of Washington politics and the Knowlands met Moody's wife, Ruth. Knowland developed few friendships in his first years in the Senate, but he considered Moody to be his closest friend.

Arthur Edson Blair Moody was born in New Haven, Connecticut, and went to public schools in Providence, Rhode Island. In his college days at Brown, he was a Phi Beta Kappa and a renowned athlete, winning nine letters in football, baseball, and track. After graduation in 1922 with a degree in economics, he taught for a year at the Moses Brown Quaker boys' school in Providence, then went to Detroit to become a reporter for the *News*, which was owned by his uncle, William E. Scripps. He was married first to Mary Williamson on June 6, 1925. They had one son, Blair Jr., born in 1928. Blair Sr. worked for a while as a sports writer, but he then began covering politics. In 1933, he was assigned to the Washington bureau of the *News*.

Ruth Curtis Amadon Lang Moody was a 112-pound bundle of energy who was dividing her time between her husband's Washington work and the couple's home in Silver Spring, Maryland, when the Knowlands met her. She handled much of the detail work for his radio program, *Meet Your Congress*. Ruth was New York born, but raised in Boston. She had married Blair Moody in 1940 after he divorced his first wife, and they had two young red-haired sons, Christopher and

Robin. She had red-gold hair and brown eyes. Blair Moody called his slim, pretty wife "sparklepuss," and apparently adored her, but he never seemed to have enough time for his family.

The Moodys spent parts of their summers in Maine on Little Lake Sebago, near North Windham. The Knowlands often joined them. Where Ruth Moody was petite and "golden," Helen was an elegant beauty—statuesque and dark-haired, with blue eyes and an appearance newspaper columnists described as "glamorous."5 Both Ruth and Helen were bright and charming women who were socially prominent in Washington. But while Helen was as strongly conservative as her husband, Ruth was a liberal Democrat. In his letters to his father, Knowland often would say he had discussed his philosophy with Blair Moody. It was rather unusual for a senator to develop a close relationship with a reporter, especially a conservative senator and a liberal reporter, but Knowland trusted the Detroit newsman.

Knowland and Moody's friendship suddenly grew stronger when Moody became a member of Knowland's exclusive men's club, the U.S. Senate—the first Washington newspaper correspondent ever to do so. He was appointed after Republican Senator Arthur H. Vandenberg of Michigan died in office, entering the Senate on April 23, 1951. Although Moody never had announced his political party, he had often written in support of President Truman's policies; Knowland thus wasn't surprised that his friend would sit across the aisle with the Democrats.

In Washington, Helen Knowland had continued the affair she started with Blair Moody in San Francisco. The friendship between the two couples took another twist when Bill Knowland fell in love with Ruth Moody and began an affair with her. "It started when I was going back to California, and Billy was going up to Maine with Ruth and Blair," Helen would recall later, according to her son, Joe. "I told Ruth to take good care of him, and I guess she did."

Although Helen learned of her husband's affair with Ruth Moody, she was able to keep her own relationship a secret. Still, she decided to write a book to describe the duplicity of the love affairs. "She was an angry woman writing this book to get it out of her system," explained Joe. The book was dedicated "To Billy." It was no accident that the description of the central character fit Ruth Moody perfectly, or that her lover was a striking figure much like Bill Knowland. She described the character as "immature, unstable, insecure, egocentric." In public appearance, he was just the opposite—he was a "senior statesman of high repute"—but Helen wrote, "That's part of it. A necessary part of it. What I'm saying doesn't mean that they can't be beautiful, handsome, what have you, and interesting and even lovable."[6] The real Knowland was handsome and "even lovable," but Helen was weary of the situation. Stuck at home with three children, and her husband often gone late into the night, she completed *Madame Baltimore* in one draft. She wrote daily in the late afternoon and completed the novel in ninety days. She said she had spent many months thinking the plot through.

An article published April 16, 1949, in the *Sacramento Bee* described the book as a "white hot whodunit—or rather a Why I Dunnit." The review by Blair Moody, which had been picked up by the *Bee*, gushed with praise for the novel:

It will take no divining rod to search out the top topic of capital cocktail conversation in the weeks just ahead. Helen Knowland has given the gals plenty to talk about. The wife of California's senator, William F. Knowland, most stylish and most articulate of Republican Senate wives, has written a book. And it's not what the inside Washington circle, distaff side, would expect from her.

The book was written in the first person singular with the heroine in the role of a love distraught murderess who kills her famous but secret sweetheart. She thinks he has fallen for a Madame Baltimore.

Thus the roles in the ordinary suspense story where the reader tries to help the sleuth think through to the culprit are reversed.

Moody noted that Helen Knowland often had been in her husband's shadow but that she had always gone along with her husband in his interest in politics. "Writing whydunits will give Helen Knowland a place in the sun of her own," Moody wrote. "For Mrs. Knowland, a leading adornment of the capital's never ending round of dinner parties, is not strong on the standard gossipy prattle. She has a penchant for moving . . . into the hot issue of the moment and more than one self fancied expert has found himself with his guard down, getting his conversational block knocked off."[7]

Helen Knowland called her book a "whydunit" because she tried to "lift the book into a psychological suspense story."[8] Bill Knowland, not an avid reader of fiction, read the book at one sitting and gave it his approval. He told his wife that a politician and his wife should never say or write anything that might embarrass them. If Knowland recognized any of the characters in the book, he didn't let on.

The 210-page book wasn't well received by most critics, and sales were poor. Not long after *Madame Baltimore* was published, Helen was back at work writing another mystery, which had as its central character a woman psychiatrist. Bill Knowland wasn't so keen on this one and he blue-penciled large parts, leaving his wife with only the bare bones of a plot. That effectively ended her literary career.

. . .

On July 14, 1950, Mamoo died suddenly after a short illness at the age of sixty-two. When she became ill, Helen and Ruth Moody were at the Moody's cabin in Maine, and Knowland was staying at Blair Moody's house in Washington. Knowland was stunned by her death. He and Helen returned to California for her funeral, and brought Mamoo's two poodles, Acey and Deucy, back with them. When a short time later they moved into an apartment where pets weren't allowed, they gave the dogs to the Moodys.

Two years after Mamoo's death, J.R. married Clarice Cook, a schoolteacher from Stockton. J.R. and "Cookie," as Clarice was known, met through their joint activities in the Native Sons and Native Daughters of the Golden West. Both were deeply involved in California history. It was his third marriage, her first. He bought her a home on the Seventeen Mile Drive in Carmel in addition to the family mansion on Seaview Avenue in Piedmont.

. . .

As Bill Knowland's Senate career was prospering, his children were growing up, going to school, and getting married. He and Helen almost missed Emelyn's December 26, 1949, marriage to Harold Jewett, the boy next door in Piedmont, because of a trip to the Far East. The senator's obligations were never far from his mind. When his son, Joe, married Dolores (Dee) Beall in 1950, Madam Chiang Kai-shek sent a wedding gift. The senator made the young couple return it lest there be a hint of political payoff for Knowland's long-standing support of the Nationalist Chinese.

In Washington, Knowland's affair with Ruth Moody was becoming an open secret. Knowland was so obsessed with Ruth that he underwent a painful circumcision surgery in his early forties in order to please her, while apparently remaining unaware of Blair Moody's continuing involvement with Helen. The double standard of behavior—integrity in public life and duplicity in private life—was accepted in the 1950s. Even the media looked the other way. The unwritten law for the press was that unless the official's job was affected, his personal life was his own business.

Moody would serve in the Senate only until January 3, 1953, as his bid for election to a full six-year term was unsuccessful. He was most noted during his brief stay in the Senate for proposing that presidential candidates debate the issues. Neither Dwight Eisenhower nor Adlai Stevenson were impressed with the idea during their 1952 presidential contest; Stevenson called it a gimmick. The Federal Communications Act, which called for equal time, was another stumbling block. Moody was eight years ahead of his time. It wasn't until Richard Nixon debated John F. Kennedy in 1960 that the idea of presidential campaign debates found favor; they soon became a national tradition.

On July 20, 1954, Blair Moody died suddenly of a heart attack while he was recuperating from an attack of viral pneumonia. He had been attempting a political comeback, campaigning for the Democratic nomination for senator from Michigan. Ruth Moody was at his side in the hospital when he died at the age of fifty-two.

Eight weeks later, on September 15, Helen Knowland was found unconscious beside her bed in her Piedmont home by her daughter-in-law, Dee Knowland. Her doctor, Robert J. McIvor, said later she had recovered consciousness and was "snapping out of it very nicely." Senator Knowland's brother, Russ, said the family did not know what had caused the condition, but added that Mrs. Knowland had been under a physician's care for several months. Apparently she still suffered pain from an automobile accident suffered earlier. The next day, newspapers called it a "cerebral seizure."[9] Her husband, who was in Long Beach, California, canceled a speech to rush to her side at Oakland's Peralta Hospital.

In truth, Knowland family members later confirmed, she had attempted suicide by overdosing on sleeping pills and alcohol. The family said she was distraught over the death of Blair Moody. Joe Knowland told us in a 1996 interview that his mother sent a suicide note to a friend, citing despair over Blair's death. Drew Pearson wrote in his diary, April 21, 1956, that he had lunch with Knowland and his wife, Helen. "Both swell people personally. Whenever I talk to her, I wonder why she wanted to take sleeping pills as she did in a suicide attempt two years ago. Yet it's probably tough living with the senator—about as tough as living with a columnist."[10]

Helen Knowland received a number of get-well letters, including one on September 18 from former president Herbert Hoover, who wrote, "I am more than solicitous over the press reports that one of the greatest

ladies in this land has been laid up. I hope you take matters in hand."
Earl Warren also wrote to Bill Knowland that it was a great shock to
hear of Helen's illness. "She seemed to be so well the last time I saw
her." In his response of November 1, Knowland replied that his wife
had recovered and that they would be returning to Washington on November 3.[11] California governor Goodwin Knight also expressed his concern. "We badly need her vivacity and spunk," he wrote Bill Knowland
on September 16, 1954. On November 20, Knowland wrote his father
that his wife was feeling fine and "has attended quite a number of sessions of the Senate."

Despite their apparent wealth, it was learned the Moodys were
deeply in debt, probably because of Blair's Senate campaigns. A memo-
rial fund was set up in Detroit to pay off campaign debts and to help
educate his younger sons. Bill Knowland got Ruth a job at the U.S. Information Agency, where she stayed for four years. In 1960, she worked
first for Lyndon Johnson's campaign for the Democratic vice presidential nomination, then later for John Kennedy's presidential campaign.
After Blair Moody's death, Helen Knowland would become much less
tolerant of her husband's continuing affair with Ruth.

The Knowlands, too, had money problems; there never seemed to
be enough to make ends meet. Bill Knowland wrote to his father on
March 8, 1948, that he hoped the *Tribune* could declare a "sufficient"
dividend. He and his wife, he said, owed almost $2,000 in back taxes on
his 1947 return and expected to owe almost $1,500 in 1948. He noted
that the tuition for his son Joe's private school was "rather stiff but I feel
that a good educational background is something that can't be taken
away by the dislocations that may be ahead." There was no mention of
economizing. Knowland's perennial financial woes surfaced again on
June 16, 1951, when he wrote to his father asking him to cash a $5,000
savings bond: "My income tax this month was $3,275; I owe you $750
and have had Helen's and Estelle's transportation to the coast. As you
know, there was no dividend this month of June. Please send it to me
AIRMAIL SPECIAL DELIVERY so I can cash it in and send deposit to the
bank."

While the senator could set financial policy on a world level, he continued to have problems with his own budget: his lifestyle always was
one rung higher than his income. He wrote to his father,

I hope we can pay $2.00 [dividend] this month at the Publishing Co. and
a fairly good dividend at the Building Co. I have been working so hard on
the public business that I have hardly had time until this weekend to check

up on mine. Running two households and doing what this job requires in a big state like California has required me to sell all of my savings bonds and borrow on my life insurance. I have some substantial insurance premiums due and other items past due and I don't want my credit rating to take a nose dive. If and when I can get disentangled from this man killing job where you have little, if any, time for relaxation and I can get back to my *Tribune* desk again no one will get me away to hold any other office public or private.

In 1956, he and his fellow senators got a significant raise—from $15,000 to $22,500 a year—along with a special tax break to cover the maintenance of a second home in Washington, plus a generous travel allowance.

.   .   .

In his years in the Senate, Bill Knowland, like all men of power, experienced the temptations of Washington, D.C.; like many of his colleagues, he succumbed to them. Because of his early marriage to Helen Herrick, he may have felt deprived of the normal youthful years of dating and experimentation, but he made up for it later with many lovers and one-night stands.

His own behavior made him tolerant of others, especially other members of the Senate club. Almost every evening, Knowland's aides James Gleason and Paul Manolis would meet with the senator in his office to discuss what had happened in the Senate and provide information to him on specific issues. At one of those meetings, they brought up a situation with a staff member that was worrying them. While the senator read through a stack of letters and memos, they told him about an attractive young woman intern in his office who was becoming involved with Senator John F. Kennedy. They described how that day they had watched her in the Senate gallery making eye contact and communicating by signs with JFK on the Senate floor. Later, they said, Kennedy was seen helping the young woman into his convertible. When Gleason and Manolis questioned her about it, she told them JFK had taken her to his home, where they had cocktails and danced.

With some apprehension, they awaited the senator's reaction. He continued to shuffle through the papers on his desk, and said, "Next item?" The subject never was brought up again.

24

The Big Switch

Knowland had been sounding out his associates about leaving the Senate for months. In December 1956, when he was sitting with staff members Paul Manolis and Jim Gleason in the lounge of the United Nations in New York, the talk turned to the 1956 election and other political issues. Casually Knowland asked his two aides, "What would you boys think if I ran for governor instead of senator in 1958?"

Gleason immediately opposed the idea. His position was that Knowland did not need to run for the presidency from the governor's office: his place in the Senate was a good forum. Even if most of the thirty-four presidents had come from the ranks of governor, Gleason argued, such a move was hardly necessary. "I felt his present platform was as good as you get," he later told us. But after the senator left to return to the UN General Assembly, Manolis told Gleason, "He has made up his mind to run for governor."

Soon after, Knowland accidentally announced his plans to leave Washington. On January 7, 1957, he was taping an interview with CBS radio reporter Griffing Bancroft. "We wonder if you are a candidate for the Republican [presidential] nomination in 1960," Bancroft asked. The senator responded, "I would say that was entirely a premature question. We haven't even inaugurated yet for the next four-year term our president that was elected last November and no one has a crystal ball to know what conditions will be four years from now."

Bancroft had finished the interview, but had a few seconds of time remaining, and filled it by asking what he surely thought was a pro forma question: "Do you plan to seek reelection to the Senate in 1958?" When Knowland replied, "I do not plan to be a candidate for reelection to the United States Senate in 1958," Bancroft asked the obvious follow-up: "What are your plans, sir?"

"Well, I do not know, except that I do not plan to be a candidate for reelection to the United States Senate."[1]

Bancroft was stunned to hear this, and Knowland instantly turned red, realizing that he had blurted out information he had not intended to make public until much later. Bancroft pressed the Senate minority leader to not make an announcement until after the show, *Capitol Cloakroom*, ran that night. Knowland agreed, but he soon realized that he had to break his word for one of the few times in his life. He couldn't let his Senate colleagues hear the announcement first on the radio. He telephoned Helen, then called Manolis and Gleason into his office. "Well, boys, I have just announced that I am not going to be a candidate for reelection to the Senate," he told them. He brought the rest of the staff together and informed them of his decision.

He then went first to Senate Majority Leader Lyndon Johnson, one of his closest friends. Both party leaders had tears in their eyes when Knowland broke the news. The following day on the Senate floor, Johnson would say, "As a human being, I know of no finer man than the senior Senator from California. Integrity and honor are words which frequently are used with little content. But when they are applied to Bill Knowland, they assume a precise accuracy that cannot be matched by Webster." He added, "In the hill country of Texas, where the Johnsons have lived for more than 100 years, we talk about the kind of people who 'will go to the well' with a man. It is an expression rarely used, and it implies the highest kind of praise. . . . Bill Knowland is that kind of man."[2] After talking to Johnson, Knowland called the national committee members for California, Edward S. Shattuck and Marjorie Benedict, and informed them of his decision. He told a group of Republican senators later in the afternoon, then went to the White House to inform President Eisenhower.

Knowland left the White House and went back to his Senate office for a 5 P.M. press conference that Manolis had scheduled. A large media group knew that the Republican leader had been to see the president and assumed he wanted to brief him on some new policy. He answered their questions about the meeting for about fifteen minutes. Then, as the conference was ending, he said, "Just a minute boys, I have one more item. I announced today that I am not going to seek reelection to the Senate after my present term of office ends." Manolis recalls that the press corps almost broke the door down rushing out to file the story.

While the Washington press corps was shocked, the media in Sacramento were stunned. California governor Goodwin Knight was delivering his annual "state of the state" address to a joint session of the legislature when the news spread through the capital. The timing of the announcement may have been accidental, but it destroyed Knight's annual day on page one throughout the state. As he tried to complete the speech, the press already was running out to follow the Knowland story. Before Knight's final lines were read, Republican State Controller Robert Kirkwood was announcing his candidacy for the Senate seat Knowland was vacating. When that news hit, Republican Robert C. McDavid of Altadena, a member of the State Board of Equalization, promptly declared he would run for Kirkwood's seat.

Governor Knight expressed complete amazement when told of Knowland's retirement by reporters just after he concluded his speech, but he declined to speculate that Knowland might challenge him for the governorship. Caught by reporters at the assembly rostrum, the governor did say he had no plans to seek Knowland's Senate seat. Still in shock, Knight said he had talked with Knowland at a luncheon in Los Angeles just three weeks earlier, and the senator made no mention of plans to retire. He obviously was shaken and said he found it hard to understand why Knowland would give up the Senate Republican leadership.[3]

Knowland's explanation to newsmen in Washington was simple. He had personal reasons for returning to private life in California. His wife, Helen, was pressuring him to get out of Washington; she wanted to take her family and go home. In addition, his father, who was nearly eighty-four, was feeling the burden of running the *Oakland Tribune*. The reasons were logical, but Washington talk immediately began to focus on one question: was Knowland preparing to go back to California to run for governor?

J. R. Knowland told the *New York Times* that he might have to retire soon and that he would like his two sons, Bill and Russ, to become joint publishers of the *Oakland Tribune*. "I'm getting along in years," he said. "I've been pretty active so far and am here at the office every day. Then, too, Bill has been in the Senate a long time and he's quite a family man."[4] He said that if the senator had any other plans he didn't know about them. Privately, J.R. was adamantly opposed to his son leaving the Senate to seek the governorship. Emelyn Jewett remembered her grandfather's anger about the senator's decision. "He felt Dad was making a dreadful mistake. He told me so personally. He was opposed to my father running for governor—not opposed to him running for governor per se, but at that particular point in time. He felt that Dad was at the pinnacle of his career, that he had a leadership position. [J.R.] did not think [his son] had a chance of being elected in California to the seat of governor."[5]

Senator Knowland's public statements were true. He did have strong personal reasons for returning to California. At the same time, he was not ready to give up the power of politics, and he believed that the governorship was the way to the White House.[6] He assumed that his popularity in California (he was reelected by a seven to one margin in 1952) would carry him into the governor's office in such a landslide that the GOP nomination in 1960 could be his. He also assumed that Knight would keep his promise to run for reelection no matter what Knowland did. By beating a popular sitting governor, Knowland reasoned, he would become the political leader of the nation's fastest-growing state, another key to the White House. The thinking was simple: history indicated that the chances of moving up from the Senate to the White House were slim. Only thirteen of its members had ever become president; most moved up from statehouses. Warren G. Harding alone in the twentieth century had gone from being senator to president.

Knowland further believed that Knight's friendship with California unions would cause him to split the vote with the Democratic candidate, and the Democrats didn't even have a candidate at that point. Attorney General Edmund G. "Pat" Brown probably was the strongest the Democrats could offer, but he showed no early interest in leaving a secure post to seek the governorship. However, Brown's interest in the governorship surely was piqued by Knowland's announcement, which opened the possibility of a real Republican battle.

It certainly put three of the most powerful Republicans in the nation in an odd triangle. Knowland and Knight had united to keep Nixon from taking over the California Republican Party in 1954. Knowland and Nixon had united against Knight to keep Nixon on the Republican national ticket in 1956. Would Nixon and Knight get back together in 1958 to derail Knowland's move on the White House?

Democratic State Chairman Roger Kent of Marin County flatly predicted that Knowland would run for governor and that his action would make it easier for Democrats to regain control of the state. He suggested that Knowland would be easier to beat than Knight; moreover, if Knight and Knowland got in a squeeze, Richard Nixon would inevitably be brought into the battle. Alan Cranston, chairman of the

California Democratic Council, said Knowland's action set the stage for a "ruthless struggle as a springboard for defeating Vice President Nixon for the presidential nomination in 1960." Nixon himself, ever cagey, was quoted as saying that he hoped Knowland would return to public service in the future: "Bill Knowland's service to his state and nation has been in the highest and best tradition of the United States Senate. I have never known a man who has worked harder or has been more dedicated in his public service."[7] But the public service both Nixon and Knowland sought was in the White House.

Although Knowland had helped Nixon when Knight opposed the vice president's renomination in 1956, relations between the California governor and the senior senator had remained good until Knowland began taking aim on Sacramento. Some California Republicans, fearing an ensuing bloodbath among their political leaders, tried to persuade Knowland to change his mind about leaving the Senate. Under the direction of Harry J. Crawford, a Pasadena lawyer, a group calling itself the Committee for Republican Victory began a letter campaign to California Republicans warning in late spring of the impending war between the senator and the governor. "It is a well-known fact to most Republicans that if Senator Knowland carries out his announced intention not to seek reelection, the probability of his being succeeded by a Democrat is very great," Crawford wrote. "In addition to this result, it is just as probable that if Senator Knowland should enter the race for governor of California, our next governor will not be a Republican."[8]

Knight denied having any part in the group and said he never had met Harry Crawford. Crawford, who backed up Knight's assertion, explained that his twenty-five-member group was made up of Republican doctors, lawyers, and businessmen who had no connections to either of the Republican leaders. He said he did not know Knowland and had not talked with him about the movement. However, independent Republicans were describing Knowland's actions as a "blueprint for disaster" for his party. The phrase was attributed to Knight, although the governor insisted that he had been speaking only about splits in the party in general. Knight also began saying that he considered it likely that Knowland would seek the presidency in 1960 if he were to win the governor's office.

For his part, Knowland said he would do a fact-finding tour through his home state in the summer of 1957, and he continued to visit California throughout the spring. In April, at a $100-a-plate Republican fund-raising event in Hollywood, he spoke not only about national issues but also about a statewide tour he would make after the congressional adjournment in late summer. When asked if it would be a vacation tour, Knowland answered, "You can't take a vacation when you're campaigning."[9]

Knight knew what Knowland was up to, and he obviously didn't like it. On April 19, the governor said he would be unable to attend two events the following week honoring Knowland. Knight denied he was snubbing the retiring senator, claiming that he had previous engagements that conflicted with the Knowland affairs. At the same time, the governor was meeting with the pro-Nixon group known as the Republican Associates, hoping to swing its members over into his camp despite Nixon's and Knight's dislike for each other.[10]

By mid-1957, Knowland still was not stating his plans, but he certainly was acting like a candidate for governor. He scheduled forty-five speeches in a statewide tour that would begin the last weekend of August and take him from the Oregon border to the edge of Mexico. He remained vague about whether he had made a decision on the governor's race, saying that he didn't want anyone to jump to conclusions. By stalling on an announcement, he prevented Knight from making open attacks. Meanwhile, the rumors and leaks continued—some from within the Knowland camp.

Even his wife, Helen, claimed that her husband had not revealed his plans to her. "But," she said, "I can read the signs." She told a reporter from *Newsweek* that she had written in a letter to her mother, "I feel as sure that Billy is going to run for governor as I've ever been of anything." She said she handed the letter to her husband to read and mail "if it's all right." He mailed it. Did Bill Knowland want to be president? "I think it's obvious," Helen answered.[11]

In the background of the senator's decision were tense family considerations. Helen Knowland had never liked Washington, D.C., and she was particularly upset about her husband's continuing affair with Ruth Moody. After Blair's death, she wanted nothing more to do with the Moody family. She wanted Bill home, away from Ruth and what she called the Washington "candy shop" of young, attractive women. There were rumors around Washington that she threatened to leave him if he didn't return home. Asked later if the rumor was true, Helen replied simply, "I don't care to comment on that." Frank Mankiewicz, a longtime Democratic Party leader remarked, "It had to be something nonpolitical because there was no political reason in it at all."[12]

As his candidacy both for the governorship and then prospectively for the presidency became apparent, Knowland moved more to the right and away from Eisenhower and his vice president, Richard Nixon. He differed with Eisenhower on the budget, foreign aid, and school construction. Even respected columnist Walter Lippman questioned whether it was good for the Senate Republican leader to be so much at odds with the Republican president of the United States.[13] On June 3, 1957, *Time* magazine stated flatly, "Bill Knowland has no known pangs of conscience. He has always made it abundantly clear that his primary obligation is to the Republican Party, not to Ike. Even so, it is the Republican Party that Knowland may in the end hurt most."

Early in August, the *Sacramento Bee* reported that Knowland had told fellow California congressmen at an off-the-record breakfast in Washington that he definitely would be a candidate for governor in 1958. Governor Knight had not officially announced his reelection bid, but he had told newsmen he would not run for Knowland's Senate seat. Knowland refused to confirm or deny the *Bee* report, but he told the Associated Press with a smile, "I did meet with the Congressional delegation and we talked over various matters of interest, but I have no comment."[14] According to Manolis, the senator not only told the California delegation of his plans, but he had to hold the members back from immediately going on record publicly urging Knowland to run for governor.

The following day, the Associated Press quoted Knight as saying, "I can only say that Senator Knowland is a distinguished Californian and until he announces his plans, I have no comment." On August 11, AP Washington reporter Jack Bell predicted not only that Knowland would declare for governor but that he would have Nixon's support.[15] The best Knight could hope for was that Nixon would stay out of the California battle. While Nixon was still seething over Knight's attempt to deny the vice presidency to him in 1956, there was also the problem of both Knowland and Nixon wanting the GOP presidential nomination in 1960: Knowland as governor would be a powerful force in controlling California's delegation to the next Republican convention.

The 1960 presidential nomination was a touchy issue for Knowland. He had to be careful not to lend credence to Knight's claims that he only wanted the governor's office for a stepping-stone to the White House. Knowland's backers started putting out the word that it would be contrary to the senator's sense of public service to win the governor's job and then neglect its duties.

On August 19, 1957, Knight declared his plans to seek reelection and issued a direct challenge to Knowland to fight it out for the nomination. Sounding more and more like a gubernatorial candidate, Knowland said on the following day that he had no qualms about challenging Knight for the governorship: "I always have assumed the governor would be a candidate for renomination. There are no changes in my plans that have been previously announced."[16] Those plans included his upcoming speaking tour, and on August 21, 1957, he announced a committee to be in charge of the five-week tour that would end October 8. In the north, Oakland businessman Robert Barkell, San Francisco attorney John Dinkelspiel, and Capitola nursery operator Worth Brown were named to head what was looking like a full-scale campaign for governor. In the south, the representatives were Los Angeles attorney M. Philip Davis, Redlands newspaper publisher William Moore, and Frank Lowe, a retired minister and chairman of the San Diego County Republican Central Committee.

The opening event was before the Commonwealth Club of California, a luncheon group well used to taking senators, governors, presidents, and foreign heads of state in its stride. Knowland's speech was both national and regional. It could have been the opening salvo of a campaign for either governor or president, or both. The next morning he was in the state capital for the Sacramento Host Breakfast in the Hotel Senator. He shared the head table with Governor Knight, who later joined him at the state fair's press-radio-television banquet. Knight was there as the state's chief executive, Knowland in a dual capacity: as the state's senior U.S. senator and as an editor of the *Oakland Tribune*. The two were cordial, but Knowland criticized Knight for injecting the governor's race into his "nonpolitical" speech that morning at breakfast.

From there, the "fact-finding" trip read like a typical campaign schedule. Redding, Shasta Dam, Red Bluff, and Chico all served as forums in the blistering heat of the upper Sacramento Valley. In Red Bluff, the dusty valley town that was the home of Democratic Congressman Clair Engle, he told the Northern California crowds, "There are grave and important issues in California which must be settled without political considerations or pussyfooting policies." He said he would amplify on those policies in the coming week, adding, "Whoever the shoe may fit, may apply it."[17] Things were going well for the powerful senator, and as if to help him more in his home state, the University of California named him "alumnus of the year" for 1957.

Knowland denied he had a political deal with Vice President Nixon to support him against Knight, but he would not say that Nixon would stay out of the California campaigns. He emphasized his long friendship with Nixon and just as pointedly recalled that Knight joined an effort to "dump Nixon" in 1956. "I thought the governor was wrong then," Knowland said, "just as I think he is wrong in his predictions now"—that a bitterly contested Republican primary might split the California GOP and allow the Democrats to take over. The senator had no such concerns. He said in mid-September of 1957 that a primary battle might stimulate GOP interest and lead it to victory in the 1958 general election.

At the same time, he was framing what he termed the two issues of the 1958 campaign—water conservation and what he termed "union democracy." To Knowland, union democracy meant the right to work without union membership. To organized labor, it meant the end of the closed shop and unionism as they saw it.

Throughout his administration, Goodwin Knight had been whipsawed by sectional jealousies and demands for water. The competing interests had deadlocked the legislature and stalled any possibility of a statewide water program. Knowland interpreted this as ineffectual leadership and Knight's inability to "chart a direct course and keep on it." Specifically, the senator cited his own authorship of federal legislation to allow joint state-federal financing for the San Luis Reservoir to transport Northern California water to huge sections of the western San Joaquin Valley, and he blamed Knight for backing off from the project. The senator said he would propose his own water development plan; it would bring together conflicting views of water surplus and deficits, help control floodwaters, and distribute surplus water to agriculture and urban needs.

Although Knowland tried to focus on the water issues, there were early warning signs that the union concerns might take over his campaign. There would be a right-to-work initiative on the November ballot, and the issue kept surfacing; moreover, Knowland would not back away from it. "No person should have to pay tribute [to a union] before he can have a job," he insisted. He talked of a time when Congress might find it necessary to regulate big unions just as corporations are regulated by antitrust regulations. While he was on his statewide "test the waters" swing, the California Federation of Labor sent a letter out to its membership accusing Knowland of running on an antilabor platform. With prescience, the state AFL group predicted that Knowland's support of right-to-work laws would make labor the dominant issue in the 1958 fight for the governor's office. The mailing also reminded its readers that Governor Knight had pledged himself to veto a right-to-work law if it came before him. In contrast, Knowland—despite terming reporters' questions "iffy"—said he would sign such legislation if it were equitable and fair.[18] The statement immediately presented the public with clear and sharp differences between the two powerful Republicans.

Although there was growing opposition from organized labor, Knowland continued to win applause from mostly Republican groups when he stated his belief that every man has a right to employment even if he does not join a union. Although the right-to-work issue was beginning to worry Republican tacticians, Knowland mentioned it in virtually every speech. Asa Call, head of Pacific Mutual and probably one of the most powerful men in the California GOP, tried to warn Knowland. He told him the issue would enrage union members and they would mobilize against him. Knowland stubbornly refused to take the advice.[19] That stubbornness delighted the Knight camp, which happily pointed out to reporters that no one had run an antilabor campaign since Republican Frank F. Merriam lost the governorship in 1938.

Republican National Committeeman Edward S. Shattuck of Los Angeles made no pretense of being objective in the governor's race. He accompanied Knowland on most of his tour through the San Joaquin Valley and stated flatly that in his opinion, Knowland would run a better campaign against Pat Brown than Knight. GOP State Chairman Alfonso Bell remained neutral, although his loyalty was with Knowland. The split began to take its toll on the Republican Party, as many leaders had predicted.

George Milias, president of the California Republican Assembly (CRA), a conservative Republican volunteer group, was a Knight supporter; but his feelings were not shared by the CRA members. When Knowland took a break from his September campaign schedule to attend a CRA meeting in Long Beach, he was met with enthusiasm and acclaim as California's great hope. Nevertheless, there was a movement started by Assemblyman Donald Doyle of Contra Costa County and CRA secretary Frances Larsen to urge Knowland to give up the governor's race and stay in the Senate: both Doyle and Larsen lost their standing among conservatives in the Republican Party as a result. Doyle, who was then vice chairman of the Republican State Central Committee, was never elevated to state chairman, and he did not seek reelection to the state assembly. Knowland, in turn, said that while he had read

Doyle's letter, he would not be intimidated into staying out of the governor's race.

Vice President Nixon's cadre also was working the CRA meeting. Senator Knowland again told reporters that there was no political bargain between them: "The vice president and I are very good friends. We see each other every day in Washington, but we have no deal or arrangement involving anything."[20] An article in the *Wall Street Journal* speculated that Nixon was up to his usual tricks, trying to manipulate the California election to benefit himself. "Vice President Nixon these days is involved in a seemingly strange political play. He is advancing his own White House ambitions by giving a boost to his only Republican rival." The reporter added, "This is neither naivete nor altruism on the part of the vice president. It may be a gamble, but it is one based on a cool calculation of the political realities."[21] By helping Knight, Nixon would have offended California conservatives whom he would need in 1960. But he believed the conservatives alone would not be strong enough to give the presidential nomination to Knowland, even if he were to win the California governorship, so helping the senator might not carry as much risk as it seemed.

There was no shortage of candidates for Knowland's senate seat. In addition to State Controller Robert Kirkwood, San Francisco mayor George Christopher, Congressman Patrick J. Hillings of Los Angeles County, and Lieutenant Governor Harold J. Powers were gearing up for the campaign. On the Democratic side, Congressman Clair Engle of Red Bluff, chairman of the House Interior and Insular Affairs Committee, was the front-runner. State Senator Robert I. McCarthy of San Francisco and Alan Cranston, chairman of the California Democratic Council, also were considering the seat. Attorney General Brown, considered the Democrat's top candidate for governor, endorsed Engle.

·   ·   ·

Knowland's stand on the right-to-work issue was producing growing concern in organized labor, and he sought to dispel it by insisting that rank-and-file members of the union movement supported his efforts to remedy union abuses. He continued to refer to his stand as "union democracy." At a September 13 press conference in San Diego, he said, "They asked me not to let up. They asked me to carry on the fight for them."[22] But he did not identify either the union members or their organizations.

Knight recognized the senator's vulnerability on the issue and went on the attack. At a September 20 press conference in Sacramento, he called Knowland's proposal "a step backward" and declared, "No politician can successfully turn the clock back in labor-management relations any more than he can reverse the trend of our rapidly expanding economy." The governor said so-called right-to-work schemes are misnamed and should be labeled anti–union shop measures.[23] Knowland was furious about Knight's comments. When both met on September 28 in Placerville at ground-breaking ceremonies for the American River Project, they greeted each other grimly, prompting one observer to say, "Icy weather came to the Sierra early today."[24]

Two days later, Knight attacked Knowland openly and by name on a Sacramento television news show, accusing the senator of "violent attacks" on organized labor. The governor said that among California's Republican and Democratic leaders, "Senator Knowland stands all alone in his attack on labor in California," and he pledged to veto any "right-to-work" bill that might come across his desk. Knowland, in turn, was saying that certain union leaders had marked him for "political liquidation" because of his stand on right-to-work, but he stated he would not be intimidated, "if I never hold public office for another day in my life."[25] In the remainder of his 1957 precampaign swing, Knowland continued to lash out at what he termed labor union racketeers, suggesting that state legislation might be necessary to curb abuses.

On October 3, 1957, U.S. Senator William F. Knowland ended his cat-and-mouse game with the people and declared his formal candidacy for governor of California. At a press conference in Sacramento's historic Hotel Senator, Knowland read his statement to a crowd of reporters, television cameras, and press photographers. At his side were his wife, Helen, and daughter Estelle McKeen.

"Twenty-five years ago, in this city, the capital of my native state, as a young man of 24, I began my public service. I thought it appropriate to return here to Sacramento to announce my decision," he said. "I shall be a candidate for governor of California in 1958. During the course of the coming months, I shall continue to frankly discuss the issues which I believe to be of importance to this state and the nation." He met head-on the question of running against a fellow Republican incumbent: "It is my belief that our citizens welcome the opportunity to nominate and elect their own public officials. The direct primary system has been in effect in California since 1910. I do not agree with those who say it is 'disruptive' or 'catastrophic' to have primary contests."

The senator tried to address the charge that he simply considered the governorship a stepping-stone to the White House, pledging that "if nominated and elected, I will devote myself faithfully to the administration of the duties of the office for the term or terms to which I might be elected." But in answer to reporters' questions as to whether that was a "General Sherman type" statement on seeking the White House, Knowland replied, "No one has a crystal ball as to 1960 or 1964."[26] (Civil War hero General William Tecumseh Sherman famously wired the Republican National Convention on June 5, 1884, "If nominated, I will not accept; if elected I will not serve.")[27]

Knight now accelerated his attacks. He accused Knowland of fighting President Eisenhower's programs, forcing the senator to defend his record in Washington and respond that he voted with Eisenhower 93 percent of the time, compared to 69 percent for the average Republican senator.[28] Meanwhile, Eisenhower's press secretary, James Hagerty, said there were no plans for the White House to get involved in the California battle. The day after Knowland's formal announcement, Knight demanded a statement from his opponent that Knowland "doesn't consider California a mere pebble on the road to the White House." He also blamed Knowland for "this intra-party struggle," adding, "If there is damage to the party or to our state, Mr. Knowland must accept full responsibility for that misfortune, as it will be of his own making."[29] That same day, California's junior senator, Thomas H. Kuchel, announced his support for Knowland for governor. The stage was set for a Republican Party donnybrook.

While Knight was expressing his fears that the Republican Party might come apart at the seams, Knowland kept insisting that a vigorous primary would be good for California. He also continued to attack organized labor. He proposed an eight-point program that would

elect union leaders by secret ballot

give union members the right to recall leaders

prevent conspiracies between management and union officials

protect welfare and pension funds

require union representation of all employees who desire membership (protection for minorities)

provide union members with a voice in the conditions, terms, and duration of strikes

prevent arbitrary control over local unions of trustees appointed by national or international unions protect union members from excessive union fees, assessments, or arbitrary actions

He even issued a pamphlet called "The Worker and Bill Knowland," which described his new program as a "Bill of Rights" for California employees.

Knowland, however, was far from at ease with workers, even his own volunteer workers. June Stephens, the Alameda County youth chairwoman for Knowland, wryly remembers: "We had a convertible, and one day we took him around the East Bay. Later, I took him to a television station in San Francisco. The next morning, we were having a train ride. Paul Manolis took me over to the senator and said, 'Do you know June Stephens?' and the senator said, 'So nice to meet you.' He didn't even remember me from the day before." In contrast, June Stephens told us, her husband, who was campaigning for Knight, had a very different experience: "Goodie remembered *everyone.*"

Vernon J. Cristina, a longtime Republican activist who would work with Knowland on the 1964 Goldwater campaign, remembered asking him to talk with some workers in Santa Clara County in 1958. "We told Paul [Manolis], 'Tomorrow morning we're going to start at 5 o'clock.' We were going to go out here to the farmer's market which always was on the agenda, or on the schedule for campaigns, because you met people who normally don't get exposed to politics." Cristina told Manolis, "But look, have him put on a pair of slacks, an open-collared shirt, and either a sport jacket or a sweater. And *not* that goddamned blue suit he always wears. [We] picked him up about a quarter to five and he was dressed up. We couldn't believe it—blue suit, shirt and tie."[30]

Knowland's campaign style, like his Senate actions, was a mixture of haste and bluster. He barreled through crowds like a fullback going off tackle, smiling and greeting supporters, but not really seeing them. But at any rate, the campaign was on schedule. Republican heavy hitters were lining up behind Knowland, and Knight was being squeezed aside. It became obvious that the *Los Angeles Times* would endorse Knowland and the Hearst newspapers would support Knight. The congressional delegation was fully in support of Knowland, and polls were beginning to show Knowland leading Knight three to one among Republican voters.

Suddenly, in the first week of November 1957, lightning struck. Governor Knight disappeared. It was rumored that he had the flu. Then it was learned that he had gone to Arizona to reassess his political future.

He was staying at the estate of Robert S. Stephens in Phoenix, where he declined to answer telephone calls. His wife, Virginia, staff member Newton Stearns, and public relations consultants Clem Whitaker and Leone Baxter went with him. Knight told them that Nixon and the Chandlers (publishers of the Los Angeles Times) had warned him they would cut off his money if he ran for governor, but would support him if he ran for the Senate. Whitaker and Baxter told him bluntly that he could not win the nomination for governor without money and the newspapers.

Knight returned to Sacramento but stayed in seclusion. He was under enormous pressure from the Los Angeles Times to get out of the governor's race. Norman Chandler sent Knight at least three messages urging him to seek the Senate seat instead of the governorship. Nixon, too, continued to work behind the scenes. The vice president called Clinton Mosher, political editor of the San Francisco Examiner, and told him the Knowland-Knight battle was threatening to tear the GOP apart. Nixon said Knight could have the Senate nomination if he wanted it, but that he surely would lose the gubernatorial nomination to Knowland. Mosher, a close friend to both Nixon and Knight, drove to Sacramento and related the vice president's comments to Knight. The governor crumbled and dutifully agreed to run for Knowland's Senate seat. Mosher had his story; Nixon had what he wanted. Knight flew to Washington, met with Eisenhower and Nixon, and then made his formal announcement. Eisenhower commended him on his decision.

"This was the beginning of the Knowland defeat," Paul Manolis now suggests, "because the senator could never shake off the charges that a deal had been made and Knight was forced to switch. Who forced the switch? Who talked Goodie into this? I have no doubt in my mind. It was the Nixon crowd and the Los Angeles Times, pointing out to Goodie the unmistakable signs of defeat that lie ahead for him. This weak man caved in and refused to face the fire of battle." Manolis adds, "The Clint Moshers were joined now by the Brown forces in shouting that the people were deprived of their right to choose, and that the checkbook Republicans had forced Goodie out. And poor Goodie Knight put himself in the position of running for any office, as long as it was a job."

Much later, in 1964, Knight publicly confirmed that there had been a deal and that Nixon had threatened to campaign against him if he didn't step aside for Knowland. "The long series of disasters which Republicans have suffered in California since 1958 can be traced to 'the big switch' in which I was denied financial aid unless I agreed to run for senator instead of governor," Knight asserted. When he went to Washington in 1957 to appeal to Eisenhower, the president told him, "I leave those California matters in Dick Nixon's hands."[31] Knowland later agreed that Nixon was largely responsible: "I think probably the vice president played a part in this, because once Knight got out of the governor's race and came into the Senate race it left the question of party leadership really undecided. Because he was still governor while running for [the Senate] whereas if we had had a primary and I had won this would have clarified the situation. It also opened up the false charge that this was a deal" in which the senator had been directly involved.[32]

.   .   .

After the battering he had taken at the hands of his party leaders, Knight and his wife took a two-week vacation in Puerto Rico. They returned November 19 looking tanned and the governor appeared again to be his jovial self.

Knowland, however, had to face talk of a deal. In a speech in Santa Barbara on November 9, he said, "Despite an amazing amount of deliberate misrepresentation and uninformed speculation, the fact of the matter is: I have not participated directly or indirectly in any discussions or communications with the incumbent governor or his representatives before, during or subsequent to his decision to retire from the gubernatorial contest. Nor have I made any private commitment, directly or indirectly, to support any candidate for the United States Senate. I will support the Republican nominee when determined by the voters at the primary next June."[33]

Knight's switch to the Senate race not only upset Knowland's plan to show strength by defeating an incumbent governor, but it also had a domino effect, disrupting other Republican elections and exacerbating the split within the GOP. Especially hard-hit was San Francisco mayor George Christopher, who had declared for the Senate only after extracting a pledge from Knight not to run for that office.

With his plans disrupted, Knowland made a grave tactical error. Whether he was overconfident after his successful late summer and fall foray through California or simply gave in to the urge to return to the comfortable surroundings of the Senate, Knowland did a curious thing in early 1958: he went back to Washington and directed his primary campaign from his Senate office. Unlike his early offensive, when he traveled throughout the state, he made only sporadic, short trips back to California during the late winter and spring. He was in the battle of his political life, and he was trying to wage it by long distance.

Knowland also pulled a switch of his own in January. After he and Senator Tom Kuchel had sponsored legislation to provide full federal funding for the Trinity River section of the Central Valley Project, he reversed himself to support a "partnership" deal whereby the Pacific Gas and Electric Company, Northern California's largest power supplier, would build the powerhouses and then sell the power at a profit. Pat Brown promptly took the other side of the issue, favoring public development of power on the river. He said he was shocked at Knowland's switch, adding, "I didn't think the senator needed the extra money for his campaign for governor that much."[34]

On April 21, 1958, Knowland took his right-to-work argument directly to organized labor. At a Fresno meeting of the California Congress of Industrial Organizations' Council on Political Education (COPE), he said he understood "how Daniel felt in the lion's den." He spoke for thirty minutes before the unsmiling audience, calling on the AFL-CIO members to support him even if their leaders did not. After the senator left the platform, convention delegates adopted resolutions opposing right-to-work legislation. By a voice vote, they adopted a straight Democratic slate, even forsaking their old friend Goodwin Knight. A motion was made for a dual endorsement of Knight and Democratic senatorial candidate Clair Engle, but it was rejected.

No matter what Knowland did, the primary campaign kept being steered back to the senator's fight with big labor. Pat Brown helped keep the pot boiling by telling California audiences that Knowland really didn't want labor reform, he merely wanted a scapegoat for workers' problems. "Knowland's attitude is, 'Why cure the patient when you can kill him?'"[35]

Brown also continued to hammer at Knowland for using the governor's office as a stepping-stone to the presidency, demanding that the senator say unequivocally whether he planned to serve a four-year term if elected. Knowland kept dodging the question by insisting that he always finished what he started, but he had no crystal ball for the future. Goodwin Knight, who was no help to the senator, even had said at an April speech in Pasadena that he believed Knowland wanted to use the governor's office as a gateway to the White House. Knowland also was forced repeatedly to deny he made a deal with Knight to switch jobs.

In Washington, the press corps watched the California election carefully; there was hardly a writer in the East who did not have some comment on Knowland. "He is unconquerably tactless, with sort of a genius for saying the wrong thing to the right people at the worst possible time," William S. White wrote in the *Washington Star*. "Far from kissing the baby, he is more likely to stonily ignore it—or to mistake its parents for quite another couple."[36]

Knowland continued his election fight in the Senate, attaching what he called his "bill of rights for labor" amendments to a broad bill aimed at regulating employee pension and welfare funds. The battle again set him against Eisenhower, who was threatening to veto an omnibus water projects bill that contained 134 flood control, navigation, and beach erosion projects, including several in California.

Attempting to keep the campaign moving back home was Knowland's family, who began a "Women for Knowland" tour through California. Accompanying Helen Knowland were her daughters Emelyn Jewett and Estelle McKeen and her daughter-in-law Dee Knowland. It was a month-long, 5,000-mile tour by bus throughout the state, launched with a May Day luncheon in Los Angeles. They would visit a hundred communities in a tour that included coffee shops, church visits, factory tours, picnics, lunch and dinner dates, and television appearances.

Estelle has mixed memories of the trip. "It was not a big budget thing, it was pretty simple. The logistics were complicated; keeping clothes cleaned and shoes polished. I remember a doughnut fry at Redding or Red Bluff. I recall a potato field in Visalia, where we took off our shoes and stockings and were walking out through the dirt to talk to workers. In San Luis Obispo we had vaqueros with mule-drawn wagons—anything to draw a crowd." The women drew good crowds and strong interest, but they were not the candidate for governor, and the campaign suffered, as Senator Knowland stayed in Washington.

Knowland flew in from Washington for a Mother's Day picnic in Sacramento, and the younger women sang for a crowd of about 300 to the tune of "I've Got Rhythm":

We've got Helen
For our mommy
We've got mommy
Who can ask for anything more?

The answer was obvious. We could ask for "Daddy more." But the candidate for governor left the picnic in Sacramento for a plane to Los Angeles, then flew back to Washington; the June 3 primary was days away. Knowland had spent just fourteen days campaigning in the state in the five months before the primary. The primary was a shocking wake-up call to the Knowland campaign. Although he easily won the Republican nomination for governor, with cross-filing in the combined primary Brown had a majority of more than 600,000 votes. Knowland reported spending $546,270, while Brown spent $402,391.

The senator called an emergency strategy meeting of his statewide Republican leaders on June 14 and 15 in San Jose to try to get back on track. On June 12 his state campaign manager, Edward S. Shattuck, who had been scheduled to preside, resigned from the Knowland organization over the disarray of the campaign. That same week, Goodwin Knight broke with the Republican campaign firm Whitaker and Baxter, his managers since his first political race for lieutenant governor in 1946; he apparently blamed them for his poor primary showing. The GOP was in shambles.

At the San Jose meeting, Knowland rejected advice from many of his 200 campaign leaders to back off from his antilabor stand. He told the Republicans he intended to stick by his principles even if that would cost him the governorship. After assuming full responsibility for not having spent more time in the state prior to the election, he left the convention and flew back to Washington without making any substantial changes in his staff. The campaign group continued to be impressed with Knowland's integrity, intelligence, and energy, but they wondered openly about his stubbornness.

Knowland proposed that all Republican candidates for statewide office join forces against the Democrats, the common enemy, and he endorsed all GOP candidates, including Knight. The governor quickly announced he would run an independent campaign in the Senate race. When Knowland announced plans to be in Sacramento on June 28 to address an American Legion convention, Knight called a press conference to say he would be out of town. The governor said he was meeting with some Democratic friends in Los Angeles. The senator countered by changing his plans to arrive in Sacramento a day early, so that he could meet with Knight.

On June 27, the two Republican rivals met for an hour and fifteen minutes in the governor's office; they emerged with no noticeable change in their stances. Afterward, Knight press secretary Tom Bright handed out a statement: "Senator Knowland and Governor Knight held a pleasant hour's talk this afternoon. They discussed questions concerning the campaign and they proposed to continue these talks either by telephone or in person during the days ahead. They have nothing further to say regarding their meeting at this time."[37] If Knowland expected Governor Knight to give in to political pressure once again, he was surprised. As London *Economist* writer William A. Clark put it in an article printed in *Frontier,* "He had not expected the irrepressible Goodwin J. Knight to be quite so irrepressible."[38]

In a press conference before the meeting, Knowland reiterated his support for Knight and other Republican nominees in the November election, but the governor did not reciprocate. On that same day, Knowland met with two other Republican nominees, Lieutenant Governor Harold J. Powers and Controller Robert C. Kirkwood, but neither agreed to endorse him. (Kirkwood gave up plans to run for the Senate after Knight decided to run, choosing instead to try for reelection.) Both opposed Knowland's right-to-work theme.

The closest Knowland came to admitting he might be on the wrong track was at a Washington press conference on July 10, when he said that if the right-to-work initiative was rejected in November and he won the governorship, he would no longer pursue the issue. In late July, Powers announced he would do whatever he could to keep the proposal from becoming part of the Republican Party platform. Pat Brown immediately accused the Republicans of trying to keep Knowland's major issue out of the GOP's summer convention. Knowland responded that the Democratic candidate and labor bosses were attempting to dictate the actions of the Republican state convention. Knowland supported Powers's move, saying that the matter should be left to the voters and that candidates should be left free to make their own decisions. The GOP delegates breathed a sigh of relief and took no stand on the right-to-work issue.

Senator Knowland's adamant refusal to leave Washington to campaign began to be a matter of widespread concern for Republican leaders. Even though he flew back to California for the August 2 and 3 GOP state convention, he made no campaign appearances. He did challenge Democratic gubernatorial nominee Pat Brown to debate, but Brown responded with derision. Casting Knowland in the role of an underdog, Brown dismissed the call for debate as a "threadbare political device used by every runnerup." He suggested that Knowland might want to debate with Goodwin Knight instead, since they disagreed so strongly on the right to work.[39] Instead of a debate, Brown urged Knowland to join him in a series of public statements presenting their views on water, schools, labor-management relations, and economic problems and giving their personal qualifications.

Back in Sacramento on August 4, Knowland said he would open his campaign about August 28. He acknowledged the difficult road ahead but expressed confidence that he could win. Then he unleashed a new type of attack on Brown, claiming that as attorney general, the Democratic nominee had allowed eastern and midwestern crime syndicates to move into California.

Republican worries over the direction of the campaign increased, and as Congress closed its session on August 20, President Eisenhower issued a strong endorsement of Knowland. While acknowledging that the two had sometimes been at odds on foreign policy, he urged the California voters to back Knowland for governor. Eisenhower also sent "Personal and Confidential" letters to big Republican fund-raisers throughout the nation, emphasizing, "Knowland *must* win." The president wrote:

I know that he has been called stubborn, a bit of a lone wolf, and likely to follow his own conclusions and decisions, disregarding the opinions and convictions of able people who would like to be his friends. In other words, he is considered by some to be a bit of a bull in a china shop.

But I feel the following is also true: Bill Knowland is impeccably honest, courageous, studious and serious, and he is physically strong and tireless. Regardless of any blunders that he may or may not have made, these attributes are not to be lightly dismissed.

Eisenhower went on to say, somewhat ruefully, that he had differences with Knowland, adding, "In fact, I think he would be of greater service to the nation, and to the Republican Party and its principles, in the governor's chair in California than he is in the U.S. Senate."[40]

The GOP alarm obviously went all the way to the White House.

Then in late August, Helen Knowland dropped a bombshell. The senator's wife came across a pamphlet written by Joseph Kamp, an eastern muckraker so far to the right that he was considered a fascist by many members of Congress. Kamp, the author of a book titled *We Must Abolish the United States* (1950), was thought to be anti-Semitic and had gone to jail for contempt of Congress after he refused to identify the backers of his poison-pen writings. Helen, however, either did not know of his reputation or didn't care. She was so enamored with his new pamphlet—*Meet the Man Who Plans to Rule America*, a virulent piece about Walter Reuther, president of the United Auto Workers—that she distributed about 500 copies to California Republicans. She was planning to mail out thousands of additional copies when the *New York Times* broke the story about a link between the Knowland campaign and

Kamp. The *Times* said financing was being provided for the pamphlets by Donaldson Brown, former vice chairman of the board of General Motors Corporation; Pierre S. du Pont II, a director of E. I. du Pont de Nemours and Company; and Charles M. White, chairman of the board of Republic Steel Corporation. Helen Knowland told the *Times* she was not aware of Kamp's background and didn't know he once had been condemned by Senator Knowland's old mentor, the late Senator Robert Taft.[41]

Brown immediately expressed outrage, saying Knowland was "doing business with elements which would not stop at imposing a Fascist dictatorship over the American people."[42] The senator ordered Helen to stop the distribution, but the damage had been done. All of the good she might have accomplished in her bus tour through California was wiped out. And even then, Knowland himself never repudiated the pamphlet outright.

.   .   .

With his Senate business finally behind him, Knowland returned to California and set about defining his candidacy. He held a press conference to declare that the new California administration would have to cut costs, seek additional revenues, and reorganize state agencies. He stopped short of saying he would raise taxes, but he made it clear that the legislature would have to find ways to support any proposals for new expenditures.

By Labor Day, he was back in Oakland declaring that hoodlum elements had infiltrated unions and that labor democracy was needed to allow members to regain control of their organizations. At a rally in downtown Los Angeles, Brown responded to Knowland's attacks, saying, "I oppose the mislabeled right-to-work law as a return to the ugly and destructive law of the economic jungle. I believe in legal or collective bargaining as a basic right of both labor and management."[43] On September 12, Knowland's own campaign manager in Santa Rosa declared himself in opposition to the proposal. Karl F. Stolting, former mayor of Santa Rosa and owner of an electrical firm employing union workers, said he was wholeheartedly for Knowland but opposed the right-to-work initiative.

A new blow to Knowland's campaign came on October 4. At a meeting of United Press International editors in Los Angeles, Goodwin Knight announced officially that he could not support the senator for governor because of his right-to-work views. "It is a rugged and hard fight in California," Knowland said when told of Knight's stand. "I personally am supporting the whole Republican ticket regardless of Knight's position in this backyard quarreling."[44] Knowland's campaign later produced a 1953 letter from Knight to a supporter in which the governor wrote, "I agree with you the right-to-work proposal should have been adopted by the legislature," but it didn't take the pressure off.

In mid-October, Vice President Richard Nixon made two trips to California to campaign for the Republican ticket. During an October 15 news conference, he said he saw no serious problem in the Knowland-Knight squabble, although he said he always found it more effective to run with and endorse other Republicans. He pointed out that Governor Earl Warren ran an independent campaign in 1950 while Nixon was running for Senate, and that both Republicans won.

Meanwhile, the rest of the nation was puzzled over all the infighting in California. Just two weeks before the election, the *Washington Post and Times-Herald* summed it up: "The one sure thing is that all this Republican infighting must be considered as manna by the Democratic candidates for governor and senator."[45]

Almost in desperation, Knowland introduced a new and confusing element into the campaign by connecting a slain Chicago underworld figure with Democratic National Committeeman Paul Ziffren, a Los Angeles attorney. The senator said Ziffren had been associated with Alex Louis Greenberg before Greenberg was murdered. He then suggested that San Francisco hotelier and Democratic fund-raiser Ben Swig had links to frontmen for Chicago gangsters. Swig, one of San Francisco's best-known civic leaders, called the senator's accusations "just another dirty, despicable character vilification." Swig added, "If Mr. Bill Knowland wants to know anything about me, all he has to do is call up Mr. Joseph Knowland, his father."[46]

With only two weeks to go before the November 4 election, political pundits were not writing about whether Bill Knowland would win or lose, but how badly he would be beaten. Some predicted Pat Brown would win the governorship by a million votes. Knowland was tired, and he must have considered how different things would have been if he had been running for his senate seat instead of for governor. He noted in a letter to Lyndon Johnson that he had had no vacation and that "one of these days when the campaign is over and I'm in your part of the world, I would like to drop down and see how you relax on your ranch."[47]

The senator, still riding his antiunion horse but arguing that rank-and-file members would vote for him, went into the Fontana United

Steelworkers Union hall on October 23 to tell his side of the story. The 1,000-seat hall had only twelve people in it—a jury commissioner and the prospective jurors he was interviewing. A nearby union office had a sign on it that said, "Offices closed. Attending Pat Brown meetings." Knowland sighed, and said, "It's what I've been saying. They only want to hear one side."[48]

The following day he was in more comfortable surroundings. At the Commonwealth Club of California's regular Friday meeting in San Francisco, he denounced Brown for claiming that Knowland would organize an ultra-right-wing third party if he lost, calling it an "unmitigated lie." He also said for the first time that if he lost the governorship bid, he probably would never seek public office again.

The 1958 campaign made clearly visible Knowland's view of the universe, which placed himself in the center. His decision to shove aside Knight was merely an extension of his belief that whatever was good for him was good for the United States and the world. As with many extremely shy and egocentric people, Knowland turned to himself for counsel, and what he heard was what he then announced as policy. He was not an easy man to advise. Moreover, his actions revealed a deep contradiction. While he presented himself as a man who would do anything for his party, his state, and his nation, he was in fact ripping apart the California Republican Party. Indeed, in the view of many California Republican leaders, he was destroying the GOP's chances for winning in 1958 or being a major factor in the 1960 presidential campaign.

William A. Clark put it bluntly in *Frontier* magazine in October 1958: "This kind of self-hypnosis—an infatuation with one's own ideas—is a common enough practice among politicians. But there are few who have been able to indulge in it as completely as Senator Knowland because a rude awakening at the polls is so often the result. So far, at least, the Senator has never had such an experience on election day—and on very few other occasions in his life either. As a result, he is known in private life and in public life in which he has risen so high as a man completely wrapped up in himself."[49]

In the final days of the campaign, Bill Knowland was already slipping badly, and then Helen got into trouble again. In a letter to 200 Republican leaders, she referred to Governor Goodwin J. Knight as a man with a "macaroni spine." In an open letter to the senator, the *Long Beach Press-Telegram* immediately accused Knowland of "a new low in tactics by using his wife, Helen, as a hatchet woman."[50] Knowland refused to apologize for his wife's actions and declared, "She has always been, as any wife should be, of great assistance to me";[51] soon afterward, the paper endorsed Brown. From inside the Knowland campaign, however, the story was different. According to Paul Manolis, the senator called Helen and shouted at her, "You've blown this election already!" The whole campaign crew was listening.

On October 30, just five days before the election, Republican William A. Burkett, state superintendent of banks, threw his support to Pat Brown, charging Knowland with destroying the Republican Party in California. He said that he would continue to support Goodwin Knight for Senate, but Knowland's mudslinging and ruthless tactics were causing Republicans to desert the GOP. The same day, the *San Francisco Chronicle* withdrew its endorsement of Knowland. The newspaper stated: "The *Chronicle* supported Senator William Knowland in the primary election. Unfortunately, however, we have been unfavorably impressed with his subsequent campaign. We now no longer feel we can unqualifiedly urge his election, and therefore suggest our readers vote for the candidate of their choice." Although the *Chronicle* made no endorsement, its action against Knowland ended the three-newspaper axis that had dominated California Republican politics for so long. The strongly Republican (but self-proclaimed "politically independent") *San Francisco Examiner*, flagship of the Hearst empire, did endorse Pat Brown.

Just before the election, in the weekend editions, the senator did gain an endorsement, from the *Los Angeles Times*. "Knowland, who didn't have to enter the fight, is staking his career and the national welfare of the Republican Party on his campaign," the editorial stated. "He will fight to the last bell and we are staying in his corner."[52] The *Los Angeles Herald Express* also endorsed Knowland the weekend before the election. The *Oakland Tribune* of course endorsed Knowland, but it endorsed no one for the U.S. Senate.

In a last-ditch effort to halt the campaign's hemorrhaging, Knowland staged a twenty-hour telethon in Southern California to try to reach voters before the November 4 election. He went on the air from Hollywood, with crews relaying questions from passersby in Hollywood, downtown Los Angeles, and Los Angeles International Airport. Actor Randolph Scott and actresses Myrna Loy, Ginger Rogers, and Zasu Pitts dropped in to wish him luck, and two dozen telephone operators took questions from television viewers. Knowland was on screen from 10:30 Friday night until 7 P.M. Saturday, November 1. Although the show originated in Southern California, it also was shown on stations in Stockton and Sacramento, covering much of the Sacramento

and San Joaquin Valleys. For the most part, the campaign was over.
Brown held his own, smaller telethon, and the candidates made a few
stops on the Monday before election day.

That night in Los Angeles, Knowland took his family and staff to
see *The Last Hurrah*, a sentimental Spencer Tracy film about a boss in
a New England town fighting for his political life. Estelle Knowland remembered: "There was an intermission, and at the intermission we went
out in the foyer for a breath of air, and who was there—Pat and Bernice
Brown."

The family returned to Oakland on Tuesday to await the returns at
the *Tribune* office. From his assistant publisher's desk, the senator kept
his own tally of votes as they came in from the precincts. The bad news
came early: the first report gave Brown 1,385 votes and Knowland 564.
Bill Knowland showed no emotion, calmly greeting family members
and friends who dropped by to watch the returns. His eighty-five-year-
old father, J. R. Knowland, also sat poker-faced as he watched the numbers roll up for Brown.

The senator chuckled once, when the tiny Sierra hamlet of Pike
came in with Knowland, 8, Brown, 1. But there was no dramatic nar-
rowing of the margin, just steadily mounting gains for Brown. With
the exception of Secretary of State Frank Jordan, the entire Republican slate was going down with Knowland. Less than two hours after
the polls closed, Brown declared victory. Knowland wasn't ready to concede. He had been in the election business twenty-six years, and although the early returns were grim, more than 80 percent of the state
still hadn't been counted.

While J. R. Knowland stayed at the newspaper, the senator and his
family drove across the Bay Bridge to his San Francisco headquarters
on lower Market Street. Shortly after they arrived, the senator took one
more look at the returns and began writing a congratulatory telegram
to Pat Brown. While Jim Gleason screamed for him not to concede,
Knowland signaled to Manolis to take the telegram down the street
to the Western Union office and send it.

At 10:32 P.M., the senator addressed his crowd of campaign workers
and the television cameras. "I have sent my congratulations to the attorney general," he said over the shouts of "No!" from his loyal followers. "He has been given the opportunity and the responsibility to be
chief executive of California for the next four years." Reporters crowded
around to ask if he would be given a federal post by President Eisenhower. He answered, "Absolutely not," and said his only plans were to

return to the *Tribune* and his family. He said he had no further political ambitions.[53]

The senator and his family walked out of the campaign headquarters and went home. There was nothing left to do. The *Tribune* held back its morning street edition deadline throughout the night, but there was no change. When the full returns came in the following morning, Brown had won by more than a million votes. The right-to-work issue went down with Knowland.

25

Citizen Knowland

As the tired old Luchenbach freighter plowed through banks of fog under the Golden Gate Bridge into the Pacific in late 1958, U.S. Senator William F. Knowland stood at the ship's railing pondering a political future as bleak as the gray November morning. Just a few days earlier, his hopes to become governor of his home state of California and position himself to seek the White House had been buried under an avalanche of votes for Edmund G. "Pat" Brown, the Democratic state attorney general.

Knowland, who had been majority leader and the most powerful Republican in the U.S. Senate, now was reduced to the status of a lame duck. He was just a passenger on a slow-moving freighter to nowhere. He chose only one companion in his defeat and loneliness—Paul Manolis, his chief aide and confidant, perhaps his only real friend. Certainly Manolis was the only one left who he felt really understood his attachment to Washington and the searing pain that he was feeling on this journey.

As the freighter rolled its way through the always-rough edge of the Pacific just west of the Golden Gate, Knowland must have silently cursed fate and pondered the reasons for his failure. There was the "right-to-work" issue that had so dominated the campaign. He considered the actions of his wife, Helen, to have been ill-timed, inappropriate, and probably fatally damaging. Republican Governor Goodwin J. Knight had refused to support him. But he placed much of the blame on Richard M. Nixon, the brooding, manipulative vice president who helped nudge Knowland toward political oblivion by encouraging the "big switch" of 1958.

The senior California senator had been Nixon's leading Republican rival for the national spotlight, and now he was finished, along with Knight, who had refused to support Nixon for the vice presidency. After the 1958 election, both were out of Nixon's path to the White House. It was Nixon who had forced Governor Knight to run for the U.S. Senate. It was Nixon who always stood in the background, manipulating and encouraging the moves that would advance his own career while destroying the California Republican Party. And it was Nixon who now would become the titular head of the party, in line for the 1960 Republican presidential nomination.

Eventually, as the freighter meandered down the California coast toward Mexico, Knowland had to come to grips with his own shortcomings. All the others had certainly contributed to his downfall, but he had his own stubbornness to blame as well. He had refused to break off an eight-year affair with Ruth Moody, wife of his close friend and fellow senator, Blair Moody, not acknowledging even to himself that it was a real problem for him. Helen knew of the affair and used his guilt to help force him to make the decision to return to California for his political destruction.

Even after he made the decision to seek the governorship, he stubbornly chose to stay in Washington, directing the campaign from there and leaving much of the personal contact with voters in California to his wife and others. It had been his decision, his disaster. Finally, he realized, he alone had led the campaign onto the minefield of the right-to-work issue, an issue that united organized labor in California as never before. That topic dominated the campaign, drawing attention away from all other stands he took.

He could have sorted out his thoughts on a train back to Washington, but the freighter seemed to be the right choice. The passenger list numbered only eight, including Knowland and Manolis. The food was spartan, and mealtimes were spent with the ship's officers. For most of the passengers, travel by freighter was a means of saving money. For Knowland, it was a way to get away from his wife, his friends, his family, and their advice.

He could come to grips with defeat on his own. Knowland spent most of his time sitting on the deck reading Ayn Rand's *Atlas Shrugged*, a just-published novel describing the importance of the world's true leaders and their treatment by those below them. "I set out to show how desperately the world needs prime movers," Rand wrote about her own most influential work, "and how viciously it treats them."[1] Indeed, Knowland felt he had been treated viciously, and Rand's probe into what the world would do without those "prime movers" fit his mood. He accepted defeat because he had known for a long time that it was coming, but this was a difficult time.

The senator was exhausted, and he did little but read, sleep, and think. A couple of drinks with Manolis at the end of the day completed the social activities. "Once in a while he would give me a few instructions on things to do, but we rarely talked," Manolis remembers. "We didn't even get off the boat in Panama City. There was very little discussion about the campaign." And when they arrived at the capital, Manolis says, "It was a sorrowful time. No one met him." Knowland returned to room 215 of the Senate Office Building to pack; his two-room suite had housed a large staff. He and Manolis then went to room P-48 in the Capitol, where he had run the operations of the Senate minority leader, and collected his personal papers. While he was cleaning out his desk in the Senate Office Building, he watched new teams moving in, setting up new staffs with new ideas and new vigor.

The words *former senator* struck home when Democratic State Central Committee Chairman William H. Rosenthal sent a telegram asking Knowland to resign early so that Senator-elect Clair Engle could be appointed and gain seniority over the new class that would be coming in January. Knowland declined, saying he had some loose ends to clean up. One of the loose ends was relinquishing his California license plate, US S 1, to Senator Thomas Kuchel, who would become California's senior senator. US S 2 would go to Engle.

He was shaken by failure—his first real failure since as a child he had started the long climb to the presidency. He had failed himself and he had failed his father, who had prodded, advised, and supported him selflessly as he moved toward his goal. Finally, it was his stubborn refusal to heed his father's advice to stay in the Senate that had cost him his political career and his chance at the White House. The one time he had gone against his father on a major issue, both his public and private worlds had begun to unravel. His very faith in himself had been rocked to the core. Was he really the powerful figure he always had believed himself to be, or just another politician trying to scratch his way to the top? He hated the very word *politician*, and *former politician* certainly was not a title he would relish.

The senator spent only ten days in Washington. There were no farewell parties. According to Manolis, Knowland was closing that chapter of his life. "He was going back [to California] to be a newspaperman—a good newspaperman. There was this feeling that his political career was all over. 'I've shut that door,' he would say."

"We spent the next few days packing," Manolis recalls. "Then about 11 o'clock one night, we went over to Union Station with Dr. and Mrs. Bailios Lambros, a couple of my friends, and the senator and I got on the train for California." Manolis remembers the leave-taking as simple and emotional. "There was no sendoff, no salute. I think his last act as U.S. Senate minority leader was to sign a picture for me.

"The senator said, 'This is quite a sad ending. What a way for it all to end,' and he and I got on the train and left Washington."

In a November 11 interview with United Press International's Lyle C. Wilson, Knowland said he had no regrets about his campaign for governor, adding, "I'd do it all over again." In a *U.S. News and World Report* interview the following week, Knowland credited organized labor for getting out the vote and opposing the right-to-work initiative and anyone who favored it. In the same *U.S. News* issue, Knight flatly placed the blame for the GOP defeat on Knowland for introducing what Knight termed a non-Republican right-to-work issue into the campaign. Both Knowland and Knight said California businessmen did not help the Republicans enough.

But it was left to Democratic Governor-elect Pat Brown to define the winners and losers and explain what had happened to the GOP. "The election has eliminated two people who very frankly, no matter what they say, don't like Mr. Nixon. And I'm referring to Mr. Knowland and Mr. Knight. He's the only one left, so you might say that helped— that left Nixon in charge of the Republican Party in California. There's no one to challenge his leadership out here now."[2]

Clair Engle had a similar interpretation, telling the Associated Press, "Knight and Knowland were fighting like men until [Nixon] interceded and ran them in tandem." Engle declined to declare Knowland politically dead, however, saying, "It's pretty hard to kill a dinosaur or a bull elephant. He's got some wiggle in him yet. He'll get up."[3]

.   .   .

Although he denied it, returning to private life was extremely painful for Bill Knowland. He was a loner in his private life, with no close friends except his trusted aide Paul Manolis. With others—even close business or political associates—he was formal and stiff. After he left

Washington and returned to Oakland, his old friend Dud Frost, whom he had known from his army days in London, worked only a few blocks away, but they seldom saw each other. Knowland worked in the same building with his brother, Russ, but they had no personal relationship. They never had lunch together. The same was true of his sister, Eleanor. The lack of communication apparently extended throughout the family. Russ's son Jay recalled years later that it was not until after his father's death that he learned that Russ attended all of his Piedmont High School football games. One of the few times the family would get together was at the Christmas command performance, when J.R. demanded attendance at his Piedmont home and got it. And Bill Knowland was also becoming more distant from Helen. They rarely did anything together. She even dropped out of his public activities that she had supported so strongly while he was in the Senate. When he got involved in community programs, Helen was rarely visible.

From his beginnings he had been shy in personal relationships and insecure in dealing closely with people. He hated confrontations on a personal level, although he easily could duel verbally with some of the most powerful individuals in the nation. He could speak to an audience of 5,000 without a quaver in his voice, but meeting a longtime employee in an elevator was very difficult for him. He could argue with Dwight Eisenhower or Lyndon Johnson, but couldn't tolerate a conversation with his own children.

"When he was fully armed in the accoutrements of power, he was comfortable," observed Dr. Franz Wassermann, a highly respected Bay Area psychiatrist whom we asked about these contrasts. "When he was just with ordinary people, he couldn't use those ploys." Some of those accoutrements remained with Knowland when he returned to private business as assistant publisher of the *Oakland Tribune*, but his confidence had suffered a shattering blow. Though in the Senate he had had an image of strength, honesty, and integrity, his life in the private sector was increasingly characterized by insecurity.

Dr. Wassermann said that the senator probably was asking himself, was his power based on feet of clay? Had he been propped up too long by his father in a position where he never had belonged? As a child, Wasserman suggested, Billy Knowland had a great burden placed on him by his parents when they selected him as their chosen son, the one who would become president. It set for him a clear and unwavering goal, but it denied him the pleasure of a normal childhood. While his brother and sister were in California enjoying ordinary lives in school, their younger brother was roaming the halls of Congress with his father. His heroes were not baseball players, film stars, or musicians; they were senators, cabinet members, and presidents. The young Knowland was physically awkward and uncomfortable with sports; that, coupled with his single-minded pursuit of his goal, channeled all his competitiveness into politics.

Joe Knowland would paraphrase Shakespeare in describing his father's personality. "All of Bill Knowland's world was a stage. All the men and women in his life were merely players. They had their exits and entrances. And one man—William Fife Knowland—played many lead parts: the infant, the school boy, the soldier . . . a man jealous in honor, sudden and quick in quarrel, seeking that bubble, reputation."

Bill Knowland's aim in life was clear-cut but limited, and it left him always dependent on his father and indebted to him in every way. When he wanted to run for public office, the *Oakland Tribune* was firmly behind him. His father quietly arranged for better assignments for him in the army during World War II. When he needed money, J.R. provided it. And when the time came, it was his father's old protégé Earl Warren who appointed Bill Knowland to the U.S. Senate.

The special treatment he received from his parents must have produced some guilt toward his siblings. Yet he followed the same path with his own children, rarely talking to them and eventually selecting as his own "favorite son" an employee, adopted much as his stepmother had adopted him. It was Manolis who became his confidant and friend, a man he once introduced at a Piedmont cocktail party as "the son I always wished I'd had." When Knowland traveled, after leaving the Senate, he took out flight insurance with Manolis as his beneficiary.

.   .   .

In the early years in his new life as a private citizen, Knowland tried things he had never done before. He took up model trains, golf, boating, duck hunting—even skiing on water and snow. He was not good at these pursuits, but he made an effort to make up for the years he had neglected his family in favor of politics. He even tried occasionally to be impulsive. "After the election, he tried to humanize himself," Joe said. "He was trying to get into the swing of family things. He bought a train set." He built a plywood platform that filled the 25-by-15-foot rumpus room in the basement. "He was not one who had nimble fingers.

When a train would break, he couldn't fix it. He would just go down and buy another one."

But the retired senator clearly missed Washington, and Washington apparently missed him. A month after Knowland left the Senate, he received a letter from Lyndon Johnson. "Events have been interesting," Johnson said, "but without you around I certainly do feel a sense of loss. Over the years that we worked together there developed between us a working relationship [and] warm bonds of friendship that can never be broken."[4]

Another tie to the Washington years was cut on June 22, 1961, however, when Ruth Moody died suddenly from an apparent stroke. Knowland had ended his affair with Ruth, but he still was quite fond of her and had visited her twice after leaving the Senate. He had Manolis go to an Oakland florist not used by the *Tribune* or the Knowland family to send flowers. At the senator's request, Manolis signed the card, "Bill and Helen Knowland."

Family problems awaited Bill Knowland at work. His brother, Russ, general manager of the *Oakland Tribune*, was dismayed that their father had welcomed Bill back as assistant publisher. Afterward, Russ Knowland's avocational alcoholism became a full-time job. As Joe Knowland recalls, "Russ never went to his office again. The bar became his office." Manolis said it wasn't quite that bad: the senator's brother came to the office for about an hour every day, then went out to meet his friends at a bar.

Russ Knowland died of a heart attack on October 6, 1961, and the senator's path to becoming publisher of the *Tribune* was clear. Two years after Russ's death, his wife Norma died, and the couple's youngest children—Joseph Russell (Jay) Knowland III, 17, and his sister, Patricia (Tish), 15—went to live with Bill and Helen Knowland. Their older sister, Penny, was a freshman in college in Colorado. Jay and Tish were never happy in their uncle's home. Where Russ and Norma had been easygoing and permissive, Bill Knowland was rigid and authoritarian. As a teenager, Jay was once arrested on a minor offense. The senator told the *Tribune* city desk to run the story; Jay never forgave him.

Bill Knowland's relationship with his own son, Joe, was also strained. His closeness to Joe's old fraternity brother, Paul Manolis, was resented bitterly, and the senator seemed intent on exacerbating the wounds. Joe was excited when his father returned to the newspaper. He had risen from reporter to assistant city editor, and he wanted to continue moving up in the *Tribune* organization. Instead, his father held him back. In contrast, after a short stint as book editor, Manolis was appointed executive editor of the paper—next in power to the assistant publisher, Bill Knowland. Joe went to his grandfather, still publisher of the *Tribune*, to protest, but J.R. would not go against his son's wishes.

Later, when managing editor Stanley Norton died, Joe wanted to take his place. The senator consulted with Manolis, then said no. City editor Stephen A. Still was promoted to managing editor, and Knowland told his son he should move into management. Joe said, "No, I'll work on the copy desk for a while." As he put it later, "We had words."

In addition to the tense family situation, there was trouble at the newspaper on another front. The *Tribune* always had been a family-oriented, paternal sort of operation. The American Newspaper Guild made a tentative thrust at organizing the news departments in the early 1950s, but staffers preferred the in-house *Oakland Tribune* Editorial Employee Association. But the aging J.R. was no longer the strong father figure he once had been to the *Tribune* staff. The senator's son, Joe, was still learning the business, and Russ was regarded as well-meaning but weak.

Shock waves went through the staff in 1958 when Knowland campaigned on the right-to-work issue, taking a stand that reporters and editors considered antilabor. When Bill Knowland lost the election and returned to Oakland to run the *Tribune* after almost twenty years away from the business, he was a virtual stranger to the staff, and he had little understanding of the paper as it was in 1959. During his first year as assistant publisher, overtime was virtually eliminated. The editorial staff shrank when no replacements were hired for reporters or editors who left. Staff morale dropped and the close-knit family divided, setting "us" against "them." When the next opportunity came in November 1959, the staff voted overwhelmingly to form a San Francisco–Oakland Newspaper Guild unit. Bill Knowland had lost another election, this one by a two-to-one margin of his own employees. Although the contract had a grandfather clause for those who wished to remain outside the guild, 95 percent of the editorial staff had joined within a year after the election. The mood at the newspaper became so tense that J.R. Knowland moved KLX, the family radio station, out of the *Tribune* Tower, fearing a strike could close down both the newspaper and his radio voice.

In the first two years after Knowland's return to the *Tribune*, ten news staffers were fired and thirteen others quit. In protest, Al Reck, legendary city editor of the *Tribune*, went on a sit-down strike at his home. When he returned, he was assigned to a rewrite desk. In all cases, Knowland carefully observed all the terms of his contract with the newspaper guild, granting full severance pay to those who left, but he remained seemingly oblivious to the reaction of his news staff.

Still, the newspaper prospered. Circulation was at 210,000 daily, 245,000 on Sunday. The San Francisco newspapers were flashy and more lively, but no one could beat the *Tribune* for thoroughness. "We cover every cat and dog bite in the East Bay," the late Russell Whitney used to say from the Contra Costa bureau in Martinez. It may have looked dull, but the people of Oakland and suburban Alameda and Contra Costa Counties loved their newspaper. Annual profits were about $1 million in 1950s dollars. J. R. Knowland was still the titular and paternal publisher.

In a 1959 interview with Lawrence Davies, San Francisco bureau chief of the *New York Times*, Bill Knowland said he had no interest in re-entering politics, adding, "I expect to be a newspaper man in a growing community and state, with a growing paper."[5] He said he planned to go to the 1960 Republican National Convention in Chicago as a newspaper man, not as a delegate.

As he settled into private life, Knowland began to put on weight again, and at one point he was up to 245 pounds, more than 20 pounds heavier than when he ran for governor. He began walking over four miles from his Piedmont home to the *Tribune* Tower to try to trim down, arriving in the office about 8:30 A.M. The already-thin Manolis had to walk with him.

He wrote editorials on everything from local to international issues with the same vigor he had demonstrated in the Senate. From his desk at the *Tribune*, one of Knowland's first actions was to advocate the end of cross-filing in California elections. Hiram Johnson's idea had worked well for Republicans for half a century, but it had failed him in his bid for governor. He sent Pat Brown a copy of his editorial endorsing legislation to eliminate cross-filing, and Brown publicly praised his former opponent. He invited Knowland to have lunch, saying the two would find many areas of agreement on California problems. Knowland also editorialized in favor of granting press access to Red China and against taxing advertising, which he portrayed as an attack on freedom of the press. He opposed inviting Soviet premier Nikita Khrushchev to the United States, calling him once again the "butcher of Budapest."

By early 1960, Knowland was convinced that Nixon would be the

Republican presidential nominee, though New York governor Nelson Rockefeller was making a strong effort. He also predicted that John F. Kennedy would win the Democratic nomination, although he considered Lyndon B. Johnson to be the most qualified Democrat. He continued to forecast that the vote in November would be extremely close. Despite his own feelings about Nixon, Knowland still campaigned loyally for the Republican ticket. He worked throughout the western states for Nixon. The Democrats countered with former president Harry S. Truman, who campaigned in the West for Kennedy.

.   .   .

Knowland went to the 1960 conventions as a newspaperman, but he couldn't shed a lifetime of political experience. As the former Senate majority leader sat in the press section with a typewriter, national reporters came by to ask him for background information.

Manolis, who accompanied him, remembers the Democratic convention in Los Angeles with particular vividness. Lyndon Johnson sent word that he wanted to see Knowland. "I went with the senator [Knowland] to the Biltmore Hotel to the Johnson suite, and the door was opened by Speaker Sam Rayburn. I sat in the other room with Speaker Rayburn, and Senator Knowland went in to speak to Lyndon Johnson. When we left—and this was the first hint we had—Senator Knowland told me that Senator Johnson asked him what he should do if the Kennedy people offered him the vice presidency and Senator Knowland told him to accept it. . . . He told me that he told Lyndon Johnson the story that Hiram Johnson had told him about not accepting the nomination for vice president," thus missing his chance to become president when Warren G. Harding died.

Knowland went back to his typewriter and wrote a story predicting that Lyndon Johnson would be the Democratic vice presidential nominee. Manolis said that the senator assumed Johnson must already have been asked by the Kennedy people or he wouldn't have been considering the vice presidency. The story was treated derisively by the national press—until Johnson was nominated, one day later.

Knowland later downplayed his part in Johnson's selection. "I can't say I had any effect on it, because I am sure that he was getting advice from people who were much closer to him than I was. I did ask for an appointment with Senator Johnson in his suite at the hotel and I told him that I thought it was not unlikely that he might be asked to be the vice presidential candidate, and personally, as an American citizen and one who had served with him in the Senate, I hoped that if that situation developed that he would accept it. Again, I think I may have discussed with him this Hiram Johnson story."[6] The senator was proved right. Johnson took the vice presidential nomination, Kennedy won the presidency, and when he was assassinated three years later, LBJ was president, as Knowland had told him he might be.

Knowland was proud of his convention reporting over the years. On one occasion, as the *Tribune* copies he always had airmailed were being brought into the press gallery, he picked one off the stack and saw his own story spread across the top of page one, with a large headline. He turned to Harry Farrell, political editor of the *San Jose Mercury*, and said, "Look, Harry, that's my story!" pointing to the William F. Knowland byline. Farrell answered, "Yeah, Senator, and you got pretty good play, too."

Sometimes Knowland the newspaperman came in conflict with Knowland the former U.S. senator. In 1962, the city desk somehow obtained photographs of a nuclear weapons test by the United States near the Christmas Islands. Fearful that the *Tribune* might be in possession of material that could jeopardize the nation's defenses, he had his staff check with the Department of Defense before using them.

Assistant Secretary of Defense Arthur Sylvester refused to clear the photographs for publication, so Knowland called him and specifically asked if running the photographs would reveal technical details of value to "the enemy." Sylvester said that publishing the pictures would not compromise the U.S. nuclear program, but he still refused to clear the photographs on the basis that no news media had been permitted on the scene.

After a week's delay, newspaperman Knowland ordered that they be published. A color photograph was published on page one of all May 27, 1962, editions, with a black-and-white photograph inside. The page one caption read, "This is the first published news photo of the nuclear bomb tests near Christmas Island. The fireball is forming in the dark haze of a Pacific dawn. It soon will turn into a mushroom-like formation, rising higher and higher. This bomb was dropped from a B-52 and the pictures [were] taken on Christmas Island."

26

Revitalizing a City

In 1962 Knowland was named Oakland's outstanding citizen of the year by the Oakland Inter Service Club Council and the Oakland Chamber of Commerce. Not only had he become a newspaperman, but he was helping his newspaper lead a city. What he could ignore as a senator, he could not overlook in his new position. He supported the Port of Oakland during its development into the second-largest containerized port in the world—only Rotterdam was bigger. While San Francisco officials were arguing over who would get the spoils from its once-thriving waterfront, Oakland stole the Bay Area's shipping industry. And during a time when Detroit and the Watts section of Los Angeles were burning, Oakland smoldered, but did not erupt in flames.

His daughter Estelle described his influence in the early 1960s. "Oakland's not the most dynamic economic city in the country, and we do have a high unemployment rate, and still have tremendous problems. But we didn't burn, we didn't riot, and the people on both sides of any fence in this town have learned how to begin to talk to each other. I think Dad's contribution was the primary one of all the individuals in this town." She added, "There was the kind of thing at the *Tribune* Tower just like his father: the door was always open. No matter who it was in town, you could go to him and say, 'We want a hotel,' or 'We've got too much unemployment, what are we going to do about it?' It wasn't that there was a pot of gold there, or any elixir, but it was a start to get people to talk about it and see what we could work out."[1]

Many things were being worked out. With industrialists Edgar Kaiser and Steve Bechtel, Knowland pushed for a stadium for the fledgling Oakland Raiders, a ragtag football team playing its home games at a junior college field near the decaying downtown center. He joined organizations; if he couldn't join himself, he sent someone. Paul Manolis became a director of the Oakland Museum and the Oakland Symphony. Whenever there was a civic cause in the East Bay (spelled "Eastbay" in the *Tribune*), Bill Knowland supported it.

Oakland was still plagued with a virtually empty downtown in the early 1960s, as buildings had been razed to make way for new developments that weren't happening. But with the *Tribune*'s support, a new museum was built six blocks from the center of town, the Bay Area Rapid Transit district headquarters was constructed in Oakland, not San Francisco, and downtown reconstruction gradually began. In 1966 the Oakland Raiders got their stadium, and the Oakland Athletics moved into town. The new stadium, the Oakland Alameda County Coliseum, was built along the Nimitz Freeway between downtown and Oakland International Airport. A new indoor sports arena was added to the Coliseum complex, allowing Oakland to draw a professional basketball team, the Golden State Warriors, away from San Francisco.

·   ·   ·

William Knowland and Richard Nixon, two of the most powerful Republicans of the mid–twentieth century, had a profound dislike for each other, and both had long memories. When Nixon was running for governor in 1962, he came across the Bay Bridge from San Francisco to Oakland with some campaign workers. One of them was June Stephens, who earlier had worked for Knowland; she pointed to an imposing structure on the Oakland skyline and said, "That's the *Tribune* Tower." Nixon looked over at the tower and said one word: "Bastard!"

Later, Nixon paid an obligatory campaign visit to Knowland in the *Oakland Tribune* offices. Nixon needed Knowland's newspaper's support in his run for governor of California. A receptionist told Knowland that Nixon was in the lobby. Knowland, who had no one in his office, kept Nixon waiting twenty minutes before inviting him in. After talking briefly, Nixon asked Knowland for permission to campaign in the *Tribune* offices. Knowland acquiesced, and instructed his receptionist to "show him around." Nixon was unceremoniously dropped off in the newsroom, where he was left to fend for himself.[2]

Nonetheless, Knowland was always loyal to the Republican Party, and he reluctantly put his personal feelings aside. Soon thereafter, the *Tribune*'s editorial writer Jack Ryan came out of a meeting with Knowland, shaking his head. "I've got to write an editorial endorsing Nixon," he said, "without saying one word against Pat Brown," Nixon's opponent in the gubernatorial race. In effect, the editorial said that Nixon was getting the nod because he was a Republican. But the day after Nixon lost to Brown, Knowland walked around with a broad smile.[3]

Ten years later, President Richard Nixon was in San Francisco at a state dinner for South Korean leader Park Chung Hee. The president exchanged pleasantries with the *Tribune* political editor and asked him to "give my best" to Senator Knowland. The next day, when the message was delivered, the senator stared straight at the editor, said nothing, then frowned and turned away.

.   .   .

Bill Knowland was obviously uncomfortable in elevators with *Tribune* employees and worked out his own way to deal with the problem.

"Have you had your vacation yet?" he would boom out as he entered the elevator. If the answer was no, he would ask, "When do you plan to go?" If the answer was yes, he would ask, "Where did you go?" Either reply was enough to get him through the interminable ride from the first floor to the fourth, where his offices shut him off from further confrontations.

One day he deviated from the routine, and asked photographer Russ Reed, "Don't I know you from somewhere?"

The nonplussed Reed answered, "Yes, Senator, I've worked for you for nearly thirty years."

After that, he returned to the tried and true, "Have you had your vacation yet?"

.   .   .

Rumors were circulating through Washington in 1963 that Bill Knowland might attempt a political comeback. They were supported in part by the senator's refusal to make an absolute statement that he would not run against Clair Engle for his old Senate seat. "I can't predict what the situation will be later this year or early in 1964, so I have no [General] Sherman like statement renouncing all political plans for all times," Knowland told the *Washington Evening Star*. "But up to today, I have not said 'yes' to anyone who has asked me to be a candidate for the Senate next year."[4]

In March, speculation on Knowland's political planning took a different turn, as a California group headed by GOP conservative Del Kirkpatrick named him as their choice as a favorite-son candidate for president. Kirkpatrick also was heading a movement to draft Senator Barry Goldwater of Arizona for president. By this time, Richard Nixon had moved to New York, and Democratic Senator Engle fueled the talk about Knowland's plans by expressing his belief that the former vice president's move would allow Knowland to take center stage in California's Republican Party. Yet a confidential report to J. Edgar Hoover out of the San Francisco FBI headquarters assessed Knowland's chances tersely: "He couldn't be elected dogcatcher in California."

By mid-1963, Knowland was announcing publicly that Goldwater would be the likely Republican nominee. With the nominating convention scheduled for San Francisco's Cow Palace, the backing of the former senator would have a powerful effect on Republicans. Thomas Kuchel, who had become California's senior senator on Knowland's retirement, was coming closer to endorsing Nelson Rockefeller for president.

On September 10, 1963, Knowland finally put an end to the talk about another run for Senate. A poll by the Citizens Committee to Support Conservative Republicans showed Knowland far out in front for the Senate seat, but he issued a statement from his Oakland office saying, "I am not a candidate for the Senate in 1964." He said he was honored, but business and personal commitments made such a campaign impossible. Later in September he went to the California Republican State Central Committee Convention to invite Goldwater to enter the 1964 Republican primary. He left no doubt that his intentions were to support the Arizona senator rather than run himself in 1964.

Knowland then embarked on a national speaking tour on which he predicted that Goldwater would be nominated on the first or second ballot. He insisted that Rockefeller could not command enough support to deadlock the San Francisco convention. By mid-October 1963, he had become chairman of the Goldwater California advisory committee and formally endorsed the Arizona senator. Despite his support of Goldwater, Knowland acknowledged that California would be a "doubtful" state for the Republicans in 1964. Although he wouldn't concede the state, he pointed out that by 1964 it would have 1.3 million more registered Democrats than Republicans. He also noted that Richard Nixon, a native Californian, had carried the state by only 30,000 votes in the 1960 presidential election, then lost the governorship in 1962. Still, he said, California would be no sure thing for President Kennedy in his reelection bid.

In November 1963 Bill and Helen Knowland were on a trip to the Far East when they received word that President Kennedy had been assassinated. From his hotel in Osaka, Japan, he told the Associated Press, "I was deeply shocked to learn of the death of the president. It is a great threat to the nation and the free world." On his return to the United States, Knowland recalled that he was majority leader of the Senate when Kennedy was elected to that body. He expressed regrets, but said he felt the nation was lucky that it had Lyndon Johnson to take over. Knowland compared the tragedy to the assassination of President Lincoln. "The government in Washington still lives," he said.[5]

As the shock of Kennedy's death lost its edge, politicians began to remember that there was an election to be won in 1964.

Both the Democrats and Republicans were having trouble in California. Senator Clair Engle, who had defeated Goodwin Knight by 730,000 votes in the "big switch" of 1958, was a shoo-in for reelection until he became incapacitated by a brain tumor. He had to drop out of the race, and State Comptroller Alan Cranston was his heir apparent. But then Pierre Salinger, Kennedy's press secretary and a former *San Francisco Chronicle* reporter, moved back to California and announced he would run for Engle's seat. California Democrats, still stunned by the president's assassination, grabbed for a last piece of JFK's Camelot and nominated Salinger. When Engle died that summer, Governor Brown appointed Salinger to the Senate, giving him the mantle of incumbency. Salinger, however, was a terrible campaigner, who didn't look or talk like a Kennedy; and by November California voters had lost much of their nostalgia for his White House connection. They elected Republican George Murphy, a former movie actor and tap dancer.

Since his 1958 defeat, Knowland had stayed in the background of California politics, but with the Goldwater campaign looming, the old political fires began to burn more fiercely. "Be gentle and understanding of a man who feels he is approaching the point where he has one good fight left in him," he scribbled in a note to his wife, Helen, in January 1964. "This is mine."

The 1964 primary was a battle of the heavyweights. On the Goldwater side were Bill Knowland; Los Angeles County sheriff Pete Pitchess; Nixon's 1960 California campaign manager, Bernard Brennan; Los Angeles financier Henry Salvatori; Schick Safety Razor Company and

Technicolor chairman Patrick J. Frawley; and industrialists Leland Kaiser and Cy Rubel of Union Oil. Goldwater also had a Hollywood cast, which included John Wayne, Raymond Massey, Walter Brennan, Efrem Zimbalist Jr., Clint Walker, Hedda Hopper, and, most important, Ronald Reagan. Rockefeller's list of heavy hitters was headed by Senator Thomas Kuchel. With Kuchel were former governor Goodwin Knight; John Krehbiel, immediate past state Republican chairman; Joseph Martin Jr., who left his post as national committeeman to join Rockefeller; former national committeeman Edward S. Shattuck; Jack McCarthy, minority leader of the state senate; former San Francisco mayor George Christopher; and James P. Mitchell, former U.S. secretary of labor.[6]

In the spring of 1964, Knowland returned to the campaign trail, going all out for Barry Goldwater. In Atlanta, Montgomery, Los Angeles, Topeka, and Washington, D.C., he carried Goldwater's banner. He returned to Northern California and campaigned in the small towns of Loyalton, Sierraville, Portola, Greenville, Chester, Likely, Cedarville, Canby, Adin, McArthur, Fall River Mills, Burney, Yuba City, Alturas, Tulelake, and Quincy. He spoke to the fortieth annual convention of the California Grain and Feed Association in Los Angeles. He battled with Joseph Martin Jr. when Martin announced he was quitting his GOP job to work for Nelson Rockefeller in the California primary. Although Goldwater had never been associated with the John Birch Society, Knowland found himself having to defend Goldwater against the Rockefeller team's attempt to link the Arizona senator with the right-wing group.

George Young, part of the Spencer-Roberts public relations team that was running Rockefeller's California effort, sympathized with Knowland. "The Goldwater people have the ready-made Republican organization and they have all those volunteer workers, but they have the problem of trying to get along with the kooks and the nuts. As I see it, that is Bill Knowland's job—he is known as the campaign manager but his job is to keep the kooks and the nuts from embarrassing the responsible people who are working for Barry. I wouldn't want the job."[7]

The California GOP was in a mean mood. The right wing had gained control and as much as told Republican moderates to get aboard or get out. After Nelson Rockefeller lost the primary to Barry Goldwater, Bill Knowland issued a warning through the press for Senator Kuchel to support Goldwater or face loss of future support, insisting, "We expect to achieve party unity and get the support of Senator Kuchel and others who supported Rockefeller." Knowland, who was to be chairman of Goldwater's California delegation to the Republican National Convention, said flatly that liberal or moderate Republicans were under a "grave obligation" to support Goldwater, and should Kuchel or any other fail to support the Arizona senator, he would lose any right to claim GOP loyalty when seeking reelection.

Kuchel, chairman of Rockefeller's unsuccessful California campaign, replied, "I am not going to respond to threats of reprisal or attempts at intimidation by Senator Knowland or anyone else. That is not the way I fulfill my public trust . . . that is the way I will remain whether I am a public servant or a private American citizen."[8] Four years later, Kuchel was a private American citizen, defeated in the 1968 primary by California State School Superintendent Max Rafferty—the smooth-talking darling of the GOP right.

The 1964 GOP convention in San Francisco's Cow Palace was an ugly display of brute force by the right-wingers. They shouted down those who disagreed with them, fought with reporters, and denounced all news media as being biased toward the Democrats. They even passed out daily lists of "Do" and "Don't Do" items. One of the things to "Do" daily was "Read the Goldwater Convention Newsletter, your state's newspapers, and the *Oakland Tribune*, which is published by Mr. Knowland. These will be available in your state headquarters."[9]

Just before the Republican convention began, Knowland summoned *Tribune* circulation director Bill Ortman to his office and told him he considered it extremely important that the *Oakland Tribune* be well represented on San Francisco newsstands. Even though Ortman put his best distributors on the job, when the senator went to the news counter at the Hilton Hotel early on the Sunday morning of the convention, he was told that the *Tribune* wouldn't be available until 11 A.M. Ortman got a call from the extremely irate Knowland telling him to get over to San Francisco and straighten out the problem. Ortman was still half asleep, but he made it from Oakland to the lobby of the downtown San Francisco Hilton in half an hour. His publisher was furiously pacing back and forth in front of the news counter. When Ortman questioned the clerk on duty, he responded, "Oh, I thought he was asking for the Chicago *Tribune*. I haven't opened the bundle of *Oakland Tribunes* yet. We actually don't open the newsstand 'til 8 A.M." As the clerk opened the bundle, Knowland snatched one off the top and thundered, "Young man, there is only one *Tribune*."

When forces supporting Pennsylvania governor William W. Scranton tried to get the convention to endorse the constitutionality of new civil rights laws, they were brushed aside. "Did any member want a stronger civil rights plank?" a reporter asked Knowland. "I would say no," replied Knowland. "They felt the platform is satisfactory as now written."[10] Just six years earlier, he had been in the Senate working with Lyndon Johnson for civil rights protections.

Goldwater was virtually shouted into nomination at the Cow Palace, with GOP National Chairman William Miller of New York as his running mate. It would be Knowland's last GOP convention as a delegate. He would go to Nixon's nominating convention in 1968 as a newsman and stay home during Nixon's renomination in 1972.

Throughout the fall in the 1964 presidential campaign, the Goldwater forces used Knowland mainly outside of California. They needed Democratic votes, and Knowland's right-to-work stance in 1958 was not forgotten by union members in his own state. He made speeches for Goldwater in fifteen other states, and he found himself continually defending the California GOP from attacks linking it to the radically conservative John Birch Society. "It is not a Republican organization," Knowland said in an October 8 speech in Columbus, Ohio. "It has never claimed to be. They do claim to have as many Democrats as Republicans."[11]

Two major international incidents in October 1964 hit an already troubled Goldwater campaign: the Chinese exploded their first atomic bomb and Nikita Khrushchev was ousted from power in the Soviet Union. Knowland called them "earth-shaking events" and predicted that they might lead Communists to take a tougher line in their relations with the West. At home they might also have brought the nation even more closely behind President Lyndon Johnson, for he defeated Goldwater easily in the November election. It was Knowland's last campaign. Although he would continue to contribute to Republicans such as Ronald Reagan for the rest of his life, he would no longer actively participate.

He returned to what was becoming a much more complex life in California. In the following months and years, the Free Speech Movement, the People's Park Rebellion, the Black Panthers, Hell's Angels, the Symbionese Liberation Army, and hundreds of what would come to be routine antidraft and antiwar demonstrations would rock the East Bay.

.   .   .

During the Goldwater campaign, Bill Knowland became enamored with a woman named Evelyn Kelley. After meeting her at the pool in the

Ambassador Hotel in Los Angeles, he began an on-again, off-again relationship that would go on for seven years and cause him a great deal
of embarrassment.

Kelley, described by Paul Manolis as a pudgy, Mediterranean-looking
woman, took the relationship far more seriously than did the senator.
Wishing to marry him, she went so far as to go to Los Angeles Superior
Court to have her name legally changed to Knowland. On January 6,
1972, when she learned he had remarried, she sent out announcements
that said in part, "The Honorable William Fife Knowland and Evelyn
Mugello Kelley no longer have a marriage."

At various times, Kelley would call and make threats to editors and
reporters at the *Oakland Tribune*, as well as to Joe Knowland and his
sister Emelyn. She would identify herself to the news staff as "the real
Mrs. Knowland." The brother and sister each went to the senator to
offer help, without the other's knowledge. Early in 1971, Kelley pan-
icked the senator by falsely saying she was pregnant. Her teenage son
told friends in Los Angeles that he was Bill Knowland's illegitimate son,
even though he was fourteen years old when she met Knowland. As late
as April 1973, the senator drew a cashier's check for $12,000 for a Bert
Kelley, who was identified in Oakland police files as the son of Evelyn
Kelley.

"I wasn't embarrassed by his women," the senator's son, Joe, told
us. "I knew presidents and kings had girlfriends." But the private life of
William F. Knowland was beginning to be known by a wider circle of his
employees and acquaintances.

.   .   .

At Senator Knowland's alma mater, the University of California at Berkeley, which in the 1960s he referred to derisively as "the Little Red School
House," trouble was brewing. It had begun before the Republican
convention when the *Oakland Tribune* city desk got a phone tip that
the W. E. B. Du Bois Club was collecting contributions for William
Scranton on university property at the Student Union Plaza. Since the
Tribune was supporting Goldwater, the tipster suggested, it might be
interested that such political solicitations were in violation of university
policy.

Because of the ban on political activities on campus, for years activ-
ists of all political stripes had set up card tables and solicited donations

on a walkway at Bancroft Way and Telegraph Avenue. When *Tribune* reporter Carl Irving checked and found the W. E. B. Du Bois Club didn't have a table set up at the time, no story was written. But although the *Tribune* had lost interest, university officials were stirred by the newspaper's inquiries. For them, the problem was complicated by the fact that while the area concerned appeared to be the city of Berkeley's sidewalk, it actually was university property; the question thus arose why political activity was permitted there that was not allowed on the rest of the campus. Alex C. Sherriffs, vice chancellor for student affairs, already had complaints that bongo drums in the Student Union Plaza were disruptive, and he decided that the dean of students was not enforcing campus rules.

Before long, University of California president Clark Kerr was drawn into the situation, and at his Charter Day speech on the university's Davis campus, he stated, "The University will not allow students or others connected with it to use it to further their non-University political or social or religious causes, nor will it allow those outside the University to use it for non-University purposes."[12] The problem was tossed in the lap of Katherine Towle, the dean of students. Though somewhat concerned about litter left in the area, she said later, "In fact, if I thought about it at all, which I think was not very often, I—it seemed to me as sort of a safety valve, and there was no harm in what they were doing."[13] The safety valve was about to be closed—and, soon after, it would blow.

As the fall semester opened, university officials still were pondering what to do about the increasingly political area. A student activist named Brad Cleveland put out a twelve-page pamphlet that called on Berkeley students to make a series of demands on the board of regents, which included the resignation of Clark Kerr and reconstitution of the board itself. The pamphlet created only a small stir, but it became the basis for a group called the Ad Hoc Committee to End Discrimination, which announced plans unrelated to the university: it would picket the Knowlands' *Oakland Tribune*. The committee accused the *Tribune* of discriminatory employment policies. Jacqueline Goldberg, head of the campus Women for Peace and a member of the ad hoc group, said that the committee didn't expect to win against Bill Knowland because he was too powerful and couldn't be frightened. She also acknowledged that a sit-in at the *Tribune* might mean a lot of jail time, because Knowland would not back down.[14]

On the same day that the ad hoc group announced its plans to picket the *Tribune,* Dean Towle sent out a letter declaring that campus rules against political solicitations would be enforced throughout the campus, including the twenty-six-foot strip of brick walkway on Bancroft Way at Telegraph Avenue. Posters, easels, and card tables would not be permitted and the area could not be used by those supporting or advocating off-campus political or social action. The effective date was September 21, 1964.

A strange coalition of radical and conservative groups joined to protest the new rules, and eighteen groups formally petitioned Dean Towle to reopen the area with limitations on the number of tables and posters, as well as on the way tables would be operated. Jackie Goldberg, who had become the official representative of this ad hoc group, met again with Towle and came away with the feeling that William Knowland was applying pressure to get rid of the political meeting place. Out of it all came a growing group called the United Front, which agreed to conduct vigils, rallies, and in some cases acts of civil disobedience if the university continued its hard line on the narrow strip at Bancroft and Telegraph. The *Daily Californian* followed with an editorial headlined "The Fight for Free Speech Begins."[15]

There is no doubt that the *Tribune* was hostile to the student agitators, but so were the other Bay Area papers. Many of the students and nonstudents involved were left-wing radicals and some were linked publicly to the Communist Party. The newspapers of the 1960s just weren't quite ready for that. It would be years before the public and press moved closer to the protesters as general opinion turned against the Vietnam War.

And Oakland was having its own problems. With a growing unemployment rate, particularly among the blacks who made up about 23 percent of its population, it was ripe for an eruption. City officials estimated they had about a year to do something about it. About $50 million in federal funds had been spent in the first half of the 1960s, much of it in job-training programs, but the city had little to show for it. When the Watts section of Los Angeles exploded into violence in 1964, many urban specialists felt it was only a matter of time before Oakland would follow.

There was a major difference between Los Angeles and Oakland, however. Watts was a relatively small area of about 65,000 residents, mostly black, surrounded by other minority communities. From the beginning of World War II to 1964, the black population in Los Angeles had increased nearly tenfold. While many of Oakland's minorities had come out from the South and the East during World War II to work in the defense industry, many of the middle-class black families making up the base of the city's population had been there for two or three generations. In addition, Oakland officials were aware of the magnitude of the problem, and when the Federal Economic Development Administration (EDA) offered them up to $23 million to stimulate industrial expansion to provide jobs, they listened. Under the guidance of Mayor John Houlihan, the leaders of Oakland were brought together. Bill Knowland, president of the Oakland Chamber of Commerce as well as publisher of the city's newspaper, generally was regarded as the most important figure in the city's power structure. He also was considered by the soldiers in Lyndon Johnson's War on Poverty to be an ultraconservative who would be difficult to deal with.

While some of the participants expected opposition or even hostility to the EDA program, Knowland listened with interest and in general terms offered assistance. A week earlier, the *Tribune* had published a large section on economic development, with a signed lead-in from Knowland that blamed unemployment for much racial unrest. He suggested that many problems would be solved when education provided skills and jobs were made available to minorities.

From this first meeting came a curious alliance of conservative business leaders, industrialists, federal bureaucrats, labor leaders, minorities, and city officials determined to see that Oakland did not suffer the fate of Detroit or Watts. Like most of the other Oakland power players, Knowland was deadly serious. A few years earlier, as a senator, he might have voted against aid to cities, but now he was ready to accept it willingly. In a meeting on the subject at the *Tribune* some time later, an editorial writer suggested that additional freeways needed for new industries in Oakland might create smog and lower air quality. "Burning cities create smog and lower air quality!" he thundered in reply.

Those outside the power structure had reason to be suspicious. For years, public elective bodies in Oakland had been selected by an "old boys" process that was self-perpetuating. From the city council to special districts to school boards, there was a common pattern: incumbents stepped down in midterm, then allowed their fellow board members to appoint a successor. From the 1930s to the 1960s, the ratio of appointees to elected officials was about seven to one. Mayor Houlihan himself was replaced by appointment when he left the mayor's office in 1966. His successor, John Reading, would be reelected twice on his own.

Every slight gain made in improving the city was tortured, highly contested, and fraught with peril. In the fall of 1966, while the Oakland–Alameda County Coliseum was being completed, the Black Panther

Party for Self Defense was being formed in Oakland by Bobby Seale and Huey Newton. There would be pickets at the *Tribune*, antidraft demonstrations, parades of Hell's Angels, petty corruption, and political battles as the city struggled to maintain a degree of equilibrium.

But Oakland did not burn.

.   .   .

Joseph R. Knowland's health had been failing for some time, and the senator was effectively running the *Tribune*. When J.R. died on February 2, 1966, at the age of ninety-two, his son Bill became publisher in name as well.

At the same time that Bill Knowland was tending to the economic recovery of Oakland, he made an unexpected decision that turned the *Oakland Tribune* inward and away from the affluent suburban areas growing rapidly in Alameda and Contra Costa Counties. At a meeting of the entire editorial department, managing editor Steve Still announced a plan to "metropolitanize" the *Tribune*.

A ripple of protest went through the staff. The *Tribune* had the best suburban coverage in the Bay Area. There were bureaus in Fremont, Hayward, Livermore, San Leandro, Alameda, and Berkeley in Alameda County. Contra Costa County, which is smaller, had bureaus in Pittsburg, Concord, Walnut Creek, Martinez, Richmond, and El Cerrito. "We had a reporter behind every rock," assistant city editor Robert Cuthbertson said. Sales of newspapers were at an all-time high. Eighty-five percent of the residents in affluent Orinda subscribed to the paper, and circulation was growing in all parts of Contra Costa and Alameda Counties. The *Tribune* was going to turn its back on a growing gold mine of advertising and circulation dollars in the suburbs.

The reason given was the high cost of maintaining circulation outside metropolitan Oakland, but the *Tribune* would never recover from the decision. Dean Lesher would immediately expand a group of small suburban Contra Costa County papers based in Walnut Creek into a rich chain of dailies, anchored to malls and laden with advertising dollars. Floyd Sparks, his Alameda County counterpart, would do the same with his small newspaper network. The *Tribune* would be left with a deteriorating city that every day was leaking businesses into the suburbs, businesses that took their advertising dollars with them. A few weeks after the announcement, a *Tribune* reporter ran into Lesher in a Concord bar. Lesher grinned and said, "Tell Bill I like what he's doing." Sparks responded similarly. "With enemies like that, who needs friends?"

The *Tribune*'s circulation went up momentarily during a San Francisco newspaper strike, then started on an inexorable downward slide. "It wasn't a decision taken lightly," Manolis recalls. "We didn't have an A.M. AP franchise. We were a P.M., and they [afternoon papers] were dropping like flies. Where we missed the boat is in not having gone A.M. ten or fifteen years earlier. [The Knowlands] would have had to invest in the future."

.   .   .

Despite his shyness and perceived aloofness to employees, Bill Knowland was a compassionate man. When science writer Henry Palm died of cancer, leaving a young widow with two small children, Knowland joined a benefit softball game with total abandon. He hit, fielded, and tripped over first base in an attempted slide before retiring to the sidelines.

Lee Susman, a mischievous member of the art staff, had brought along a large thermos full of martinis, and he offered one to the senator as he huffed and puffed to the bench. The thermos was one of the old-fashioned kind, with a metal cup that both formed the top of the container and served as a drinking glass.

Knowland gratefully accepted the cup Susman filled, drank the martini in a gulp, and in one powerful motion crushed the cup as if it were paper and tossed it aside.

"Thank you, Lee," he said.

"You're welcome, Senator," Susman said wryly as he stared at the remains of his thermos cup.

On another occasion, a raucous retirement party was held in a downtown Oakland restaurant for an editor who was leaving the *Tribune*. Two of the participants ended up in the Oakland jail for driving under the influence. One of them—a rather insecure sports columnist—had smashed his *Tribune* car into a couple of parked autos on the way home. Knowland, knowing of the columnist's tendency to worry, called him into his office the following morning and assured him that his job was not in danger. Then as the columnist left, the senator added, "It must have been a helluva party!"

.   .   .

Knowland was drifting further and further away from the political scene. He respected Ronald Reagan, whose reelection as governor he supported in 1970. Editorially, he supported George Murphy's attempt to hold on to his old Senate seat, but he virtually dismissed the incumbent senator as incompetent. Even a dozen years after he had left the Senate, the *Tribune* publisher was vitally concerned with the seat he had represented.

When John V. Tunney, a young Kennedy clan Democratic congressman from Southern California, challenged Murphy in 1970, Knowland invited Murphy to Oakland for a strategy session. Tunney, son of the world heavyweight boxing champion Gene Tunney, was the former college roommate and close friend of Senator Edward Kennedy; he was expected to be a strong Democratic candidate. Over a luncheon catered by Trader Vic's restaurant in the *Tribune*'s twentieth-floor executive suite, Knowland vigorously described Murphy's problems in Northern California in general and the Bay Area in particular. He outlined several moves the senator could make to raise both money and his level of support in the north. The *Tribune* publisher offered to help, pointedly remarking that Northern Californians still considered Murphy to be a lightweight movie actor more noted for tap dancing than for his legislative career.

Murphy appeared to be totally unaware of the advice Knowland was offering; instead, he started a rambling discourse on how well things were going. "You know, Bill," he said in the raspy voice left scarred by an operation for throat cancer, "as I was coming home the other night, I ran into Frank Sinatra. I said 'How you doing, Frank?' He said, 'Fine, George. You know, I've been thinking of endorsing you.' I said, 'Frank, that's wonderful.'" Turning to Knowland, Murphy asked, "What do you think, Bill, isn't that wonderful?"

Bill Knowland's neck turned first red, then purple. He rose from a half-finished lunch and said in a firm, cold voice, "Well, Senator, I'm sure you have more important things to do. We don't want to keep you any longer." He then almost physically forced Murphy to the elevator and the street below.

That November, John V. Tunney was elected to the U.S. Senate, and Murphy retired to private life.

During this time, Knowland was trying to turn his paper away from its image as a right-wing mouthpiece. When Dave Hope, the respected but extremely conservative *Tribune* political editor, died at his typewriter in the city room on February 14, 1969, the senator appointed a young registered Democrat as his new political editor and immediately ordered him to give equal coverage to both parties. The editorial pages remained Republican, but the *Tribune* began to endorse an occasional Democrat. The senator himself even grew a stylish mustache.

His family noticed the change. "I'd have to say that when Dad aged, he moved more to the left," his daughter Estelle recalled. "For example, his feeling on Nixon's trip to China was, 'It's about time.' He had tremendous praise and admiration for the trip and for the beginning of opening the door. We were together the morning that the news broke." She said that he turned away from the Republican right wing. "Dad just couldn't tolerate that kind of conservatism any longer as he got older. As a result, he may have become someone who was believable by both the moderates and conservatives in the party. He was the elder statesman, the only one left in town, so to speak." When there was an attempt to revive the right-to-work movement in the early 1970s, Knowland quietly discouraged it.

The senator continued to have disagreements with his son over the operation of the *Tribune* and over Joe's part in the newspaper. In particular, Joe continued to question Manolis's high place in the newspaper's chain of command. In a letter to his son, Bill Knowland defended Manolis, saying, "I owe him more than I could repay in a lifetime. Outside of my immediate family he was closer to me than any other person. He was the bridge between my life in Washington and Oakland. He knows my political, economic and civic policies and aspirations. He has given me loyal and dedicated service over and beyond that of a valued employee and beyond the call of duty."

Curiously, he described Manolis in the same way his daughter Emelyn described her mother, Helen—as a "brutal friend." And twice in his letter, the elder Knowland referred to himself as "Stubby," a nickname hung on him not by his son, but by Manolis, in reference to his stubbornness. He insisted that every leader needs such a friend "who will tell his principal the facts, good and bad, who has the guts to say what the timid 'ass kissers' don't dare to say. [Manolis] was invaluable to me, let him be to you. He can do things for you that at times you can't do as well for yourself."

           ·   ·   ·

The senator began casino gambling as early as 1962. "All the years when he was in the Senate, he never went to Reno or Las Vegas," Manolis said. But at a quarterly meeting of the California Newspaper Publishers Association at Lake Tahoe, he recalls, the senator said, "Let's go do some gambling." They played some blackjack. At that time, Manolis suggested, it was secondary in the senator's life; he had never seen him gamble before. Soon, however, Knowland was making trips to Las Vegas just to visit the casinos.

In the beginning, he was winning. He would send notes to Manolis: "Please deposit in my account at United California Bank," or "Please deposit Crocker-Citizens Account. Having a good time. Wish you were here." One such note said, "Dear Paul. You doubled your $5.00. The $10.00 is yours. Please deposit $100.00 for me in Crocker-Citizens. Deposit tag in upper left hand drawer in back of check book. Bill." Another note, on a greeting card, said, "Dear Paul, Profitable delay! Our plane was 2 hours late leaving Las Vegas—We went to the Tropicana [near the airport] and I won $300.00. Here is $100.00 to deposit for me in Crocker account."

Knowland's chief editorial writer in the late 1960s and early 1970s was Virgil Meibert, a talented horse handicapper who would spend hours at night studying racing forms. When he would go to the senator's office to discuss editorials, they also would talk about horses. Later, at Golden Gate Field in Albany, Meibert would go to the two-dollar window to collect his meager winnings and look over at the fifty-dollar window where the senator was collecting stacks of large bills on his bigger bets.

Knowland may have tried to break the gambling cycle. He wrote to Helen in November 1969, "I'm seeking a different vacation spot that we both would enjoy once a year. I have 'had it' with Las Vegas." He suggested trying Bermuda, Acapulco, or New Orleans. But a year later, he was traveling to Las Vegas to gamble on his own. "He would play craps," says his son, Joe. "He wasn't a logical [gambling] person. I never saw him playing roulette, or even 21 [blackjack]." Joe recalls, "He loved to win, and throughout his life, he played each staged role to 'win.' Furthermore, throughout his life he never lost. He was never taught to lose."

The gambling would turn deadly serious in the early 1970s, and Bill Knowland would learn about losing.

27

Ann

Bill Knowland met Ann Dickson in a bar at the Tropicana Hotel in Las Vegas on July 7, 1970. He was taking a break from the gambling tables, and he noticed her immediately. She was a stunningly beautiful woman in her late thirties who stood out in a city filled with beautiful women. He sat at the bar beside her and began a casual conversation. Despite his stilted manner of small talk, when he introduced himself and offered a drink, Ann accepted readily.

Although he usually had difficulty talking one on one, even with people he knew well, Ann was different. She made conversation easy, letting him know she knew who he was, how important he was, and that she remembered his background. He was flattered. Sometimes even in Oakland, where he should have been recognized, the senator felt he was ignored. With Ann, he felt important, and they got along from the start. She touched the right buttons and he reacted. He liked to drink, and she kept up with him, drink for drink. He liked to dance, and she danced beautifully. He liked to gamble, and she knew her way around Las Vegas.

They spent the night in her nearby apartment, which she called "the Pit." Within days they were into a torrid affair. The senator and Ann quickly became part of the Las Vegas Strip scene.

He soon would know that Ann was a mistake, a horribly messy mistake. Ann wanted more than an affair. She quickly let him know she wanted marriage and a chance at the rich Knowland life. His past affairs for the most part had been quiet, pleasant interludes. He had truly loved Ruth Moody, but most of the women were just entertainment outside his marriage. Now, he found himself looking at divorce and remarriage, not an affair, and despite everything he had done for her, Ann was out of control. She was drinking constantly, throwing tantrums, and abusing him verbally in front of his friends. She wanted him to leave Oakland, leave the *Tribune*, and move to Las Vegas. She knew he couldn't do that, but she kept demanding it.

Ruth Ann Dickson was born November 28, 1931, in Tulsa, Oklahoma. She was a beauty from the start: old family photos show her as striking, modeling an Easter hat when she was scarcely more than a baby. She was an only child and the center of the family's attention.

She began doing television commercials for a Tulsa car dealer when she was barely in her teens. Friends recalled that she never left the family's neat, middle-class house unless her hair was done and her makeup was perfect.

Her daughter, Kay Sessinghaus Paolinctti, who after college became a successful businesswoman in Colorado Springs, Colorado, remembers Ann as "a product of the '50s, where if you had a pretty face, men fell at your heels and would do anything." She was the belle of her Catholic high school and later of Tulsa University. As a Chi Omega sorority pledge at the university, she learned to drink, an aptitude that would both help her and drag her down. "She had her choice of boyfriends, even then," her daughter recalls older family members saying. Her favorite was Lawrence Sessinghaus, a fellow student, and they began dating seriously a few weeks after they met. Girls of the '50s were expected to get married, and in 1952, when she was twenty-one years old, Ann became Mrs. Sessinghaus.

Kay was born the following year, and Ann was totally unprepared for this change in her life. While Ann found her role as mother especially difficult, marriage was not easy for either her or Lawrence. Both were young, self-centered, and unready for a suburban family life. Ann resented the marriage and resented having to take care of a child. Kay said her father told her later that Ann would call him home from work to change diapers.

Before, life had been easy for Ann, but now it became more and more arduous. Sessinghaus was restless and moved the young family constantly. They lived in Oklahoma, California, and Kansas. They had a second child, Steve, in 1958, but Sessinghaus never really settled down. When he announced that they were moving to Arizona, Ann decided she had had enough. She felt she deserved a better life and she knew it wouldn't be with Sessinghaus. She filed for divorce and let Sessinghaus take the children with him to Arizona.

Ann went to Las Vegas to try to get her life on track again. She was still young, beautiful, and ambitious, and in the late 1950s, Las Vegas was a mecca for the young and restless. There she met Jack Wilson, a high flier who was rich one year, poor the next. She caught him on an upward swing, and she began to experience the life she had always wanted. Life in Las Vegas was exciting, and the possibilities seemed limitless. They were married, and while their success lasted they enjoyed a life of luxury. Ann won parts in television commercials for Schlitz beer, MetraCal, and Kentucky Fried Chicken. They bought a country club in El Centro, California. Then the downward slide began. Wilson tried various business ventures, but few were successful. Ann felt herself falling into the same unsettled pattern that she had experienced in her earlier marriage.

As she moved from place to place, Ann saw her children occasionally, but they remained in Arizona with Sessinghaus. They remember little of Wilson. Her daughter, Kay, told us, "I don't know who he was, or when they got married. They divorced and married again. They fought a lot over money. They had a lot and lost it all. . . . [It was] feast or famine. One summer I went out to visit them. They had a gorgeous home off Sunset in the Hollywood hills. It was beautiful, with a swimming pool."

Wilson and Ann separated a final time, and she returned to Las Vegas, living with a man named Nick Lorenzo. Ann's son, Steve Sessinghaus, remembers Lorenzo as an old "Italian type guy, kind of a rough-hewn character, what you might think of as old Las Vegas." Wilson mailed her a Mexican divorce in 1970, and she never heard from him again. Back in Las Vegas, she began doing some bit parts in movies in addition to television commercials. She met Elvis Presley when she had a small part in *Viva Las Vegas*, and did some dancing in clubs, but she never really caught on. "I think Mom always had in herself the thought that she could be [another] Elizabeth Taylor. But as far back as I can remember, she didn't have any skills," her daughter recalls. "She thought the only assets she had were her looks." Ann started dropping years off her age; once she introduced Kay as her sister so no one would know that she was old enough to have a teenage daughter.

The young divorcée definitely was ready for something better when former senator William F. Knowland approached her in the Tropicana casino bar.

The Las Vegas Strip in 1970 was nothing like the Disneyland-like high-rise carnival of today. Most of the hotels and casinos were two- or three-story buildings set back from the streets. It was still a small town,

a place where the rich and famous could be entertained. James Seagrave, vice president of public affairs at the Stardust Hotel and casino,
remembers the era with some nostalgia. He can't recall meeting Knowland, but he says, "It was not uncommon at all for prominent people
to lose lots of money, and feel perfectly safe that no one would know
about it. There was an aura of privacy. [Hotels and casinos] were stylish, low-key getaways. People wore dinner jackets. Women wore evening dresses." Typically, a big spender would be met at the airport and
brought by limousine to his or her casino of choice. Rooms, food, and
drinks were complimentary. Sometimes, even major officials at a hotel
might be unaware of well-known guests and their gambling habits.

Organized crime still ran the town in the late 1960s and early '70s
when Knowland was gambling heavily. "It was mob controlled," says
Myram Borders, longtime United Press International Las Vegas reporter
and currently chief of the Las Vegas Convention/Visitors Authority
news bureau. "But it was freewheeling for the patrons. You could drop
out of sight and have a wonderful time." Borders worked in the UPI
Las Vegas bureau from the time of the mob buildup into the corporate
era of the 1990s.

As far as the outside world was concerned, Bill Knowland was able
to drop out of sight and have a wonderful time, at least until his relationship with Ann became public. After he met Ann, they gambled together. The Knowland family believed she had been working for the
casinos as a shill to entice customers to the table. Her son, Steve, who
now is an attorney in Tulsa, rejects the notion: "She had a friend who
did that, but I don't think she did." Nevertheless, Knowland began to
be invited to parties for high rollers at the Tropicana and Riviera. When
the MGM casino opened, the senator and Ann were invited. Everything was complimentary.

Kay remembers, "Every holiday, he'd have a suite and everything
was comped. Steve and I would have parties, and when room service
came, we'd say, 'Oh, he's in the shower, can we sign for it?' We always
had the nicest rooms. You don't get those things without being a big
spender. He'd always have a lot of chips in his pocket when he was in
Vegas." To Ann and her children, Knowland appeared rich. "He was a
fountain of money," Kay says of the time. "His own kids had gorgeous
homes in Piedmont."

What they did not know was that the gambling and the expense of
maintaining two lives were dragging him down. In the next three years,
he would spend every dollar he could get his hands on, then borrow
more. He sold his holdings in the Tribune Building Company and the

Franklin Investment Company, a business associated with the *Tribune*. He sold his Russian River home to the Tribune Building Company. Using his influential position as publisher of the *Tribune*, he was able to borrow $1 million from Oakland banks. He even borrowed from Helen. By 1974, he had to ask for his entire annual salary from the *Tribune* in January. A month later, the money was all gone.

His dream romance, a sixty-two-year-old man with a beautiful younger woman, began to collapse almost from the beginning. Knowland started living in a plastic world in more ways than one. He had fourteen credit cards when he met Ann, and he would add thirty-five more in the next three years. In 1971, he cashed $52,354 in checks just at the Tropicana, Riviera, and Sands casinos. Like most gamblers, his bad luck ran in streaks. On March 4, 1971, he cashed a $200 check at the Tropicana and another for $400 at the Riviera. Two days later, he cashed checks for $600 and $400 at the Riviera. A day later, it was $500 at the Sands and $500 at the Tropicana. In April, he cashed $2,700 in checks at the same casinos in a three-day period. Most of the checks ranged from $300 to $600, and sometimes he cashed more than $1,000 a day. He also was paying Ann's bills and commuting most weekends to Las Vegas. They occasionally took trips to New York and Puerto Rico.

While the senator liked set rules, organization, and order, Ann was impetuous, extravagant, and totally unstructured in her life. Knowland tried to put her on a schedule, establish her lifestyle, and set her on a straight course, but it was an impossible situation for both of them. He had been in control all of his life, and she was uncontrollable. Still, the smitten senator went ahead with plans to get a divorce from Helen, his wife of forty-four years, and marry Ann. Joe remembers both his parents at that time as being terribly distraught: "Helen, like most women who really love 'their man' for more than sex and security, was indeed in her own way in love with her 'Billy' until the day she died. And, believe it or not, HE remained in love with HER, in his own way, until the day he died. Note—when he asked for the divorce, reluctantly she gave it to him by filing 'irreconcilable differences' rather than adultery." An interlocutory, or intermediate, decree was issued on October 5, 1971. The final dissolution of the marriage to Helen was ordered on March 15, 1972.

Knowland began planning for a new marriage; to get Ann's correct ring size, he borrowed the wedding ring Jack Wilson had given her. He lost the ring and Ann became furious. He finally calmed her by giving her a check for $1,500.

Adjusting to his new family was difficult for the senator. Ann was having trouble with her adolescent son, Steve, and wanted to send him back to Tulsa to stay with her mother. Ann wouldn't move to Oakland, but she would call or fly up on a moment's notice. He kept trying to make order out of what rapidly was becoming a totally disordered life. But nothing was working as he planned. Ann again was being difficult. Early in March, they tried to come up with a wedding date, but in a note to himself, Knowland wrote that problems with Steve, Ann's temper, and her medical problems indicated that they should postpone marriage until "we both knew there was a reasonable chance for happiness for all of us." When he told Ann this in a phone call to Las Vegas, she hung up on him. Knowland also noted that Ann had slapped his face four times; she sometimes berated him crudely and profanely. Nevertheless, he clung to her and the hope that the relationship could be saved. She told him they would be married in April "or not at all," and on April 29, they were married in Oakland at the Park Bellview apartments. The senator's daughter Emelyn put the small ceremony together; Paul Manolis was best man. The senator was devastated when his only son, Joe, refused to attend. Manolis's wife, Elene, remembers seeing Ann's mother and thinking, "That's who he should be marrying. She was very dignified, with gray hair."

The honeymoon that followed was a disaster. Instead of going to the Caribbean, they booked a luxury cruise through the Mediterranean on the Incres Lines' *Victoria*. Ann disliked her cabin and hated the ship, which she immediately labeled an "old tub." She did like the ship's food, and she loved the champagne. She drank heavily and loudly insulted people around her on the liner. Knowland repeatedly pleaded with her to keep her voice down and not to disturb the other passengers. In his letters home to Manolis, now the *Tribune*'s executive editor, he referred to Ann's having a serious "change of life problem," but he remained blind to what was clear to others—Ann was a full-blown alcoholic.

The situation became so intolerable that the captain of the *Victoria* threatened to remove the Knowlands from the ship when it reached Greece. The senator decided he was not going to be pushed around. It was his honeymoon, and he was determined to finish it. He wrote to Manolis, "If we are put off, I shall inform those responsible that I intend to use all the resources at my command to take civil action against the Incres Lines, its officers, ship and corporate [headquarters]." He called both his lawyer son-in-law, Hal Jewett, and Manolis and ordered them to be prepared to fly to Athens. He told them the shock and embarrassment of being kicked off the ship might cause his blood pressure to go so high it might kill him, and his heirs would "have a strong case, as do the [*Tribune*] corporation[s] for damage done to them." The *Victoria*'s captain relented, and the remainder of the trip settled down to a pattern of pleasant visits ashore and distressing periods aboard the ship.

In a letter to his daughter Emelyn, Knowland wrote: "It has been a yo yo existence almost every single day since we stepped foot aboard the Victoria. The shore visits, in many cases were all that could be desired. But on the return to the ship, she would be upset by such a variety of major things to her, but relatively minor to any other human being, that I was baffled, troubled and now [I am] convinced that she is a very upset, immature and perhaps dangerous woman."

Ann threatened to leave the ship in Spain and take off on her own. "Ann is two completely different personalities," Knowland told Emelyn. "One is sweet, kind and most lovable. The other is violent, abusive and more bitchy than any woman or man I have ever known." He added, "After one of her tantrum sessions which must be seen to be believed, a veil seems to fall before her eyes and she is living in another world. The next day, or perhaps even later the same day, the veil lifts and she is her other lovable self. At least she seems contrite and not to remember what she has said or done."

Early in the affair with Ann, Knowland had met still another woman. Lee Carter was something of a mystery woman, known to Knowland's *Oakland Tribune* staff only as a voice on the telephone. According to his family, he went to see her when he was having trouble with Ann, and she had a sympathetic ear for his problems. He would drop everything when she called the *Tribune*. Knowland kept pictures of her in his desk drawer, but even Manolis never met her. The senator's daughter Estelle listed Paul Manolis as the telephone contact for Carter, but he says he cannot recall anything about her. Although the affair lasted more than three years, she never was seen with him publicly. The day after the honeymoon ended, Knowland went to visit Lee Carter in San Francisco. He told her of the troubles throughout the trip. He was obsessed with death, and he brought a copy of his own obituary that he had prepared for her to read.

Once back in Oakland, the senator worked on getting to know his new family. He and Ann flew to Scottsdale to an eighth-grade graduation ceremony for her son, Steve. Then the three flew to Tulsa for the high school graduation of Steve's sister, Kay.

They returned to Oakland and moved into a third-floor luxury apartment at 311 Wayne Avenue near Lake Merritt, even though the senator still had a lease at the Park Bellview apartments nearby. Steve had a room in the apartment and Kay lived in a separate apartment next door.

"I thought he was quite nice," Steve recalls. "I liked him very much. He treated me very well. He was always wanting to give me advice on things. I was a pretty good student; I think he was pleased about that." To the public, the senator appeared stern, almost humorless at times, but Steve says he didn't have that impression at all; "seemed like he laughed at a lot of things, enjoyed things that made him laugh."

His sister, Kay, has similar memories. "I thought he was a wonderful man. I would have liked him [even] had he not paid my tuition and everything, and he still made me work." One of Kay's favorite stories about the senator concerned his voracious appetite. "He was a big man, and he had a big appetite. My mom had this lemon cream makeup she put on her face. He ate it." Kay later opened the refrigerator and saw a big sign on the cream, "NOT FOOD! DON'T EAT!"

Kay wanted to go back to Tulsa for college, but Knowland insisted she stay in the Bay Area. She was too late to register at Stanford University, her first choice, and he convinced her that she should attend Mills College in Oakland. While at Mills, Kay was holding down a job in a greasy spoon on University Avenue in Berkeley. The senator would go up to visit her in his limousine. "I was working at this little barbecue dump. . . . About once a week he'd be sure to come and have dinner there—in his suit, and everybody else in jeans and T-shirt, and here he'd try to order a decent dinner and always leave me a big tip."

Kay was aware of the couple's stormy relationship, but she cautioned, "Don't show my mother in too terrible a light. I don't believe she drove Bill into bankruptcy." She added, "Bill truly loved my mother, and in her way she loved him. It's a fact she drank, but she didn't do anything differently after they were married than before they were married."

It was as if Knowland was trying to have a relationship with Ann's children that he never had with his own. He communicated with them constantly and advised instead of ordering. Steve recalls driving through the San Joaquin Valley once with Knowland on a trip from Oakland to Las Vegas. "We drove through Merced and Kern County. He was telling me about all the political factions in them. I found it an interesting conversation. It was a long time ago, but I remember it." In contrast, Knowland's younger daughter, Estelle, remembers a summer in Washington, D.C., when she and her father commuted together—she to school and he to the Capitol: "We never talked about anything. We rode in silence."

Ann hated Oakland. She was not accepted in the senator's old social circles and was barely tolerated by most of his family. The couple's closest friends were Charles and Irene Sargent, and the Knowland family said that Ann bought her way into that friendship with her lavish spending at Irene Sargent's specialty apparel store. She also was running up charge accounts at other exclusive Bay Area shops. Ann was jealous of the lifestyle of the senator's two daughters and his son. They were high in the East Bay social strata and she was not.

The senator's son, Joe, was the most rigid. He made it clear that at best he considered Ann an opportunist. He didn't say what his worst thoughts were. His relationship with his father worsened, both in the family and at the *Tribune*. Joe now reflects, "Where what he once touched turned to gold, now it turned to stone. Everything he tried to do failed him."

The senator was short of money again, and he wanted the newspaper's board of directors to sell its holdings in a newsprint company in Tacoma, Washington. Joe didn't want to lose the *Tribune*'s source of newsprint. "I asked for a one-month delay," Joe says. "Dad said to the board, 'If you don't support my resolution, I will resign.'" They took one gasp of breath and went along with him; Joe cast the only dissenting vote. According to Joe, the decision cost the company $1 million. The senator removed his son as assistant publisher, saying, "There is only one publisher at the *Tribune*, and I am he."

That dictatorial attitude did not reflect personal animus; he took the same approach toward his own *Oakland Tribune* editorial board, a group of editors that made recommendations on endorsements. During one election, a $47 million Peralta Community College District bond issue was on the ballot; Knowland's editors felt they could not justify it. Knowland, always a strong supporter of education, listened patiently as the editors explained their points of view. Then he stated, "The vote is one to five, and I win. We endorse the bonds."

When ground was broken on a new campus financed by the bonds, Knowland was there with a shovel.

.   .   .

Ann began to exploit the senator's friendship with her own children. In a note to himself, Knowland said she had called him from Las Vegas and threatened to link him romantically with her teenage daughter. He wrote a note for his files: "During the course of the phone conversation, she said she would accuse me of spending more time with Kay than with her. 'How will that look in print?' said she. It was a bald-faced threat of blackmail and I told her so. She calmed down some after I told her I could not be threatened or intimidated by any such move on her part. I told her I would inform Kay of what had transpired and arrange for her to re-enter Mills as a boarding student. She asked me not to tell Kay, but I feel tonight that there is no alternative left to me now." During the same period, Ann often complained that he was spending too much time with the Knowland family. He told her he had divorced his wife for her, but not his family. In a later note, he wrote, "Dear God, I have never dreamed a marriage in 'paradise crest' could turn out to be made up of so much 'hell.' Maybe man makes his own heaven or hell on earth."

Ann sought the recognition in Las Vegas that she couldn't have in Oakland or Piedmont. The senator bought her a house on Ridgecrest Drive in southeast Las Vegas; it was a large home resembling tract housing, about five miles east of the strip, near the intersection of Boulder Highway and Flamingo Road. She decorated the living room in pinks and golds, with a baby grand piano as the focal point. In the family room, she placed the senator's political mementos. The master bedroom was in blues and whites. A red and white bedroom with imported wicker furniture was done for Kay, but she never lived there permanently. In November 1972, the Knowlands' Las Vegas home was included in the Clark County Attorneys' Wives Thirteenth Annual Tour of Homes.

The senator bought Ann a Pontiac Grand Prix. She didn't like it, so he bought her a new Lincoln Continental Mark IV and gave the Grand Prix to Kay. He sent Ann on two trips to Hawaii in the first months after their marriage, joining her on the second. She asked for boats, a car for Steve when he reached his sixteenth birthday, and a new car for Kay in place of the Grand Prix. "The more I did for her, the more she wanted," he complained in a note to Paul Manolis in December 1972.

She responded by continuing her attempts to spend her way to social approval, and Knowland suffered more. "I am not Aristotle Onassis," he protested to her at one point. He considered selling the *Tribune* to raise money. He talked to the Gannett newspaper group, but they couldn't reach an agreement. He wanted $20 million, and they offered $8 million. By this time, he was behind $68,000 on a commercial loan, owed Helen for part of the divorce settlement, and was trying to pay nearly $30,000 in back income taxes.

"By December [1972], I had come to realize that unless the situation was corrected soon, the situation was headed for disaster for both of us, in one way or another," Knowland wrote in another memo.

He told Manolis that things were moving to a crisis stage. Ann was demanding a $3,200 set of diamond drop earrings for Christmas, and said if Knowland didn't buy them for her, "I might as well not come to Las Vegas." On Christmas Day, he gave her a different set of diamond earrings and she threw them at him. "It was this Christmas disaster that was the straw that broke the camel's back of our marriage," he wrote in a memo. "I knew then that we had come to the end of the road." The despondent senator wrote a letter to Manolis outlining plans for his own funeral.

On December 30, he wrote again to Manolis, saying Ann was going to hire Los Angeles attorney Paul Ziffren to handle any divorce action. Ziffren was a former California Democratic Party leader that Knowland had treated harshly in the 1958 campaign for governor. "He hates your guts," Ann had told the senator. Knowland also told Manolis that he was concerned for the *Tribune*. He said Ann had threatened to destroy him and the family business. "She is capable to do [*sic*] the first and perhaps to make a real attempt to do the second through some strange connections she has," he told his executive editor. He did not explain the "strange connections."

Ann was more comfortable with her old friends in Las Vegas than in California, and even as she threatened divorce, she wanted Knowland to get more involved there. In January 1973, she called the senator with a problem. She had been out with Phil Daly, a friend who had been fired from his job as manager of the slot machine operation at the Tropicana Hotel when new management took over. The two had been drinking together, and he had been arrested for driving under the influence of alcohol. Ann said there had been no accident, and no one was hurt, but the police had taken Daly to jail and impounded his car. When the senator called the Las Vegas police, he was told that Daly had been booked and bail was set at $500. With the help of his son-in-law, Hal Jewett, Knowland arranged for bail through a Las Vegas bondsman. Because of a delay in wiring the money through Western Union, Jewett ended up flying to Las Vegas with the bail money. But by the time he arrived, Daly already was out of jail.

·   ·   ·

The pressures of his foundering marriage and worsening financial condition continued, and on February 7 the senator collapsed at his

Oakland apartment. His daughter Emelyn brought him to Peralta Hospital in Oakland unconscious and unable to sign his admittance papers. He had been working on labor negotiations regarding new equipment in the *Tribune*'s composing room and was exhausted from his trips back and forth from Las Vegas. The diagnosis was high blood pressure.

Ann flew to Oakland and was enraged when the Knowland family was allowed to see the senator and she was not. The family battle that ensued further troubled the senator. When he was released from the hospital, he filed for divorce. Knowland's attorney was Suren Toomajian, known then in Oakland as "the great separator" because of his success in divorces of the rich and famous. Toomajian, who had occupied offices in the *Tribune* Tower since it was built, advised a lump settlement for Ann so that a clean cut could be made. The senator wanted to set up some sort of an annuity for her and her children.

But the divorce would never become final. On March 3, Ann fell against a table in her Las Vegas home and suffered a severe head injury; as a result, the senator was drawn back into the quagmire. Ann had been drinking and arguing with her son throughout the day. Ann's mother, Ruth Dickson, took Steve out to dinner to get him away from Ann. When they returned at about 11 P.M., they found her on the floor near the dining room with a deep puncture wound in her forehead. Both Steve and his grandmother thought she was dead. They called police for an ambulance. Because of the depth of the wound, Las Vegas police thought she had been shot. Knowland flew to her side at Sunrise Hospital.

As Ann recovered, they continued to discuss a divorce settlement, but the senator moved back into the cycle of commuting to Las Vegas. Ann insisted she did not want a divorce. The senator told her he could not continue his busy life and come home to turmoil. He offered a number of suggestions, including that she return to Tulsa to live with her mother. She rejected them all.

The man who had argued with presidents and set national policy had more than met his match in this second wife. In another memo to himself, he wrote: "It is one of the few times in my life I have run up against an impasse with every alternative door apparently blocked. Yet, there must be a reasonable and proper answer. Perhaps with God's help, one can be found before a great tragedy takes place."

28

"Not Much Time"

The senator became increasingly obsessed with thoughts of his own mortality; he wrote repeated instructions to Paul Manolis on what to do after his death, and he was fearful for his own and his family's safety. He became morbid, hinting that his own entanglement with Las Vegas might be more sinister than just gambling losses.

In an October 17, 1973, letter to Manolis, he discussed selling the *Tribune* but noted, "There will be forces at work who will seek to divide and conquer. Some may have connections with the crime syndicate. . . . Pull together and not apart. There are elements that do not have the best interest of this community at heart who would like to gain control over the TRIBUNE." In an earlier letter to his son, Joe, he had warned that "some from the criminal underworld may seek to gain control." He never discussed his gambling debts with the family or Manolis, but they were a growing problem for him, and he may well have been worried about problems from the Las Vegas mob.

In addition, both the FBI and the Oakland Police Department had warned him in 1973 that certain groups might try to kidnap him or a family member. Since the *Tribune* had openly opposed some of the Black Panthers' tactics, he may have feared them as well as other radical groups. At the time, the threats were very real. In rapid succession, *Atlanta Constitution* publisher Reginald Murphy was kidnapped, then Hearst newspaper heiress Patty Hearst was abducted from her Berkeley apartment by a group calling itself the "Symbionese Liberation Army" (SLA). The same band that kidnapped Hearst had assassinated the popular Oakland school superintendent, Marcus Foster, with cyanide-tipped bullets and had wounded his assistant, Bob Blackburn. There were reports that the SLA had a "hit list" that included Knowland, the industrialist Edgar Kaiser, and other prominent East Bay residents.

Knowland hired round-the-clock security for his family and drew up his own funeral plans. He issued orders that in the event that he was kidnapped, no deals be made with the kidnappers, even preparing an elaborate plan on how he would handle his own kidnapping. He ordered that no payment be made for his return and threatened that should he survive, he would fire anyone who paid ransom. He suggested he might fake a heart attack and fall to the pavement to give police a clear shot at his assailants.

The Oakland police and FBI investigated at least one death threat against the senator, but results were inconclusive. The threatening letter later disappeared from the police department files. Meanwhile, the senator developed secret knocks so that Ann and her children would know when he was at the door of their Wayne Avenue apartment.

On January 3, 1974, Knowland sold 100 shares of stock in the Tribune Building Company for $80,000. He told the family that the money would be used "to pay off a substantial bank loan, to prepare for payment of income taxes, and to do estate planning." He borrowed $36,000 from his former wife, Helen. She said later, "He made a statement to me that he never expected to get out of debt as long as he lived. That was just said once and it was not amplified or explained."[1] Even with Manolis, the senator became silent and uncommunicative, and he began to take on the physical appearance of a very sick man.

On Thursday, February 14, he and Ann had a Valentine's Day dinner at Trader Vic's in Emeryville with Ed Daly, president of World Airways, and his wife; Oakland Symphony conductor Harold Farberman and his wife; and Charles and Irene Sargent. The next night, at an informal dinner thrown by industrialist Steve Bechtel at the Banker's Club in San Francisco, he was distant and preoccupied. Knowland looked so haggard that Kaiser executive Nils Eklund took Estelle aside to discuss her father's health.

During that day, too, the senator had seemed disturbed and had talked very little. Manolis was so concerned he went to the *Tribune* over the weekend, leaving a note in Knowland's office asking to talk with him. Knowland usually arrived at the *Tribune* early, and at 7:30 A.M. Monday, he called Manolis from his office in answer to the note. When they met at 8:30 A.M., Manolis asked point-blank about Knowland's health and assured the senator that everyone wanted to help him. Knowland tried to talk, but apparently he could not unburden himself. He did say he was worried that Ann would make a scene at the paper's centennial celebration planned for the following Thursday, and that he would be embarrassed in front of Governor Reagan and all of his friends. Manolis noticed that the senator was not smoking and that all ashtrays had been removed from his office.

On Tuesday, *Tribune* employees described their publisher as "zombie-like," although he appeared to be in a slightly more cheerful mood than he had on Monday. Still, he looked tired and was unusually quiet; his typically booming voice was almost inaudible. When he saw several editors and department managers throughout the day, he seemed to be using his desk as a prop to keep himself from falling. He had a lengthy telephone conversation with Bob Beritzhoff of the Oakland Chamber of Commerce, apparently about the centennial celebration. He went to the bank, returned to the office briefly, then drove to Irene Sargent's upscale specialty dress shop to pick up Ann, who was shopping again. When a store employee came in to say the senator was outside, she said, "Tell the old fart to wait. I will be out when I feel like it." Knowland left, and a store janitor drove her home.

That night, Ann embarrassed the senator again. An Oakland police officer saw a woman walking in a traffic lane along Lakeshore Avenue. He described her as "intoxicated and belligerent." When he attempted to question her, she pointed to a man in a blue Cadillac, and screamed, "I'm not going to ride with him." The driver identified himself as "Mr. Knowland" and the woman said, "We are on our way to the Paramount." She got into the car and they drove toward Broadway.[2]

When they stopped at the Mirabeau Restaurant in Oakland's Kaiser Center for dinner, they were seated at Nils Eklund's table. Ann became loud and quarrelsome and had to be removed from the Mirabeau. The couple had planned to attend an Oakland Symphony performance at the Paramount Theatre of the Arts, and they were driven there from the Mirabeau in Irene Sargent's chauffeured limousine. Friends outside said that when the Knowlands arrived, they heard Ann direct a stream of profanity at the senator. The Knowlands did not go inside, and they did not go to a reception they were scheduled to attend after the concert.

On Wednesday morning, Knowland was in his office by 7:10 A.M. A 10 A.M. meeting of the Tribune Publishing Company board had been moved up an hour because the funeral of Dudley Frost, one of the senator's few close friends, also was at 10. The meeting was short, and when Manolis went to the senator's office at 10:10 that morning, he was surprised to find Knowland still there. He asked Knowland why he hadn't attended the funeral of Frost, whom he had known since his army days.

The senator replied, "I don't know. I wanted to. I just couldn't." Manolis said Knowland looked "absolutely exhausted."

Knowland asked for a glass of water, saying he felt "dried out." When Manolis asked if he wanted him to call a doctor, the senator replied, "No, that is the last thing I want." The senator told Manolis he still had not written his remarks for the centennial celebration to be held the next day, and that he was concerned about it. Manolis offered to put together the remarks, assuring Knowland that he knew the history of the paper and had all the information he needed. Knowland's response to the offer wasn't clear, but Joanne Eskenberry, one of his secretaries, said that the staff already was preparing the senator's speech.

When Manolis continued to press the senator about his health, Knowland told him he had slept only two hours the night before. "There is not much time left," he told Manolis. He didn't explain whether he was talking about the anniversary celebration, his marriage, or his own life.

Knowland canceled two other *Tribune* meetings scheduled for that afternoon. He had lunch with Ann at the Mirabeau, then returned to the *Tribune* and told his executive secretary, Bertha Farris, that he would be out most of the afternoon. After leaving, he called in several times, saying he was in a phone booth in San Francisco, mainly to discuss the seating at the family tables for the centennial luncheon. Joe and Emelyn talked to each other about their father's condition Wednesday evening, noting that he appeared to be under unusual stress. Knowland returned to his office after ten that night, and marked a memo for filing. He left a few minutes later.

At 7:50 A.M. Thursday, the day of the centennial, Knowland entered through the back elevator, which took him through the fourth-floor newsroom before he came into his own office. The staff said he seemed to be forcing himself to be upbeat. Later, when departmental ceremonies to mark the paper's one hundred years began, he appeared not to recognize people. He asked Joe to take his place in cutting the cakes and retreated into his office. Joe asked Emelyn to follow the senator, and her father told her, "I am just so tired."

Joe asked that Dr. Sid Priday, the senator's physician, be called in, but when Knowland heard about it, he refused. Nevertheless, Priday was contacted by Knowland's son-in-law, Hal Jewett, about 9:30 A.M. Though Priday was afraid that his arrival at the *Tribune* might upset the senator even more, he promised that he would come if the senator wanted him. The senator emphatically did not want the doctor. He then went back to the cake-cutting ceremonies. After they were over, Joe, Emelyn, and security manager King Collins accompanied the senator to advertising director Roy Boody's second-floor office. Knowland was worried about picking up Ann, and he said he intended to drive over himself and bring her to the *Tribune*. Jewett offered to drive Knowland home, and although he balked at first, the senator finally gave his car keys to his son-in-law.

The main public ceremonies were held on the marquee in front of the *Tribune*'s entrance at Thirteenth and Franklin streets. Raymond L. Spangler, former publisher of the Redwood City *Tribune*, presented a plaque naming the original *Tribune* building on Ninth Street as a historic site in journalism, as officially designated by the national journalism society, Sigma Delta Chi. Ann was shaking visibly, and the senator appeared to be unsure of what was going on. When he came to the microphone to deliver his remarks, he obviously was unaware that the plaque presentation already had been made.

A bus drove the dignitaries to Jack London Square, where the Chamber of Commerce celebration luncheon was planned at the cavernous Goodman Hall. Knowland again told Emelyn he was worried about Ann making a scene. He asked that Estelle sit next to Kay Sessinghaus at one of the family tables. Ann sat quietly at the head table through the luncheon without incident, as Governor Reagan delivered a glowing speech about the newspaper and the Knowland family. After the luncheon, family members closed in on Knowland to support him. Three times he seemed ready to collapse. His daughter Estelle said later his eyes were glazed and he appeared to be oblivious to his surroundings.

Back in his office with Ann, the senator said to Manolis, "I wasn't very good, was I?" He seemed in better spirits, though, and was relieved that the ceremonies were over. Shortly after 4 P.M., he told Manolis that he and Ann were going to the home of his stepmother, Clarice "Cookie" Cook, for a family gathering. Hal Jewett drove them to the Seaview Avenue home. While there, Cookie made the excuse of taking the senator and Estelle to the basement to look at some early editions of the *Tribune*, so that they could talk to him privately. They both told him they were worried about his health, and asked him to allow himself to be hospitalized that night. He wouldn't answer. Cookie asked him if he had been threatened. He didn't speak, but indicated "yes" by nodding. He wouldn't explain further.

After they returned to the main floor, Estelle again asked her father privately if he would go to the hospital that night. He paused, then said, "No." She pressed him, urging him to go the next day. He answered slowly, "I'll think about it." Knowland agreed not to attend cake-cutting ceremonies for the night shifts at the *Tribune*, letting Joe handle the program. Privately, he also agreed to take a walkie-talkie radio set to his apartment. Both Hal and Estelle said they were not sure that Ann would call a doctor if he became ill. The senator accepted a list with the names of three doctors from Estelle, putting them in the left breast pocket of his suit coat, though Estelle doubted that he would use them. Hal and Estelle drove Ann and the senator back to their apartment, then went to the *Tribune* to pick up the walkie-talkie transceiver. Knowing his difficulty with mechanical devices, they marked the "on" button with red ink. Back at the apartment, they had a drink with the senator and Ann; he was "virtually unresponsive," they said later.

Later in the evening, Knowland's spirits picked up, and he and Ann went to Victor's restaurant at the St. Francis Hotel in San Francisco. Ann later described it to Emelyn as a beautiful evening, saying they had a good dinner, danced, and "closed up the place." But Ann became concerned about Knowland during the night. About 5 A.M. Friday, she called Irene Sargent to see if she could get Irene's doctor, Paul Jones, but he did not come to the apartment. At 6 A.M., Knowland was up and having coffee at the Quarter Pounder on Grand Avenue near Magnolia in Piedmont. Dr. Karl Stucki, an orthodontist who had offices nearby, also was in the restaurant. He told the family later that the senator "looked terrible."

The senator had left a note with Ann, saying, "Dearest Ann, I've gone out to get the morning and evening papers. Do not make any engagements or appointments until I return." Knowland didn't reach his office until 10:30 A.M. Repeated attempts by family members to find him earlier were unsuccessful. Manolis asked the senator if he had slept, and he answered, "No, I hardly slept, did not get much sleep."

King Collins came in to give Knowland better instructions on the use of the walkie-talkie. Joe Knowland arrived to talk with his father, and asked if there was anything he could do. The senator answered, "No, these are personal problems." Then he told Joe, "She [Ann] has some strange friends." Later in the morning, some color returned to the senator's face, and he began to look more cheerful. Emelyn said that she heard him on the telephone with his sister, Eleanor, and he was laughing. He told Emelyn that he was feeling better. Emelyn asked him if he would get medical help for his stress. "If a person is not under one kind of stress, he is under another," he grumbled to his daughter. But he promised her he would not allow himself to get so rundown again.

When she asked him what the family could do if he did, he answered, "Hit me with a club."

At noon, the senator, Emelyn, and Manolis had lunch in the *Tribune* Tower twentieth-floor board room. They talked about the centennial and the Patty Hearst kidnapping. Knowland returned to his office and spent the balance of the day working on personal papers, writing checks, and balancing his checkbook. He was smoking, and the ashtrays were out again. He told Manolis that Ann had planned parties for them to attend over the weekend, and he was not enthusiastic about it. When the *Tribune*'s political editor stopped by Knowland's office in midafternoon to discuss some upcoming news coverage, he noticed a marked improvement in the senator's appearance.

Knowland talked with Emelyn and Estelle by telephone, and again declined to have himself hospitalized. He told Estelle he hoped to go to the Russian River in the next week, and said their weekend plans included a dinner dance Saturday night at the Claremont Country Club and a Sunday night dinner party in San Francisco. Estelle told him to take care of himself, and said, "I love you." He answered, "I love you." He had several calls from Ann during the rest of the afternoon, but declined other calls. Before he left the *Tribune*, the senator had Bertha Farris take a deposit to the bank and he wrote some checks, including $150 cash for himself. He told the office staff to have a good weekend and left at 5:30 P.M. On his way out of the building, Knowland ran into his nephew, George Church, and told him he looked forward to a birthday party for Church's brother-in-law, Edgar Lion. A short time later, Ann called Eleanor Lion in Arizona to accept the invitation to Edgar's party.

The senator had shown extraordinary interest in the Hearst kidnapping. One of the SLA demands had been that the Hearst family buy more than $1 million of groceries and distribute it in the inner city. The senator was concerned about disturbances in connection with that distribution in East Oakland. He called city editor Roy Grimm about 9:30 P.M. to tell him he wanted to be kept informed about the situation.

Ann told Emelyn later that they had argued that evening over her demands that she be given a substantial amount of *Tribune* stock. She also told Emelyn that Knowland had a phone conversation, perhaps as long as fifteen minutes, with an unidentified person that evening. The senator went to bed in the guest bedroom about 10 P.M.; it was the last time she would see him alive.

29

Powder Burns

Emelyn and Hal Jewett had arrived at the Knowland Russian River compound about 1 A.M. the day of William Knowland's death. After hearing from neighbors that someone had been cutting down redwood trees for firewood, they had driven up from Oakland to check out the report. They went over to the senator's house about 2:30 A.M. to get some canned soup for a snack.

Back at their own residence, they slept late, arising about 11. They checked out the redwood grove along the river and found nothing indicating unauthorized timber harvesting. A half hour later, they went by the senator's home and were met by the caretaker, Gilbert Michael Baxter, who told them that the gate to the path leading to the river had been unlocked. It turned out that Baxter had been hauling some oak trees from up the coast onto the property, where he was cutting them up for sale.

Emelyn noticed her father's car in the driveway, but when she checked, he was not in the house. She left a note for him, then walked with her husband to the Northwood Lodge, which was just west of the family compound. Glenwood Parker, the lodge manager, told them that he had seen the senator pass at approximately 10:10 A.M., and that he was alone. Another neighbor, Otis John Schubel, and his wife told Emelyn they had not seen the senator, but their house guest, Natalie Lavin of Sonoma, had seen a gray-haired man drive up to the house shortly after 10. The Jewetts spent about twenty minutes talking with the Schubels, then walked over to the nearby golf course clubhouse to see if anyone had seen the senator, thinking he might have stopped there for breakfast.

Hal and Emelyn returned to the senator's home, and Baxter led them through the gate and down to the river. The path was overgrown as it usually was in the winter, but it was easy to see a single set of widely spaced footprints going down to the dock—the strong stride typical of the senator on a mission. At the edge of the river, the footprints were muddied, as if he had slipped.

By now, Emelyn was frightened. She called Paul Manolis, but he said he hadn't known the senator was going to the family compound. She was afraid her father might have fallen into the fast-moving water. Baxter waded into the edge of the river and felt around, but found nothing. By this time, Harold Jewett III, the senator's grandson, arrived and launched a small boat the family kept at the compound. His search, too, was fruitless, although he worked his way downstream to Monte Rio. At 1:40 P.M., fully recognizing the seriousness of the situation, Hal Jewett called the Sonoma County Sheriff's Department. Emelyn called Manolis again and asked him to call her brother, Joe, because she couldn't remember his phone number.

Torn scraps of paper were found around the dock. When pieced together, they showed part of an invitation to a reception in Hillsborough in honor of U.S. Attorney General and Mrs. William Saxbe, from 4 to 6 P.M. Saturday. No note was found.

Scuba divers David Nagel and Kenneth Anderson of Rohnert Park Police Department arrived shortly after 3 P.M., and they were in the water by 3:30. It took them only thirty seconds to find the body, about six feet from the shore on the east side of the dock. Knowland was still dressed in his familiar blue suit, wearing a neatly tied tie and dress shoes. A single bullet had entered his right temple and exited on the left side of his head. There were powder burns around the entry wound. The divers went back in the water, and within fifteen minutes Nagel had found the .32-caliber Colt automatic on one of the stairs leading into the water. The safety was off and a live round was in the firing chamber, but the weapon was jammed. A small paper clip, wedged between the remaining three cartridges, would have prevented the gun from firing again.[1]

An autopsy was performed by Dr. John C. Leissring under the direction of Sonoma County Deputy Coroner Pat Boling. Leissring noted the powder burns on the right temple, indicating that the muzzle of the gun had been at very close range. There also were powder burns on the senator's right fingers. No water was in his lungs, and blood tests indicated no trace of alcohol or drugs. There were no indications of any serious illness; indeed, for a sixty-five-year-old man, Knowland had been in excellent health. His haggard appearance in the final week of his life apparently was caused by stress.

Officers from Sonoma notified the Oakland Police Department and the FBI. The Oakland police sent a copy of the report to the Las Vegas Police Department. Although there was immediate suspicion of foul play, the evidence was overwhelming that the wound was self-inflicted. Only one set of footprints led to the water; the powder burns were obvious; and the only fingerprints on the weapon were Knowland's.

Various individuals contacted the FBI concerning the death, saying there must have been a murder. They offered no evidence—they simply couldn't believe that the senator had committed suicide.

· · ·

The day after the senator's death, the news staff started drifting into the *Tribune* by midmorning. It was a Sunday, but those from all shifts worked to put out a fitting tribute to the man they sometimes disagreed with but always respected. "There Were Giants in the Congress," said a page one headline on February 25, 1974, over a story that described the senators Knowland had served with and his legislative accomplishments. Although the reporters and editors worked most of the day, not one turned in an overtime slip.

Tributes began to arrive from all over the country. Perhaps Senator John Stennis of Mississippi summed it up best: "I knew him as a man of deep conviction and great determination. He was a great party man, always, but he was always ready to break with the position of his party when he felt strongly that his own conflicting position was right. I recall that while he was serving as majority leader the Senate became evenly divided as between the major parties, Senator Knowland remarked, 'I am the only man who has served as majority leader without a majority.' A few of us will remember him fondly, streaking down the Senate aisle with his giant steps as if there was always more to be accomplished than we knew about."[2]

A simple funeral service was held in Oakland's First Methodist Church, where his father's services were held. At Knowland's own request, the songs "I Love You, California" and "Stout-Hearted Men" were played. Former California senator Thomas Kuchel was the only representative of the U.S. Senate present.

Lee Carter made a last call to the *Tribune* to ask about funeral services. She said she wanted to bring flowers, without a card. She disappeared as mysteriously as she had appeared.

Epilogue

Three days after Knowland's death, nearly $1 million in bank loans came due. The family eventually would repay them and reclaim the stock.

Joe Knowland, the senator's only son, became editor and publisher of the *Tribune*. His sister Emelyn became president of the board of directors. Unlike her brother, Emelyn had never worked at the *Tribune* until her father died, but she started out at the top. She remembered sitting at her typewriter trying to write a book to be titled "The End of an Era"; she quit after four chapters.

Despite bringing new ideas, new energies, and a new lively format to the paper, Joe was unable to lead the *Tribune* back to its previous levels of power and financial stability. He was named "Publisher of the Year" by the California Press Association in December of 1975. Yet just a year later, his cousins, aunt, and uncle put enough stock together to force the sale of the paper.

Combined Communications, a Phoenix corporation noted more for outdoor advertising than for newspapers, purchased the *Tribune*, and on July 1, 1977, the Knowland family relinquished control. The same day, Lionel Wilson, Oakland's first black mayor, was sworn in at city hall. Although the usual public pronouncement was made by Combined Communications that no administrative staff changes were contemplated, Joe Knowland was fired as editor and publisher the following Monday.

The new *Tribune* owners threw a big party for the staff at the Paramount Theatre of the Arts on Broadway, a theater that the Knowlands had worked hard to restore. The centerpiece was an ice sculpture of the *Tribune* Tower. After the party, the sculpture was tossed into the street in front of the Paramount, where it melted slowly into the gutter.

Two years later, Gannett Corporation acquired the *Tribune* by swallowing Combined Communications. They used it to try out a new format in a paper called *Eastbay Today*—the experimental forerunner of Gannett's *USA Today*. They brought in former *Washington Post* national reporter Robert Maynard to edit the *Tribune* and eventually made him the nation's first black publisher of a metropolitan daily newspaper. But the *Tribune* was not a typical Gannett cash cow, and in early 1983, the chain financed Maynard's purchase of the paper so that it could get out from under the *Tribune*'s increasing red ink.

Maynard tried to keep the newspaper going, but in 1993, his failing health and the paper's continuing deficits forced him to sell to a suburban chain, Alameda Newspaper Group. Maynard died of cancer just months after the sale. The *Tribune* now runs as an edition of the Alameda Newspaper Group, operating out of a Port of Oakland office at Jack London Square.

The senator's sister, Eleanor Knowland Lion, died in 1978 at the age of eighty-three.

Helen Herrick Knowland died in 1981 of cancer.

Happiness and success continued to evade Ann Dickson Knowland. After the senator's death, she ran a small country-western working man's bar in Las Vegas for a while; she married twice more. She developed lung cancer and returned to her hometown of Tulsa in 1984. Her mother took care of her, and she died in a tiny bedroom in the back of the house where she grew up. She was fifty-two.

Hal Jewett died in 1986 and Emelyn died in 1988, both after long bouts with cancer.

The phone numbers that the senator had for Lee Carter and Evelyn Kelley have been disconnected, and attempts to contact them were unsuccessful.

Paul Manolis gathered more than 400 boxes of the senator's papers for the Bancroft Library of the University of California at Berkeley. Manolis now is director of the Patriarchal Orthodox Institute at the Graduate Theological University on Hearst Street in Berkeley, where he also serves as an adjunct professor at the university across the street.

Estelle, a writer, has reclaimed the Knowland name; she lives in Alameda.

Joe Knowland and his wife, Dee, also live in Alameda, a few blocks from Estelle; they sell real estate.

The twenty-one-story Tribune Tower, once the pride of Oakland, stands dark in the center of the city.

Notes

Chapter 2. Heading West

1. J. R. Knowland, unfinished autobiography (written ca. 1950), in family possession (copy in Joseph R. Knowland papers, Bancroft Library, University of California at Berkeley).

2. Joseph E. Baker, *The History of Alameda County* (Chicago: Clarke, 1914), p. 69.

3. Daniel E. Wyatt, "Joseph R. Knowland: The Political Years, 1899–1915" (master's thesis, University of San Francisco, 1982), p. 4.

4. *History of Alameda County* (n.p.: N. W. Wood, 1883), p. 778.

Chapter 3. Newspapers and Politics

1. Daniel E. Wyatt, "Joseph R. Knowland: The Political Years, 1899–1915" (master's thesis, University of San Francisco, 1982), p. 7.

2. Ibid., p. 10.

3. J. R. Knowland, unfinished autobiography (written ca. 1950), in family possession (copy in Joseph R. Knowland papers, Bancroft Library, University of California at Berkeley).

4. Ibid.

5. Thomas Storke, *California Editor* (Los Angeles: Westernlore Press, 1958), p. 153.

6. George Mowry, *The California Progressives* (Chicago: Quadrangle Books, 1951), p. 59.

7. Quoted in "The Battle for California's Toga," *Sunset, the Pacific Monthly*, October 1914, p. 654.

8. Roland DeWolk, "The Knowland Family and the *Oakland Tribune*" (unpublished), Bancroft Library, University of California at Berkeley.

9. William F. Knowland, oral history, p. 1, interview by Raymond Henle, October 4, 1967, Herbert Hoover Library, West Branch, Iowa.

10. Quoted in *Washington Post*, February 25, 1974.

11. *Time*, January 18, 1954.

Chapter 4. After Politics

1. John A. Gothberg, "The Local Influence of J. R. Knowland's *Oakland Tribune*," *Journalism Quarterly* 45 (1968): 494–95.

2. *Oakland Tribune Yearbook 1924* (Oakland, Calif.: Oakland Tribune, 1925).

3. Gothberg, "Local Influence," p. 491.

4. Quoted in *Editor and Publisher*, August 8, 1959.

5. *Time*, August 14, 1939.

6. Harold Ickes, *America's House of Lords: An Inquiry into the Freedom of the Press* (New York: Harcourt, Brace, 1939), pp. 139–45.

7. *Time*, August 14, 1939.

8. J. R. Knowland, letter to publishers, October 28, 1939, Joseph R. Knowland papers, Bancroft Library, University of California at Berkeley.

9. *Time*, August 14, 1939.

10. Gothberg, "Local Influence," p. 495.

11. Edward C. Hayes, *Power Structure and Urban Policy: Who Rules in Oakland?* (New York: McGraw-Hill, 1972), p. 133.

12. Quoted in Gothberg, "Local Influence," p. 488.

13. Quoted in *Oakland Tribune*, January 13, 1923.

14. Quoted in *Editor and Publisher*, September 20, 1930.

15. Quoted in Gothberg, "Local Influence," p. 489.

Chapter 5. "That Look in His Eyes"

1. Quoted in *Time*, January 14, 1957.

2. Paul Healy, "The Grim Senator from California," *Saturday Evening Post*, April 25, 1953, p. 27.

3. Ibid.

4. Geraldine McConnell, "Earl Warren: Views and Episodes," p. 13, interviews by Willa K. Baum, Amelia Fry, Caroline Gallacci, Catherine Harroun, Hannah Josephson, Rosemary Levenson, Garielle Morris, and Ruth Teiser, March 29, 1970, Regional Oral History Office, Bancroft Library, University of California at Berkeley.

5. William F. Knowland, oral history, interview by Raymond Henle, October 4, 1967, p. 3, Herbert Hoover Library, West Branch, Iowa.

6. Quoted in *Time*, January 14, 1957.

7. Herbert L. Phillips, *Big Wayward Girl* (Garden City, N.Y.: Doubleday, 1968), p. 177.

8. Walton Bean, *California: An Interpretive History* (New York: McGraw-Hill, 1968), p. 410.

9. Greg Mitchell, *The Campaign of the Century* (New York: Random House, 1992), p. xii.

10. Ibid., p. 226.

11. William F. Knowland, in "Earl Warren's Campaigns," vol. 2, p. 20, interview by Amelia Fry, August 2, 1973, Regional Oral History Office, Bancroft Library, University of California at Berkeley.

12. Ruth A. Ross and Barbara S. Stone, *California's Political Process* (New York: Random House, 1973), p. 167.

13. Knowland, interview in "Earl Warren's Campaigns," p. 26.

14. Earl Warren, *Memoirs of Earl Warren* (Garden City, N.Y.: Doubleday, 1977), pp. 68–69.

15. Quoted in Irving Stone, *Earl Warren: A Great American Story* (Englewood Cliffs, N.J.: Prentice-Hall, 1948), pp. 88–89.

16. Ibid.

17. Oscar J. Jahnsen, oral history, in "Enforcing the Law against Gambling, Bootlegging, Graft, Fraud, and Subversion, 1922–1942," p. 32, interviews by Alice King and Miriam Feingold, 1976, Regional Oral History Office, Bancroft Library, University of California at Berkeley.

18. Knowland, interview in "Earl Warren's Campaigns," p. 35.

19. Ibid., p. 33.

20. Knowland, oral history, p. 5; interview in "Earl Warren's Campaigns," p. 34.

21. *Oakland Tribune*, April 10, 1938.

22. Charles Fisher, oral history, p. 12, interview by Raymond Henle, July 31, 1971, Herbert Hoover Library, West Branch, Iowa.

23. Quoted in *New York Times*, August 9, 1938.

24. Quoted in *Oakland Tribune*, April 10, 1938.

25. California Republican Assembly newsletter, July 28, 1938, Herbert Hoover Library, West Branch, Iowa.

26. William F. Knowland, letter to Henry S. McKee, July 16, 1938, William F. Knowland file, Herbert Hoover Library, West Branch, Iowa.

27. Fisher, oral history, p. 24.

28. William F. Knowland papers, Bancroft Library, University of California at Berkeley.

29. Gladwin Hill, *Dancing Bear: An Inside Look at California Politics* (Cleveland: World Publishing, 1968), p. 96.

30. Ibid., p. 97.

31. William F. Knowland, interview by James Bassett, associate editor of the *Los Angeles Times*, June 12, 1973, Bancroft Library, University of California at Berkeley.

32. Gardiner Johnson, oral history, interview by Gabrielle Morris, 1973, p. 66, Regional Oral History Office, Bancroft Library, University of California at Berkeley.

33. Healy, "Grim Senator," p. 27.

34. William F. Knowland, letter to Wendell Willkie, April 23, 1942, and Willkie, undated letter to Knowland, William F. Knowland papers, Bancroft Library, University of California at Berkeley.

Chapter 6. Billy Goes Off to War

1. William F. Knowland, letter to Herbert Hoover, June 16, 1942, and Hoover, letter to Knowland, June 18, 1842, Herbert Hoover Library, West Branch, Iowa.
2. Marilynn S. Johnson, *The Second Gold Rush: Oakland and the East Bay in World War II* (Berkeley: University of California Press, 1993), p. 8.
3. Quoted in ibid., p. 30.

Chapter 7. From Major to Senator

1. Quoted in Fletcher Knebel and Dan Fowler, "He Would Rather Be Right and President," *Look*, April 5, 1955, p. 44.
2. *San Francisco News*, February 13, 1945.
3. *New York Times*, August 8, 1945.
4. *New York Times*, August 12, 1945.
5. Royce D. Delmatier, Clarence F. McIntosh, and Earl G. Waters, *The Rumble of California Politics, 1848–1970* (New York: John Wiley, 1970), p. 308.
6. *New Yorker*, July 7, 1956.
7. *New York Times*, August 15, 1945.
8. Geraldine McConnell, "Earl Warren: Views and Episodes," p. 13, interviews by Willa K. Baum, Amelia Fry, Caroline Gallacci, Catherine Harroun, Hannah Josephson, Rosemary Levenson, Garielle Morris, and Ruth Teiser, March 29, 1970, Regional Oral History Office, Bancroft Library, University of California at Berkeley.
9. *Time*, August 27, 1945.
10. *Newsweek*, August 27, 1945.
11. Leo Katcher, *Earl Warren: A Political Biography* (New York: McGraw-Hill, 1967), p. 193.
12. McIntyre Faries, "California Republicans, 1934–1953," p. 38, interviews by Amelia Fry and Elizabeth Kerby, June 29, 1970, Regional Oral History Office, Bancroft Library, University of California at Berkeley.
13. William F. Knowland, interview by James Bassett, associate editor of the *Los Angeles Times*, June 12, 1973, Bancroft Library, University of California at Berkeley.
14. Associated Press Biographical Service, August 1, 1971.

Chapter 8. A Freshman Senator

1. David G. McCullough, *Truman* (New York: Simon and Schuster, 1992), p. 468.
2. *Time*, March 10, 1947.
3. Donald R. Matthews, *U.S. Senators and Their World* (Chapel Hill: University of North Carolina Press, 1960), p. 110.
4. Quoted in Fletcher Knebel and Dan Fowler, "He Would Rather Be Right and President," *Look*, April 5, 1955, p. 44.
5. Tom Wicker, *One of Us: Richard Nixon and the American Dream* (New York: Random House, 1991), p. 45.

6. Quoted in Leo Katcher, *Earl Warren: A Political Biography* (New York: McGraw-Hill, 1967), pp. 203–4.

7. Quoted by Murray Chotiner in "Fundamentals of Campaign Organizations," pp. 8–9 (a speech delivered to Republican state chairmen during a training session in Washington, D.C., September 7–10, 1955), National Archives, Southwest Division, Laguna Niguel, California.

8. Roger Morris, *Richard Milhous Nixon: The Rise of an American Politician* (New York: Henry Holt, 1990), p. 29.

9. *Nation*, July 2, 1955.

10. *Fortnight*, November 4, 1946, pp. 18–21; quoted in Royce D. Delmatier, Clarence F. McIntosh, and Earl G. Waters, *The Rumble of California Politics, 1848–1970* (New York: John Wiley, 1970), p. 311.

11. Quoted in *PIC*, June 1948.

12. Oliver J. Carter, oral history, interview by James R. Fuchs, February 26, 1970, p. 44, Harry S. Truman Library, Independence, Missouri.

13. David M. Oshinsky, *A Conspiracy So Immense: The World of Joe McCarthy* (New York: Free Press, 1983), p. 53.

14. Philip J. Wolman, "The Oakland General Strike of 1946," *Southern California Quarterly* 57 (1975): 157.

15. Bob Ash, "Alameda County Central Labor Council during the Warren Years," in "Labor Leaders View the Warren Era," interview by Mariam Stein and Amelia Fry, 1970, p. 29, Regional Oral History Office, Bancroft Library, University of California at Berkeley.

Chapter 9. Making His Mark

1. James T. Patterson, *Mr. Republican: A Biography of Robert Taft* (Boston: Houghton Mifflin, 1972), p. 339.

2. *Time*, March 10, 1947.

3. Quoted in ibid.

4. "Should the Congress Reduce the Public Debt Before Reducing Taxes?" *Congressional Digest*, February 28, 1947, p. 126.

5. William F. Knowland, letter to George C. Marshall, September 26, 1947, Herbert Hoover Library, West Branch, Iowa.

6. Quoted in *PIC*, June 1948.

7. Merrill Small, "The Earl Warren Era in California, 1925–1963," interview by Amelia Fry, *California Historical Quarterly* 54 (1975): 83–84.

8. Henry Z. Scheele, *Charlie Halleck: A Political Biography* (New York: Exposition Press, 1966), p. 123.

9. *Time*, January 14, 1957.

10. Sen. William F. Knowland, letter to Sen. Arthur H. Vandenberg of Michigan, September 2, 1948, Bentley Historical Library, University of Michigan, Ann Arbor, Michigan.

11. Sen. William F. Knowland, letter to Sen. Arthur H. Vandenberg, December 8, 1948, Bentley Historical Library, University of Michigan, Ann Arbor, Michigan.

12. Sen. Arthur H. Vandenberg, letter to Sen. William F. Knowland, December 11, 1948, Bentley Historical Library, University of Michigan, Ann Arbor, Michigan.

Chapter 10. Moving Up in the Senate

1. Frank Rogers, "Washington Letter," *Fortnight*, January 7, 1949, p. 10.
2. William F. Knowland, oral history, p. 11, interview by Joe B. Frantz, March 23, 1970, Lyndon Baines Johnson Library, Austin, Texas.
3. William Bragg Ewald Jr., *Who Killed Joe McCarthy?* (New York: Simon and Schuster, 1984), p. 42.
4. *Newsweek*, August 5, 1957.
5. Quoted in *Frontier*, October 1958.
6. Quoted in Fletcher Knebel and Dan Fowler, "He Would Rather Be Right and President," *Look*, April 5, 1955, p. 53.
7. Knowland, oral history, p. 14.
8. Richard Nixon, *RN: The Memoirs of Richard Nixon* (New York: Grosset and Dunlap, 1978), pp. 110–12.
9. Foster Rhea Dulles, *American Foreign Policy toward Communist China, 1949–1969* (New York: Thomas Y. Crowell, 1972), p. 36.
10. David S. McLellan, *Dean Acheson: The State Department Years* (New York: Dodd, Mead, 1976), p. 190.
11. Richard M. Fried, *Nightmare in Red* (New York: Oxford University Press, 1990), p. 89.
12. Quoted in ibid.
13. Knowland, oral history, p. 12.
14. William F. Knowland, telegram to Harry S Truman, November 29, 1949, Harry S Truman Library, Independence, Missouri.
15. Knowland, oral history, p. 12.
16. Dumas Malone and Basil Rauch, *American and World Leadership, 1940–65* (New York: Appleton-Century-Crofts, 1965), pp. 112–13.
17. Quoted in Dulles, *American Foreign Policy*, p. 5.
18. Dean Acheson, *Present at the Creation: My Years in the State Department* (New York: W. W. Norton, 1969), p. 101.
19. Quoted in "Another Side of Bill Knowland," *California Journal*, April 1974, p. 114.
20. Philip S. Sprouse, oral history, p. 14, interview by James R. Fuchs, February 11, 1974, p. 14, Harry S Truman Library, Independence, Missouri.
21. Allen Griffin, oral history, p. 52, interview by James R. Fuchs, February 15, 1974, Harry S Truman Library, Independence, Missouri.
22. Paul Healy, "The Grim Senator from California," *Saturday Evening Post*, April 25, 1953, p. 81.
23. *Nation*, December 30, 1950.
24. Dulles, *American Foreign Policy*, p. 73.
25. Quoted in Healy, "Grim Senator," p. 81.
26. Quoted in *Collier's*, October 1, 1954.

Chapter 11. Formosa and Korea

1. Quoted in Foster Rhea Dulles, *American Foreign Policy toward Communist China, 1949–1969* (New York: Thomas Y. Crowell, 1972), p. 63.

2. Quoted in David S. McLellan, *Dean Acheson: The State Department Years* (New York: Dodd, Mead, 1976), p. 206.

3. Quoted in ibid., p. 208.

4. Quoted in ibid., p. 209.

5. *U.S. News and World Report,* January 13, 1950.

6. *Congressional Record,* 82nd Cong., 1st sess., 1951, 97, pts. 11–12:A2255.

7. *Time,* January 26, 1950.

8. Richard Nixon, *RN: The Memoirs of Richard Nixon* (New York: Grosset and Dunlap, 1978), p. 75.

9. J.R. Knowland, letter to Herbert Hoover, September 27, 1950, Herbert Hoover Library, West Branch, Iowa.

10. Quoted in Robert J. Donovan, *The Tumultuous Years: The Presidency of Harry S. Truman, 1949–53* (New York: W. W. Norton, 1982), p. 256.

11. William F. Knowland, oral history, p. 50, interview by Ed Edwin, June 22, 1967, Oral History Office, Butler Library, Columbia University.

12. William F. Knowland, oral history, interview by Joe B. Frantz, March 23, 1970, p. 13, Lyndon Baines Johnson Library, Austin, Texas.

13. Quoted in William Manchester, *The Glory and the Dream* (Boston: Little, Brown, 1974), p. 536.

14. Quoted in David McCullough, *Truman* (New York: Simon and Schuster, 1992), p. 782.

15. Quoted in Trumbull Higgins, *Korea and the Fall of MacArthur* (New York: Oxford University Press, 1960), p. 23.

Chapter 12. "Bill, You Don't Kiss Babies"

1. *Congressional Record,* 82nd Cong., 1st sess., 1951, 97, pts. 11–12:A3519.

2. Quoted in Dumas Malone and Basil Rauch, *American and World Leadership, 1940–65* (New York: Appleton-Century-Crofts, 1965), p. 124.

3. Herman Perry, letter to Richard M. Nixon, July 26, 1951, Richard Nixon Library, Yorba Linda, California.

4. Robert D. Adams, letter to U.S. Senate, May 17, 1952, Harry S. Truman Library, Independence, Missouri.

5. Herman Perry, letter to Bernard C. Brennan (Warren delegate to the 1952 convention), May 17, 1952, Richard Nixon Library, Yorba Linda, California.

6. William F. Knowland, "The Survival of Our Nation," *Vital Speeches of the Day,* 1951–52, p. 556.

7. Quoted in Paul Healy, "The Grim Senator from California," *Saturday Evening Post,* April 25, 1953, p. 81.

8. Ibid.

9. Gladwin Hill, *Dancing Bear: An Inside Look at California Politics* (Cleveland: World Publishing, 1968), pp. 58–61.

10. Healy, "Grim Senator," p. 81.
11. Quoted in *Time*, January 14, 1957.

Chapter 13. Betrayed Loyalty

1. Telegram, November 7, 1951, National Archives, Pacific Southwest Region, Laguna Niguel, California.
2. Quoted in Stephen Ambrose, *Nixon: The Education of a Politician, 1913–1962* (New York: Simon and Schuster, 1987), p. 254.
3. Quoted in Roger Morris, *Richard Milhous Nixon: The Rise of an American Politician* (New York: Henry Holt, 1990), p. 702.
4. Quoted in ibid., p. 703.
5. Quoted in ibid., p. 676.
6. Nixon papers, National Archives, Pacific Southwest Region, Laguna Niguel, California.
7. Quoted in James D. Weaver, *Warren: The Man, the Court, the Era* (Boston: Little, Brown, 1967), p. 180.
8. William F. Knowland, oral history, p. 13, interview by Raymond Henle, October 4, 1967, Herbert Hoover Library, West Branch, Iowa.
9. Earl Warren, *The Memoirs of Earl Warren* (Garden City, N.Y.: Doubleday, 1977), p. 251.
10. Quoted in Morris, *Nixon*, p. 696.
11. Ambrose, *Nixon*, p. 259.
12. Quoted in Morris, *Nixon*, pp. 707, 719.
13. Ibid., p. 719.
14. Richard M. Nixon, *RN: The Memoirs of Richard Nixon* (New York: Grosset and Dunlap, 1978), p. 83.
15. William F. Knowland, oral history, p. 21, interview by Ed Edwin, June 20, 1967, Oral History Office, Butler Library, Columbia University.
16. Quoted in Morris, *Nixon*, p. 693.
17. Thomas J. Mellon, in "Earl Warren's Campaigns," vol. 2, p. 38, interview by Amelia Fry and Elizabeth Kerby, June 29, 1970, Regional Oral History Office, Bancroft Library, University of California at Berkeley.
18. Quoted in Morris, *Nixon*, p. 724.
19. Ibid., p. 725.
20. Knowland, oral history, p. 20, interview by Edwin.
21. Quoted in Jess Edward Smith, *Lucius D. Clay: An American Life* (New York: Henry Holt, 1990), p. 602.
22. Nixon, *Memoirs*, p. 88.
23. Quoted in Morris, *Nixon*, p. 724.
24. Quoted in Roland DeWolk, "The Knowland Family and the *Oakland Tribune*" (unpublished), Bancroft Library, University of California at Berkeley.
25. Warren, *Memoirs*, p. 252.
26. Quoted in Morris, *Nixon*, p. 713.
27. Warren, *Memoirs*, p. 254.
28. Knowland, oral history, p. 28, interview by Edwin.

29. Paul G. Manolis, "A Friend and an Aide Reminisces," p. 2, in "Remembering William F. Knowland," interview by Ruth Teiser, April 24, 1979, Regional Oral History Office, Bancroft Library, University of California at Berkeley.

30. Emelyn Knowland Jewett, in "My Father's Political Philosophy and Colleagues," p. 2, in "Remembering William F. Knowland," interview by Ruth Teiser, June 11, 1979, Regional Oral History Office, Bancroft Library, University of California at Berkeley.

31. *Time*, June 16, 1952.

32. *Collier's*, February 3, 1956.

33. Quoted in Earl Mazo and Stephen Hess, *Nixon, a Political Portrait* (New York: Harper and Row, 1967), pp. 84–85.

34. Quoted in Morris, *Nixon*, p. 692.

35. Ibid., p. 705.

36. Frank Jorgensen, "Richard M. Nixon in the Warren Era," p. 72, interview by Amelia Fry, April 1–22, 1975, Regional Oral History Office, Bancroft Library, University of California at Berkeley.

37. Quoted in Morris, *Nixon*, pp. 727–28.

38. *Politics in America, 1945–65* (Washington, D.C.: Congressional Quarterly Service, 1967), p. 14.

39. Quoted in Leonard Lurie, *The King Makers* (New York: Coward, McCann, and Geoghegan, 1971), p. 94.

40. Knowland, oral history, p. 19, interview by Edwin.

41. Morris, *Nixon*, p. 729.

42. Quoted in Earl Mazo, *Richard Nixon: A Political and Personal Portrait* (New York: Avon Books, 1960), p. 90.

43. McIntyre Faries, "California Republicans, 1934–1953," p. 24, interviews by Amelia Fry and Elizabeth Kerby, 1970, Regional Oral History Office, Bancroft Library, University of California at Berkeley.

44. Nixon, *Memoirs*, p. 89.

45. Keith McCormac, in "Earl Warren's Campaigns," vol. 3, p. 8, interview by Amelia Fry, 1978, Regional Oral History Office, Bancroft Library, University of California at Berkeley.

46. Sherman Adams, *Firsthand Report* (New York: Harper, 1961), p. 41.

47. Earl C. Adams, "Financing Richard Nixon's Campaigns in 1946 to 1960," in "Richard M. Nixon in the Warren Era," p. 10, interview by Amelia Fry, February 20, 1975, Regional Oral History Office, Bancroft Library, University of California at Berkeley.

48. Quoted in Ralph De Toledano, *One Man Alone: Richard Nixon* (New York: Funk and Wagnalls, 1969), p. 146.

49. Herbert D. Parmet, *Richard Nixon and His America* (Boston: Little, Brown, 1990), p. 238.

50. Quoted in Mazo, *Richard Nixon*, p. 121.

51. Jewett, "My Father," p. 16.

52. Faries, "California Republicans," p. 22a (this document was inserted following p. 22 only after Faries's death).

53. Knowland, oral history, p. 29, interview by Henle.

Chapter 14. The Republicans Take Over

1. Jack Bell, *The Splendid Misery* (Garden City, N.Y.: Doubleday, 1960), p. 32.
2. William F. Knowland, oral history, p. 31, interview by Ed Edwin, June 20, 1967, Oral History Office, Butler Library, Columbia University.
3. Ibid., June 22, 1967, pp. 38–39.
4. Ibid., November 16, 1970, p. 132.
5. Ibid., June 20, 1967, p. 32.
6. Ibid., November 16, 1970, pp. 137–39.
7. Leonard Mosley, *Dulles* (New York: Dell, 1978), pp. 333–34.
8. L. B. Nichols, memorandum to FBI Director J. Edgar Hoover, March 16, 1954, FBI files, Washington, D.C.
9. William Bragg Ewald Jr., *Who Killed Joe McCarthy?* (New York: Simon and Schuster, 1984), p. 57.
10. Quoted in *Reporter*, March 8, 1956.
11. Nichols, memorandum.
12. Ewald, *Who Killed Joe McCarthy?* p. 43.
13. William F. Knowland, oral history, pp. 21, 22, interview by Joe B. Frantz, March 23, 1970, Lyndon Baines Johnson Library, Austin, Texas.
14. William F. Knowland, oral history, p. 20, interview by Raymond Henle, October 4, 1967, Herbert Hoover Library, West Branch, Iowa.
15. Quoted in Stephen Ambrose, *Eisenhower the President*, vol. 2 (New York: Simon and Schuster, 1984), p. 100.
16. Dwight D. Eisenhower, *Mandate for Change* (New York: Signet Books, 1963), p. 273.

Chapter 15. Nobody Can Push Him Around

1. Quoted in William S. White, *The Taft Story* (New York: Harper and Row, 1954), p. 259.
2. Ibid., p. 261.
3. William F. Knowland, oral history, p. 4, interview by Joe B. Frantz, March 23, 1970, Lyndon Baines Johnson Library, Austin, Texas.
4. Quoted in *Time*, December 13, 1954.
5. Quoted in *Time*, January 14, 1957.
6. Quoted in White, *The Taft Story*, p. 268.
7. Quoted in Arthur J. Schlesinger Jr., *History of U.S. Political Parties*, vol. 4, *1945–72* (New York: Chelsea House, 1973), p. 2994.
8. Quoted in William Manchester, *The Glory and the Dream* (Boston: Little, Brown, 1974), p. 608.
9. Dwight D. Eisenhower, *Mandate for Change* (New York: Signet Books, 1963), pp. 363–64.
10. William F. Knowland, oral history, pp. 34–35, interview by Ed Edwin, June 20, 1967, Oral History Office, Butler Library, Columbia University.
11. Quoted in *New York Times*, August 5, 1953.
12. Knowland, oral history, p. 6, interview by Frantz.

13. *New York Times*, August 6, 1953.

14. Quoted in *U.S. News and World Report*, July 24, 1953.

15. Quoted in *Newsweek*, August 9, 1953.

16. Rowland Evans and Robert Novak, *Lyndon Johnson: The Exercise of Power* (New York: New American Library, 1966), p. 169.

17. *Newsweek*, August 5, 1957.

18. Quoted in Evans and Novak, *Lyndon Johnson*, p. 169.

19. Quoted in Schlesinger, *History of U.S. Political Parties*, vol. 4, p. 2294.

20. Barry M. Goldwater, oral history, pp. 42–43, interview by Ed Edwin, June 15, 1967, Oral History Office, Butler Library, Columbia University.

21. Barry M. Goldwater, *With No Apologies* (New York: William Morrow, 1979), p. 68.

22. Quoted in Hedrick Smith, *The Power Game: How Washington Works* (New York: Random House, 1988), p. 453.

23. Quoted in Emmet John Hughes, *The Ordeal of Power: A Political Memoir of the Eisenhower Years* (New York: Atheneum, 1963), p. 128.

24. Sherman Adams, *Firsthand Report* (New York: Harper, 1961), p. 26.

25. Quoted in Alfred Steinberg, *Sam Johnson's Boy: A Close-up of the President from Texas* (New York: Macmillan, 1968), p. 353.

26. Jack Bell, *The Splendid Misery* (Garden City, N.Y.: Doubleday, 1960), p. 33.

27. Knowland, oral history, pp. 35–36, interview by Edwin.

28. James Hagerty, oral history, p. 3, interview by Michael Gillette, November 16, 1971, Lyndon Baines Johnson Library, Austin, Texas.

29. Steve Neal, *The Eisenhowers: Reluctant Dynasty* (Garden City, N.Y.: Doubleday, 1978), p. 324.

30. Knowland, oral history, p. 18, interview by Frantz.

31. Hubert H. Humphrey, oral history, interview 3, p. 19, interview by Michael Gillette, June 21, 1977, Lyndon Baines Johnson Library, Austin, Texas.

32. Walter W. Rostow, oral history, interview 1, p. 11, interview by Paige E. Mulhollan, March 1, 1979, Lyndon Baines Johnson Library, Austin, Texas.

33. Clifford Case, oral history, interview 1, p. 8, interview by Michael Gillette, March 1, 1979, Lyndon Baines Johnson Library, Austin, Texas.

34. Knowland, oral history, pp. 142–43, interview by Edwin.

35. *Time*, January 14, 1957.

36. Walter Jenkins, oral history, interview 3, p. 7, interview by Michael Gillette, September 23, 1976, Lyndon Baines Johnson Library, Austin, Texas.

37. Ibid., p. 27.

38. William S. White, oral history, interview 3, p. 26, interview by Michael Gillette, July 21, 1978, Lyndon Baines Johnson Library, Austin, Texas; William S. White, *The Citadel: The Story of the U.S. Senate* (New York: Harper and Row, 1956), p. 210.

39. Booth Mooney, *The Politicians, 1945–60* (New York: Lippincott, 1970), pp. 219, 226.

40. Quoted in Steinberg, *Sam Johnson's Boy*, p. 484.

41. Lyndon Johnson, letter to William F. Knowland, February 13, 1967, Lyndon Baines Johnson Library, Austin, Texas.

42. Douglass Cater, "Knowland: The Man Who Wants to Be Taft," *Reporter*, March 8, 1956, p. 32.

43. White, *The Taft Story*, pp. 256–57.

44. Cater, "Knowland," p. 32.

45. Russell B. Long, oral history, interview 2, p. 7, interview by Michael Gillette, June 20, 1977, Lyndon Baines Johnson Library, Austin, Texas.

46. White, *The Citadel*, pp. 92, 200.

47. Ibid., p. 89.

48. Ibid., p. 105.

49. Cater, "Knowland," p. 32.

50. Quoted in Neal, *The Eisenhowers*, p. 325.

51. Dwight D. Eisenhower, letter to William F. Knowland, February 1, 1954, Dwight D. Eisenhower Library, Abilene, Kansas.

52. Quoted in David B. Truman, *The Congressional Party: A Case Study* (London: John Wiley, 1959), p. 340.

53. Duane Tananbaum, *The Bricker Amendment Controversy* (Ithaca, N.Y.: Cornell University Press, 1988), pp. 179–80.

54. Eisenhower, *Mandate for Change*, p. 227.

55. Quoted in G. Edward White, *Earl Warren: A Public Life* (New York: Oxford University Press, 1982), p. 151.

56. Quoted in William O. Douglas, *The Autobiography of William O. Douglas* (New York: Random House, 1980), p. 227.

57. William F. Knowland, "Communism, a Global Menace," *Vital Speeches of the Day*, 1953–54, pp. 167–71.

58. Quoted in Neal, *The Eisenhowers*, p. 382.

59. Quoted in *New York Times*, December 8, 1953.

60. Quoted in Martin Hall, "Knowland of California: Playmate for McCarthy," *Frontier*, February 1954, p. 8.

61. Ibid.

62. Eisenhower, *Mandate for Change*, p. 366.

63. Knowland, oral history, p. 19, interview by Frantz.

64. Memorandum of conversation between Secretary of State John Foster Dulles and William F. Knowland, October 5, 1953, Dwight D. Eisenhower Library, Abilene, Kansas.

Chapter 16. The McCarthy Era

1. *San Francisco Chronicle*, December 13, 1953.

2. Dwight D. Eisenhower, *The Eisenhower Diaries*, edited by Robert H. Ferrell (New York: W. W. Norton, 1981), p. 270.

3. Dwight D. Eisenhower, *Waging Peace, 1956–61* (Garden City, N.Y.: Doubleday, 1965), pp. 384–85.

4. Dumas Malone and Basil Rauch, *America and World Leadership, 1940–65* (New York: Appleton-Century-Crofts, 1960), pp. 164–65.

5. Quoted in William Bragg Ewald Jr., *Who Killed Joe McCarthy?* (New York: Simon and Schuster, 1984), p. 261.

6. Quoted in David M. Oshinsky, *A Conspiracy So Immense: The World of Joe McCarthy* (New York: Free Press, 1983), p. 403.

7. Quoted in Ewald, *Who Killed Joe McCarthy?* p. 261.

8. James C. Hagerty, *The Diary of James C. Hagerty* (Bloomington: Indiana University Press, 1983), p. 29; Eisenhower quoted in Ewald, *Who Killed Joe McCarthy?* p. 261.

9. Sherman Adams, *Firsthand Report* (New York: Harper, 1961), p. 27.

10. William F. Knowland, oral history, p. 26, interview by Raymond Henle, October 4, 1967, Herbert Hoover Library, West Branch, Iowa.

11. William F. Knowland, oral history, p. 37, interview by Joe B. Frantz, March 23, 1970, Lyndon Baines Johnson Library, Austin, Texas.

12. Quoted in Fred I. Greenstein, *The Hidden Hand Presidency: Eisenhower as Leader* (New York: Basic Books, 1982), p. 188.

13. Quoted in Robert Griffith, *The Politics of Fear: Joseph R. McCarthy and the Senate* (Lexington: University of Kentucky Press, 1970), p. 274.

14. Quoted in *Sacramento Bee*, May 14, 1954.

15. Quoted in William Safire, *Safire's Political Dictionary*, 3rd ed. (New York: Ballantine Books, 1980), p. 658.

16. Dwight D. Eisenhower, *Mandate for Change* (New York: Signet Books, 1963), p. 396.

17. Quoted in Stephen E. Ambrose, *Nixon: The Education of a Politician, 1913–1962* (New York: Simon and Schuster, 1987), pp. 334–35.

18. Quoted in Lately Thomas, *When Angels Wept* (New York: William Morrow, 1983), p. 596.

19. Quoted in Arthur Watkins, *Enough Rope* (Englewood Cliffs, N.J.: Prentice-Hall, 1969), p. 25.

20. *New York Times*, July 31, 1954.

21. *New Republic*, August 23, 1954.

22. William F. Knowland, oral history, p. 165, interview by Ed Edwin, November 16, 1970, Oral History Office, Butler Library, Columbia University.

23. William S. White, oral history, interview 3, p. 29, interview by Michael Gillette, July 21, 1978, Lyndon Baines Johnson Library, Austin, Texas.

24. Rowland Evans and Robert Novak, *Lyndon Johnson: The Exercise of Power* (New York: New American Library, 1966), p. 85.

25. Watkins, *Enough Rope*, p. 33.

26. Quoted in Eisenhower, *Mandate for Change*, p. 400.

27. Knowland, oral history, p. 165, interview by Edwin.

28. Ibid., pp. 161–63, 165–66.

29. Ibid., pp. 161–63.

30. Quoted in *Time*, December 13, 1954.

31. Jeff Broadwater, *Eisenhower and the Anti-Communist Crusade* (Chapel Hill: University of North Carolina Press, 1992), p. 103.

32. Quoted in Douglass Cater, "Knowland: The Man Who Wants to Be Taft," *Reporter*, March 8, 1956, pp. 32–35.

33. *Time*, December 13, 1954.

34. Eisenhower quoted in Hagerty, *Diary*, p. 120; ibid.

35. Ibid., p. 123.

36. Griffith, *The Politics of Fear*, p. 311.

37. Broadwater, *Eisenhower and the Anti-Communist Crusade*, p. 164.

38. Quoted in *Sacramento Bee*, September 27, 1954.

Chapter 17. Politics at Home

1. *American Mercury*, October 1954.
2. *Newsweek*, December 13, 1954.
3. *American Mercury*, October 1954; *Newsweek*, December 13, 1954.
4. Quoted in *U.S. News and World Report*, December 24, 1954.
5. Quoted in *Frontier*, October 1954, p. 5.
6. Quoted in ibid.
7. *Frontier*, October 1957.
8. Fletcher Knebel and Dan Fowler, "He Would Rather Be Right and President," *Look*, April 5, 1955, p. 52.
9. Quoted in *Los Angeles Times*, October 10, 1954.
10. Quoted in *New York Times*, September 24, 1954.

Chapter 18. Standing Up to Ike

1. Jack Anderson, memorandum to Drew Pearson, undated, Drew Pearson papers, Lyndon Baines Johnson Library, Austin, Texas.
2. Hugh Gregory Gallagher, *Advise and Obstruct* (New York: Delacorte Press, 1969), p. 288.
3. Ibid., p. 294.
4. Ibid., pp. 291–92.
5. Anderson, memorandum.
6. Ibid.
7. William F. Knowland, oral history, pp. 64–65, interview by Ed Edwin, June 22, 1967, Oral History Office, Butler Library, Columbia University.
8. *Sacramento Bee*, May 7, 1954.
9. Quoted in Foster Rhea Dulles, *American Foreign Policy toward Communist China, 1949–1969* (New York: Thomas Y. Crowell, 1972), pp. 145–46.
10. Quoted in Sherman Adams, *Firsthand Report* (New York: Harper, 1961), p. 123.
11. Knowland, oral history, June 22, 1967, p. 60.
12. Quoted in *U.S. News and World Report*, July 9, 1954.
13. Quoted in *Time*, July 12, 1954.
14. Knowland, oral history, June 22, 1967, p. 60.
15. Ibid.
16. Quoted in Gallagher, *Advise and Obstruct*, p. 295.
17. Quoted in David B. Truman, *The Congressional Party: A Case Study* (London: John Wiley, 1959), p. 305.
18. James C. Hagerty, *The Diary of James C. Hagerty* (Bloomington: Indiana University Press, 1983), p. 84.
19. Quoted in Malcolm E. Jewell, *Senatorial Politics and Foreign Policy* (Lexington: University of Kentucky Press, 1962), p. 64.
20. Dwight D. Eisenhower, memorandum to Allen Foster Dulles, July 8, 1954, Dwight D. Eisenhower Library, Abilene, Kansas.
21. Summary of a telephone conversation between John Foster Dulles and

William F. Knowland, July 17, 1954, Dwight D. Eisenhower Library, Abilene, Kansas.

22. Michael R. Beschloss, *Mayday: Eisenhower, Khrushechev, and the U-2 Affair* (New York: Harper and Row, 1986), pp. 82–84.

23. Dwight D. Eisenhower, letter to William F. Knowland, September 7, 1954, Dwight D. Eisenhower Library, Abilene, Kansas.

24. Quoted in *U.S. News and World Report*, December 24, 1954.

25. Dwight D. Eisenhower, *The Eisenhower Diaries*, edited by Robert H. Ferrell (New York: W. W. Norton, 1981), p. 174.

26. Quoted in Douglass Cater, "Knowland: The Man Who Wants to Be Taft," *Reporter*, March 8, 1956, pp. 34–35.

27. "We Must Be Willing to Fight Now," *Collier's*, October 1, 1954, p. 24.

28. "Knowland's Turn," *Reporter*, October 7, 1954, p. 4.

29. Ferreus and Knowland quoted in *Los Angeles Times*, December 24, 1954.

30. *Congressional Record*, 83rd Cong., 2nd sess., 1954, 100, pts. 11–12:14904.

31. Quoted in *New York Times*, December 3, 1954.

32. Quoted in *Fortnight*, November 17, 1954.

33. Ibid.

34. Quoted in William S. White, *The Citadel: The Story of the U.S. Senate* (New York: Harper and Row, 1956), p. 98.

35. Quoted in *New York Times*, December 3, 1954.

36. *Los Angeles Times*, July 21, 1954.

37. Adams, *Firsthand Report*, p. 129.

38. Quoted in Hagerty, *Diary*, p. 165.

39. Memorandum of a conversation between President Eisenhower and William F. Knowland, November 23, 1954, Dwight D. Eisenhower Library, Abilene, Kansas.

40. Quoted in the *New York Times*, December 3, 1954.

41. Quoted in *U.S. News and World Report*, December 24, 1954.

42. *Sacramento Bee*, December 7, 1954.

43. Quoted in *U.S. News and World Report*, December 24, 1954.

44. *Newsweek*, December 13, 1954.

45. Knowland, oral history, June 22, 1967, p. 46.

46. *Christian Century*, December 15, 1954.

47. *America*, December 18, 1954.

Chapter 19. Waiting in the Wings

1. "Republicans, Democrats: Who's Who," *New York Times Magazine*, January 2, 1955, p. 5.

2. Jack Bell, *The Splendid Misery* (Garden City, N.Y.: Doubleday, 1960), pp. 28–31.

3. John Foster Dulles, confidential memorandum of a conversation between Dulles and William F. Knowland, January 15, 1955, Dwight D. Eisenhower Library, Abilene, Kansas.

4. Quoted in *Newsweek*, March 28, 1955.

5. Quoted in Foster Rhea Dulles, *American Foreign Policy toward Communist China, 1949–1969* (New York: Thomas Y. Crowell, 1972), p. 154.

6. Quoted in *Newsweek*, February 7, 1955.

7. William F. Knowland, oral history, p. 56, interview by Ed Edwin, June 22, 1967, Oral History Office, Butler Library, Columbia University.

8. Quoted in Alfred Steinberg, *Sam Johnson's Boy: A Close-up of the President from Texas* (New York: Macmillan, 1968), p. 401.

9. Notes from telephone call between John Foster Dulles and William F. Knowland, April 27, 1955, Dwight D. Eisenhower Library, Abilene, Kansas.

10. John Foster Dulles, memorandum of meeting with Sens. William F. Knowland, Bourke Hickenlooper, and Alexander Smith, April 27, 1955, Dwight D. Eisenhower Library, Abilene, Kansas.

11. Quoted in *U.S. News and World Report*, May 6, 1955.

12. William F. Knowland, oral history, p. 28, interview by Joe B. Frantz, March 23, 1970, Lyndon Baines Johnson Library, Austin, Texas.

13. William F. Knowland, letter to Lyndon B. Johnson, July 12, 1955; Johnson, letter to Knowland, September 27, 1955, Lyndon Baines Johnson Library, Austin, Texas.

14. Quoted in Peter Lyon, *Eisenhower: Portrait of a Hero* (Boston: Little, Brown, 1974), p. 586.

15. Quoted in *U.S. News and World Report*, January 21, 1955.

16. Quoted in *Sacramento Bee*, June 8, 1955.

17. Ibid.

18. Quoted in William Costello, *The Facts about Nixon* (New York: Viking Press, 1960), p. 145.

19. Quoted in William L. Roper, "Can Nixon Make It?" *Frontier*, November 1955, p. 8.

20. Quoted in ibid., p. 9.

21. Ibid., p. 8.

22. Quoted in Associated Press, October 5, 1955.

23. Knowland, oral history, p. 122, interview by Edwin.

24. Ibid., p. 78.

25. Quoted in Stephen E. Ambrose, *Eisenhower the President*, vol. 2 (New York: Simon and Schuster, 1984), p. 281.

26. *Sacramento Bee*, May 30, 1955.

27. Quoted in James C. Hagerty, *The Diary of James C. Hagerty* (Bloomington: Indiana University Press, 1983), p. 241.

28. Quoted in ibid.

29. Quoted in *Newsweek*, December 19, 1955.

30. This poster is in the Richard Nixon Papers, Knowland file, National Archives, Pacific Southwest Region, Laguna Niguel, California.

Chapter 20. Stepping Aside

1. Dwight D. Eisenhower, *The Eisenhower Diaries*, edited by Robert H. Ferrell (New York: W. W. Norton, 1981), p. 291.

2. James L. Wick, "Knowland ('Mr. Integrity') Enters the Race," *Human Events*, February 4, 1956.

3. William S. White, "What Bill Knowland Stands For," *New Republic*, February 27, 1956, p. 10.

4. Quoted in William B. Ewald Jr., *Eisenhower, the President: Crucial Days, 1951–60* (Englewood Cliffs, N.J.: Prentice-Hall, 1981), p. 179.

5. William F. Knowland, oral history, p. 124, interview by Ed Edwin, June 22, 1967, Oral History Office, Columbia University.

6. Quoted in Charles A. H. Thomson and Frances M. Shattuck, *The 1956 Presidential Campaign* (Westport, Conn.: Greenwood Press, 1960), p. 81.

7. Knowland, oral history, p. 124.

8. Quoted in *U.S. News and World Report*, July 14, 1956.

9. Emelyn Knowland Jewett, in "My Father's Political Philosophy and Colleagues," in "Remembering William F. Knowland," interview by Ruth Teiser, June 11, 1979, Regional Oral History Office, Bancroft Library, University of California at Berkeley.

10. Knowland, oral history, p. 82.

11. Herbert L. Phillips, *Big Wayward Girl* (New York: Doubleday, 1968), p. 174.

12. Merle Miller, *Lyndon: An Oral Biography* (New York: G. P. Putnam's Sons, 1980), p. 201.

Chapter 21. The Suez Crisis

1. Quoted in Donald Neff, *Warriors at Suez* (New York: Simon and Schuster, 1981), pp. 260–62.

2. Quoted in ibid., p. 285.

3. John Foster Dulles, memorandum of conversation with Senator Knowland at a luncheon meeting, September 8, 1956, Dwight D. Eisenhower Library, Abilene, Kansas.

4. Quoted in Robert A. Divine, *Foreign Policy and U.S. Presidential Elections, 1952–1960* (New York: New Viewpoints, 1974), p. 149.

5. Quoted in *Time*, January 14, 1957.

6. Jack Bell, *The Splendid Misery* (Garden City, N.Y.: Doubleday, 1960), pp. 33–34.

7. Herman Finer, *Dulles over Suez* (Chicago: Quadrangle Books, 1964), p. 475.

8. Extracts of a speech given at Georgetown University, Washington, D.C., February 11, 1957, from Knowland files, Lyndon Baines Johnson Library, Austin, Texas.

9. Knowland files, Johnson Library.

10. William F. Knowland, oral history, p. 36, interview by Joe B. Frantz, March 23, 1970, Lyndon Baines Johnson Library, Austin, Texas.

11. Sherman Adams, *Firsthand Report* (New York: Harper, 1961), p. 281.

12. Alfred Steinberg, *Sam Johnson's Boy: A Close-up of the President from Texas* (New York: Macmillan, 1968), p. 467.

13. Quoted in Stephen E. Ambrose, *Eisenhower the President*, vol. 2. (New York: Simon and Schuster, 1984), p. 391.

14. Dwight D. Eisenhower, diary, August 29, 1957, Dwight D. Eisenhower Library, Abilene, Kansas.

15. Dwight D. Eisenhower, letter to Meade Alcorn, August 30, 1957, Dwight D. Eisenhower Library, Abilene, Kansas.

16. Adams, *Firsthand Report*, p. 380.

17. Eisenhower, letter to Alcorn.

18. John Foster Dulles, top-secret memorandum of conversation with Senator William F. Knowland, August 30, 1957, declassified on January 26, 1989, Dwight D. Eisenhower Library, Abilene, Kansas.

19. John Foster Dulles, memorandum of conversation with Senator William F. Knowland, May 28, 1957, Dwight D. Eisenhower Library, Abilene, Kansas.

20. Quoted in Adams, *Firsthand Report*, p. 410.

21. Quoted in ibid., p. 411.

22. Quoted in Bell, *Splendid Misery*, p. 36.

23. Quoted in Piers Brendan, *Ike: His Life and Times* (New York: Harper and Row, 1986), p. 349.

24. William F. Knowland, oral history, p. 113, interview by Ed Edwin, June 22, 1967, Oral History Office, Butler Library, Columbia University.

25. Quoted in Adams, *Firsthand Report*, pp. 416–17.

Chapter 22. Civil Rights

1. Quoted in J. W. Anderson, *Eisenhower, Brownell, and the Congress* (Tuscaloosa: University of Alabama Press, 1964), p. 47.

2. Quoted in *Time*, January 14, 1957.

3. Clinton Anderson, *Outsider in the Senate* (New York: World Publishing, 1970), p. 146.

4. Joseph S. Clark, *Congress: The Sapless Branch* (New York: Harper and Row, 1964), p. 4.

5. William F. Knowland, oral history, p. 38, interview by Joe B. Frantz, March 23, 1970, Lyndon Baines Johnson Library, Austin, Texas.

6. Quoted in *Sacramento Bee*, May 28, 1957.

7. Knowland, oral history, p. 39.

8. Quoted in *New York Times*, January 5, 1958.

9. "Congress Approves Civil Rights Act of 1957," *Congressional Quarterly Almanac* (Washington, D.C.: Congressional Quarterly Newsfeatures, 1958), pp. 566, 567.

10. *New York Times*, August 13, 1957, quoted in Taylor Branch, *Parting the Waters: America in the King Years*, vol. 1, *1954–63* (New York: Simon and Schuster, 1988), p. 221.

11. Ibid.

12. Branch, *Parting the Waters*, p. 20.

13. Herbert Brownell, oral history, p. 213, interview by Ed Edwin, January 31, 1968, Oral History Office, Butler Library, Columbia University.

14. Dwight D. Eisenhower, letter to William F. Knowland, August 2, 1957, Dwight D. Eisenhower Library, Abilene, Kansas.

Chapter 23. The Private Man

1. George Reedy, oral history, interview 6, p. 34, interview by Michael Gillette, October 27, 1982, Lyndon Baines Johnson Library, Austin, Texas.
2. Associated Press, August 1, 1971.
3. *PIC*, June 1948.
4. *Detroit News*, April 29, 1951.
5. *San Francisco Chronicle*, November 18, 1951.
6. Helen Knowland, *Madam Baltimore* (New York: Dodd, Mead, 1949), p. 58.
7. *Sacramento Bee*, April 16, 1949.
8. Quoted in *Los Angeles Times*, April 3, 1949.
9. *New York Times*, September 17, 1954.
10. Drew Pearson, *Diaries, 1949–59*, edited by Tyler Abell (New York: Holt, Rinehart, and Winston, 1974), p. 357.
11. William F. Knowland papers, Bancroft Library, University of California at Berkeley.

Chapter 24. The Big Switch

1. Quoted in *U.S. News and World Report*, January 18, 1957.
2. *Congressional Record*, 85th Cong., 1st sess., 1957, 103, pts. 1–2:333.
3. *Sacramento Bee*, January 8, 1957.
4. Quoted in *New York Times*, January 8, 1957.
5. Emelyn Knowland Jewett, "My Father's Philosophy and Colleagues," in "Remembering William Knowland," p. 4, interview by Ruth Teiser, 1981, Regional Oral History Office, Bancroft Library, University of California at Berkeley.
6. Paul Manolis, interview by authors, December 8, 1995.
7. Quoted in *Sacramento Bee*, January 8, 1957.
8. *Sacramento Bee*, May 18, 1957.
9. Quoted in *Sacramento Bee*, April 23, 1957.
10. *New York Times*, April 20, 1957.
11. Quoted in *Newsweek*, August 5, 1957.
12. Quoted in Roland DeWolk, "The Knowland Family and the *Oakland Tribune*" (unpublished), Bancroft Library, University of California at Berkeley.
13. *Time*, June 3, 1957.
14. Quoted in *Sacramento Bee*, August 8, 1957.
15. *Sacramento Bee*, August 12, 1957.
16. Quoted in *Sacramento Bee*, August 20, 1957.
17. Quoted in *Sacramento Bee*, September 2, 1957.
18. *Sacramento Bee*, September 4, 1957.
19. *Los Angeles Times*, August 2, 1996.

20. Quoted in United Press International, September 16, 1957.

21. Quoted in *Sacramento Bee*, May 18, 1957.

22. Quoted in *Sacramento Bee*, September 13, 1957.

23. Quoted in *Sacramento Bee*, September 20, 1957.

24. *Sacramento Bee*, September 28, 1957.

25. Quoted in *Sacramento Bee*, September 30, 1957.

26. Quoted in *Sacramento Bee*, October 3, 1957.

27. William Safire, *Safire's Political Dictionary*, 3rd ed. (New York: Ballantine Books, 1980), p. 643.

28. *Sacramento Bee*, October 3, 1957.

29. Quoted in *Sacramento Bee*, October 4, 1957.

30. Vernon J. Cristina, in "Republican Campaigns and Party Issues," pp. 24–25, interview by Sarah Sharpe, August 15, 1983, Regional Oral History Office, Bancroft Library, University of California at Berkeley.

31. Quoted in United Press International, March 5, 1964.

32. William F. Knowland, oral history, interview by Joe B. Frantz, March 23, 1970, Lyndon Baines Johnson Library, Austin, Texas.

33. Quoted in *Sacramento Bee*, November 10, 1957.

34. Quoted in *Sacramento Bee*, January 30, 1958.

35. Quoted in Associated Press, May 6, 1958.

36. *Washington Star*, March 28, 1958.

37. Quoted in *Sacramento Bee*, June 27, 1958.

38. William A. Clark, "Leader of the Beat Generation," *Frontier*, October 1958, p. 6.

39. *Sacramento Bee*, August 4, 1958.

40. Dwight D. Eisenhower, letter to Charles S. Jones, August 22, 1958, Dwight D. Eisenhower Library, Abilene, Kansas.

41. *New York Times*, September 24, 1958.

42. Quoted in *Sacramento Bee*, September 25, 1958.

43. Quoted in Associated Press, September 8, 1958.

44. Quoted in United Press International, October 7, 1958.

45. *Washington Post and Times-Herald*, October 17, 1958.

46. Quoted in *Sacramento Bee*, October 18, 1958.

47. William F. Knowland, letter to Lyndon B. Johnson, September 20, 1958, Lyndon Baines Johnson Library, Austin, Texas.

48. Quoted in *San Francisco Chronicle*, October 24, 1958.

49. Clark, "Leader of the Beat Generation," p. 6.

50. *Long Beach Press-Telegram*, October 28, 1957.

51. United Press International, October 28, 1958.

52. *Los Angeles Times*, November 2, 1958.

53. Paul Manolis, interview by authors, December 6, 1995.

Chapter 25. Citizen Knowland

1. Ayn Rand, *Atlas Shrugged* (New York: Signet Books, 1957), p. ii.

2. Quoted in *U.S. News and World Report*, November 14, 1958.

3. Quoted in *Sacramento Bee*, November 5, 1958.

4. Lyndon B. Johnson, letter to William F. Knowland, February 3, 1959, Lyndon Baines Johnson Library, Austin, Texas.

5. *New York Times*, May 24, 1959, p. 52.

6. William F. Knowland, oral history, interview by Joe B. Frantz, March 23, 1970, Lyndon Baines Johnson Library, Austin, Texas.

Chapter 26. Revitalizing a City

1. Estelle Johnson Knowland, "My Father as Senator, Campaigner, and Civic Leader," in "Remembering William F. Knowland," p. 17, interview by Ruth Teiser, 1981, Regional Oral History Office, Bancroft Library, University of California at Berkeley.

2. Ed Salzman, "A Personal Perspective," *California Journal*, April 1974, p. 114.

3. Ibid.

4. Quoted in *Washington Evening Star*, February 2, 1963.

5. Quoted in *Sacramento Bee*, November 23, 1963.

6. F. Clifton White, *Suite 3505* (New York: Arlington House, 1967), p. 337.

7. Quoted in Charles McDowell Jr., *Campaign Fever* (New York: William Morrow, 1965), p. 62.

8. Quoted in Associated Press, June 15, 1964.

9. Quoted in McDowell, *Campaign Fever*, p. 98.

10. Quoted in *Sacramento Bee*, July 10, 1964.

11. Quoted in *Sacramento Bee*, October 8, 1964.

12. Quoted in Max Heirich, *The Spiral of Conflict* (New York: Columbia University Press, 1971), p. 94.

13. Quoted in ibid., p. 96.

14. Ibid., p. 101.

15. Ibid., p. 107.

Chapter 28. "Not Much Time"

1. Helen Knowland, testimony in Alameda County Superior Court, September 29, 1976.

2. Oakland Police Department Report, February 20, 1974.

Chapter 29. Powder Burns

1. Mac Scott, Sonoma County Sheriff's Department Report, February 24, 1974.

2. *Congressional Record*, 93rd Cong., 2nd sess., 1974, 120, pt. 3:4044.

Bibliography

Published Sources

Acheson, Dean. *Among Friends: Personal Letters of Dean Acheson*, edited by David S. McLellan and David C. Acheson. New York: Dodd, Mead, 1980.
———. *Present at the Creation: My Years in the State Department*. New York: W. W. Norton, 1969.
Adams, Sherman. *Firsthand Report*. New York: Harper, 1961.
Allen, Robert S., and William V. Shannon. *The Truman Merry-Go-Round*. New York: Vanguard Press, 1950.
Ambrose, Stephen E. *Eisenhower: Soldier and President*. New York: Touchstone, 1990.
———. *Eisenhower the President*. Vol. 2. New York: Simon and Schuster, 1984.
———. *Nixon: The Education of a Politician, 1913–1962*. New York: Simon and Schuster, 1987.
Anderson, Clinton. *Outsider in the Senate*. New York: World Publishing, 1970.
Anderson, J. W. *Eisenhower, Brownell, and the Congress*.Tuscaloosa: University of Alabama Press, 1964.
Anderson, Jack. *Confessions of a Muckraker*. New York: Random House, 1979.
Anderson, Totton J. "The 1958 Election in California." *Western Political Quarterly* 12: 276–300.
Arnold, James R. *The First Domino*. New York: William Morrow, 1991.
Aronson, James. *The Press and the Cold War*. Indianapolis: Bobbs-Merrill, 1970.
Bagwell, Beth. *Oakland: The Story of a City*. Oakland, Calif.: Oakland Heritage Alliance, 1982.
Baker, Joseph E. *The History of Alameda County*. Chicago: Clarke, 1914.
Baker, Ross K. *Friend and Foe in the U.S. Senate*. New York: Free Press, 1980.
Bean, Walton. *California: An Interpretive History*. New York: McGraw-Hill, 1968.

Bell, Jack. *The Splendid Misery.* Garden City, N.Y.: Doubleday, 1960.

Beschloss, Michael R. *Mayday: Eisenhower, Khrushchev, and the U-2 Affair.* New York: Harper and Row, 1986.

Branch, Taylor. *Parting the Waters: America in the King Years.* Vol. 1, *1954–63.* New York: Simon and Schuster, 1988.

Branyan, Robert L., and Lawrence H. Larson. *The Eisenhower Administration, 1953–61.* New York: Random House, 1971.

Brendan, Piers. *Ike: His Life and Times.* New York: Harper and Row, 1986.

Broadwater, Jeff. *Eisenhower and the Anti-Communist Crusade.* Chapel Hill: University of North Carolina Press, 1992.

Brodie, Fawn M. *Richard Nixon: The Shaping of His Character.* New York: W. W. Norton, 1981.

Byrd, Robert C. *The Senate, 1789–1989: Addresses on the History of the U.S. Senate.* Washington, D.C.: U.S. Government Printing Office, 1988.

Cannon, Lou. *Reagan.* New York: G. P. Putnam's Sons, 1982.

Chao, Ena. "The China Bloc, Congress, and the Making of Foreign Policy, 1947–52." Ph.D. diss., University of North Carolina, 1983.

Clark, Joseph S. *Congress: The Sapless Branch.* New York: Harper and Row, 1964.

Cohen, Warren. "The China Lobby." In *Encyclopedia of American Foreign Policy,* 104–9. New York: Charles Scribners Sons, 1978.

Conmy, Peter T. *The Beginnings of Oakland.* Oakland, Calif.: California A.U.C., Oakland Public Library, 1961.

Cook, Blanche W. *The Declassified Eisenhower.* Garden City, N.Y.: Doubleday, 1981.

Costello, William. *The Facts about Nixon.* New York: Viking Press, 1960.

Crocker, Florence. *Who Made Oakland?* Oakland, Calif.: Florence Crocker, 1925.

Dallek, Robert. *Lone Star Rising: Lyndon Johnson and His Times, 1908–1960.* New York: Oxford University Press, 1991.

David, Paul T., Malcolm Moos, and Ralph Goldman. *Presidential Nominating Politics in 1952.* Baltimore: Johns Hopkins University Press, 1954.

Delmatier, Royce D., Clarence F. McIntosh, and Earl G. Waters. *The Rumble of California Politics, 1848–1970.* New York: John Wiley, 1970.

Demaris, Ovid. *The Last Mafioso.* New York: Times Books, 1981.

De Toledono, Ralph. *One Man Alone: Richard Nixon.* New York: Funk and Wagnalls, 1969.

Divine, Robert A. *Foreign Policy and U.S. Presidential Elections, 1952–1960.* New York: New Viewpoints, 1974.

Donovan, Robert J. *Conflict and Crisis.* New York: W. W. Norton, 1977.

———. *Eisenhower: The Inside Story.* New York: Harper, 1956.

———. *The Tumultuous Years: The Presidency of Harry S. Truman, 1949–53.* New York: W. W. Norton, 1982.

Douglas, William O. *The Autobiography of William O. Douglas.* New York: Random House, 1980.

Dulles, Foster Rhea. *American Foreign Policy toward Communist China, 1949–1969.* New York: Thomas Y. Crowell, 1972.

Dunne, John Gregory. *Vegas: A Memoir of a Dark Season.* New York: Random House, 1974.

Edwards, Lee. *The Man Who Made a Revolution.* Washington, D.C.: Regnery, 1995.

Eisenhower, Dwight D. *The Eisenhower Diaries,* edited by Robert H. Ferrell. New York: W. W. Norton, 1981.

———. *Mandate for Change.* New York: Signet Books, 1963.

———. *Waging Peace, 1956–61.* Garden City, N.Y.: Doubleday, 1965.

Evans, Rowland, and Robert Novak. *Lyndon Johnson: The Exercise of Power.* New York: New American Library, 1966.

Ewald, William Bragg, Jr. *Eisenhower, the President: Crucial Days, 1951–60.* Englewood Cliffs, N.J.: Prentice-Hall, 1981.

———. *Who Killed Joe McCarthy?* New York: Simon and Schuster, 1984.

Faber, Harold, ed. *The Road to the White House.* New York: McGraw-Hill, 1964.

Finer, Herman. *Dulles over Suez.* Chicago: Quadrangle Books, 1964.

Fowle, Eleanor. *Cranston, the Senator from California.* Boston: Houghton Mifflin, 1980.

Fried, Richard M. *Nightmare in Red.* New York: Oxford University Press, 1990.

Gallagher, Hugh Gregory. *Advise and Obstruct.* New York: Delacorte Press, 1969.

Gentry, Curt. *J. Edgar Hoover: The Man and His Secrets.* New York: W. W. Norton, 1991.

Goines, David L. *The Free Speech Movement.* Berkeley, Calif.: Ten Speed Press, 1993.

Goldwater, Barry M., with Jack Casserly. *Goldwater.* New York: Doubleday, 1988.

———. *With No Apologies.* New York: William Morrow, 1979.

Gothberg, John A. "The Local Influence of J. R. Knowland's *Oakland Tribune.*" *Journalism Quarterly* 45 (1968): 487–95.

Gottlieb, Robert, and Irene Wolt. *Thinking Big: The Story of the "Los Angeles Times," Its Publishers, and Their Influence on Southern California.* New York: G. P. Putnam's Sons, 1977.

Goulden, Joseph C. *Korea: The Untold Story of the War.* New York: Times Books, 1982.

Greenstein, Fred I. *The Hidden Hand Presidency: Eisenhower as Leader.* New York: Basic Books, 1982.

Griffith, Robert. *The Politics of Fear: Joseph R. McCarthy and the Senate.* Lexington: University of Kentucky Press, 1970.

Groennings, Sven, and Jonathan P. Hawley. *To Be a Congressman: The Promise and the Power.* Washington, D.C.: Acropolis Books, 1973.

Hagerty, James C. *The Diary of James C. Hagerty,* edited by Robert H. Ferrell. Bloomington.: Indiana University Press, 1983.

Halberstam, David. *The Fifties.* New York: Villard Books, 1993.

———. *The Powers That Be.* New York: Alfred A. Knopf, 1979.

Hayes, Edward C. *Power Structure and Urban Policy: Who Rules in Oakland?* New York: McGraw-Hill, 1972.

Heirich, Max. *The Spiral of Conflict.* New York: Columbia University Press, 1971.

Higgins, Trumbull. *Korea and the Fall of MacArthur.* New York: Oxford University Press, 1960.

Hill, Gladwin. *Dancing Bear: An Inside Look at California Politics.* Cleveland: World Publishing, 1968.

History of Alameda County. N.p.: N. W. Wood, 1883.

Hoopes, Towsend. *The Devil and John Foster Dulles.* Boston: Little, Brown, 1973.

Hughes, Emmet John. *The Living Presidency.* New York: Coward, McCann, and Geoghegan, 1973.

———. *The Ordeal of Power: A Political Memoir of the Eisenhower Years.* New York: Atheneum, 1963.

Ickes, Harold. *America's House of Lords: An Inquiry into the Freedom of Press.* New York: Harcourt, Brace, 1939.

Jacobs, John. *A Rage for Justice.* Berkeley: University of California Press, 1995.

Jewell, Malcolm E. *Senatorial Politics and Foreign Policy.* Lexington: University of Kentucky Press, 1962.

Johnson, Marilynn S. *The Second Gold Rush: Oakland and the East Bay in World War II.* Berkeley: University of California Press, 1993.

Jonas, Frank H. *Western Politics.* Salt Lake City: University of Utah Press, 1961.

Katcher, Leo. *Earl Warren: A Politicial Biography.* New York: McGraw-Hill, 1967.

Kleindienst, Richard. *Justice: The Memoirs of an Attorney General.* Ottawa, Ill.: Jameson Books, 1985.

Knowland, Helen. *Madame Baltimore.* New York: Dodd, Mead, 1949.

Krich, John. *Bump City: Winners and Losers in Oakland.* Berkeley, Calif.: City Miner Books, 1979.

Krieg, Joann P. *Dwight David Eisenhower: Soldier, President, Statesman.* New York: Greenwood Press, 1987.

LaFeber, Walter. *America, Russia, and the Cold War, 1945–1990.* New York: McGraw-Hill, 1991.

Larson, Arthur. *The President Nobody Knew.* New York: Charles Scribner's Sons, 1968.

Lately, Thomas. *When Even Angels Wept.* New York: William Morrow, 1983.

Lurie, Leonard. *The King Makers.* New York: Coward, McCann, and Geoghegan, 1971.

———. *The Running of Richard Nixon.* New York: Coward, McCann, and Geoghegan, 1972.

Lyon, Peter. *Eisenhower: Portrait of a Hero.* Boston: Little, Brown, 1974.

Malone, Dumas, and Basil Rauch. *American and World Leadership, 1940–65.* New York: Appleton-Century-Crofts, 1965.

Manchester, William. *The Glory and the Dream.* Boston: Little, Brown, 1974.

Martin, Joe. *My First 50 Years in Congress.* New York: McGraw-Hill, 1960.

Matthews, Donald R. *U.S. Senators and Their World.* Chapel Hill: University of North Carolina Press, 1960.

Mazo, Earl. *Richard Nixon: A Political and Personal Portrait*. New York: Avon Books, 1960.

Mazo, Earl, and Stephen Hess. *Nixon, a Political Portrait*. New York: Harper and Row, 1967.

McCullough, David G. *Truman*. New York: Simon and Schuster, 1992.

McDowell, Charles, Jr. *Campaign Fever*. New York: William Morrow, 1965.

McLellan, David S. *Dean Acheson: The State Department Years*. New York: Dodd, Mead, 1976.

McPherson, Harry. *A Political Education*. Boston: Little, Brown, 1972.

Medhurst, Martin J. *Eisenhower's War of Words*. Lansing: Michigan State University Press, 1994.

Melendey, H. Brett, and Benjamin F. Gilbert. *The Governors of California*. Georgetown, Calif.: Talisman Press, 1965.

Millard, Baily. *The History of the San Francisco Bay Region*. San Francisco: American Historical Society, 1924.

Miller, Merle. *Lyndon: An Oral Biography*. New York: G. P. Putnam's Sons, 1980.

Mitchell Greg. *The Campaign of the Century*. New York: Random House, 1992.

Mooney, Booth. *LBJ, an Irreverent Choice*. New York: Crowell, 1976.

———. *The Politicians, 1945–60*. New York: Lippincott, 1970.

Morgan, Irvin W. *Eisenhower versus the Spenders*. London: Pinter Publishers, 1990.

Morris, Roger. *Richard Milhous Nixon: The Rise of an American Politician*. New York: Henry Holt, 1990.

Mosley, Leonard. *Dulles*. New York: Dell, 1978.

Mowry, George E. *The California Progressives*. Chicago: Quadrangle Books, 1951.

Nash, Lee. *Understanding Herbert Hoover: Ten Perspectives*. Stanford, Calif.: Hoover Institution Press, 1987.

Neal, Steve. *The Eisenhowers: Reluctant Dynasty*. Garden City, N.Y.: Doubleday, 1978.

Neff, Donald. *Warriors at Suez*. New York: Simon and Schuster, 1981.

Nixon, Richard M. *In the Arena: A Memoir of Victory, Defeat, and Renewal*. New York: Simon and Schuster, 1990.

———. *RN: The Memoirs of Richard Nixon*. New York: Grosset and Dunlap, 1978.

Oshinsky, David M. *A Conspiracy So Immense: The World of Joe McCarthy*. New York: Free Press, 1983.

Owens, John R., Edmond Costantini, and Louis F. Weschler. *California Politics and Parties*. New York: Macmillan, 1970.

Parmet, Herbert S. *Richard Nixon and His America*. Boston: Little, Brown, 1990.

Patterson, James T. *Mr. Republican: A Biography of Robert A. Taft*. Boston: Houghton Mifflin, 1972.

Pearson, Drew. *Diaries, 1949–59*, edited by Tyler Abell. New York: Holt, Rinehart, and Winston, 1974.

Peirce, Neal R. *The Pacific States of America.* New York: W. W. Norton, 1972.

Pettit, Lawrence K., and Edward Keynes. *The Legislative Process in the U.S. Senate.* Chicago: Rand McNally, 1969.

Phillips, Cabell. *The Truman Presidency.* New York: Macmillan, 1966.

Phillips, Herbert L. *Big Wayward Girl.* Garden City, N.Y.: Doubleday, 1968.

Pollack, Jack Harrison. *Earl Warren, the Judge Who Changed America.* Englewood Cliffs, N.J.: Prentice-Hall, 1979.

Rand, Ayn. *Atlas Shrugged.* New York: Signet Books, 1957.

Rapoport, Roger. *California Dreaming: The Political Odyssey of Pat and Jerry Brown.* Berkeley, Calif.: Nolo Press, 1982.

Reedy, George E. *The U.S. Senate: Paralysis or a Search for Consensus?* New York: Crown Publishers, 1986.

Reeves, Thomas C. *The Life and Times of Joe McCarthy.* New York: Stein and Day, 1982.

Reichard, George W. *The Reaffirmation of Republicanism.* Knoxville: University of Tennessee Press, 1975.

Reichley, James. *States in Crisis: Politics in Ten American States, 1950–1962.* Chapel Hill: University of North Carolina Press, 1964.

Reid, Ed, and Ovid Demaris. *The Green Felt Jungle.* New York: Trident Press, 1963.

Richardson, Elmo. *The Presidency of Dwight D. Eisenhower.* Lawrence: Regents Press of Kansas, 1979.

Riedel, Richard Langhorn. *Halls of the Mighty.* Washington, D.C.: Robert B. Luce, 1969.

Ripley, Randall B. *Majority Party Leadership in Congress.* Boston: Little, Brown, 1969.

———. *Power in the Senate.* New York: St. Martin's Press, 1969.

Rorabaugh, W. J. *Berkeley at War: The 1960s.* New York: Oxford University Press, 1989.

Ross, Ruth A., and Barbara S. Stone. *California's Political Process.* New York: Random House, 1973.

Safire, William. *Safire's Political Dictionary.* 3rd ed. New York: Ballantine Books, 1980.

Schapsmeier, Edward L., and Frederick Schapsmeier. *Dirksen of Illinois: Senatorial Statesman.* Champaign: University of Illinois Press, 1985.

Scheele, Henry Z. *Charlie Halleck: A Political Biography.* New York: Exposition Press, 1966.

Schlesinger, Arthur, Jr. *Dynamics of World Power.* New York: Chelsea House, 1973.

———. *History of U.S. Political Parties.* Vol. 4, *1945–72.* New York: Chelsea House, 1973.

Schoenebaum, Eleanora W., ed. *Political Profiles: The Eisenhower Years.* New York: Facts on File, 1977.

Sevareid, Eric. *Candidates 1960.* New York: Basic Books, 1959.

Small, Merrill. "The Earl Warren Era in California, 1925–1963." Interview by Amelia Fry. *California Historical Quarterly* 54 (1975): 83–84.

Smith, Hedrick. *The Power Game: How Washington Works.* New York: Random House, 1988.

Smith, Jess Edward. *Lucius D. Clay: An American Life.* New York: Henry Holt, 1990.

Spalding, Henry D. *The Nixon Nobody Knows.* Middle Village, N.Y.: Jonathan David, 1972.

Steinberg, Alfred. *Sam Johnson's Boy: A Close-up of the President from Texas.* New York: Macmillan, 1968.

Stone, Irving. *Earl Warren: A Great American Story.* Englewood Cliffs, N.J.: Prentice-Hall, 1948.

Tananbaum, Duane. *The Bricker Amendment Controversy.* Ithaca, N.Y.: Cornell University Press, 1988.

Theoharis, Athan G. *The Yalta Myths.* Columbia: University of Missouri Press, 1970.

Thomas, Lately. *When Angels Wept.* New York: William Morrow, 1983.

Thomson, Charles A. H., and Frances M. Shattuck. *The 1956 Presidential Campaign.* Westport, Conn.: Greenwood Press, 1960.

Truman, David B. *The Congressional Party: A Case Study.* London: John Wiley, 1959.

Vandenberg, Arthur H. *The Private Papers of Senator Vandenberg*, edited by Arthur H. Vandenberg Jr. Boston: Houghton Mifflin, 1952.

Vogt, Robert C. *LBJ and the Uses of Power.* New York: Greenwood Press, 1988.

Warren, Earl. *The Memoirs of Earl Warren.* Garden City, N.Y.: Doubleday, 1977.

Watkins, Arthur V. *Enough Rope.* Englewood Cliffs, N.J.: Prentice-Hall, 1969.

Weaver, John D. *Warren: The Man, the Court, the Era.* Boston: Little, Brown, 1967.

White, F. Clifton. *Suite 3505.* New York: Arlington House, 1967.

White, G. Edward. *Earl Warren, a Public Life.* New York: Oxford University Press, 1982.

White, Theodore H. *Breach of Faith: The Fall of Richard Nixon.* New York: Atheneum, 1978.

———. *The Making of the President 1964.* New York: Atheneum, 1965.

White, William S. *The Citadel: The Story of the U.S. Senate.* New York: Harper and Row, 1956.

———. *The Professional.* Boston: Houghton Mifflin, 1964.

———. *The Taft Story.* New York: Harper and Row, 1954.

Wicker, Tom. *One of Us: Richard Nixon and the American Dream.* New York: Random House, 1991.

Wiley, Alexander. *Laughing with Congress.* New York: Crown Publishers, 1947.

Wills, Garry. *Nixon Agonistes.* Boston: Houghton Mifflin, 1970.

Wolman, Philip J. "The Oakland General Strike of 1946." *Southern California Quarterly* 57 (1975): 148–78.

Wyatt, Daniel E. "Joseph R. Knowland: The Political Years, 1899–1915." Master's thesis, University of San Francisco, 1982.

Zauner, Phyllis, and Lou Zauner. *California Gold.* Tahoe Paradise, Calif.: Zanel Publications, 1980.

Interviews and Personal Papers

INTERVIEWS BY THE AUTHORS

Myram Borders
George Christopher
Robert Cuthbertson
Harvey Diederich
Harry Farrell
Bill Fiset
James Gleason
Lou Grant
Roy Grimm
Arthur Hakel
June Stephens Hannon
David Hunter
William Jaeger
Emelyn Jewett
Harold Jewett
Virginia Knight
Estelle Knowland
Joseph W. Knowland
Sydney Kossen
Dean Lesher
Ed Levitt
Elene Manolis
Paul Manolis
Ray Marta
Al Martinez
Virgil Meibert
Ruth Narfi
Bill Ortman
Kay Sessinghaus Paolinetti
Billy Ray
Russ Reed
Penny Robb
John Rothman
James Seagrave
Steve Sessinghaus
Floyd Sparks
Steve Still
Lee Susman
Dr. Franz Wassermann
Edgar West
Frank Wootten

BANCROFT LIBRARY, UNIVERSITY
OF CALIFORNIA, BERKELEY

Archives

William F. Knowland papers
Joseph R. Knowland papers
Sheldon Sackett papers
Roland DeWolk, "The Knowland Family and the *Oakland
    Tribune*" (unpublished)

Regional Oral History Office

Earl C. Adams, "Financing Richard Nixon's Campaigns from
    1946 to 1960," in "Richard M. Nixon in the Warren Era,"
    interview by Amelia Fry, 1975.
Bob Ash, "Alameda County Central Labor Council during the
    Warren Years," in "Labor Leaders View the Warren Era,"
    interview by Mariam Stein and Amelia Fry, 1970.
Vernon J. Cristina, "Republican Campaigns and Party Issues,"
    interview by Sarah Sharp, 1983, in "Republican Campaigns
    and Party Issues, 1964–1976," 1986.
McIntrye Faries, in "California Republicans, 1934–1953," inter-
    views by Amelia Fry and Elizabeth Kerby, June 29, 1970.
Victor R. Hansen, in "Earl Warren's Campaigns," vol. 2, in-
    terview by Amelia Fry, 1977.
Preston Hotchkis Sr., "One Man's Dynamic Role in California
    Politics, Water Development, and World Affairs," interview
    by Mariam Stein and Sarah Sharp, 1980.
Oscar J. Jahnsen, oral history, in "Enforcing the Law against
    Gambling, Bootlegging, Graft, Fraud, and Subversion,
    1922–1942," interviews by Alice King and Miriam Feingold,
    1976.
Emelyn Knowland Jewett, "My Father's Philosophy and Col-
    leagues," in "Remembering William Knowland," interview
    by Ruth Teiser, June 11, 1979.
Estelle Knowland Johnson, "My Father as Senator, Cam-
    paigner, and Civic Leader," in "Remembering William
    Knowland," interview by Ruth Teiser, 1981.
Gardiner Johnson, untitled oral history, interview by Gabrielle
    Morris, 1973.
Frank Jorgensen, "Richard M. Nixon in the Warren Era," in-
    terview by Amelia Fry, April 1–22, 1975.
Clark Kerr, in "Earl Warren's Campaigns," vol. 2, interview by
    Amelia Fry, 1977.
William F. Knowland, in "Earl Warren's Campaigns," vol. 2,
    interview by Amelia Fry, 1977.

Paul G. Manolis, "A Friend and Aide Reminisces," in "Remembering William Knowland," interview by Ruth Teiser, April 24, 1979.

Geraldine McConnell, in "Earl Warren: Views and Episodes," interview by Ruth Teiser, 1976.

Keith McCormac, in "Earl Warren's Campaigns," vol. 3, interview by Amelia Fry, 1978.

Thomas J. Mellon, in "Earl Warren's Campaigns," vol. 2, interview by Amelia Fry, 1977.

Homer Spence, in "Perspectives on the Alameda County District Attorney's Office," vol. 2, interview by Miriam Feingold, 1973.

COLUMBIA UNIVERSITY

Oral History Office, Butler Library

Herbert Brownell, untitled oral history, interview by Ed Edwin, January 31, 1968.

Barry Goldwater, untitled oral history, interview by Ed Edwin, 1967.

William F. Knowland, untitled oral history, interviews by Ed Edwin, June 20 and 22, 1967, November 16, 1970.

Wilton B. "Jerry" Persons, untitled oral history, interview by Jack Luther, June 24, 1970.

HERBERT HOOVER LIBRARY

Charles W. Fisher, untitled oral history, interview by Raymond Henle, July 31, 1971.

William F. Knowland, untitled oral history, interview by Raymond Henle, October 4, 1967.

HARRY S TRUMAN LIBRARY

Oliver J. Carter, untitled oral history, interview by James R. Fuchs, February 26, 1970.

Allen Griffin, untitled oral history, interview by James R. Fuchs, February 15, 1974.

Philip S. Sprouse, untitled oral history, interview by James R. Fuchs, February 11, 1974.

LYNDON BAINES JOHNSON LIBRARY

Archives

William F. Knowland files
Drew Pearson papers

Oral Histories

Clifford Case, untitled oral history, interview 1, interview by
Michael Gillette, March 1, 1979.

Barry M. Goldwater, untitled oral history, interview by Ed
Edwin, June 15, 1967.

James Hagerty, untitled oral history, interview by Michael
Gillette, November 16, 1971.

Hubert H. Humphrey, untitled oral history, interview 3, interview by Michael Gillette, June 21, 1977.

Walter Jenkins, oral history, interview 3, interview by Michael
Gillette, September 23, 1976.

William F. Knowland, untitled oral history, interview by Joe B.
Frantz, March 23, 1970.

Russell B. Long, oral history, interview 2, interview by
Michael Gillette, June 20, 1977.

George Reedy, oral history, interview 5 on October 14, 1983,
and 6 on October 27, 1982, interviews by Michael Gillette.

Walter W. Rostow, untitled oral history, interview 1, interview
by Paige E. Mulhollan, March 1, 1979.

William S. White, untitled oral history, interview 3, interview
by Michael Gillette, July 21, 1978.

BENTLEY HISTORICAL LIBRARY, UNIVERSITY
OF MICHIGAN, ANN ARBOR

Sen. Arthur H. Vandenberg papers

NATIONAL ARCHIVES, WESTERN DIVISION,
LAGUNA NIGUEL, CALIFORNIA

Richard Nixon papers

RICHARD NIXON LIBRARY, YORBA LINDA,
CALIFORNIA

Richard Nixon papers

EISENHOWER PRESIDENTIAL LIBRARY,
ABILENE, KANSAS

John Foster Dulles papers
Dwight D. Eisenhower papers

LIBRARY OF CONGRESS, WASHINGTON, D.C.

NATIONAL ARCHIVES, WASHINGTON, D.C.

FRANKLIN D. ROOSEVELT LIBRARY,
HYDE PARK, NEW YORK

Franklin D. Roosevelt papers

Index

Indexer:	Carol Roberts
Compositor:	Prestige Typography
Text:	10/13 Galliard
Display:	Galliard
Printer and binder:	Haddon Craftsmen, Inc.